NON-LEAGUE FOOTBALL TABLES 1889-2008

EDITOR
Michael Robinson

FOREWORD

In selecting the Leagues to be included in this seventh edition of Non-League Football Tables we have again chosen those forming the pinnacle of the Non-League Football Pyramid, i.e. The Football Conference and it's three direct feeders.

In addition we have once more included the briefly-lived Football Alliance which became, effectively, the 2nd Division of the Football League in 1892 together with the North-West Counties League, Manchester League, Norfolk & Suffolk League, Warwickshire Combination, Wessex League, Corinthian League, Delphian League and 5 of the early but short-lived Leagues which arose in the East Midlands area.

Furthermore, as league sponsors change frequently, we have not used sponsored names (eg. Rymans League) other than in an indicative way on the cover.

We are indebted to Mick Blakeman for providing tables for the new Leagues included in this edition of the book.

British Library Cataloguing in Publication Data
A catalogue record for this book is available from the British Library

ISBN: 978-1-86223-171-9

Manufactured in the UK by LPPS Ltd, Wellingborough, NN8 3PJ

CONTENTS

FOOTBALL ALLIANCE

1889-90

Sheffield Wednesday	22	15	2	5	70	39	32
Bootle	22	13	2	7	66	39	28
Sunderland Albion	21	12	2	7	64	39	28
Grimsby Town	22	12	2	8	58	47	26
Crewe Alexandra	22	11	2	9	68	59	24
Darwen	22	10	2	10	70	75	22
Birmingham St George	21	9	3	9	62	49	21
Newton Heath	22	9	2	11	40	44	20
Walsall Town Swifts	22	8	3	11	44	59	19
Small Heath	22	6	5	11	44	67	17
Nottingham Forest	22	6	5	11	31	62	17
Long Eaton Rangers	22	4	2	16	35	73	10

Sunderland Albion record includes 2 points awarded when Birmingham St George refused to fulfil a fixture which the Alliance committee had ordered to be replayed.

1890-91

Stoke	22	13	7	2	57	39	33
Sunderland Albion	22	12	6	4	69	28	30
Grimsby Town	22	11	5	6	43	27	27
Birmingham St George	22	12	2	8	64	62	26
Nottingham Forest	22	9	7	6	66	39	25
Darwen	22	10	3	9	64	59	23
Walsall Town Swifts	22	9	3	10	34	61	21
Crewe Alexandra	22	8	4	10	59	67	20
Newton Heath	22	7	3	12	37	55	17
Small Heath	22	7	2	13	58	66	16
Bootle	22	3	7	12	40	61	13
Sheffield Wednesday	22	4	5	13	39	66	13

1891-92

Nottingham Forest	22	14	5	3	59	22	33
Newton Heath	22	12	7	3	69	33	31
Small Heath	22	12	5	5	53	36	29
Sheffield Wednesday	22	12	4	6	65	35	28
Burton Swifts	22	12	2	8	54	52	26
Grimsby Town	22	6	6	10	40	39	18
Crewe Alexandra	22	7	4	11	44	49	18
Ardwick	22	6	6	10	39	51	18
Bootle	22	8	2	12	42	64	18
Lincoln City	22	6	5	11	37	65	17
Walsall Town Swifts	22	6	3	13	33	59	15
Birmingham St George	22	5	3	14	34	64	13

SOUTHERN LEAGUE

1894-95

First Division

Millwall Athletic	16	12	4	0	68	19	28
Luton Town	16	9	4	3	36	22	22
Southampton St Mary's	16	9	2	5	34	25	20
Ilford	16	6	3	7	26	40	15
Reading	16	6	2	8	33	38	14
Chatham	16	4	5	7	22	25	13
Royal Ordnance Factories	16	3	6	7	20	30	12
Clapton	16	5	1	10	22	38	11
Swindon Town	16	4	1	11	24	48	9

Second Division

New Brompton	12	11	0	1	57	10	22
Sheppey United	12	6	1	5	25	23	13
Old St Stephen's	12	6	0	6	26	26	12
Uxbridge	12	4	3	5	14	20	11
Bromley	12	4	1	7	23	30	9
Chesham	12	3	3	6	20	42	9
Maidenhead	12	2	4	6	19	33	8

1895-96

First Division

Millwall Athletic	18	16	1	1	75	16	33
Luton Town	18	13	1	4	68	14	27
Southampton St Mary's	18	12	0	6	44	23	24
Reading	18	11	1	6	45	38	23
Chatham	18	9	2	7	43	45	20
New Brompton	18	7	4	7	30	37	18
Swindon Town	18	6	4	8	38	41	16
Clapton	18	4	2	12	30	67	10
Royal Ordnance Factories	18	3	3	12	23	44	9
Ilford	18	0	0	18	10	81	0

Second Division

Wolverton L & NW Railway	16	13	1	2	43	10	27
Sheppey United	16	11	3	2	60	19	25
1st Scots Guards	16	8	5	3	37	22	21
Uxbridge	16	9	1	6	28	23	19
Old St Stephen's	16	6	3	7	34	21	15
Guildford	16	7	1	8	29	41	15
Maidenhead	16	4	1	11	20	49	9
Chesham	16	2	3	11	15	48	7
Bromley	16	2	2	12	16	49	6

1896-97

First Division

Southampton St Mary's	20	15	5	0	63	18	35
Millwall Athletic	20	13	5	2	63	24	31
Chatham	20	13	1	6	54	29	27
Tottenham Hotspur	20	9	4	7	43	29	22
Gravesend United	20	9	4	7	35	34	22
Swindon Town	20	8	3	9	33	37	19
Reading	20	8	3	9	31	49	19
New Brompton	20	7	2	11	32	42	16
Northfleet	20	5	4	11	24	46	14
Sheppey United	20	5	1	14	34	47	11
Wolverton L & NW Railway	20	2	0	18	17	74	4

Second Division

Dartford	24	16	4	4	83	19	36
Royal Engineers Training Battalion	24	11	9	4	49	37	31
Freemantle	24	12	4	8	58	40	28
Uxbridge	24	11	5	8	62	37	27
Wycombe Wanderers	24	10	6	8	37	54	26
Chesham	24	11	3	10	41	55	25
Southall	24	9	6	9	55	52	24
1st Scot Guards	24	9	6	9	49	50	24
West Herts	24	11	1	12	41	49	23
Warmley (Bristol)	24	10	2	12	44	43	22
Old St Stephen's	24	5	7	12	36	52	17
Maidenhead	24	4	8	12	33	64	16
1st Coldstream Guards	24	3	6	15	30	66	12

1897-98

First Division

Southampton	22	18	1	3	53	18	37
Bristol City	22	13	7	2	67	33	33
Tottenham Hotspur	22	12	4	6	52	31	28
Chatham	22	12	4	6	50	34	28
Reading	22	8	7	7	39	31	23
New Brompton	22	9	4	9	37	37	22
Sheppey United	22	10	1	11	40	49	21
Gravesend United	22	7	6	9	28	39	20
Millwall Athletic	22	8	2	12	48	45	18
Swindon Town	22	7	2	13	36	48	16
Northfleet	22	4	3	15	29	60	11
Wolverton L & NW Railway	22	3	1	18	28	82	7

Second Division

Royal Artillery (Portsmouth)	22	19	1	2	75	22	39
Warmley (Bristol)	22	19	0	3	108	15	38
West Herts	22	11	6	5	50	48	28
Uxbridge	22	11	2	9	39	57	24
St Albans	22	9	5	8	47	41	23
Dartford	22	11	0	11	68	55	22
Southall	22	8	2	12	49	61	18
Chesham	22	8	2	12	38	48	18
Olsd St Stephen's	22	7	2	13	47	66	16
Wycombe Wanderers	22	7	2	13	37	55	16
Maidenhead	22	4	4	14	27	81	12
Royal Engineers Training Battalion	22	4	2	16	26	62	10

1898-99

First Division

Southampton	24	15	5	4	54	24	35
Bristol City	24	15	3	6	55	12	33
Millwall Athletic	24	12	6	6	59	35	30
Chatham	24	10	8	6	32	23	28
Reading	24	9	8	7	31	24	26
New Brompton	24	10	5	9	38	30	25
Tottenham Hotspur	24	10	4	10	40	36	24
Bedminster	24	10	4	10	35	39	24
Swindon Town	24	9	5	10	43	49	23
Brighton United	24	9	2	13	37	48	20
Gravesend United	24	7	5	12	42	52	19
Sheppey United	24	5	3	16	23	53	13
Royal Artillery (Portsmouth)	24	4	4	16	17	60	12

Second Division (London Section)

Thames Ironworks	22	19	1	2	64	16	39
Wolverton L & NW Railway	22	13	4	5	88	43	30
Watford	22	14	2	6	62	35	30
Brentford	22	11	3	8	59	39	25
Wycombe Wanderers	22	10	2	10	55	57	22
Southall	22	11	0	11	44	55	22
Chesham	22	9	2	11	45	62	20
St Albans	22	8	3	11	45	59	19
Shepherds Bush	22	7	3	12	37	53	17
Fulham	22	6	4	12	36	44	16
Uxbridge	22	7	2	13	29	48	16
Maidenhead	22	3	2	17	33	86	8

Second Division (South West Section)

Cowes	10	10	0	0	58	8	20
Ryde	10	7	0	3	30	11	14
Freemantle	10	4	1	5	18	31	9
Sandown	10	4	0	6	20	29	8
Eastleigh	10	2	1	7	17	37	5
Andover	10	2	0	8	14	41	4

1899-1900

First Division

Tottenham Hotspur	28	20	4	4	67	26	44
Portsmouth	28	20	1	7	58	27	41
Southampton	28	17	1	10	70	33	35
Reading	28	15	2	11	41	28	32
Swindon Town	28	15	2	11	50	42	32
Bedminster	28	13	2	13	44	45	28
Millwall Athletic	28	12	3	13	36	37	27
Queens Park Rangers	28	12	2	14	49	57	26
Bristol City	28	9	7	12	43	47	25
Bristol Rovers	28	11	3	14	46	55	25
New Brompton	28	9	6	13	39	49	24
Gravesend United	28	10	4	14	38	58	24
Chatham	28	10	3	15	38	58	23
Thames Ironworks	28	8	5	15	30	45	21
Sheppey United	28	3	7	18	24	66	13

Second Division

Watford	20	14	2	4	57	25	30
Fulham	20	10	4	6	44	23	24
Chesham Town	20	11	2	7	43	37	24
Wolverton L & NW Railway	20	9	6	5	46	36	21
Grays United	20	8	6	6	63	29	22
Shepherds Bush	20	9	4	7	45	37	22
Dartford	20	8	3	9	36	44	19
Wycombe Wanderers	20	8	3	9	35	50	19
Brentford	20	5	7	8	31	48	17
Southall	20	6	3	11	21	44	15
Maidenhead	20	1	2	17	16	64	4

1900-01

First Division

Southampton	28	18	5	5	58	26	41
Bristol City	28	17	5	6	54	27	39
Portsmouth	28	17	4	7	56	32	38
Millwall Athletic	28	17	2	9	55	32	36
Tottenham Hotspur	28	16	4	8	55	33	36
West Ham United	28	14	5	9	40	28	33
Bristol Rovers	28	14	4	10	46	35	32
Queens Park Rangers	28	11	4	13	43	48	26
Reading	28	8	8	12	24	25	24
Luton Town	28	11	2	15	43	49	24
Kettering	28	7	9	12	33	46	23
New Brompton	28	7	5	16	34	51	19
Gravesend United	28	6	7	15	32	85	19
Watford	28	6	4	18	24	52	16
Swindon Town	28	3	8	17	19	47	14

Second Division

Brentford	16	14	2	0	63	11	30
Grays United	16	12	2	2	62	12	26
Sheppey United	16	8	1	7	44	26	17
Shepherds Bush	16	8	1	7	30	30	17
Fulham	16	8	0	8	38	26	16
Chesham Town	16	5	1	10	26	39	11
Maidenhead	16	4	1	11	21	49	9
Wycombe Wanderers	16	4	1	11	23	68	9
Southall	16	4	1	11	22	68	9

1901-02

First Division

Portsmouth	30	20	7	3	67	24	47
Tottenham Hotspur	30	18	6	6	61	22	42
Southampton	30	18	6	6	71	28	42
West Ham United	30	17	6	7	45	28	40
Reading	30	16	7	7	57	24	39
Millwall Athletic	30	13	6	11	48	31	32
Luton Town	30	11	10	9	31	35	32
Kettering	30	12	5	13	44	39	29
Bristol Rovers	30	12	5	13	43	39	29
New Brompton	30	10	7	13	39	38	27
Northampton	30	11	5	14	53	64	27
Queens Park Rangers	30	8	7	15	34	56	23
Watford	30	9	4	17	36	60	22
Wellingborough	30	9	4	17	34	75	22
Brentford	30	7	6	17	34	61	20
Swindon Town	30	2	3	25	17	93	7

Second Division

Fulham	16	13	0	3	51	19	26
Grays United	16	12	1	3	49	14	25
Brighton & Hove Albion	16	11	0	5	34	17	22
Wycombe Wanderers	16	7	3	6	36	30	17
West Hampstead	16	6	4	6	39	29	16
Shepherds Bush	16	6	1	9	31	31	13
Southall	16	5	2	9	28	52	12
Maidenhead	16	3	1	12	23	59	7
Chesham Town	16	2	2	12	24	64	6

1902-03

First Division

Team							
Southampton	30	20	8	2	83	20	48
Reading	30	19	7	4	72	30	45
Portsmouth	30	17	7	6	69	32	41
Tottenham Hotspur	30	14	7	9	47	31	35
Bristol Rovers	30	13	8	9	46	34	34
New Brompton	30	11	11	8	37	35	33
Millwall Athletic	30	14	3	13	52	37	31
Northampton Town	30	12	6	12	39	48	30
Queens Park Rangers	30	11	6	13	34	42	28
West Ham United	30	9	10	11	35	49	28
Luton Town	30	10	7	13	43	44	27
Swindon Town	30	10	7	13	38	46	27
Kettering	30	8	11	11	33	40	27
Wellingborough	30	11	3	16	36	56	25
Watford	30	6	4	20	35	87	16
Brentford	30	2	1	27	16	84	5

Second Division

Team							
Fulham	10	7	1	2	27	7	15
Brighton & Hove Albion	10	7	1	2	34	11	15
Grays United	10	7	0	3	28	12	14
Wycombe Wanderers	10	3	3	4	13	19	9
Chesham Town	10	2	1	7	9	37	5
Southall	10	1	0	9	10	35	2

1903-04

First Division

Team							
Southampton	34	22	6	6	75	30	50
Tottenham Hotspur	34	16	11	7	54	37	43
Bristol Rovers	34	17	8	9	66	42	42
Portsmouth	34	17	8	9	41	38	42
Queens Park Rangers	34	15	11	8	53	37	41
Reading	34	14	13	7	48	35	41
Millwall	34	16	8	10	64	42	40
Luton Town	34	14	12	8	38	33	40
Plymouth Argyle	34	13	10	11	44	34	36
Swindon Town	34	10	11	13	30	42	31
Fulham	34	9	12	13	33	34	30
West Ham United	34	10	7	17	38	43	27
Brentford	34	9	9	16	34	48	27
Wellingborough	34	11	5	18	44	63	27
Northampton Town	34	10	7	17	36	69	27
New Brompton	34	6	13	15	26	43	25
Brighton & Hove Albion	34	6	12	16	45	79	24
Kettering	34	6	7	21	30	78	19

Second Division

Team							
Watford	20	18	2	0	70	15	38
Portsmouth Reserves	20	15	2	3	85	25	32
Millwall Reserves	20	9	4	7	35	39	22
Southampton Reserves	20	9	3	8	59	35	21
Grays United	20	9	3	8	25	55	21
Fulham Reserves	20	8	4	8	40	34	20
Swindon Town Reserves	20	8	3	9	50	44	19
Reading Reserves	20	8	2	10	43	42	18
Wycombe Wanderers	20	5	5	10	29	64	15
Southall	20	4	2	14	25	62	10
Chesham Town	20	1	2	17	19	65	4

1904-05

First Division

Team							
Bristol Rovers	34	20	8	6	74	36	48
Reading	34	18	7	9	57	38	43
Southampton	34	18	7	9	54	40	43
Plymouth Argyle	34	18	5	11	57	39	41
Tottenham Hotspur	34	15	8	11	53	34	38
Fulham	34	14	10	10	46	34	38
Queens Park Rangers	34	14	8	12	51	46	36
Portsmouth	34	16	4	14	61	56	36
New Brompton	34	11	11	12	40	41	33
West Ham United	34	12	8	14	48	42	32
Brighton & Hove Albion	34	13	6	15	44	45	32
Northampton Town	34	12	8	14	43	54	32
Watford	34	14	3	17	41	44	31
Brentford	34	10	9	15	33	38	29
Millwall	34	11	7	16	38	47	29
Swindon Town	34	12	5	17	41	59	29
Luton Town	34	12	3	19	45	54	27
Wellingborough	34	5	3	26	25	104	13

Second Division

Team							
Fulham Reserves	22	16	4	2	78	25	36
Portsmouth Reserves	22	14	2	6	75	28	30
Swindon Town Reserves	22	12	3	7	54	47	27
Grays United	22	11	3	8	61	40	25
Southampton Reserves	22	10	5	7	52	35	25
Brighton & Hove Albion	22	9	3	10	48	49	21
West Ham United Reserves	22	8	5	9	45	47	21
Clapton Orient	22	7	7	8	47	56	21
Watford Reserves	22	5	6	11	30	62	16
Southall	22	7	2	13	31	66	16
Wycombe Wanderers	22	6	2	14	37	70	14
Reading Reserves	22	4	4	14	24	57	12

1905-06

First Division

Team							
Fulham	34	19	12	3	44	15	50
Southampton	34	19	7	8	58	39	45
Portsmouth	34	17	9	8	61	35	43
Luton Town	34	17	7	10	64	40	41
Tottenham Hotspur	34	16	7	11	46	29	39
Plymouth Argyle	34	16	7	11	52	33	39
Norwich City	34	13	10	11	46	38	36
Bristol Rovers	34	15	5	14	56	56	35
Brentford	34	14	7	13	43	52	35
Reading	34	12	9	13	53	46	33
West Ham United	34	14	5	15	42	39	33
Millwall	34	11	11	12	38	41	33
Queens Park Rangers	34	12	7	15	58	44	31
Watford	34	8	10	16	38	57	26
Swindon Town	34	8	9	17	31	52	25
Brighton & Hove Albion	34	9	7	18	30	55	25
New Brompton	34	7	8	19	20	62	22
Northampton Town	34	8	5	21	32	79	21

Second Division

Team							
Crystal Palace	24	19	4	1	66	14	42
Leyton	24	16	6	2	61	18	38
Portsmouth Reserves	24	12	8	4	52	24	32
Fulham Reserves	24	11	6	7	52	39	28
Southampton Reserves	24	7	9	8	39	41	23
Southern United	24	8	7	9	45	49	23
St Leonard's United	24	9	4	11	54	50	22
Watford Reserves	24	8	5	11	43	47	21
West Ham United Reserves	24	7	5	12	46	48	19
Grays United	24	8	3	13	24	77	19
Reading Reserves	24	6	5	13	36	49	15
Swindon Town Reserves	24	5	5	14	36	51	15
Wycombe Wanderers	24	5	3	16	36	83	13

1906-07

First Division

Fulham	38	20	13	5	58	32	53
Portsmouth	38	22	7	9	64	36	51
Brighton & Hove Albion	38	18	9	11	53	43	45
Luton Town	38	18	9	11	52	52	45
West Ham United	38	15	14	9	60	41	44
Tottenham Hotspur	38	17	9	12	63	45	43
Millwall	38	18	6	14	71	50	42
Norwich City	38	15	12	11	57	48	42
Watford	38	13	16	9	46	43	42
Brentford	38	17	8	13	57	56	42
Southampton	38	13	9	16	49	56	35
Reading	38	14	6	18	57	47	34
Leyton	38	11	12	15	38	60	34
Bristol Rovers	38	12	9	17	55	54	33
Plymouth Argyle	38	10	13	15	43	50	33
New Brompton	38	12	9	17	47	59	33
Swindon Town	38	11	11	16	43	54	33
Queens Park Rangers	38	11	10	17	47	55	32
Crystal Palace	38	8	9	21	46	66	25
Northampton Town	38	5	9	24	29	88	19

Second Division

Southend United	22	14	5	3	58	23	33
West Ham United Reserves	22	14	3	5	64	30	31
Portsmouth Reserves	22	11	6	5	53	24	28
Fulham Reserves	22	11	4	7	47	32	26
Hastings & St Leonards	21	10	4	7	46	31	24
Tunbridge Wells Rangers	22	10	1	11	46	36	21
Salisbury City	22	9	2	11	40	42	20
Southampton Reserves	22	8	2	12	37	56	18
Swindon Town Reserves	22	7	3	12	35	43	17
Reading Reserves	22	6	4	12	32	47	16
Royal Engineers (Aldershot)	21	5	4	12	27	58	14
Wycombe Wanderers	22	4	6	12	28	68	14

The match between Tunbridge Wells Rangers and Royal Engineers (Aldershot) was not completed.

1907-08

First Division

Queens Park Rangers	38	21	9	8	82	57	51
Plymouth Argyle	38	19	11	8	50	31	49
Millwall	38	19	8	11	49	32	46
Crystal Palace	38	17	10	11	54	51	44
Swindon Town	38	16	10	12	55	40	42
Bristol Rovers	38	16	10	12	59	56	42
Tottenham Hotspur	38	17	7	14	59	48	41
Northampton Town	38	15	11	12	50	41	41
Portsmouth	38	17	6	15	63	52	40
West Ham United	38	15	10	13	47	48	40
Southampton	38	16	6	16	51	60	38
Reading	38	15	6	17	55	50	36
Bradford Park Avenue	38	12	12	14	53	54	36
Watford	38	12	10	16	47	49	34
Brentford	38	14	5	19	49	52	33
Norwich City	38	12	9	17	46	49	33
Brighton & Hove Albion	38	12	8	18	46	59	32
Luton Town	38	12	6	20	33	56	30
Leyton	38	8	11	19	51	73	27
New Brompton	38	9	7	22	44	75	25

Second Division

Southend	18	13	3	2	47	16	29
Portsmouth Reserves	18	10	5	3	39	22	25
Croydon Common	18	10	3	5	35	25	23
Hastings & St Leonard's	18	10	2	6	43	29	22
Southampton Reserves	18	7	4	7	54	46	18
Tunbridge Wells Rangers	18	7	3	8	42	38	17
Salisbury City	18	6	4	8	35	46	16
Swindon Town Reserves	18	5	5	8	36	40	15
Brighton & Hove Albion Reserves	18	4	4	10	34	47	12
Wycombe Wanderers	18	1	1	16	16	72	3

1908-09

First Division

Northampton Town	40	25	5	10	90	45	55
Swindon Town	40	22	5	13	96	55	49
Southampton	40	19	10	11	67	58	48
Portsmouth	40	18	10	12	68	60	46
Bristol Rovers	40	17	9	14	60	63	43
Exeter City	40	18	6	16	56	65	42
New Brompton	40	17	7	16	48	59	41
Reading	40	11	18	11	60	57	40
Luton Town	40	17	6	17	59	60	40
Plymouth Argyle	40	15	10	15	46	47	40
Millwall	40	16	6	18	59	61	38
Southend United	40	14	10	16	52	54	38
Leyton	40	15	8	17	52	55	38
Watford	40	14	9	17	51	64	37
Queens Park Rangers	40	12	12	16	52	50	36
Crystal Palace	40	12	12	16	62	62	36
West Ham United	40	16	4	20	56	60	36
Brighton & Hove Albion	40	14	7	19	60	61	35
Norwich City	40	12	11	17	59	75	35
Coventry City	40	15	4	21	64	91	34
Brentford	40	13	7	20	59	74	33

Second Division

Croydon Common	12	10	0	2	67	14	20
Hastings & St Leonard's	12	8	1	3	42	18	17
Depot Battalion Royal Engineers	12	8	1	3	23	22	17
2nd Grenadier Guards	12	5	0	7	21	33	10
South Farnborough Athletic	12	2	4	6	20	39	8
Salisbury City	12	3	1	8	24	36	7
Chesham Town	12	2	1	9	17	52	5

1909-10

First Division

Brighton & Hove Albion	42	23	13	6	69	28	59
Swindon Town	42	22	10	10	92	46	54
Queens Park Rangers	42	19	13	10	56	47	51
Northampton Town	42	22	4	16	90	44	48
Southampton	42	16	16	10	64	55	48
Portsmouth	42	20	7	15	70	63	47
Crystal Palace	42	20	6	16	69	50	46
Coventry City	42	19	8	15	71	60	46
West Ham United	42	15	15	12	69	56	45
Leyton	42	16	11	15	60	46	43
Plymouth Argyle	42	16	11	15	61	54	43
New Brompton	42	19	5	18	76	74	43
Bristol Rovers	42	16	10	16	37	48	42
Brentford	42	16	9	17	50	58	41
Luton Town	42	15	11	16	72	92	41
Millwall	42	15	7	20	45	59	37
Norwich City	42	13	9	20	59	78	35
Exeter City	42	14	6	22	60	69	34
Watford	42	10	13	19	51	76	33
Southend United	42	12	9	21	51	90	33
Croydon Common	42	13	5	24	52	96	31
Reading	42	7	10	25	38	73	24

Second Division - Section A

Stoke	10	10	0	0	48	9	20
Ton Pentre	10	4	2	4	17	21	10
Merthyr Town	9	4	1	4	16	21	9
Salisbury City	8	2	1	5	7	18	5
Burton United	6	2	0	4	8	21	4
Aberdare	7	1	0	6	6	11	2

Second Division - Section B

Hastings & St Leonard's	9	6	3	0	26	11	15
Kettering	10	6	0	4	34	19	12
Chesham Town	10	5	2	3	25	25	12
Peterborough City	10	4	2	4	16	23	10
South Farnborough Athletic	10	4	1	5	23	19	9
Romford	9	0	0	9	7	33	0

1910-11

First Divison

Swindon Town	38	24	5	9	80	31	53
Northampton Town	38	18	12	8	54	27	48
Brighton & Hove Albion	38	20	8	10	58	35	48
Crystal Palace	38	17	13	8	55	48	47
West Ham United	38	17	11	10	63	46	45
Queens Park Rangers	38	13	14	11	52	41	40
Leyton	38	16	8	14	57	52	40
Plymouth Argyle	38	15	9	14	54	55	39
Luton Town	38	15	8	15	67	63	38
Norwich City	38	15	8	15	46	48	38
Coventry City	38	16	6	16	65	68	38
Brentford	38	14	9	15	41	42	37
Exeter City	38	14	9	15	51	53	37
Watford	38	13	9	16	49	65	35
Millwall	38	11	9	18	42	54	31
Bristol Rovers	38	10	10	18	42	55	30
Southampton	38	11	8	19	42	67	30
New Brompton	38	11	8	19	34	65	30
Southend United	38	10	9	19	47	64	29
Portsmouth	38	8	11	19	34	53	27

Second Division

Reading	22	16	3	3	55	11	35
Stoke	22	17	1	4	72	21	35
Merthyr Town	22	15	3	4	52	22	33
Cardiff City	22	12	4	6	48	29	28
Croydon Common	22	11	3	8	61	26	25
Treharris	22	10	3	9	38	31	23
Aberdare	22	9	5	8	38	33	23
Ton Pentre	22	10	3	9	44	40	23
Walsall	22	7	4	11	37	41	18
Kettering	22	6	1	15	34	68	13
Chesham Town	22	1	3	18	16	93	5
Salisbury City	22	0	3	19	16	92	3

1911-12

First Division

Queens Park Rangers	38	21	11	6	59	35	53
Plymouth Argyle	38	23	6	9	63	31	52
Northampton Town	38	22	7	9	82	41	51
Swindon Town	38	21	6	11	82	50	48
Brighton & Hove Albion	38	19	9	10	73	35	47
Coventry City	38	17	8	13	66	54	42
Crystal Palace	38	15	10	13	70	46	40
Millwall	38	15	10	13	60	57	40
Watford	38	13	10	15	56	68	36
Stoke	38	13	10	15	51	63	36
Reading	38	11	14	13	43	69	36
Norwich City	38	10	14	14	40	60	34
West Ham United	38	13	7	18	64	69	33
Brentford	38	12	9	17	60	65	33
Exeter City	38	11	11	16	48	62	33
Southampton	38	10	11	17	46	63	31
Bristol Rovers	38	9	13	16	41	62	31
New Brompton	38	11	9	18	35	72	31
Luton Town	38	9	10	19	49	61	28
Leyton	38	7	11	20	27	62	25

Second Division

Merthyr Town	26	19	3	4	60	14	41
Portsmouth	26	19	3	4	73	20	41
Cardiff City	26	15	4	7	55	26	34
Southend United	26	16	1	9	73	24	33
Pontypridd	26	13	6	7	39	24	32
Ton Pentre	26	12	3	11	56	45	27
Walsall	26	13	1	11	44	41	27
Treharris	26	11	5	10	44	47	27
Aberdare	26	10	3	13	39	44	23
Kettering	26	11	0	15	37	62	22
Croydon Common	26	8	2	15	43	45	18
Mardy	26	6	6	12	37	51	18
Cwm Albion	26	5	1	16	27	70	11
Chesham Town	26	1	0	25	18	131	2

1912-13

First Division

Plymouth Argyle	38	27	6	10	77	36	50
Swindon Town	38	20	8	10	66	41	48
West Ham United	38	18	12	8	66	43	48
Queens Park Rangers	38	18	10	10	46	35	43
Crystal Palace	38	17	11	10	55	36	45
Millwall	38	19	7	12	62	43	45
Exeter City	38	18	8	12	48	44	44
Reading	38	17	8	13	59	55	42
Brighton & Hove Albion	38	13	12	13	48	47	38
Northampton Town	38	12	12	14	61	48	36
Portsmouth	38	14	8	16	41	49	36
Merthyr Town	38	12	12	14	42	60	36
Coventry City	38	13	8	17	53	59	34
Watford	38	12	10	16	43	50	34
Gillingham	38	12	10	16	36	53	34
Bristol Rovers	38	12	9	17	55	64	33
Southampton	38	10	11	17	40	72	31
Norwich City	38	10	9	19	39	50	29
Brentford	38	11	5	22	42	55	27
Stoke	38	10	4	24	39	75	24

Second Division

Cardiff City	24	18	5	1	54	15	41
Southend United	24	14	6	4	43	23	34
Swansea Town	24	12	7	5	29	23	31
Croydon Common	24	13	4	7	51	29	30
Luton Town	24	13	4	7	52	39	30
Llanelly	24	9	6	9	33	39	24
Pontypridd	24	6	11	7	30	28	23
Mid Rhondda	24	9	4	11	33	31	22
Aberdare	24	8	6	10	38	40	22
Newport County	24	7	5	12	29	36	19
Mardy	24	6	3	15	38	38	15
Treharris	24	5	2	17	18	60	12
Ton Pentre	24	3	3	18	22	69	9

1913-14

First Division

Swindon Town	38	21	8	9	81	41	50
Crystal Palace	38	17	16	5	60	32	50
Northampton Town	38	14	19	5	50	37	47
Reading	38	17	10	11	43	36	44
Plymouth Argyle	38	15	13	10	46	42	43
West Ham United	38	15	12	11	61	60	42
Brighton & Hove Albion	38	15	12	11	43	45	42
Queens Park Rangers	38	16	9	13	45	43	41
Portsmouth	38	14	12	12	57	48	40
Cardiff City	38	13	12	13	46	42	38
Southampton	38	15	7	16	55	54	37
Exeter City	38	10	16	12	39	38	36
Gillingham	38	13	9	16	48	49	35
Norwich City	38	9	17	12	49	51	35
Millwall	38	11	12	15	51	56	34
Southend Unied	38	10	12	16	41	66	32
Bristol Rovers	38	10	11	17	46	67	31
Watford	38	10	9	19	50	56	29
Merthyr Town	38	9	10	19	38	61	28
Coventry City	38	6	14	18	43	68	26

Second Division

Croydon Common	30	23	5	2	76	14	51
Luton Town	30	24	3	3	92	22	51
Brentford	30	20	4	6	80	18	44
Swansea Town	30	20	4	6	66	23	44
Stoke	30	19	2	9	71	34	40
Newport County	30	14	8	8	49	38	36
Mid Rhondda	30	13	7	10	55	37	33
Pontypridd	30	14	5	11	43	38	33
Llanelly	30	12	4	14	45	39	28
Barry	30	9	8	13	44	70	26
Abertillery	30	8	4	18	44	57	20
Ton Pentre	30	8	4	18	33	61	20
Mardy	30	6	6	18	30	60	18
Caerphilly	30	4	7	19	21	103	15
Aberdare	30	4	5	21	33	87	13
Treharris	30	2	4	24	19	106	8

1914-15

First Division

Watford	38	22	8	8	68	46	52
Reading	38	21	7	10	68	43	49
Cardiff City	38	22	4	12	72	38	48
West Ham United	38	18	9	11	58	47	45
Northampton Town	38	16	11	11	56	51	43
Southampton	38	19	5	14	78	74	43
Portsmouth	38	16	10	12	54	42	42
Millwall	38	16	10	12	50	51	42
Swindon Town	38	15	11	12	77	59	41
Brighton & Hove Albion	38	16	7	15	46	47	39
Exeter City	38	15	8	15	50	41	38
Queens Park Rangers	38	13	12	13	55	56	38
Norwich City	38	11	14	13	53	56	36
Luton Town	38	13	8	17	61	73	34
Crystal Palace	38	13	8	17	47	61	34
Bristol Rovers	38	14	3	21	53	75	31
Plymouth Argyle	38	8	14	16	51	61	30
Southend United	38	10	8	20	44	64	28
Croydon Common	38	9	9	20	47	63	27
Gillingham	38	6	8	24	43	82	20

Second Division

Stoke	24	17	4	3	62	15	38
Stalybridge Celtic	24	17	3	4	47	22	37
Merthyr Town	24	15	5	4	46	20	35
Swansea Town	24	16	1	7	48	21	33
Coventry City	24	13	2	9	56	33	28
Ton Pentre	24	11	6	7	42	43	28
Brentford	24	8	7	9	35	45	23
Llanelly	24	10	1	13	39	32	21
Barry	24	6	5	13	30	35	17
Newport County	24	7	3	14	27	42	17
Pontypridd	24	5	6	13	31	58	16
Mid Rhondda	24	3	6	15	17	40	12
Ebbw Vale	24	3	1	20	23	88	7

1919-20

First Division

Portsmouth	42	23	12	7	73	27	58
Watford	42	26	6	10	69	42	58
Crystal Palace	42	22	12	8	69	43	56
Cardiff City	42	18	17	7	70	43	53
Plymouth Argyle	42	20	10	12	57	29	50
Queens Park Rangers	42	18	10	14	62	50	46
Reading	42	16	13	13	51	43	45
Southampton	42	18	8	16	72	63	44
Swansea Town	42	16	11	15	53	45	43
Exeter City	42	17	9	16	57	51	43
Southend United	42	13	17	12	46	48	43
Norwich City	42	15	11	16	64	57	41
Swindon Town	42	17	7	18	65	68	41
Millwall	42	14	12	16	52	55	40
Brentford	42	15	10	17	52	59	40
Brighton & Hove Albion	42	14	8	20	60	72	36
Bristol Rovers	42	11	13	18	61	78	35
Newport County	42	13	7	22	45	70	33
Northampton Town	42	12	9	21	64	103	33
Luton Town	42	10	10	22	51	76	30
Merthyr Town	42	9	11	22	47	78	29
Gillingham	42	10	7	25	34	74	27

Second Division

Mid Rhondda	20	17	3	0	79	10	37
Ton Pentre	20	12	7	1	50	14	31
Llanelly	20	10	5	5	47	30	25
Pontypridd	20	10	3	7	33	29	23
Ebbw Vale	20	7	7	6	38	40	21
Barry	20	7	5	8	32	27	19
Mardy	20	7	5	8	29	30	19
Abertillery	20	6	5	9	29	40	17
Porth Athletic	20	4	4	12	30	74	12
Aberaman Athletic	20	4	3	13	28	48	11
Caerphilly	20	1	3	16	20	74	5

1920-21

English Section

Brighton & Hove Albion Reserves	24	16	3	5	65	29	35
Portsmouth Reserves	24	13	7	4	44	20	33
Millwall Reserves	24	12	4	8	40	24	28
Southampton Reserves	24	10	7	7	53	35	27
Boscombe	24	10	6	8	25	40	26
Reading Reserves	24	11	3	10	41	34	25
Luton Town Reserves	24	8	8	8	38	35	24
Charlton Athletic	24	8	8	8	41	41	24
Watford Reserves	24	9	4	11	43	45	22
Norwich City Reserves	24	7	7	10	31	39	21
Gillingham Reserves	24	6	5	13	32	47	17
Chatham	24	5	6	13	24	47	16
Thornycrofts	24	4	6	14	29	74	14

Welsh Section

Barry	20	13	4	3	35	12	30
Aberdare Athletic	20	12	3	5	29	23	27
Ebbw Vale	20	10	5	5	34	23	25
Pontypridd	20	10	3	7	34	23	23
Mid Rhondda	20	10	3	7	26	18	23
Abertillery Town	20	8	5	7	35	24	21
Ton Pentre	20	7	5	8	32	34	19
Aberaman Athletic	20	5	7	8	30	33	17
Llanelly	20	7	2	11	28	46	16
Mardy	20	2	6	12	18	39	10
Porth Athletic	20	3	3	14	28	54	9

1921-22

English Section

Plymouth Argyle Reserves	36	22	5	9	91	38	49
Bristol City Reserves	36	18	8	10	73	50	44
Portsmouth Reserves	36	17	10	9	63	41	44
Southampton Reserves	36	19	5	12	70	47	43
Gillingham Reserves	36	17	9	10	65	47	43
Charlton Athletic Reserves	36	18	6	12	69	54	42
Boscombe	36	17	5	14	38	55	39
Luton Town Reserves	36	17	4	15	50	54	38
Watford Reserves	36	15	7	14	65	53	37
Brighton & Hove Albion Reserves	36	12	13	11	60	52	37
Bath City	36	16	5	15	55	53	37
Swindon Town Reserves	36	14	7	15	59	46	35
Bristol Rovers Reserves	36	13	7	16	50	82	33
Millwall Reserves	36	13	4	19	49	53	30
Reading Reserves	36	11	7	18	46	59	29
Exeter City Reserves	36	10	9	17	42	63	29
Guildford United	36	11	6	19	44	56	28
Norwich City Reserves	36	10	6	20	47	86	26
Southend United Reserves	36	9	3	24	47	92	21

Welsh Section

Ebbw Vale	16	11	3	2	33	11	25
Ton Pentre	16	9	4	3	35	14	22
Aberaman Athletic	16	7	5	4	25	19	19
Porth Athletic	16	6	6	4	31	20	18
Pontypridd	16	7	4	5	28	19	18
Swansea Town Reserves	16	7	4	5	24	17	18
Barry	16	3	3	10	14	35	9
Abertillery Town	16	3	2	11	21	45	8
Mardy	16	2	3	11	14	43	7

1922-23

English Section

Bristol City Reserves	38	24	5	9	84	39	53
Boscombe	38	22	7	9	67	34	51
Portsmouth Reserves	38	23	3	12	93	51	49
Bristol Rovers Reserves	38	20	8	10	59	41	48
Plymouth Argyle Reserves	38	20	7	11	74	41	47
Torquay United	38	18	8	12	63	38	44
Brighton & Hove Albion Reserves	38	20	3	15	95	60	43
Luton Town Reserves	38	16	11	11	67	56	43
Southend United Reserves	38	18	6	14	69	68	42
Southampton Reserves	38	18	5	15	65	54	41
Millwall Reserves	38	15	10	13	61	55	40
Coventry City Reserves	38	15	8	15	56	61	38
Guildford Town Reserves	38	15	7	16	65	59	37
Swindon Town Reserves	38	13	6	19	54	73	32
Bath City	38	10	8	20	44	71	28
Watford Reserves	38	11	6	21	34	79	28
Yeovil & Petters United	38	10	6	22	56	104	26
Norwich City Reserves	38	9	7	22	42	68	25
Exeter City Reserves	38	10	5	23	43	81	25
Reading Reserves	38	7	6	25	43	95	20

Welsh Section

Ebbw Vale	12	6	5	1	22	15	17
Aberaman Athletic	12	7	2	3	30	19	16
Swansea Town Reserves	12	6	2	4	25	14	14
Pontypridd	12	6	2	4	18	18	14
Barry	12	4	3	5	15	11	11
Bridgend Town	12	4	2	6	15	21	10
Porth Athletic	12	0	2	10	18	24	2

1923-24

Eastern Section

Peterborough & Fletton United	30	20	2	8	54	31	42
Leicester City Reserves	30	19	3	8	72	30	41
Southampton Reserves	30	18	5	7	60	36	41
Millwall Reserves	30	18	3	9	56	38	39
Portsmouth Reserves	30	16	2	12	66	37	34
Brighton & Hove Albion Reserves	30	13	7	10	55	42	33
Norwich City Reserves	30	13	6	11	46	34	32
Folkestone	30	12	5	13	61	51	29
Coventry City Reserves	30	10	8	12	39	4	28
Watford Reserves	30	11	6	13	36	48	28
Reading Reserves	30	11	6	13	32	43	28
Northampton Town Reserves	30	9	10	11	32	47	28
Luton Town Reserves	30	10	7	13	40	49	27
Guildford United	30	7	5	18	38	72	19
Kettering	30	5	8	17	30	67	18
Bournemouth Reserves	30	4	5	21	40	85	13

Western Section

Yeovil & Petters United	34	25	3	6	71	30	53
Plymouth Argyle Reserves	34	21	5	8	74	37	47
Pontypridd	34	19	8	7	81	44	46
Torquay United	34	19	7	8	59	25	45
Bristol City Reserves	34	17	9	8	63	39	43
Swansea Town Reserves	34	19	5	10	62	38	43
Bristol Rovers Reserves	34	17	6	11	69	43	40
Cardiff City Reserves	34	15	4	15	55	31	34
Exeter City Reserves	34	11	11	12	48	47	33
Weymouth	34	15	3	16	48	60	33
Llanelly	34	14	5	15	47	62	33
Swindon Town Reserves	34	11	6	17	36	60	28
Bridgend Town	34	11	5	18	57	72	27
Newport County Reserves	34	10	7	17	57	79	27
Ebbw Vale	34	8	8	18	38	62	24
Bath City	34	6	9	19	32	71	21
Barry	34	6	7	21	36	74	19
Aberaman Athletic	34	6	4	24	41	87	16

1924-25

Eastern Section

Southampton Reserves	32	17	10	5	65	30	44
Kettering Town	32	17	6	9	67	39	40
Brighton & Hove Albion Reserves	32	15	10	7	68	42	40
Millwall Reserves	32	15	10	7	65	48	40
Peterborough & Fletton United	32	15	9	8	56	29	39
Bournemouth Reserves	32	15	9	8	66	48	39
Leicester City Reserves	32	15	7	10	61	45	37
Portsmouth Reserves	32	15	7	10	51	40	37
Folkestone	32	13	11	8	55	46	37
Norwich City Reserves	32	13	8	11	65	58	34
Coventry City Reserves	32	12	9	11	51	41	33
Luton Town Reserves	32	15	2	15	48	63	32
Northampton Town Reserves	32	10	5	17	38	59	25
Watford Reserves	32	7	7	18	44	71	21
Nuneaton Town	32	8	2	22	37	62	18
Reading Reserves	32	8	1	23	38	87	17
Guildford United	32	4	3	25	40	107	11

Western Section

Swansea Town Reserves	38	25	4	9	73	26	54
Plymouth Argyle Reserves	38	22	10	6	97	35	54
Pontypridd	38	24	4	10	81	39	52
Bridgend Town	38	20	11	7	74	52	51
Mid Rhondda United	38	21	6	11	79	48	48
Weymouth	38	21	4	13	77	50	46
Cardiff City Reserves	38	18	6	14	56	44	42
Newport County Reserves	38	17	8	13	71	60	42
Swindon Town Reserves	38	17	8	13	48	46	42
Bristol City Reserves	38	18	5	15	51	43	41
Yeovil & Petters United	38	15	10	13	49	50	40
Exeter City Reserves	38	16	6	16	78	55	38
Taunton Unied	38	15	6	17	55	51	36
Bristol Rovers Reserves	38	13	6	19	45	50	32
Torquay United	38	9	11	18	41	73	29
Llanelly	38	6	12	20	49	94	24
Ebbw Vale	38	9	6	23	40	91	24
Bath City	38	8	8	22	28	85	24
Barry	38	8	6	24	38	82	22
Aberaman Athletic	38	6	7	25	39	95	19

1925-26

Eastern Section

Millwall Reserves	34	24	6	4	106	37	54
Leicester City Reserves	34	23	2	9	105	60	48
Brighton & Hove Albion Reserves	34	21	4	9	105	69	46
Kettering Town	34	19	5	10	98	68	43
Peterborough & Fletton United	34	19	3	12	76	62	41
Portsmouth Reserves	34	17	5	12	76	67	39
Norwich City Reserves	34	17	4	13	85	90	38
Bournemouth Reserves	34	15	7	12	76	67	37
Southampton Reserves	34	14	7	13	65	72	35
Fulham Reserves	34	13	6	15	86	77	32
Grays Thurrock United	34	13	5	16	63	77	31
Guildford United	34	11	8	15	71	87	30
Watford Reserves	34	12	2	20	62	94	26
Luton Town Reserves	34	11	3	20	70	78	25
Folkestone	34	9	6	19	67	93	24
Reading Reserves	34	10	3	21	58	84	23
Coventry City Reserves	34	9	5	20	54	93	23
Nuneaton Town	34	7	3	24	61	113	17

Western Section

Plymouth Argyle Reserves	26	20	1	5	67	31	41
Bristol City Reserves	26	16	4	6	48	28	36
Bristol Rovers Reserves	26	13	4	9	51	35	30
Swindon Town Reserves	26	13	4	9	57	40	30
Ebbw Vale	26	13	3	10	60	46	29
Torquay United	26	12	5	9	59	46	29
Yeovil & Petters United	26	9	8	9	43	48	26
Mid Rhondda	26	12	1	13	47	49	25
Weymouth	26	10	3	13	64	60	23
Exeter City Reserves	26	8	5	13	40	49	21
Barry	26	8	4	14	47	55	20
Taunton United	26	9	2	15	44	60	20
Pontypridd	26	7	5	14	44	77	19
Bath City	26	7	1	18	38	86	15

1926-27

Eastern Section

Brighton & Hove Albion Reserves	32	21	6	5	86	47	48
Peterborough & Fletton United	32	18	9	5	80	39	45
Portsmouth Reserves	32	19	6	7	95	65	44
Kettering Town	32	15	10	7	66	41	40
Millwall Reserves	32	16	5	11	67	56	37
Bournemouth Reserves	32	14	6	12	69	64	34
Norwich City Reserves	32	14	5	13	79	74	33
Dartford	32	13	7	12	60	71	33
Reading Reserves	32	12	8	12	75	79	32
Luton Town Reserves	32	10	11	11	75	70	1
Leicester City Reserves	32	12	5	15	94	72	29
Watford Reserves	32	10	8	14	74	84	28
Southampton Reserves	32	10	6	16	57	77	26
Poole	32	9	6	17	55	86	24
Grays Thurrock United	32	10	3	19	49	66	23
Guildford United	32	6	7	19	57	106	19
Folkestone	32	7	4	21	57	98	18

Western Section

Torquay United	26	17	4	5	63	30	38
Bristol City Reserves	26	14	10	2	77	37	38
Plymouth Argyle Reserves	26	15	4	7	56	38	34
Ebbw Vale	26	14	2	10	67	45	30
Bristol Rovers Reserves	26	12	4	10	51	43	28
Swindon Town Reserves	26	11	5	10	60	57	27
Barry	26	11	4	11	65	50	26
Essex City Reserves	26	10	6	10	62	49	26
Weymouth	26	12	2	12	48	65	26
Newport County Reserves	26	9	6	11	57	53	24
Bath City	26	7	9	10	44	52	23
Yeovil & Petters United	26	9	5	12	49	66	23
Taunton United	26	4	4	18	36	83	12
Mid Rhondda United	26	2	5	19	22	89	9

1927-28

Easter Section

Kettering Town	34	23	6	5	90	39	52
Peterborough & Fletton United	34	21	3	10	73	43	45
Northfleet United	34	17	7	10	83	54	41
Brighton & Hove Albion Reserves	34	20	0	14	90	63	40
Norwich City Reserves	34	17	6	11	69	69	40
Southampton Reserves	34	16	7	11	92	70	39
Aldershot Town	34	17	5	12	85	66	39
Sittingbourne	34	16	5	13	64	70	37
Millwall Reserves	34	15	6	13	66	59	36
Poole	34	15	5	14	69	84	35
Folkestone	34	12	6	16	71	91	30
Guildford City	34	12	5	17	65	89	29
Dartford	34	12	4	18	46	49	28
Gillingham Reserves	34	10	7	17	72	84	27
Sheppey United	34	11	3	20	57	87	25
Chatham	34	10	4	20	49	70	24
Grays Thurrock United	34	10	3	21	48	88	23
Bournemouth Reserves	34	9	4	21	48	62	22

Western Section

Bristol City Reserves	30	20	3	7	95	51	43
Exeter City Reserves	30	18	4	8	104	56	40
Bristol Rovers Reserves	30	16	3	11	80	64	35
Plymouth Argyle Reserves	30	16	2	12	88	53	34
Newport County Reserves	30	13	8	9	99	70	34
Ebbw Vale	30	15	3	12	67	74	33
Swindon Town Reserves	30	13	4	13	80	74	30
Aberdare & Aberaman	30	12	6	12	62	68	30
Yeovil & Petters United	30	11	7	12	64	57	29
Torquay United Reserves	30	11	6	13	51	67	28
Bath City	30	12	3	15	64	68	27
Taunton Town	30	11	5	14	60	65	27
Weymouth	30	10	6	14	50	83	26
Merthyr Town Reserves	30	9	4	17	50	77	22
Barry	30	8	6	16	45	87	22
Mid Rhondda United	30	7	6	17	36	81	20

1928-29

Eastern Section

Kettering Town	36	24	4	8	96	46	52
Peterborough & Fletton United	36	21	5	10	86	44	47
Brighton & Hove Albion Reserves	36	19	9	8	91	56	47
Millwall Reserves	36	21	4	11	90	67	46
Bournemouth Reserves	36	20	5	11	82	58	45
Aldershot Town	36	18	5	13	68	52	41
Sheppey United	36	17	7	12	58	58	41
Folkestone	36	17	6	13	83	80	40
Northfleet United	36	17	4	15	87	65	38
Gillingham Reserves	36	15	8	13	68	70	38
Guildford City	36	13	11	12	85	78	37
Southampton Reserves	36	14	6	16	86	79	34
Poole	36	13	8	15	62	66	34
Thames Association	36	13	5	18	67	74	31
Dartford	36	10	6	20	55	106	26
Chatham	36	8	8	20	47	81	24
Sittingbourne	36	11	1	24	59	98	23
Norwich City Reserves	36	8	6	22	48	96	22
Grays Thurrock United	36	6	6	24	47	91	18

Western Section

Plymouth Argyle Reserves	26	15	6	5	69	27	36
Newport County Reserves	26	15	2	9	64	58	32
Bristol Rovers Reserves	26	14	3	9	54	45	31
Bristol City Reserves	26	14	2	10	70	46	30
Torquay United Reserves	26	13	4	9	52	42	30
Bath City	26	13	4	9	43	59	30
Exeter City Reserves	26	11	6	9	69	53	28
Lovells Athletic	26	11	6	9	54	48	28
Swindon Town Reserves	26	11	5	10	68	74	27
Yeovil & Petters United	26	11	2	13	49	57	24
Taunton Town	26	9	5	12	58	66	23
Ebbw Vale	26	9	5	12	56	66	23
Barry	26	6	3	17	38	66	15
Merthyr Town Reserves	26	3	1	22	37	92	7

1929-30

Eastern Section

Aldershot Town	32	21	6	5	84	39	48
Millwall Reserves	32	21	3	8	75	56	45
Thames Association	32	17	6	9	80	60	40
Peterborough & Fletton United	32	18	3	11	66	39	39
Northampton Town Reserves	32	17	4	11	86	60	38
Southampton Reserves	32	14	7	11	73	62	35
Sheppey United	32	15	5	12	76	69	35
Kettering Town	32	13	7	12	70	69	33
Dartford	32	14	5	13	57	59	33
Norwich City Reserves	32	14	3	15	69	69	31
Guildford City	32	13	2	17	65	97	28
Bournemouth Reserves	32	10	7	15	59	63	27
Brighton & Hove Albion Reserves	32	12	2	18	56	79	26
Folkestone	32	13	0	19	56	82	26
Sittingbourne	32	10	5	17	55	59	25
Northfleet United	32	6	7	19	53	77	19
Grays Thurrock United	32	7	2	23	54	101	16

Western Section

Bath City	28	16	6	6	85	52	38
Bristol Rovers Reserves	28	16	4	8	66	50	36
Taunton Town	28	14	7	7	50	40	35
Barry	28	15	3	10	65	55	33
Yeovil & Petters United	28	12	7	9	63	47	31
Plymouth Argyle Reserves	28	14	3	11	68	52	31
Newport County Reserves	28	13	4	11	68	76	30
Lovells Athletic	28	13	2	13	59	57	28
Exeter City Reserves	28	11	6	11	49	54	28
Bristol City Reserves	28	11	5	12	59	63	27
Swindon Town Reserves	28	10	6	12	69	67	26
Torquay United Reserves	28	10	6	12	76	77	26
Llanelly	28	10	4	14	55	52	24
Ebbw Vale	28	5	6	17	52	97	16
Merthyr Town Reserves	28	5	1	22	48	93	11

1930-31

Eastern Section

Dartford	16	9	5	2	39	18	23
Aldershot Town	16	10	3	3	50	28	23
Norwich City Reserves	16	9	1	6	47	38	19
Peterborough & Fletton United	16	6	5	5	35	29	17
Thames Association Reserves	16	7	2	7	38	31	16
Millwall Reserves	16	7	0	9	47	40	14
Folkestone	16	4	3	9	31	46	11
Guildford City	16	5	1	10	28	53	11
Sheppey United	16	4	2	10	31	63	10

Western Section

Exeter City Reserves	22	15	2	5	59	28	32
Llanelly	22	10	8	4	72	39	28
Merthyr Town	22	12	3	7	62	49	27
Plymouth Argyle Reserves	22	12	2	8	55	34	26
Bath City	22	10	6	6	47	39	26
Torquay United Reserves	22	9	5	8	66	49	23
Swindon Town Reserves	22	7	7	8	48	52	21
Bristol Rovers Reserves	22	7	6	9	58	64	20
Barry	22	7	5	10	29	39	19
Taunton Town	22	5	7	10	36	62	17
Newport County Reserves	22	6	2	14	36	66	14
Ebbw Vale	22	5	1	16	32	79	11

1931-32

Eastern Section

Dartford	18	12	3	3	53	18	27
Folkestone	18	12	2	4	58	27	26
Guildford City	18	11	1	6	33	24	23
Norwich City Reserves	18	9	2	7	46	33	20
Millwall Reserves	18	9	2	7	41	39	20
Tunbridge Wells Rangers	18	7	5	6	23	25	19
Bournemouth Reserves	18	6	4	8	43	61	16
Peterborough & Fletton United	18	4	5	9	28	29	13
Aldershot Town	18	3	5	10	17	30	11
Sheppey United	18	2	1	15	16	72	5

Western Section

Yeovil & Petters United	24	16	4	4	65	31	36
Plymouth Argyle Reserves	24	15	5	4	81	31	35
Bath City	24	12	7	5	50	33	31
Llanelly	24	12	4	8	65	46	28
Taunton Town	24	13	2	9	53	58	28
Newport County Reserves	24	10	6	8	70	51	26
Exeter City Reserves	24	9	7	8	59	43	25
Merthyr Town	24	9	4	11	66	73	22
Bristol Rovers Reserves	24	8	4	12	54	47	20
Swindon Town Reserves	24	8	4	12	54	95	20
Barry	24	7	3	14	58	76	17
Torquay United Reserves	24	5	6	13	43	66	16
Ebbw Vale	24	3	2	19	34	102	8

1932-33

Eastern Section

Norwich City Reserves	14	9	2	3	34	22	20
Dartford	14	8	2	4	26	23	18
Folkestone	14	7	1	6	35	32	15
Bournemouth Reserves	14	5	4	5	36	33	14
Tunbridge Wells Rangers	14	5	2	7	23	24	12
Guildford City	14	5	2	7	22	28	12
Millwall Reserves	14	5	1	8	27	31	11
Aldershot Reserves	14	3	4	7	24	34	10

Western Section

Bath City	20	13	4	3	62	34	30
Exeter City Reserves	20	12	3	5	62	46	27
Torquay United Reserves	20	12	1	7	56	37	25
Plymouth Argyle Reserves	20	11	2	7	68	38	24
Yeovil & Petters United	20	11	2	7	59	44	24
Llanelly	20	10	2	8	53	33	22
Bristol Rovers Reserves	20	7	3	10	53	65	17
Newport County Reserves	20	6	4	10	42	55	16
Merthyr Tydfil	20	7	1	12	39	58	15
Barry	20	3	4	13	30	72	10
Taunton Town	20	4	2	14	21	63	10

1933-34

Eastern Section

Norwich City Reserves	16	9	4	3	41	15	22
Margate	16	8	3	5	23	20	19
Millwall Reserves	16	7	4	5	28	28	18
Clapton Orient Reserves	16	8	1	7	33	34	17
Bournemouth Reserves	16	6	3	7	28	30	15
Tunbridge Wells Rangers	16	6	2	8	25	36	14
Folkestone	16	5	3	8	26	26	13
Guildford City	16	5	3	8	27	33	13
Dartford	16	4	5	7	15	24	13

Western Section

Plymouth Argyle Reserves	20	13	6	1	62	22	32
Bristol Rovers Reserves	20	14	3	3	56	27	31
Bath City	20	11	3	6	43	25	25
Torquay United Reserves	20	9	4	7	54	36	22
Yeovil & Petters United	20	10	1	9	35	39	21
Exeter City Reserves	20	8	3	9	54	47	19
Merthyr Town	20	8	2	10	39	50	18
Llanelly	20	8	1	11	25	39	17
Barry	20	4	5	11	37	64	13
Newport County Reserves	20	4	3	13	36	54	11
Taunton Town	20	5	1	14	27	65	11

Central Section

Plymouth Argyle Reserves	18	16	1	1	47	14	33
Clapton Orient Reserves	18	9	3	6	35	25	21
Norwich City Reserves	18	8	4	6	41	27	20
Yeovil & Petters United	18	7	4	7	34	38	18
Bath City	18	7	3	8	31	36	17
Dartford	18	6	4	8	28	26	16
Tunbridge Wells Rangers	18	7	1	10	26	37	15
Llanelly	18	6	2	10	28	39	14
Folkestone	18	6	1	11	30	41	13
Guildford City	18	6	1	11	28	45	13

1934-35

Eastern Section

Norwich City Reserves	18	12	1	5	52	21	25
Dartford	18	8	6	4	36	22	22
Margate	18	7	6	7	38	30	20
Bournemouth Reserves	18	8	3	8	34	26	19
Guildford City	18	7	5	6	41	34	19
Aldershot Reserves	18	7	3	8	29	43	17
Folkestone	18	5	6	7	30	39	16
Tunbridge Wells Rangers	18	6	4	8	32	56	16
Clapton Orient Reserves	18	5	4	9	33	35	14
Millwall Reserves	18	3	6	9	26	45	12

Western Section

Yeovil & Petters United	16	11	2	3	49	18	24
Newport County Reserves	16	8	5	3	45	29	21
Plymouth Argyle Reserves	16	7	5	4	40	24	19
Exeter City Reserves	16	7	2	7	38	32	16
Bath City	16	6	4	6	35	32	16
Bristol Rovers Reserves	16	5	5	6	33	37	15
Barry	16	6	3	7	30	40	15
Torquay United Reserves	16	5	3	8	24	29	13
Taunton Town	16	1	3	12	13	66	5

Central Section

Folkestone	20	11	4	5	43	31	26
Guildford City	20	11	4	5	43	39	26
Plymouth Argyle Reserves	20	6	9	5	40	28	21
Torquay United Reserves	20	7	6	7	34	35	20
Bristol Rovers Reserves	20	8	4	8	38	46	20
Margate	20	8	3	9	40	34	19
Dartford	20	8	3	9	43	38	19
Aldershot Reserves	20	8	3	9	33	44	19
Tunbridge Wells Rangers	20	8	2	10	33	37	18
Yeovil & Petters United	20	8	1	11	45	51	17
Bath City	20	6	3	11	34	43	15

1935-36

Eastern Section

Margate	18	13	2	3	49	16	28
Folkestone	18	11	3	4	46	23	25
Dartford	18	9	3	6	47	25	21
Tunbridge Wells Rangers	18	9	1	8	26	41	19
Clapton Orient Reserves	18	7	4	7	39	31	18
Millwall Reserves	18	7	3	8	42	39	17
Norwich City Reserves	18	8	0	10	39	38	16
Guildford City	18	6	3	9	32	52	15
Aldershot Reserves	18	6	1	11	24	45	13
Bournemouth Reserves	18	3	2	13	25	59	8

Western Section

Plymouth Argyle Reserves	16	12	3	1	51	18	27
Bristol Rovers Reserves	16	8	3	5	35	30	19
Newport County Reserves	16	8	3	5	29	30	19
Torquay United Reserves	16	7	1	8	25	28	15
Bath City	16	5	5	6	18	26	15
Cheltenham Town	16	6	2	8	32	28	14
Yeovil & Petters United	16	5	3	8	31	35	13
Barry	16	5	2	9	29	41	12
Exeter City Reserves	16	4	2	10	24	38	10

Central Section

Margate	20	14	3	3	57	18	31
Bristol Rovers Reserves	20	13	1	6	51	37	27
Plymouth Argyle Reserves	20	12	2	6	53	32	26
Aldershot Reserves	20	9	4	7	37	37	22
Folkestone	20	9	3	8	51	36	21
Tunbridge Wells Rangers	20	7	4	9	40	41	18
Dartford	20	7	3	10	34	42	17
Guildford City	20	7	3	10	33	47	17
Cheltenham Town	20	5	5	10	32	45	15
Bath City	20	5	5	10	34	52	15
Yeovil & Petters United	20	3	5	12	40	75	11

1936-37

Ipswich Town	30	19	8	3	68	35	46
Norwich City Reserves	30	18	5	7	70	35	41
Folkestone	30	17	4	9	71	62	38
Margate	30	15	4	11	64	49	34
Guildford City	30	15	4	11	54	60	34
Bath City	30	14	5	11	65	55	33
Yeovil & Petters United	30	15	3	12	77	69	33
Plymouth Argyle Reserves	30	11	8	11	64	58	30
Newport County Reserves	30	11	8	11	72	68	30
Barry	30	12	4	14	58	72	28
Cheltenham Town	30	10	4	16	61	70	24
Dartford	30	9	5	16	41	55	23
Exeter City Reserves	30	8	7	15	57	78	23
Tunbridge Wells Rangers	30	8	6	16	62	64	22
Torquay United Reserves	30	8	5	17	46	76	21
Aldershot Reserves	30	7	6	17	47	74	20

Midweek Section

Margate	18	12	1	5	48	24	25
Bath City	18	10	5	3	38	28	25
Norwich City Reserves	18	9	5	4	44	27	23
Folkestone	18	7	6	5	32	36	20
Millwall Reserves	18	8	3	7	44	47	19
Portsmouth Reserves	18	6	5	7	40	27	17
Tunbridge Wells Rangers	18	5	4	9	30	41	14
Aldershot Reserves	18	6	2	10	20	30	14
Guildford City	18	3	6	9	24	36	12
Dartford	18	4	3	11	19	43	11

1937-38

Guildford City	34	22	5	7	94	60	49
Plymouth Argyle Reserves	34	18	9	7	98	58	45
Ipswich Town	34	19	6	9	89	54	44
Yeovil & Petters United	34	14	14	6	72	45	42
Norwich City Reserves	34	15	11	8	77	55	41
Colchester United	34	15	8	11	90	58	38
Bristol Rovers Reserves	34	14	8	12	63	62	36
Swindon Town Reserves	34	14	7	13	70	76	35
Tunbridge Wells Rangers	34	14	6	14	68	74	34
Aldershot Reserves	34	10	12	12	42	55	32
Cheltenham Town	34	13	5	16	72	68	31
Exeter City Reserves	34	13	5	16	71	75	31
Dartford	34	9	11	14	51	70	29
Bath City	34	9	9	16	45	65	27
Folkestone	34	10	6	18	58	82	26
Newport County Reserves	34	10	6	18	56	86	26
Barry	34	8	7	19	50	88	23
Torquay United Reserves	34	8	7	19	46	81	23

Midweek Section

Millwall Reserves	18	13	3	2	59	21	29
Colchester United	18	13	1	4	42	23	27
Aldershot Reserves	18	11	3	4	38	29	25
Norwich City Reserves	18	9	1	8	45	39	19
Portsmouth Reserves	18	5	5	8	31	30	15
Dartford	18	6	3	9	32	35	15
Folkestone	18	6	3	9	34	38	15
Tunbridge Wells Rangers	18	5	4	9	28	36	14
Bath City	18	5	3	10	27	45	13
Guildford City	18	4	0	14	21	61	8

1938-39

Colchester United	44	31	5	8	110	37	67
Guildford City	44	30	6	8	126	52	66
Gillingham	44	29	6	9	104	57	64
Plymouth Argyle Reserves	44	26	5	13	128	63	57
Yeovil & Petters United	44	22	10	12	85	70	54
Arsenal Reserves	44	21	9	14	92	57	51
Cardiff City Reserves	44	24	3	17	105	72	51
Tunbridge Wells Rangers	44	22	6	16	93	76	50
Norwich City Reserves	44	23	4	17	86	76	50
Chelmsford City	44	18	8	18	74	73	44
Bath City	44	16	12	16	58	74	44
Barry	44	18	7	19	76	90	43
Cheltenham Town	44	16	9	19	76	105	41
Ipswich Town Reserves	44	14	12	18	64	76	40
Worcester City	44	13	14	17	72	90	40
Folkestone	44	16	6	22	74	85	38
Newport County Reserves	44	13	10	21	74	108	36
Exeter City Reserves	44	12	9	23	51	107	33
Torquay United Reserves	44	12	8	24	53	89	32
Swindon Town Reserves	44	11	9	24	66	101	31
Aldershot Reserves	44	12	6	26	69	92	30
Bristol Rovers Reserves	44	9	11	24	66	85	29
Dartford	44	8	5	31	53	119	21

Midweek Section

Tunbridge Wells Rangers	16	8	7	1	37	18	23
Colchester United	16	9	2	5	36	21	20
Norwich City Reserves	16	7	4	5	40	26	18
Millwall Reserves	16	7	4	5	33	23	18
Portsmouth Reserves	16	5	4	7	21	29	14
Guildford City	16	4	6	6	24	39	14
Aldershot Reserves	16	4	5	7	22	25	13
Folkestone	16	4	5	7	24	35	13
Dartford	16	4	3	9	24	45	11

1939-40

Eastern Section

Chelmsford City	7	5	0	2	29	9	10
Guildford City	8	4	1	3	26	13	9
Tunbridge Wells Rangers	7	2	3	2	21	16	7
Dartford	7	2	1	4	17	30	5
Norwich City Reserves	7	2	1	4	9	34	5

Western Section

Lovells Athletic	14	11	1	2	53	22	23
Worcester City	14	9	2	3	55	30	20
Hereford United	14	8	0	6	45	31	16
Yeovil & Petters United	14	7	2	5	30	24	16
Gloucester City	14	5	0	9	35	49	10
Barry	14	4	1	9	31	56	9
Cheltenham Town	13	3	2	8	21	38	8
Bath City	13	3	2	8	21	41	8

1945-46

Chelmsford City	18	15	1	2	66	23	34
Hereford United	20	13	3	4	59	31	29
Bath City	20	12	2	6	62	32	26
Cheltenham Town	18	9	1	8	35	54	22
Barry Town	20	8	4	8	42	42	20
Yeovil & Petters United	18	7	1	10	57	52	18
Worcester City	20	8	2	10	60	58	18
Colchester United	20	7	3	10	29	47	17
Bedford Town	16	4	1	11	30	49	15
Swindon Town Reserves	18	4	3	11	36	65	14
Cardiff City Reserves	20	4	5	11	39	60	13

1946-47

Gillingham	31	20	6	5	103	45	47
Guildford City	32	21	4	7	86	39	46
Merthyr Tydfil	31	21	2	8	104	37	45
Yeovil Town	32	19	6	7	100	49	44
Chelmsford City	31	17	3	11	90	60	38
Gravesend & Northfleet	32	17	4	11	82	58	38
Barry Town	30	14	6	10	89	61	36
Colchester United	31	15	4	12	65	60	35
Cheltenham Town	31	14	3	14	68	75	32
Millwall	24	8	5	11	59	57	29
Dartford	32	10	5	17	71	100	25
Bedford Town	32	8	8	16	63	98	24
Hereford United	32	8	7	17	37	85	23
Worcester City	31	8	5	18	55	90	22
Exeter City Reserves	32	10	2	20	69	126	22
Bath City	32	7	7	18	52	93	21
Gloucester City	32	8	1	23	57	120	17

1947-48

Merthyr Tydfil	34	23	7	4	84	38	53
Gillingham	34	21	5	8	81	43	47
Worcester City	34	21	3	10	74	45	45
Colchester United	34	17	10	7	88	41	44
Hereford United	34	16	10	8	77	53	42
Lovells Athletic	34	17	6	11	74	50	40
Exeter City Reserves	34	15	7	12	65	57	37
Yeovil Town	34	12	11	11	56	50	35
Chelmsford City	34	14	7	13	62	58	35
Cheltenham Town	34	13	9	12	71	71	35
Bath City	34	12	8	14	55	62	32
Barry Town	34	10	9	15	60	70	29
Gravesend & Northfleet	34	11	6	17	52	81	28
Guildford City	34	11	4	19	69	74	26
Dartford	34	10	6	18	35	62	26
Gloucester City	34	8	6	20	45	78	22
Torquay United Reserves	34	6	9	19	43	95	21
Bedford Town	34	6	3	25	41	104	15

1948-49

Gillingham	42	26	10	6	104	48	62
Chelmsford City	42	27	7	8	115	64	61
Merthyr Tydfil	42	26	8	8	133	54	60
Colchester United	42	21	10	11	94	61	52
Worcester City	42	22	7	13	87	56	51
Dartford	42	21	9	12	73	53	51
Gravesend & Northfleet	42	20	9	13	60	46	49
Yeovil Town	42	19	9	14	90	53	47
Cheltenham Town	42	19	9	14	71	64	47
Kidderminster Harriers	42	19	6	17	77	96	44
Exeter City Reserves	42	18	7	17	83	73	43
Hereford United	42	17	6	19	83	84	40
Bath City	42	15	8	19	72	87	38
Hastings United	42	14	10	18	69	93	38
Torquay United Reserves	42	15	7	20	73	93	37
Lovells Athletic	42	14	8	20	73	74	36
Guildford City	42	12	12	18	58	85	36
Gloucester City	42	12	10	20	78	100	34
Barry Town	42	12	10	20	55	95	34
Tonbridge	42	9	7	26	54	105	25
Chingford Town	42	6	9	27	43	94	21
Bedford Town	42	5	8	29	32	101	18

1949-50

Merthyr Tydfil	46	34	3	9	143	62	71
Colchester United	46	31	9	6	109	51	71
Yeovil Town	46	29	7	10	104	45	65
Chelmsford City	46	26	9	11	121	64	61
Gillingham	46	23	9	14	93	61	55
Dartford	46	20	9	17	70	65	49
Worcester City	46	21	7	18	85	80	49
Guildford City	46	18	11	17	79	73	47
Weymouth	46	19	9	18	80	82	47
Barry Town	46	18	10	18	78	72	46
Exeter City Reserves	46	16	14	16	73	83	46
Lovells Athletic	46	17	10	19	86	78	44
Tonbridge	46	16	12	18	65	76	44
Hastings United	46	17	8	21	92	140	42
Gravesend & Northfleet	46	16	9	21	88	82	41
Torquay United Reserves	46	14	12	20	80	89	40
Bath City	46	16	7	23	61	78	39
Gloucester City	46	14	11	21	72	101	39
Hereford United	46	15	8	23	74	76	38
Cheltenham Town	46	13	11	22	75	96	37
Headington United	46	15	7	24	72	97	37
Bedford Town	46	12	11	23	63	79	35
Kidderminster Harriers	46	12	11	23	65	108	35
Chingford Town	46	10	6	30	61	151	26

1950-51

Merthyr Tydfil	44	29	8	7	156	66	66
Hereford United	44	27	7	10	110	69	61
Guildford City	44	23	8	13	88	60	54
Chelmsford City	44	21	12	11	84	58	54
Llanelly	44	19	13	12	89	73	51
Cheltenham Town	44	21	8	15	91	61	50
Headington United	44	18	11	15	84	83	47
Torquay United Reserves	44	20	6	18	93	79	46
Exeter City Reserves	44	16	12	16	90	94	44
Weymouth	44	16	12	16	82	88	44
Tonbridge	44	16	12	16	79	87	44
Gloucester City	44	16	11	17	81	76	43
Yeovil Town	44	13	15	16	72	72	41
Worcester City	44	15	11	18	69	78	41
Bath City	44	15	10	19	66	73	40
Dartford	44	14	11	19	61	70	39
Bedford Town	44	15	9	20	64	94	39
Gravesend & Northfleet	44	12	14	18	65	83	38
Kettering Town	44	13	11	20	87	87	37
Lovells Athletic	44	12	13	19	81	93	37
Kidderminster Harriers	44	13	9	22	58	103	35
Barry Town	44	13	7	24	54	104	33
Hastings United	44	11	6	27	91	143	28

1951-52

Merthyr Tydfil	42	27	6	9	128	60	60
Weymouth	42	22	13	7	81	42	57
Kidderminster Harriers	42	22	10	10	70	40	54
Guildford City	42	18	16	8	66	47	52
Hereford United	42	21	9	12	00	59	51
Worcester City	42	23	4	15	86	73	50
Kettering Town	42	18	10	14	83	56	46
Lovells Athletic	42	18	10	14	87	68	46
Gloucester City	42	19	8	15	68	55	46
Bath City	42	19	6	17	75	67	44
Headington United	42	16	11	15	55	53	43
Bedford Town	42	16	10	16	75	64	42
Barry Town	42	18	6	18	84	89	42
Chelmsford City	42	15	10	17	67	80	40
Dartford	42	15	9	18	63	65	39
Tonbridge	42	15	6	21	63	84	36
Yeovil Town	42	12	11	19	56	76	35
Cheltenham Town	42	15	4	23	59	85	34
Exeter City Reserves	42	13	7	22	76	106	33
Llanelly	42	13	6	23	70	111	32
Gravesend & Northfleet	42	12	7	23	68	88	31
Hastings United	42	3	5	34	41	131	11

1952-53

Headington United	42	23	12	7	93	50	58
Merthyr Tydfil	42	25	8	9	117	66	58
Bedford Town	42	24	8	10	91	61	56
Kettering Town	42	23	8	11	88	50	54
Bath City	42	22	10	10	71	46	54
Worcester City	42	20	11	11	100	66	51
Llanelly	42	21	9	12	95	72	51
Barry Town	42	22	3	17	89	69	47
Gravesend & Northfleet	42	19	7	16	83	76	45
Gloucester City	42	17	9	16	50	78	43
Guildford City	42	17	8	17	64	60	42
Hastings United	42	18	5	19	75	66	41
Cheltenham Town	42	15	11	16	70	89	41
Weymouth	42	15	10	17	70	75	40
Hereford United	42	17	5	20	76	73	39
Tonbridge	42	12	9	21	62	88	33
Lovells Athletic	42	12	8	22	68	81	32
Yeovil Town	42	11	10	21	75	99	32
Chelmsford City	42	12	7	23	58	92	31
Exeter City Reserves	42	13	4	25	71	94	30
Kidderminster Harriers	42	12	5	25	54	85	29
Dartford	42	6	5	31	40	121	17

1953-54

Merthyr Tydfil	42	27	8	7	97	55	62
Headington United	42	22	9	11	68	43	53
Yeovil Town	42	20	8	14	87	76	48
Bath City	42	17	12	13	73	67	46
Kidderminster Harriers	42	18	9	15	62	59	45
Weymouth	42	18	8	16	83	72	44
Barry Town	42	17	9	16	108	91	43
Bedford Town	42	19	5	18	80	84	43
Gloucester City	42	16	11	15	69	77	43
Hastings United	42	16	10	16	73	67	42
Kettering Town	42	15	12	15	65	63	42
Hereford United	42	16	9	17	66	62	41
Llanelly	42	16	9	17	80	85	41
Guildford City	42	15	11	16	56	60	41
Gravesend & Northfleet	42	16	8	18	76	77	40
Worcester City	42	17	6	19	66	71	40
Lovells Athletic	42	14	11	17	62	60	39
Tonbridge	42	15	9	18	85	91	39
Chelmsford City	42	14	10	18	67	71	38
Exeter City Reserves	42	11	13	18	61	72	35
Cheltenham Town	42	11	12	19	56	83	34
Dartford	42	6	13	23	42	89	25

1954-55

Yeovil Town	42	23	9	10	105	66	55
Weymouth	42	24	7	11	105	84	55
Hastings United	42	21	9	12	94	60	51
Cheltenham Town	42	21	8	13	85	72	50
Guildford City	42	20	8	14	72	59	48
Worcester City	42	19	10	13	80	73	48
Barry Town	42	16	15	11	82	87	47
Gloucester City	42	16	13	13	66	54	45
Bath City	42	18	9	15	73	80	45
Headington Town	42	18	7	17	82	62	43
Kidderminster Harriers	42	18	7	17	84	86	43
Merthyr Tydfil	42	17	8	17	97	94	42
Exeter City Reserves	42	19	4	19	67	78	42
Lovells Athletic	42	15	11	16	71	68	41
Kettering Town	42	15	11	16	70	69	41
Hereford United	42	17	5	20	91	72	39
Llanelly	42	16	7	19	78	81	39
Bedford Town	42	16	3	23	75	103	35
Tonbridge	42	11	8	23	68	91	30
Dartford	42	9	12	21	55	76	30
Chelmsford City	42	11	6	25	73	111	28
Gravesend & Northfleet	42	9	9	24	62	97	27

1955-56

Guildford City	42	26	8	8	74	34	60
Cheltenham Town	42	25	6	11	82	53	56
Yeovil Town	42	23	9	10	98	55	55
Bedford Town	42	21	9	12	99	69	51
Dartford	42	20	9	13	78	62	49
Weymouth	42	19	10	13	83	63	48
Gloucester City	42	19	9	14	72	60	47
Lovells Athletic	42	19	9	14	91	78	47
Chelmsford City	42	18	10	14	67	55	46
Kettering Town	42	16	11	15	105	86	43
Exeter City Reserves	42	17	9	16	75	76	43
Gravesend & Northfleet	42	17	8	17	79	75	42
Hereford United	42	17	7	18	90	90	41
Hastings United	42	15	10	17	90	76	40
Headington United	42	17	6	19	82	86	40
Kidderminster Harriers	42	14	7	21	86	108	35
Llanelly	42	14	6	22	64	98	34
Barry Town	42	11	11	20	91	108	33
Worcester City	42	12	9	21	66	83	33
Tonbridge	42	11	11	20	53	74	33
Merthyr Tydfil	42	7	10	25	52	127	24
Bath City	42	7	10	25	43	107	24

1956-57

Kettering Town	42	28	10	4	106	47	66
Bedford Town	42	25	8	9	89	52	58
Weymouth	42	22	10	10	92	71	54
Cheltenham Town	42	19	15	8	73	46	53
Gravesend & Northfleet	42	21	11	10	74	58	53
Lovells Athletic	42	21	7	14	99	84	49
Guildford City	42	18	11	13	68	49	47
Hereford United	42	19	8	15	96	60	46
Headington United	42	19	7	16	64	61	45
Gloucester City	42	18	8	16	74	72	44
Hastings United	42	17	9	16	70	58	43
Worcester City	42	16	10	16	81	80	42
Dartford	42	16	10	16	79	88	42
Chelmsford City	42	16	9	17	73	85	41
Tonbridge	42	14	12	16	74	65	40
Yeovil Town	42	14	11	17	83	85	39
Bath City	42	15	8	19	56	78	38
Exeter City Reserves	42	10	10	22	52	89	30
Merthyr Tydfil	42	9	11	22	72	95	29
Barry Town	42	6	11	25	39	84	23
Kidderminster Harriers	42	7	10	25	60	83	20
Llanelly	42	5	8	29	39	123	18

1957-58

Gravesend & Northfleet	42	27	5	10	109	71	59
Bedford Town	42	25	7	10	112	64	57
Chelmsford City	42	24	9	9	93	57	57
Weymouth	42	25	5	12	90	61	55
Worcester City	42	23	7	12	95	59	53
Cheltenham Town	42	21	10	11	115	66	52
Hereford United	42	21	6	15	79	56	48
Kettering Town	42	18	9	15	99	76	45
Headington Town	42	18	7	17	90	83	43
Poole Town	42	17	9	16	82	81	43
Hasting United	42	13	15	14	78	77	41
Gloucester City	42	17	7	18	70	70	41
Yeovil Town	42	16	9	17	70	84	41
Dartford	42	14	9	19	66	92	37
Lovells Athletic	42	15	6	21	60	83	36
Bath City	42	13	9	20	65	64	35
Guildford City	42	12	10	20	58	92	34
Tonbridge	42	13	7	22	77	100	33
Exeter City Reserves	42	12	8	22	60	94	32
Barry Town	42	11	9	22	72	101	31
Kidderminster Harriers	42	10	10	22	60	101	30
Merthyr Tydfil	42	9	3	30	69	137	21

1958-59

North-Western Zone

Hereford United	34	22	5	7	80	37	49
Kettering Town	34	20	7	7	83	63	47
Boston United	34	18	8	8	73	47	44
Cheltenham Town	34	20	4	10	65	47	44
Worcester City	34	19	4	11	74	47	42
Bath City	34	17	5	12	89	62	39
Wellington Town	34	15	9	10	74	58	39
Nuneaton Borough	34	17	5	12	76	66	39
Wisbech Town	34	16	5	13	77	54	37
Headington United	34	16	3	15	76	61	35
Barry Town	34	15	5	14	64	67	35
Merthyr Tydfil	34	16	3	15	54	59	35
Gloucester City	34	12	6	16	50	65	30
Corby Town	34	10	8	16	59	79	28
Lovells Athletic	34	10	3	21	51	70	23
Rugby Town	34	7	6	21	45	93	20
Kidderminster Harriers	34	7	3	24	42	94	17
Burton Albion	34	3	3	28	41	104	9

South-Eastern Zone

Bedford Town	32	21	6	5	90	41	48
Gravesend & Northfleet	32	21	2	9	79	54	44
Dartford	32	20	3	9	77	41	43
Yeovil Town	32	17	8	7	60	41	42
Weymouth	32	13	11	8	61	43	37
Chelmsford City	32	12	12	8	74	53	36
King's Lynn	32	14	5	13	70	63	33
Poole Town	32	12	8	12	60	65	32
Cambridge City	32	12	7	13	61	54	31
Hastings United	32	13	5	14	60	59	31
Tonbridge	32	14	3	15	51	59	31
Cambridge United	32	11	8	13	55	77	30
Trowbridge Town	32	12	4	16	53	75	28
Exeter City Reserves	32	7	12	13	47	71	26
Guildford City	11	7	6	19	45	67	20
Clacton Town	32	6	7	19	44	81	19
Yiewsley	32	3	7	22	36	78	13

1959-60

Premier Division

Bath City	42	32	3	7	116	50	67
Headington United	42	23	8	11	78	61	54
Weymouth	42	22	9	11	93	69	53
Cheltenham Town	42	21	6	15	82	68	48
Cambridge City	42	18	11	13	81	72	47
Chelmsford Town	42	19	7	16	90	70	45
Bedford Town	42	21	3	18	97	85	45
King's Lynn	42	17	11	14	89	78	45
Boston United	42	17	10	15	83	80	44
Wisbech Town	42	17	10	15	81	84	44
Yeovil Town	42	17	8	17	81	73	42
Hereford United	42	15	12	15	70	74	42
Tonbridge	42	16	8	18	79	73	40
Hastings United	42	16	8	18	63	77	40
Wellington Town	42	13	11	18	63	78	37
Dartford	42	15	7	20	64	82	37
Gravesend & Northfleet	42	14	8	20	69	84	36
Worcester City	42	13	10	19	72	89	36
Nuneaton Borough	42	11	11	20	64	78	33
Barry Town	42	14	5	23	78	103	33
Poole Town	42	10	8	24	69	96	28
Kettering Town	42	9	10	23	60	90	28

First Division

Clacton Town	42	27	5	10	106	69	59
Romford	42	21	11	10	65	40	53
Folkestone Town	42	23	5	14	93	71	51
Exeter City Reserves	42	23	3	16	85	62	49
Guildford City	42	19	9	14	79	56	47
Sittingbourne	42	20	7	15	66	55	47
Margate	42	20	6	16	88	77	46
Trowbridge Town	42	18	9	15	90	78	45
Cambridge United	42	18	9	15	71	72	45
Yiewsley	42	17	10	15	83	69	44
Bexleyheath & Welling	42	16	11	15	85	77	43
Merthyr Tydfil	42	16	10	16	63	65	42
Ramsgate Athletic	42	16	8	18	83	84	40
Ashford Town	42	14	12	16	61	70	40
Tunbridge Wells United	42	17	5	20	77	73	39
Hinckley Athletic	42	14	8	20	62	75	36
Gloucester City	42	13	9	20	56	84	35
Dover	42	14	6	22	59	85	34
Kidderminster Harriers	42	14	6	22	59	97	34
Corby Town	42	15	3	24	75	91	33
Burton Albion	42	11	10	21	52	79	32
Rugby Town	42	10	11	21	67	91	31

1960-61

Premier Division

Oxford United	42	27	10	5	104	43	64
Chelmsford City	42	23	11	8	91	55	57
Yeovil Town	42	23	9	10	109	54	55
Hereford United	42	21	10	11	83	67	52
Weymouth	42	21	9	12	78	63	51
Bath City	42	18	14	10	74	52	50
Cambridge City	42	16	12	14	101	71	44
Wellington Town	42	17	9	16	66	68	43
Bedford Town	42	18	7	17	94	97	43
Folkestone Town	42	18	7	17	75	86	43
King's Lynn	42	13	16	13	68	66	42
Worcester City	42	15	11	16	69	69	41
Clacton Town	42	15	11	16	82	83	41
Romford	42	13	15	14	66	69	41
Guildford City	42	14	11	17	65	62	39
Tonbridge	42	16	6	20	79	85	38
Cheltenham Town	42	15	7	20	81	81	37
Gravesend & Northfleet	42	15	7	20	75	101	37
Dartford	42	13	11	18	57	90	37
Hastings United	42	8	9	25	60	100	25
Wisbech Town	42	9	6	27	58	112	24
Boston United	42	6	8	28	62	123	20

Oxford United were previously known as Headington United.

First Division

Kettering Town	40	26	7	7	100	55	59
Cambridge United	40	25	5	10	100	53	55
Bexleyheath & Welling	40	22	8	10	93	46	52
Merthyr Tydfil	40	23	6	11	88	65	52
Sittingbourne	40	21	10	9	77	63	52
Hinckley Athletic	40	17	13	10	74	59	47
Ramsgate Athletic	40	19	7	14	77	56	45
Rugby Town	40	18	9	13	89	71	45
Corby Town	40	16	10	14	82	73	42
Poole Town	40	18	5	17	71	65	41
Barry Town	40	16	9	15	65	74	41
Yiewsley	40	17	7	16	65	76	41
Trowbridge Town	40	14	10	16	71	73	38
Ashford Town	40	14	8	18	61	67	36
Margate	40	11	12	17	62	75	34
Dover	40	12	7	21	67	74	31
Canterbury City	40	10	10	20	52	75	30
Nuneaton Borough	40	11	7	22	60	91	29
Burton Albion	40	12	4	24	63	85	28
Tunbridge Wells United	40	8	5	27	56	115	21
Gloucester City	40	7	7	26	40	102	21

1961-62

Premier Division

Oxford United	42	28	5	9	118	46	61
Bath City	42	25	7	10	102	70	57
Guildford City	42	24	8	10	79	49	56
Yeovil Town	42	23	8	11	97	59	54
Chelmsford City	42	19	12	11	74	60	50
Weymouth	42	20	7	15	80	64	47
Kettering Town	42	21	5	16	90	84	47
Hereford United	42	21	2	19	81	68	44
Cambridge City	42	18	8	16	70	71	44
Bexleyheath & Welling	42	19	5	18	69	75	43
Romford	42	15	9	18	63	70	39
Cambridge United	42	13	12	17	76	78	38
Wellington United	42	14	10	18	75	78	38
Gravesend & Northfleet	42	17	4	21	59	92	38
Bedford Town	42	16	5	21	73	79	37
Worcester City	42	15	7	20	51	64	37
Merthyr Tydfil	42	13	11	18	62	80	37
Clacton Town	42	13	10	19	74	91	36
Tonbridge	42	10	14	18	71	92	34
King's Lynn	42	12	8	22	59	74	32
Folkestone Town	42	12	6	24	64	103	30
Cheltenham	42	9	7	26	48	86	25

First Division

Wisbech Town	38	21	11	6	76	42	53
Poole Town	38	23	6	9	81	47	52
Dartford	38	21	8	9	89	50	50
Rugby Town	38	20	9	9	82	49	49
Margate	38	20	6	12	73	55	46
Corby Town	38	19	6	13	82	60	44
Sittingbourne	38	16	12	10	69	51	44
Dover	38	19	6	13	66	55	44
Yiewsley	38	18	6	14	64	51	42
Barry Town	38	14	11	13	55	51	39
Ashford Town	38	14	11	13	66	70	39
Hinckley Athletic	38	15	8	15	75	65	38
Burton Albion	38	16	5	17	70	79	37
Nuneaton Borough	38	12	12	14	63	69	36
Tunbridge Wells United	38	12	7	19	60	85	31
Canterbury City	38	11	8	19	60	82	30
Ramsgate Athletic	38	10	9	19	48	70	29
Trowbridge Town	38	9	9	20	45	69	27
Gloucester City	38	6	4	28	46	104	16
Hastings United	38	5	4	29	45	115	14

1962-63

Premier Division

Cambridge City	40	25	6	9	99	64	56
Cambridge United	40	23	7	10	74	50	53
Weymouth	40	20	11	9	82	43	51
Guildford City	40	20	11	9	70	50	51
Kettering Town	40	22	7	11	66	49	51
Wellington Town	40	19	9	12	71	49	47
Dartford	40	19	9	12	61	54	47
Chelmsford City	40	18	10	12	63	50	46
Bedford Town	40	18	8	14	61	45	44
Bath City	40	18	6	16	58	56	42
Yeovil Town	40	15	10	15	64	54	40
Romford	40	14	11	15	73	68	39
Bexleyheath & Welling	40	13	11	16	55	63	37
Hereford United	40	14	7	19	56	66	35
Merthyr Tydfil	40	15	4	21	54	71	34
Rugby Town	40	14	5	21	65	76	33
Wisbech Town	40	15	3	22	64	84	33
Worcester City	40	12	9	19	47	65	33
Poole Town	40	10	12	18	54	66	32
Gravesend & Northfleet	40	10	3	27	62	91	23
Clacton Town	40	3	7	30	50	135	13

First Division

Margate	38	21	13	4	86	47	55
Hinckley Athletic	38	22	9	7	66	38	53
Hastings United	38	22	8	8	86	36	52
Nuneaton Borough	38	21	10	7	82	41	52
Tonbridge	38	22	8	8	81	51	52
Dover	38	22	7	9	78	56	51
Corby Town	38	19	8	11	79	50	46
King's Lynn	38	19	7	15	76	66	45
Cheltenham Town	38	18	7	13	83	52	43
Folkestone Town	38	15	10	13	79	57	40
Canterbury City	38	14	8	16	42	56	36
Yiewsley	38	11	10	17	63	71	32
Ramsgate Athletic	38	12	7	19	58	82	31
Trowbridge Town	38	11	9	18	50	81	31
Burton Albion	38	10	10	18	48	76	30
Gloucester City	38	9	11	18	42	78	29
Sittingbourne	38	12	3	23	56	75	27
Ashford Town	38	9	6	23	58	76	24
Barry Town	38	6	5	27	35	75	17
Tunbridge Wells United	38	6	2	30	43	118	14

1963-64

Premier Division

Yeovil Town	42	29	5	8	93	36	63
Chelmsford City	42	26	7	9	99	55	59
Bath City	42	24	9	9	88	51	57
Guildford City	42	21	9	12	90	55	51
Romford	42	20	9	13	71	58	49
Hastings United	42	20	8	14	75	61	48
Weymouth	42	20	7	15	65	53	47
Bedford Town	42	19	9	14	71	68	47
Cambridge United	42	17	9	16	92	77	43
Cambridge City	42	17	9	16	76	70	43
Wisbech Town	42	17	8	17	64	68	42
Bexley United	42	16	10	16	70	77	42
Dartford	42	16	8	18	56	71	40
Worcester City	42	12	15	15	70	74	39
Nuneaton Borough	42	15	8	19	58	61	38
Rugby Town	42	15	8	19	68	86	38
Margate	42	12	13	17	68	81	37
Wellington Town	42	12	9	21	73	85	33
Merthyr Tydfil	42	12	8	22	69	108	32
Hereford United	42	12	7	23	58	86	31
Kettering Town	42	10	5	27	49	89	25
Hinckley Athletic	42	7	6	29	51	104	20

First Division

Folkstone Town	42	28	7	7	82	38	63
King's Lynn	42	28	5	9	94	44	61
Cheltenham Town	42	25	10	7	92	49	60
Tonbridge	42	24	11	7	98	54	59
Corby town	42	24	7	11	114	56	55
Stevenage Town	42	21	6	15	70	59	48
Ashford Town	42	19	9	14	73	57	47
Burton Albion	42	19	8	15	76	70	46
Poole Town	42	17	11	14	75	61	45
Dover	42	18	9	15	86	75	45
Canterbury City	42	16	12	14	66	66	44
Crawley Town	42	20	2	20	81	71	42
Trowbridge Town	42	16	9	17	71	78	41
Clacton Town	42	19	1	22	76	88	39
Gloucester City	42	17	4	21	88	89	38
Yiewsley	42	15	8	19	63	77	38
Sittingbourne	42	15	8	19	52	70	38
Ramsgate Athletic	42	13	9	20	57	55	35
Tunbridge Wells Rangers	42	10	8	24	47	89	28
Gravesend & Northfleet	42	7	9	26	43	96	23
Deal Town	42	5	7	30	48	106	17
Barry Town	42	3	6	33	33	137	12

1964-65

Premier Division

Weymouth	42	24	8	10	99	50	56
Guildford City	42	21	12	9	73	49	54
Worcester City	42	22	6	14	100	62	50
Yeovil Town	42	18	14	10	76	55	50
Chelmsford City	42	21	8	13	86	77	50
Margate	42	20	9	13	88	79	49
Dartford	42	17	11	14	74	64	45
Nuneaton Borough	42	19	7	16	57	55	45
Cambridge United	42	16	11	15	78	66	43
Bedford Town	42	17	9	16	66	70	43
Cambridge City	42	16	9	17	72	69	41
Cheltenham Town	42	15	11	16	72	78	41
Folkestone Town	42	17	7	18	72	79	41
Romford	42	17	7	18	61	70	41
King's Lynn	42	13	13	16	56	79	39
Tonbridge	42	10	16	16	66	75	36
Wellington Town	42	13	10	19	63	78	36
Rugby Town	42	15	6	21	71	98	36
Wisbech Town	42	14	6	22	75	91	34
Bexley United	42	14	5	23	67	74	33
Hastings United	42	9	14	19	58	86	32
Bath City	42	13	3	26	60	86	29

First Division

Hereford United	42	34	4	4	124	39	72
Wimbledon	42	24	13	5	108	52	61
Poole Town	42	26	6	10	92	56	58
Corby Town	42	24	7	11	88	55	55
Stevenage Town	42	19	13	10	83	43	51
Hillingdon Borough	42	21	7	14	105	63	49
Crawley Town	42	22	5	15	83	52	49
Merthyr Tydfil	42	20	9	13	75	59	49
Gloucester City	42	19	10	13	68	65	48
Burton Albion	42	20	7	15	83	75	47
Canterbury City	42	13	16	13	73	53	42
Kettering Town	42	14	13	15	74	64	41
Ramsgate Athletic	42	16	8	18	51	59	40
Dover	42	14	10	18	54	59	38
Hinckley Athletic	42	13	9	20	56	81	35
Trowbridge Town	42	13	5	24	68	106	31
Ashford Town	42	11	8	23	60	98	30
Barry Town	42	11	7	24	47	103	29
Deal Town	42	7	13	22	61	127	27
Tunbridge Wells Rangers	42	10	6	26	51	107	26
Gravesend & Northfleet	42	9	7	26	57	101	25
Sittingbourne	42	8	5	29	58	103	21

1965-66

Premier Division

Weymouth	42	22	13	7	70	35	57
Chelmsford City	42	21	12	9	74	50	54
Hereford United	42	21	10	11	81	49	52
Bedford Town	42	23	6	13	80	57	52
Wimbledon	42	20	10	12	80	47	50
Cambridge City	42	19	11	12	67	52	49
Romford	42	21	7	14	87	72	49
Worcester City	42	20	8	14	69	54	48
Yeovil Town	42	17	11	14	91	70	45
Cambridge United	42	18	9	15	72	64	45
King's Lynn	42	18	7	17	75	72	43
Corby Town	42	16	9	17	66	73	41
Wellington Town	42	13	13	16	65	70	39
Nuneaton Borough	42	15	8	19	60	74	38
Folkestone Town	42	14	9	19	53	75	37
Guildford City	42	14	8	20	70	84	36
Poole Town	42	14	7	21	61	75	35
Cheltenham Town	42	13	9	20	69	99	35
Dartford	42	13	7	22	62	69	33
Rugby Town	42	11	10	21	67	95	32
Tonbridge	42	11	6	25	63	101	28
Margate	42	8	10	24	66	111	26

First Division

Barnet	46	30	9	7	114	49	69
Hillingdon Borough	46	27	10	9	101	46	64
Burton Albion	46	28	8	10	121	60	64
Bath City	46	25	13	8	88	50	63
Hastings United	46	25	10	11	104	59	60
Wisbech Town	46	25	9	12	98	54	59
Canterbury City	46	25	8	13	89	66	58
Stevenage Town	46	23	9	14	86	49	55
Kettering Town	46	22	9	15	77	74	53
Merthyr Tydfil	46	22	6	18	95	68	50
Dunstable Town	46	15	14	17	76	72	44
Crawley Town	46	17	10	19	72	71	44
Bexley United	46	20	4	22	65	71	44
Trowbridge Town	46	16	11	19	79	81	43
Dover	46	17	8	21	59	62	42
Barry Town	46	16	10	20	72	94	42
Gravesend & Northfleet	46	16	9	21	84	86	41
Gloucester City	46	14	12	20	75	98	40
Sittingbourne	46	11	12	23	77	121	34
Ramsgate Athletic	46	9	15	22	35	76	33
Hinckley Athletic	46	10	12	24	59	93	32
Tunbridge Wells Rangers	46	12	8	26	47	88	32
Ashford Town	46	9	10	27	44	92	28
Deal Town	46	3	4	39	29	165	10

1966-67

Premier Division

Romford	42	22	8	12	80	60	52
Nuneaton Borough	42	21	9	12	82	54	51
Weymouth	42	18	14	10	64	40	50
Wimbledon	42	19	11	12	88	60	49
Barnet	42	18	13	11	86	66	49
Guildford City	42	19	10	13	65	51	48
Wellington Town	42	20	7	15	70	67	47
Cambridge United	42	16	13	13	75	67	45
Chelmsford City	42	15	15	12	66	59	45
Hereford United	42	16	12	14	79	61	44
King's Lynn	42	15	14	13	78	72	44
Cambridge City	42	15	13	14	66	70	43
Cheltenham Town	42	16	11	15	60	71	43
Yeovil Town	42	14	14	14	66	72	42
Burton Albion	42	17	5	20	63	71	39
Corby Town	42	15	9	18	60	75	39
Poole Town	42	14	11	17	52	65	39
Hillingdon Borough	42	11	13	18	49	70	35
Bath City	42	11	12	19	51	74	34
Worcester City	42	11	8	23	59	79	30
Bedford Town	42	8	13	21	54	72	29
Folkestone Town	42	6	15	21	44	81	27

First Division

Dover	46	29	12	5	92	35	70
Margate	46	31	7	8	127	54	69
Stevenage Town	46	29	8	9	90	32	66
Hastings United	46	25	16	5	89	45	66
Kettering Town	46	27	9	10	105	62	63
Crawley Town	46	26	8	12	81	48	60
Ramsgate Athletic	46	23	8	15	79	62	54
Dartford	46	19	15	12	92	67	53
Tonbridge	46	21	10	15	91	69	52
Trowbridge Town	46	20	12	14	73	60	52
Ashford Town	46	18	8	20	74	68	44
Merthyr Tydfil	46	17	9	20	81	71	43
Gloucester City	46	18	6	22	69	83	42
Canterbury City	46	17	8	21	57	75	42
Wisbech Town	46	16	9	21	87	93	41
Bexley United	46	13	15	18	53	69	41
Banbury United	46	13	14	19	88	100	40
Rugby Town	46	15	7	24	57	77	37
Dunstable Town	46	14	6	26	55	87	34
Barry Town	46	11	11	24	62	89	33
Gravesend & Northfleet	46	11	9	26	63	106	31
Hinckley Athletic	46	10	8	28	44	100	28
Tunbridge Wells Rangers	46	4	15	27	31	96	23
Sittingbourne	46	5	10	31	44	136	20

1967-68

Premier Division

Chelmsford City	42	25	7	10	85	50	57
Wimbledon	42	24	7	11	85	47	55
Cambridge United	42	20	13	9	73	42	53
Cheltenham Town	42	23	7	12	97	67	53
Guildford City	42	18	13	11	56	43	49
Romford	42	20	8	14	72	60	48
Barnet	42	20	8	14	81	71	48
Margate	42	19	8	15	80	71	46
Wellington Town	42	16	13	13	70	66	45
Hillingdon Borough	42	18	9	155	53	54	45
King's Lynn	42	18	8	16	66	57	44
Yeovil Town	42	16	12	14	45	43	44
Weymouth	42	17	8	17	65	62	42
Hereford United	42	17	7	18	58	62	41
Nuneaton Borough	42	13	14	15	62	64	40
Dover	42	17	6	19	54	56	40
Poole Town	42	13	10	19	55	74	36
Stevenage Town	42	13	9	20	57	75	35
Burton Albion	42	14	6	22	51	73	34
Corby Town	42	7	13	22	40	77	27
Cambridge City	42	10	6	26	51	81	26
Hastings United	42	4	8	30	33	94	16

First Division

Worcester City	42	23	14	5	92	35	60
Kettering Town	42	24	10	8	88	40	58
Bedford Town	42	24	7	11	101	40	55
Rugby Town	42	20	15	7	72	44	55
Dartford	42	23	9	10	70	48	55
Bath City	42	21	12	9	78	51	54
Banbury United	42	22	9	11	79	59	53
Ramsgate Athletic	42	17	7	8	70	37	51
Merthyr Tydfil	42	18	13	11	80	66	49
Tonbridge	42	18	9	15	76	71	45
Canterbury City	42	16	11	15	66	63	43
Ashford Town	42	18	6	18	73	78	42
Brentwood Town	42	16	9	17	63	73	41
Bexley United	42	12	13	17	56	64	37
Trowbridge Town	42	12	11	19	64	70	35
Gloucester City	42	12	9	21	54	68	33
Wisbech Town	42	11	10	21	43	78	32
Crawley Town	42	10	8	24	54	85	28
Folkestone Town	42	10	7	25	49	80	27
Dunstable Town	42	8	10	24	44	94	26
Barry Town	42	7	12	23	36	81	26
Gravesend & Northfleet	42	6	7	29	28	112	19

1968-69

Premier Division

Cambridge United	42	27	5	10	72	39	59
Hillingdon Borough	42	24	10	8	68	47	58
Wimbledon	42	21	12	9	66	48	54
King's Lynn	42	20	9	13	68	60	49
Worcester City	42	19	11	12	53	47	49
Romford	42	18	12	12	58	52	48
Weymouth	42	16	15	11	52	41	47
Yeovil Town	42	16	13	13	52	50	45
Kettering Town	42	18	8	16	51	55	44
Dover	42	17	9	16	66	61	43
Nuneaton Borough	42	17	7	18	74	58	41
Barnet	42	15	10	17	72	66	40
Chelmsford City	42	17	6	19	56	58	40
Hereford United	42	15	9	18	66	62	39
Telford United	42	14	10	18	62	61	38
Poole Town	42	16	6	20	75	76	38
Burton Albion	42	16	5	21	55	71	37
Margate	42	14	7	21	79	90	35
Cheltenham Town	42	15	5	22	55	64	35
Bedford Town	42	11	12	19	46	63	34
Rugby Town	42	10	6	26	38	83	26
Guildford City	42	7	11	24	41	73	25

First Division

Brentwood Town	42	26	12	4	44	37	64
Bath City	42	26	10	6	96	40	62
Gloucester City	42	25	9	8	100	53	59
Crawley Town	42	21	13	8	65	32	55
Corby Town	42	22	6	14	81	65	50
Dartford	42	20	8	14	79	51	48
Ramsgate Athletic	42	19	9	14	72	57	47
Salisbury	42	20	6	16	69	52	46
Cambridge City	42	18	10	14	73	63	46
Banbury United	42	16	12	14	67	72	44
Trowbridge Town	42	15	8	19	70	60	44
Folkestone Town	42	19	5	18	53	59	43
Canterbury City	42	17	7	18	67	63	41
Ashford Town	42	16	8	18	72	73	40
Bexley United	42	15	9	18	62	75	39
Hastings United	42	15	9	18	58	69	39
Wisbech Town	42	11	13	18	57	70	35
Dunstable Town	42	14	6	22	73	99	34
Merthyr Tydfil	42	10	7	25	49	101	27
Barry Town	42	8	10	24	39	78	26
Gravesend & Northfleet	42	8	9	25	51	79	25
Tonbridge	42	2	6	34	36	137	10

1969-70

Premier Division

Cambridge United	42	26	6	10	86	49	58
Yeovil Town	42	25	7	10	78	48	57
Chelmsford City	42	20	11	11	76	58	51
Weymouth	42	18	14	10	59	37	50
Wimbledon	42	19	12	11	64	52	50
Hillingdon Borough	42	19	12	11	56	50	50
Barnet	42	16	15	11	71	54	47
Telford United	42	18	10	14	61	62	46
Brentwood Town	42	16	13	13	61	38	45
Hereford United	42	18	9	15	74	65	45
Bath City	42	18	8	16	63	55	44
King's Lynn	42	16	11	15	72	68	43
Margate	42	17	8	17	70	64	42
Dover	42	15	10	17	51	50	40
Kettering Town	42	18	3	21	64	75	39
Worcester City	42	14	10	18	35	44	38
Romford	42	13	11	18	50	62	37
Poole Town	42	8	19	15	48	57	35
Gloucester City	42	12	9	21	53	73	33
Nuneaton Borough	42	11	10	21	52	74	32
Crawley Town	42	6	15	21	53	101	27
Burton Albion	42	3	9	30	24	82	15

First Division

Bedford Town	42	26	9	7	93	37	61
Cambridge City	42	26	8	8	104	43	60
Dartford	42	24	11	7	33	46	58
Ashford Town	42	19	15	8	71	43	53
Rugby Town	42	20	10	12	82	66	50
Trowbridge Town	42	20	8	14	72	65	48
Hastings United	42	18	11	13	67	51	47
Guildford City	42	19	9	14	68	58	47
Banbury United	42	19	8	15	86	72	46
Cheltenham Town	42	20	5	17	78	81	45
Canterbury City	42	15	13	14	61	57	43
Corby Town	42	14	15	13	58	53	43
Folkestone Town	42	19	5	18	57	55	43
Ramsgate Athletic	42	14	13	15	53	57	41
Salisbury	42	13	13	16	48	53	39
Gravesend & Northfleet	42	13	11	18	62	71	37
Bexley United	42	10	11	21	58	76	31
Dunstable Town	42	11	9	22	52	82	31
Merthyr Tydfil	42	9	11	22	40	80	29
Barry Town	42	11	6	25	39	76	28
Wisbech Town	42	8	9	25	58	116	25
Tonbridge	42	4	10	28	46	101	18

1970-71

Premier Division

Yeovil Town	42	25	7	10	66	31	57
Cambridge City	42	22	11	9	67	38	55
Romford	42	23	9	10	63	42	55
Hereford United	42	23	8	11	71	53	54
Chelmsford City	42	20	11	11	61	32	51
Barnet	42	18	14	10	69	49	50
Bedford Town	42	20	10	12	62	46	50
Wimbledon	42	20	8	14	72	54	48
Worcester City	42	20	8	14	61	46	48
Weymouth	42	14	16	12	64	48	44
Dartford	42	15	12	15	53	51	42
Dover	42	16	9	17	64	63	41
Margate	42	15	10	17	64	70	40
Hillingdon Borough	42	17	6	19	61	68	40
Bath City	42	13	12	17	48	68	38
Nuneaton Borough	42	12	12	18	43	66	36
Telford United	42	13	8	21	64	70	34
Poole Town	42	14	6	22	57	75	34
King's Lynn	42	11	7	24	44	67	29
Ashford Town	42	8	13	21	52	86	29
Kettering Town	42	8	11	23	48	84	27
Gloucester City	42	6	10	26	34	81	21

First Division

Guildford City	38	22	10	6	76	36	54
Merthyr Tydfil	38	19	12	7	52	33	50
Gravesend & Northfleet	38	19	10	9	74	42	48
Folkestone	38	20	8	10	83	53	48
Burton Albion	38	19	10	9	56	37	48
Rugby Town	38	17	14	7	58	40	48
Ramsgate Athletic	38	20	5	13	83	54	45
Trowbridge Town	38	19	7	12	78	55	45
Bexley United	38	17	11	10	57	45	45
Crawley Town	38	15	11	12	84	68	41
Hastings United	38	13	12	13	51	50	38
Banbury United	38	13	11	14	58	53	37
Corby Town	38	14	8	16	57	60	36
Salisbury	38	13	7	18	56	60	33
Cheltenham Town	38	8	15	15	44	58	31
Stevenage Athletic	38	12	7	19	55	79	21
Tonbridge	38	8	8	22	48	83	24
Barry Town	38	9	6	23	35	82	24
Dunstable Town	38	8	4	26	32	81	20
Canterbury City	38	5	4	29	37	105	14

1971-72

Premier Division

Chelmsford City	42	28	6	8	109	46	62
Hereford United	42	24	12	6	68	30	60
Dover	42	20	11	11	67	45	51
Barnet	42	21	7	14	80	57	49
Dartford	42	20	8	14	75	68	48
Weymouth	42	21	5	16	69	43	47
Yeovil Town	42	18	11	13	67	51	47
Hillingdon Borough	42	20	6	16	64	58	46
Margate	42	19	8	15	74	68	46
Wimbledon	42	19	7	16	75	64	45
Romford	42	16	13	13	54	49	45
Guildford City	42	20	5	17	71	65	45
Telford United	42	18	7	17	83	68	43
Nuneaton Borough	42	16	10	16	46	47	42
Bedford Town	42	16	9	17	59	66	41
Worcester City	42	17	7	18	46	57	41
Cambridge City	42	12	14	16	68	71	38
Folkestone	42	14	7	21	58	64	35
Poole Town	42	9	11	22	43	72	29
Bath City	42	11	4	27	45	86	26
Merthyr Tydfil	42	7	8	27	29	93	22
Gravesend & Northfleet	42	5	6	31	30	110	16

First Division (North)

Kettering Town	34	23	6	5	70	27	52
Burton Albion	34	18	13	3	58	27	49
Cheltenham Town	34	20	4	10	72	51	44
Rugby Town	34	18	7	9	52	36	43
Wellingborough Town	34	15	10	9	73	44	40
Stourbridge	34	13	14	7	59	42	40
King's Lynn	34	14	11	9	62	45	39
Corby Town	34	15	9	10	47	35	39
Ilkeston Town	34	14	11	9	44	38	39
Banbury United	34	14	5	15	54	46	33
Bury Town	34	14	5	15	47	44	33
Wealdstone	34	14	5	15	51	58	33
Lockheed Leamington	34	15	3	16	41	52	33
Gloucester City	34	8	8	18	46	61	24
Stevenage Athletic	34	8	8	18	41	69	24
Bletchley	34	7	7	20	36	70	21
Dunstable Town	34	5	7	22	29	75	17
Barry Town	34	1	7	26	22	84	9

First Division (South)

Waterlooville	30	15	9	6	40	22	39
Ramsgate Athletic	30	14	11	5	42	27	39
Maidstone United	30	14	10	6	48	28	38
Crawley Town	30	15	5	10	67	55	35
Metropolitan Police	30	15	3	12	48	41	33
Tonbridge	30	12	9	9	37	34	33
Bexley United	30	14	4	12	52	46	32
Basingstoke Town	30	14	4	12	37	36	32
Andover	30	11	9	10	32	34	31
Ashford Town	30	12	4	14	43	48	28
Salisbury	30	10	7	13	45	44	27
Winchester City	30	10	7	13	40	47	27
Hastings United	30	10	7	13	28	42	27
Trowbridge Town	30	8	7	15	41	49	23
Canterbury City	30	7	8	15	39	56	22
Woodford Town	30	4	6	20	22	52	14

1972-73

Premier Division

Kettering Town	42	20	17	5	74	44	57
Yeovil Town	42	21	14	7	67	61	56
Dover	42	23	9	10	61	68	55
Chelmsford City	42	23	7	12	75	43	53
Worcester City	42	20	13	9	68	47	53
Weymouth	42	20	12	10	72	51	52
Margate	42	17	15	10	80	60	49
Bedford Town	42	16	15	11	43	36	47
Nuneaton Borough	42	16	14	12	51	41	46
Telford United	42	12	20	10	57	47	44
Cambridge City	42	14	15	13	64	53	43
Wimbledon	42	14	14	14	50	50	42
Barnet	42	15	11	16	60	59	41
Romford	42	17	5	20	51	65	39
Hillingdon Borough	42	16	6	20	52	58	38
Dartford	42	12	11	19	49	63	35
Folkestone	42	11	11	20	41	72	33
Guildford City	42	10	11	21	59	84	31
Ramsgate	42	9	13	20	35	61	31
Poole Town	42	10	10	22	50	88	30
Burton Albion	42	9	7	26	43	81	25
Waterlooville	42	4	16	22	33	63	24

First Division (North)

Grantham	42	29	8	5	113	41	66
Atherstone Town	42	23	11	8	82	48	57
Cheltenham Town	42	24	8	10	87	47	56
Rugby Town	42	20	10	12	60	47	50
Kidderminster Harriers	42	19	12	11	67	56	50
Merthyr Tydfil	42	17	12	13	51	40	46
Corby Town	42	14	16	12	62	56	44
Stourbridge	42	16	11	15	70	64	43
Gloucester City	42	18	7	17	55	64	43
Bromsgrove Rovers	42	17	8	17	63	54	42
Redditch United	42	18	6	18	58	59	42
Banbury United	42	18	5	19	60	53	41
Wellingborough Town	42	17	7	18	58	71	41
King's Lynn	42	14	12	16	45	49	40
Lockheed Leamington	42	13	12	17	51	58	38
Enderby Town	42	12	14	16	50	61	38
Stevenage Athletic	42	12	13	17	50	63	37
Tamworth	42	14	8	20	45	65	36
Bury Town	42	13	9	20	52	69	35
Barry Town	42	11	10	21	45	71	32
Ilkeston Town	42	9	6	27	35	68	24
Bedworth United	42	10	3	29	42	94	23

First Division (South)

Maidstone United	42	25	12	5	90	38	62
Tonbridge	42	26	7	9	70	44	59
Ashford Town	42	24	7	11	90	40	55
Bideford	42	19	14	9	70	43	52
Minehead	42	20	12	10	65	47	52
Gravesend & Northfleet	42	22	7	13	81	55	51
Bath City	42	18	11	13	56	54	47
Wealdstone	42	16	12	14	81	61	44
Bletchley Town	42	14	13	15	54	51	41
Hastings United	42	14	13	15	53	53	41
Andover	42	15	11	16	62	70	41
Canterbury City	42	14	12	16	51	59	40
Basingstoke Town	42	14	12	16	48	57	40
Crawley Town	42	14	11	17	59	76	39
Metropolitan Police	42	15	8	19	82	75	38
Trowbridge Town	42	15	8	19	65	77	38
Bexley United	42	12	14	16	54	64	38
Salisbury	42	14	10	18	49	60	38
Bognor Regis Town	42	12	9	21	41	66	33
Dorchester Town	42	10	12	20	47	73	32
Winchester City	42	7	11	24	41	79	25
Dunstable Town	42	4	10	28	38	105	18

1973-74

Premier Division

Dartford	42	22	13	7	67	37	57
Grantham	42	18	13	11	70	49	49
Chelmsford City	42	19	10	13	62	49	48
Kettering Town	42	16	16	10	62	51	48
Maidstone United	42	16	14	12	54	43	46
Yeovil Town	42	13	20	9	45	39	46
Weymouth	42	19	7	16	60	41	45
Barnet	42	18	9	15	55	46	45
Nuneaton Borough	42	13	19	10	54	47	45
Cambridge City	42	15	12	15	45	54	42
Atherstone Town	42	16	9	17	61	59	41
Wimbledon	42	15	11	16	50	56	41
Telford United	42	12	16	14	51	57	40
Dover	42	11	17	14	41	46	39
Tonbridge	42	12	15	15	38	45	39
Romford	42	11	17	14	39	52	39
Margate	42	15	8	19	56	63	38
Guildford City	42	13	11	18	48	67	37
Worcester City	42	11	14	17	53	67	36
Bedford Town	42	11	14	17	38	51	36
Folkestone	42	11	12	19	56	65	34
Hillingdon Borough	42	9	15	18	44	65	33

First Division (North)

Stourbridge	42	29	11	2	103	36	69
Burton Albion	42	27	9	6	88	32	63
Cheltenham Town	42	24	8	10	75	51	56
AP Leamington	42	21	12	9	82	45	54
Enderby Town	42	19	14	9	60	36	52
Witney Town	42	20	10	12	69	55	50
Stevenage Athletic	42	19	11	12	65	46	49
Banbury United	42	19	11	12	69	57	49
King's Lynn	42	19	10	13	65	50	48
Kidderminster Harriers	42	15	14	13	67	53	44
Merthyr Tydfil	42	16	12	14	70	61	44
Redditch United	42	14	11	17	56	73	39
Bromsgrove Rovers	42	14	10	18	54	61	38
Bedworth United	42	14	10	18	50	77	38
Tamworth	42	13	11	18	42	51	37
Corby Town	42	12	11	19	40	57	35
Bletchley Town	42	10	15	17	47	71	35
Barry Town	42	10	8	24	53	85	29
Bury Town	42	10	6	26	57	84	26
Gloucester City	42	10	6	26	52	81	26
Wellingborough Town	42	7	9	26	42	87	23
Dunstable Town	42	5	11	26	26	83	21

First Division (South)

Wealdstone	38	26	7	5	75	35	59
Bath City	38	20	8	10	55	34	48
Waterlooville	38	16	15	7	55	38	47
Minehead	38	16	15	7	69	52	47
Bideford	38	17	12	9	61	51	46
Poole Town	38	18	9	11	67	47	45
Bexley United	38	18	7	13	50	42	43
Hastings United	38	16	9	13	45	36	41
Basingstoke Town	38	14	11	13	55	44	39
Gravesend & Northfleet	38	13	13	12	58	52	39
Bognor Regis Town	38	13	12	13	48	54	38
Ashford Town	38	14	8	16	41	42	36
Ramsgate	38	13	9	16	46	44	35
Dorchester Town	38	10	13	15	40	48	33
Canterbury City	38	9	12	17	37	46	30
Trowbridge Town	38	8	14	16	44	61	30
Salisbury	38	10	9	19	40	60	29
Metropolitan Police	38	9	11	18	37	61	29
Andover	38	11	3	24	38	70	25
Crawley Town	38	6	9	23	35	79	21

1974-75

Premier Division

Wimbledon	42	25	7	10	63	33	57
Nuneaton Borough	42	23	8	11	56	37	54
Yeovil Town	42	21	9	12	64	34	51
Kettering Town	42	20	10	12	73	41	50
Burton Albion	42	18	13	11	54	48	49
Bath City	42	20	8	14	63	50	48
Margate	42	17	12	13	64	64	46
Wealdstone	42	17	11	14	62	61	45
Telford United	42	16	13	13	55	56	45
Chelmsford City	42	16	12	14	62	51	44
Grantham	42	16	11	15	70	62	43
Dover	42	15	13	14	43	53	43
Maidstone United	42	15	12	15	52	50	42
Atherstone Town	42	14	14	14	48	53	42
Weymouth	42	13	13	16	66	58	39
Stourbridge	42	13	12	17	56	70	38
Cambridge	42	11	14	17	51	56	36
Tonbridge	42	11	12	19	44	66	34
Romford	42	10	13	19	46	62	33
Dartford	42	9	13	20	52	70	31
Barnet	42	10	9	23	44	76	29
Guildford & Dorking United	42	10	5	27	45	82	25

First Division (North)

Bedford Town	42	28	9	5	85	33	65
Dunstable Town	42	25	8	9	105	61	58
AP Leamington	42	25	7	10	68	48	57
Redditch United	42	22	12	8	76	40	56
Worcester City	42	24	8	10	84	50	56
Cheltenham Town	42	21	9	12	72	53	51
Tamworth	42	21	8	13	74	53	50
King's Lynn	42	19	10	13	71	64	48
Enderby Town	42	17	12	13	61	48	46
Banbury United	42	18	10	14	52	51	46
Stevenage Athletic	42	16	13	13	62	48	45
Bromsgrove Rovers	42	18	9	15	63	52	45
Merthyr Tydfil	42	11	15	16	53	64	37
Witney Town	42	16	4	22	57	76	36
Corby Town	42	11	13	18	60	57	35
Kidderminster Harriers	42	12	11	19	50	66	35
Gloucester City	42	13	8	21	55	75	34
Wellingborough Town	42	9	13	20	42	61	31
Barry Town	42	10	10	22	49	73	30
Bedworth United	42	9	9	24	60	91	27
Milton Keynes City	42	7	5	30	48	100	19
Bury Town	42	5	7	30	36	119	17

First Division (South)

Gravesend & Northfleet	38	24	12	2	70	30	60
Hillingdon Borough	38	22	8	8	87	45	52
Minehead	38	21	9	8	74	33	51
Ramsgate	38	19	11	8	70	37	49
Bexley United	38	19	7	12	61	44	45
Waterlooville	38	17	11	10	67	49	45
Ashford Town	38	16	12	10	64	55	44
Basingstoke Town	38	16	11	11	64	50	43
Canterbury City	38	16	9	13	54	43	41
Hastings United	38	13	14	11	54	45	40
Poole Town	38	11	13	14	50	60	35
Metropolitan Police	38	11	13	14	54	66	35
Folkestone & Shepway	38	10	14	14	53	57	34
Andover	38	12	8	18	52	71	32
Bognor Regis Town	38	10	11	17	49	64	31
Salisbury	38	9	11	18	45	66	29
Trowbridge Town	38	10	9	19	48	76	29
Bideford	38	10	8	20	40	71	28
Dorchester Town	38	8	10	20	40	63	26
Crawley Town	38	3	5	30	31	102	11

1975-76

Premier Division

Wimbledon	42	26	10	6	74	29	62
Yeovil Town	42	21	12	9	68	35	54
Atherstone Town	42	18	15	9	56	55	51
Maidstone United	42	17	16	9	52	39	50
Nuneaton Borough	42	16	18	8	41	33	50
Gravesend & Northfleet	42	16	18	8	49	47	50
Grantham	42	15	14	13	56	47	44
Dunstable Town	42	17	9	16	52	43	43
Bedford Town	42	13	17	12	55	51	43
Burton Albion	42	17	9	16	52	53	43
Margate	42	15	12	15	62	60	42
Hillingdon Borough	42	13	14	15	61	54	40
Telford United	42	14	12	16	54	51	40
Chelmsford City	42	13	14	15	52	57	40
Kettering Town	42	11	17	14	48	52	39
Bath City	42	11	16	15	62	57	38
Weymouth	42	13	9	20	51	67	35
Dover	42	8	18	16	51	60	34
Wealdstone	42	12	9	21	61	82	33
Tonbridge AFC	42	11	11	20	45	70	33
Cambridge City	42	8	15	19	41	67	31
Stourbridge	42	10	9	23	38	72	29

First Division (North)

Redditch United	42	29	11	2	101	39	69
AP Leamington	42	27	10	5	85	31	64
Witney Town	42	24	9	9	66	40	57
Worcester City	42	24	8	10	90	49	56
Cheltenham Town	42	20	10	12	87	55	50
Barry Town	42	19	10	13	52	47	48
King's Lynn	42	17	14	11	52	48	48
Tamworth	42	18	11	13	65	43	47
Barnet	42	15	12	15	56	56	42
Oswestry Town	42	16	8	18	63	71	40
Enderby Town	42	16	6	20	48	51	38
Banbury United	42	15	8	19	58	67	38
Merthyr Tydfil	42	11	15	16	59	67	37
Bromsgrove Rovers	42	13	11	18	49	65	37
Milton Keynes City	42	15	6	21	51	63	36
Bury Town	42	12	11	19	52	72	35
Gloucester City	42	13	9	20	49	78	35
Kidderminster Harriers	42	13	8	21	54	70	34
Bedworth United	42	8	18	16	41	66	34
Corby Town	42	11	10	21	50	65	32
Wellingborough Town	42	9	11	22	42	68	29
Stevenage Athletic	42	6	6	30	46	105	18

First Division (South)

Minehead	38	27	8	3	102	35	62
Dartford	38	26	4	8	84	46	56
Romford	38	21	9	8	66	37	51
Salisbury	38	17	11	10	73	53	45
Hastings United	38	15	15	8	67	51	45
Poole United	38	20	2	16	57	57	42
Bexley United	38	14	13	11	62	53	41
Waterlooville	38	13	13	12	62	54	39
Basingstoke Town	38	13	12	13	69	71	38
Ashford Town	38	14	8	16	67	73	36
Canterbury City	38	11	13	14	53	60	35
Folkestone & Shepway	38	10	14	14	36	51	34
Metropolitan Police	38	9	14	15	46	58	32
Trowbridge Town	38	11	10	17	48	75	32
Guildford & Dorking United	38	9	13	16	43	50	31
Bognor Regis Town	38	6	17	15	44	72	29
Ramsgate	38	9	10	19	57	76	28
Crawley Town	38	9	10	19	46	66	28
Andover	38	9	10	19	42	62	28
Dorchester Town	38	11	6	21	45	69	28

1976-77

Premier Division

Wimbledon	42	28	7	7	64	22	63
Minehead	42	23	12	7	73	39	58
Kettering Town	42	20	16	6	66	46	56
Bath City	42	20	15	7	51	30	55
Nuneaton Borough	42	20	11	11	52	35	51
Bedford Town	42	17	14	11	54	47	48
Yeovil Town	42	15	16	11	54	42	46
Dover	42	13	16	13	46	43	42
Grantham	42	14	12	16	55	50	40
Maidstone United	42	13	14	15	46	50	40
Gravesend & Northfleet	42	13	13	16	38	43	39
AP Leamington	42	12	15	15	44	53	39
Redditch United	42	12	14	16	45	54	38
Wealdstone	42	13	12	17	54	66	38
Hillingdon Borough	42	14	10	18	45	59	38
Atherstone Town	42	14	9	19	41	49	37
Weymouth	42	16	5	21	53	73	37
Dartford	42	13	10	19	52	57	36
Telford United	42	11	12	19	36	50	34
Chelmsford City	42	9	13	20	56	68	31
Burton Albion	42	10	10	22	41	52	30
Margate	42	9	10	23	47	85	28

First Division (North)

Worcester City	38	32	5	1	97	22	69
Cheltenham Town	38	23	8	7	85	35	54
Witney Town	38	21	8	9	48	31	50
Bromsgrove Rovers	38	20	8	10	61	37	48
Barry Town	38	19	8	11	62	45	46
Cambridge City	38	17	10	11	68	43	44
Stourbridge	38	17	9	12	48	35	43
Kidderminster Harriers	38	17	6	15	74	65	40
Banbury United	38	15	10	13	51	47	40
Gloucester City	38	18	4	16	70	81	40
Enderby Town	38	15	9	14	50	44	39
King's Lynn	38	13	11	14	47	53	37
Corby Town	38	11	13	14	56	64	35
Tamworth	38	11	13	14	49	58	35
Merthyr Tydfil	38	12	6	20	60	69	30
Oswestry Town	38	8	10	20	30	60	26
Wellingborough Town	38	8	7	23	37	73	23
Dunstable	38	7	7	24	38	84	21
Bedworth United	38	5	10	23	28	68	20
Milton Keynes City	38	7	6	25	31	76	20

First Division (South)

Barnet	34	23	8	3	65	25	54
Hastings United	34	18	11	5	47	18	47
Waterlooville	34	19	6	9	50	25	44
Dorchester Town	34	16	11	7	48	30	43
Salisbury	34	15	11	8	57	39	41
Romford	34	18	5	11	47	32	41
Poole Town	34	17	7	10	40	35	41
Trowbridge Town	34	15	8	11	47	39	38
Crawley Town	34	14	9	11	53	42	37
Folkestone & Shepway	34	12	11	11	39	42	35
Basingstoke Town	34	12	10	12	51	43	34
Canterbury City	34	6	16	12	36	46	28
Bognor Regis Town	34	9	9	16	33	50	27
Tonbridge AFC	34	9	9	16	33	50	27
Metropolitan Police	34	5	12	17	37	61	22
Andover	34	4	11	19	17	49	19
Ashford Town	34	5	8	21	32	65	18
Aylesbury United	34	5	6	23	27	68	16

1977-78

Premier Division

Bath City	42	22	18	2	83	32	62
Weymouth	42	21	16	5	64	36	58
Maidstone United	42	20	11	11	59	41	51
Worcester City	42	20	11	11	67	50	51
Gravesend & Northfleet	42	19	11	12	57	42	49
Kettering Town	42	18	11	13	58	48	47
Barnet	42	18	11	13	63	58	47
Wealdstone	42	16	14	12	54	48	46
Telford United	42	17	11	14	52	45	45
Nuneaton Borough	42	15	14	13	38	36	44
Dartford	42	14	15	13	57	65	43
Yeovil Town	42	14	14	14	57	49	42
Hastings United	42	15	9	18	49	60	39
Cheltenham Town	42	12	14	16	43	52	38
Hillingdon Borough	42	13	9	20	45	54	35
Atherstone Town	42	10	15	17	41	56	35
Redditch United	42	15	5	22	40	55	35
AP Leamington	42	11	13	18	34	57	35
Minehead	42	11	12	19	43	48	34
Dover	42	9	13	20	41	63	31
Bedford Town	42	8	13	21	51	75	29
Grantham	42	11	6	25	40	66	28

First Division (North)

Witney Town	38	20	15	3	54	27	55
Bridgend Town	38	20	9	9	59	45	49
Burton Albion	38	17	11	10	48	32	45
Enderby Town	38	17	10	11	59	44	44
Bromsgrove Rovers	38	16	12	10	56	41	44
Banbury United	38	17	10	11	52	47	44
Kidderminster Harriers	38	16	11	11	58	41	43
Merthyr Tydfil	38	18	6	14	85	62	42
Cambridge City	38	14	12	12	56	45	40
Barry Town	38	14	11	13	58	48	39
Wellingborough Town	38	11	15	12	47	43	37
King's Lynn	38	12	13	13	55	55	37
Gloucester City	38	14	8	16	68	75	36
Corby Town	38	9	17	12	46	48	35
Dunstable Town	38	11	13	14	49	59	35
Stourbridge	38	9	15	14	52	53	33
Tamworth	38	10	11	17	37	48	31
Bedworth United	38	8	14	16	36	58	30
Milton Keynes City	38	5	11	22	26	74	21
Oswestry Town	38	6	8	24	29	85	20

First Division (South)

Margate	38	24	10	4	92	32	58
Dorchester Town	38	23	10	5	67	31	56
Salisbury	38	21	10	7	60	27	52
Waterlooville	38	19	13	6	66	36	51
Romford	38	17	15	6	58	37	49
Aylesbury United	38	20	7	11	56	42	47
Trowbridge Town	38	16	11	11	65	59	43
Chelmsford City	38	15	11	12	58	46	41
Folkestone & Shepway	38	16	9	13	64	56	41
Taunton Town	38	15	10	13	57	54	40
Addlestone	38	14	10	14	57	60	38
Crawley Town	38	14	9	15	61	60	37
Basingstoke Town	38	11	11	16	44	50	33
Tonbridge AFC	38	13	5	20	64	77	31
Ashford Town	38	9	13	16	39	60	31
Hounslow	38	10	10	18	43	62	30
Bognor Regis Town	38	9	8	21	52	69	26
Poole Town	38	8	10	20	43	68	26
Andover	38	4	12	22	30	68	20
Canterbury City	38	2	6	30	31	113	10

1978-79

Premier Division

Worcester City	42	27	11	4	92	33	65
Kettering Town	42	27	7	8	109	43	61
Telford United	42	22	10	10	60	39	54
Maidstone United	42	18	18	6	55	35	54
Bath City	42	17	19	6	59	41	53
Weymouth	42	18	15	9	71	51	51
AP Leamington	42	19	11	12	65	53	49
Redditch United	42	19	10	13	70	57	48
Yeovil Town	42	15	16	11	59	49	46
Witney Town	42	17	10	15	53	52	44
Nuneaton Borough	42	13	17	12	59	50	43
Gravesend & Northfleet	42	15	12	15	56	55	42
Barnet	42	16	10	16	52	64	42
Hillingdon Borough	42	12	16	14	50	41	40
Wealdstone	42	12	12	18	51	59	36
Atherstone Town	42	9	17	16	46	65	35
Dartford	42	10	14	18	40	56	34
Cheltenham Town	42	11	10	21	38	72	32
Margate	42	10	9	23	44	75	29
Dorchester Town	42	7	11	24	46	86	25
Hastings United	42	5	13	24	37	85	23
Bridgend Town	42	6	6	30	39	90	18

First Division (North)

Grantham	38	21	10	7	70	45	52
Merthyr Tydfil	38	22	7	9	90	53	51
Alvechurch	38	20	10	8	70	42	50
Bedford Town	38	19	9	10	74	49	47
King's Lynn	38	17	11	10	57	46	45
Oswestry Town	38	18	8	12	63	43	44
Gloucester City	38	18	8	12	76	59	44
Burton Albion	38	16	10	12	51	40	42
Kidderminster Harriers	38	13	14	11	70	60	40
Bedworth United	38	13	14	11	41	34	40
Tamworth	38	15	8	15	47	45	38
Stourbridge	38	15	7	16	64	61	37
Barry Town	38	14	9	15	51	53	37
Enderby Town	38	14	8	16	46	55	36
Banbury United	38	10	13	15	42	58	33
Wellingborough Town	38	13	6	19	50	71	32
Cambridge City	38	9	9	20	37	62	27
Bromsgrove Rovers	38	6	14	18	33	61	26
Milton Keynes City	38	7	9	22	37	87	23
Corby Town	38	5	6	27	40	85	16

First Division (South)

Dover	40	28	9	3	88	20	65
Folkestone & Shepway	40	22	6	12	84	50	50
Gosport Borough	40	19	11	10	62	47	49
Chelmsfor d City	40	20	7	13	65	61	47
Minehead	40	16	13	11	58	39	45
Poole Town	40	15	15	10	48	44	45
Hounslow	40	16	12	12	56	45	44
Waterlooville	40	17	10	13	52	43	44
Trowbridge Town	40	15	12	13	65	61	42
Aylesbury United	40	16	9	15	54	52	41
Taunton Town	40	16	9	15	53	51	41
Bognor Regis Town	40	17	7	16	58	58	41
Dunstable	40	18	4	18	57	55	40
Tonbridge AFC	40	15	10	15	43	47	40
Salisbury	40	13	10	17	47	51	36
Basingstoke Town	40	12	11	17	49	62	35
Addlestone	40	12	9	19	56	64	33
Andover	40	12	6	22	47	69	30
Ashford Town	40	10	10	20	28	53	30
Crawley Town	40	9	9	22	44	75	27
Canterbury City	40	6	3	31	31	98	15

1979-80

Midland Division

Bridgend Town	42	28	6	8	85	39	62
Minehead	42	22	15	5	70	42	59
Bedford Town	42	20	12	10	71	42	52
Kidderminster Harriers	42	23	6	13	81	59	52
Merthyr Tydfil	42	20	11	11	70	47	51
Enderby Town	42	21	8	13	62	50	50
Stourbridge	42	19	11	12	67	49	49
Alvechurch	42	17	14	11	78	60	48
Trowbridge Town	42	19	9	14	62	61	47
Bromsgrove Rovers	42	18	10	14	67	56	46
Barry Town	42	15	12	15	64	58	42
King's Lynn	42	15	11	16	48	55	41
Banbury United	42	13	14	15	56	56	40
Taunton Town	42	16	8	18	55	62	40
Witney Town	42	10	19	13	43	45	39
Bedworth United	42	12	15	15	40	42	39
Milton Keynes City	42	15	7	20	46	59	37
Gloucester City	42	10	14	18	55	68	32
Cheltenham Town	42	13	5	24	49	70	31
Wellingborough Town	42	9	7	26	54	106	25
Cambridge City	42	6	9	27	30	73	21
Corby Town	42	5	9	28	40	94	19

Gloucester City had points deducted

Southern Division

Dorchester Town	46	25	12	9	81	53	62
Aylesbury United	46	25	11	10	73	40	61
Dover	46	22	13	11	78	47	57
Gosport Borough	46	21	15	10	70	50	57
Dartford	46	21	14	11	66	45	56
Bognor Regis Town	46	20	15	11	66	38	55
Hillingdon Borough	46	19	16	11	64	41	54
Dunstable	46	17	19	10	93	64	53
Addlestone	46	20	13	13	72	57	53
Hastings United	46	19	15	12	74	65	53
Fareham Town	46	16	16	14	61	53	48
Waterlooville	46	17	12	17	67	64	46
Andover	46	16	13	17	65	65	45
Poole Town	46	16	13	17	49	64	45
Canterbury City	46	15	15	17	56	60	44
Hounslow	46	14	14	17	44	57	43
Margate	46	17	8	21	51	62	42
Folkestone & Shepway	46	14	11	21	54	63	39
Ashford Town	46	12	14	20	54	71	38
Crawley Town	46	13	11	22	55	72	37
Chelmsford City	46	9	18	19	47	69	36
Basingstoke Town	46	9	15	22	48	79	33
Salisbury	46	10	12	24	47	59	32
Tonbridge AFC	46	3	9	34	30	128	15

1980-81

Midland Division

Alvechurch	42	26	9	7	76	40	61
Bedford Town	42	25	11	6	63	32	61
Trowbridge Town	42	24	9	9	69	39	57
Kidderminster Harriers	42	23	9	10	67	41	55
Barry Town	42	21	9	12	60	40	51
Stourbridge	42	17	16	9	75	49	50
Enderby Town	42	21	8	13	71	47	50
Cheltenham Town	42	18	12	12	70	59	48
Bromsgrove Rovers	42	19	9	14	65	50	47
Corby Town	42	19	7	16	69	58	45
Bridgend Town	42	19	7	16	74	64	45
Minehead	42	19	7	16	54	60	45
Gloucester City	42	19	6	17	82	72	44
Merthyr Tydfil	42	15	12	15	60	50	42
Bedworth United	42	14	12	16	49	46	40
Banbury United	42	11	11	20	51	65	33
Taunton Town	42	10	9	23	48	68	29
Cambridge City	42	8	12	22	46	87	28
Witney Town	42	9	9	24	44	65	27
Wellingborough Town	42	10	7	25	43	91	27
Redditch United	42	11	4	27	54	92	26
Milton Keynes City	42	3	7	32	28	103	13

Southern Division

Dartford	46	26	14	6	76	39	66
Bognor Regis Town	46	25	13	8	95	43	63
Hastings United	46	24	14	8	87	43	62
Gosport Borough	46	24	12	10	84	52	60
Waterlooville	46	19	21	6	67	50	59
Dorchester Town	46	21	13	12	84	56	55
Dover	46	22	10	14	70	50	54
Poole Town	46	19	14	13	70	56	52
Addlestone & Weybridge	46	21	9	16	66	57	51
Dunstable	46	19	13	14	73	68	51
Aylesbury United	46	20	10	16	66	60	50
Hounslow	46	17	13	16	65	55	47
Hillingdon Borough	46	16	15	15	50	49	47
Basingstoke Town	46	16	14	16	69	58	46
Crawley Town	46	18	4	24	64	78	40
Ashford Town	46	12	15	19	55	76	39
Tonbridge AFC	46	12	15	19	44	68	39
Chelmsford City	46	13	12	21	54	78	38
Canterbury City	46	12	13	21	40	59	37
Salisbury	46	14	8	24	57	76	36
Folkestone	46	11	11	24	47	65	33
Margate	46	11	7	28	65	117	29
Fareham Town	46	5	18	23	31	73	28
Andover	46	6	10	30	41	94	22

1981-82

Midland Division

Nuneaton Borough	42	27	11	4	88	32	65
Alvechurch	42	26	10	6	79	34	62
Kidderminster Harriers	42	22	12	8	71	40	56
Stourbridge	42	21	10	11	69	47	52
Gloucester City	42	21	9	12	64	48	51
Bedworth United	42	20	10	12	59	40	50
Enderby Town	42	20	10	12	79	66	50
Witney Town	42	19	8	15	71	49	46
Barry Town	42	16	14	12	59	46	46
Corby Town	42	19	8	15	70	59	46
Merthyr Tydfil	42	16	12	14	63	54	44
Wellingborough Town	42	15	12	15	50	45	42
Bridgend Town	42	13	13	16	50	62	39
Bromsgrove Rovers	42	15	8	19	57	63	38
Bedford Town	42	12	13	17	45	54	37
Cheltenham Town	42	11	14	17	65	68	36
Taunton Town	42	12	8	22	46	76	32
Banbury United	42	11	8	23	63	91	30
Minehead	42	12	6	24	38	69	30
Cambridge City	42	10	8	24	38	80	28
Milton Keynes City	42	6	11	25	34	70	23
Redditch United	42	8	5	29	37	103	21

Southern Division

Wealdstone	46	32	8	6	100	32	72
Hastings United	46	31	9	6	79	34	71
Dorchester Town	46	21	18	7	76	41	60
Gosport Borough	46	26	8	12	76	45	60
Fareham Town	46	20	14	12	58	48	54
Poole Town	46	19	15	12	92	63	53
Waterlooville	46	22	9	15	75	53	53
Welling United	46	19	13	14	70	48	51
Addlestone & Weybridge	46	17	17	12	71	53	51
Chelmsford City	46	20	11	15	64	53	51
Aylesbury United	46	19	12	15	79	61	50
Basingstoke Town	46	18	12	16	75	61	48
Dover	46	19	8	19	61	63	46
Ashford Town	46	16	14	16	52	56	46
Tonbridge AFC	46	19	7	20	62	70	45
Dunstable	46	18	8	20	63	68	44
Salisbury	46	16	10	20	64	81	42
Hounslow	46	15	11	20	59	83	41
Hillingdon Borough	46	14	10	22	46	58	38
Canterbury City	46	10	16	20	49	78	36
Crawley Town	46	9	12	25	46	81	30
Folkestone	46	10	6	30	49	101	26
Andover	46	4	11	31	39	100	19
Thanet United	46	5	7	34	37	110	17

1982-83

Premier Division

AP Leamington	38	25	4	9	78	50	79
Kidderminster Harriers	38	23	7	8	69	40	76
Welling United	38	21	6	11	63	40	69
Chelmsford City	38	16	11	11	57	40	59
Bedworth United	38	16	11	11	47	39	59
Dartford	38	16	8	14	48	38	56
Gosport Borough	38	14	13	11	47	43	55
Fareham Town	38	16	7	15	73	82	55
Dorchester Town	38	14	12	12	52	50	54
Gravesend & Northfleet	38	14	12	12	49	50	54
Gloucester City	38	13	12	13	61	57	51
Witney Town	38	12	13	13	60	48	47
Alvechurch	38	13	8	17	60	66	47
Stourbridge	38	12	11	15	48	54	47
Corby Town	38	12	11	15	58	67	47
Hastings United	38	11	11	16	48	61	44
Enderby Town	38	11	9	18	44	62	42
Waterlooville	38	10	9	19	62	83	39
Poole Town	38	9	9	20	57	73	36
Addlestone & Weybridge	38	5	10	23	24	62	25

Witney Town had 2 points deducted for fielding an ineligible player

Midland Division

Cheltenham Town	32	22	5	5	65	29	71
Sutton Coldfield Town	32	21	7	4	62	24	70
Forest Green Rovers	32	21	3	8	68	32	66
Merthyr Tydfil	32	17	7	8	64	45	58
Willenhall Town	32	17	6	9	74	49	57
Oldbury United	32	16	6	10	52	49	54
Banbury United	32	15	3	14	59	55	48
Bridgend Town	32	12	11	9	46	37	47
Wellingborough Town	32	13	7	12	49	37	46
Bromsgrove Rovers	32	13	5	14	47	47	44
Dudley Town	32	12	7	13	40	45	43
Bridgwater Town	32	12	6	14	42	43	42
Aylesbury United	32	12	5	15	37	51	41
Redditch United	32	8	6	18	51	73	30
Taunton Town	32	5	7	20	30	64	22
Minehead	32	5	7	20	24	62	22
Milton Keynes City	32	0	4	28	22	90	4

Southern Division

Fisher Athletic	34	23	5	6	79	34	74
Folkestone	34	22	6	6	79	41	72
RS Southampton	34	21	7	6	66	30	70
Dunstable	34	19	5	10	57	39	62
Hillingdon Borough	34	14	11	9	41	30	53
Salisbury	34	14	10	10	59	49	52
Crawley Town	34	14	9	11	51	43	51
Ashford Town	34	13	10	11	51	41	49
Tonbridge AFC	34	14	5	15	57	57	47
Hounslow	34	11	12	11	46	47	45
Canterbury City	34	12	9	13	52	63	45
Cambridge City	34	12	5	17	56	63	41
Dover	34	11	7	16	35	52	40
Thanet United	34	10	5	19	30	61	35
Basingstoke Town	34	8	10	16	37	56	34
Woodford Town	34	6	9	19	29	57	27
Andover	34	6	8	20	28	53	26
Erith & Belvedere	34	5	9	20	26	62	24

1983-84

Premier Division

Dartford	38	23	9	6	67	32	78
Fisher Athletic	38	22	9	7	80	42	75
Chelmsford City	38	19	9	10	67	45	66
Gravesend & Northfleet	38	18	9	11	50	38	63
Witney Town	38	18	6	14	75	50	60
King's Lynn	38	18	6	14	42	45	60
Folkestone	38	16	9	13	60	56	57
Cheltenham Town	38	16	7	15	63	56	55
Gloucester City	38	13	15	10	55	50	54
Hastings United	38	15	9	14	55	57	54
Bedworth United	38	15	9	14	51	55	54
Welling United	38	15	7	16	61	61	52
AP Leamington	38	14	9	15	73	83	51
Corby Town	38	12	14	12	55	54	50
Fareham Town	38	13	11	14	65	70	50
Alvechurch	38	12	12	14	56	62	48
Sutton Coldfield Town	38	10	14	14	49	53	44
Gosport Borough	38	6	15	17	31	64	33
Dorchester Town	38	4	8	26	40	69	20
Stourbridge	38	4	7	27	30	82	19

Midland Division

Willenhall Town	38	27	4	7	100	44	85
Shepshed Charterhouse	38	25	5	8	88	37	80
Bromsgrove Rovers	38	20	8	10	73	43	68
Dudley Town	38	18	13	7	71	43	67
Aylesbury United	38	17	15	6	62	35	66
Moor Green	38	18	12	8	63	44	66
Rushden Town	38	17	12	9	68	42	63
Merthyr Tydfil	38	18	8	12	63	44	62
Redditch United	38	17	9	12	67	67	60
VS Rugby	38	15	12	11	68	51	57
Forest Green Rovers	38	15	12	11	67	51	57
Bridgnorth Town	38	16	9	13	64	52	57
Leicester United	38	12	9	17	58	58	45
Oldbury United	38	10	13	15	53	51	43
Coventry Sporting	38	11	7	20	40	67	40
Bridgwater Town	38	10	8	20	39	65	38
Wellingborough Town	38	7	9	22	43	80	30
Banbury United	38	6	11	21	37	78	29
Milton Keynes City	38	3	9	26	31	110	18
Tamworth	38	2	7	29	25	118	13

Southern Division

RS Southampton	38	26	6	6	83	35	84
Crawley Town	38	22	9	7	68	28	75
Basingstoke Town	38	20	9	9	54	36	69
Tonbridge AFC	38	20	9	9	61	44	69
Addlestone & Weybridge	38	19	11	8	58	34	68
Poole Town	38	20	7	11	68	42	67
Hillingdon Borough	38	18	11	9	43	20	65
Ashford Town	38	19	5	14	65	47	62
Salisbury	38	17	8	13	61	48	59
Cambridge City	38	13	9	16	43	53	48
Canterbury City	38	12	9	17	44	52	45
Waterlooville	38	12	9	17	56	69	45
Dover Athletic	38	12	9	17	51	74	45
Chatham Town	38	11	10	17	46	56	43
Andover	38	12	6	20	35	54	42
Erith & Belvedere	38	11	9	18	43	68	42
Dunstable	38	10	8	20	38	65	38
Thanet United	38	9	8	21	40	65	35
Woodford Town	38	7	8	23	30	69	29
Hounslow	38	4	12	22	30	58	24

1984-85

Premier Division

Cheltenham Town	38	24	5	9	83	41	77
King's Lynn	38	23	6	9	73	48	75
Crawley Town	38	22	8	8	76	52	74
Willenhall Town	38	20	8	10	57	38	68
RS Southampton	38	21	4	13	76	52	67
Welling United	38	18	11	9	55	38	65
Folkestone	38	19	6	13	70	54	63
Fisher Athletic	38	19	5	14	67	57	62
Chelmsford City	38	17	10	11	52	50	61
Shepshed Charterhouse	38	18	5	15	67	50	59
Corby Town	38	15	6	17	56	54	51
Bedworth United	38	14	8	16	48	52	50
Gravesend & Northfleet	38	12	12	14	46	46	48
Fareham Town	38	13	8	17	52	55	47
Alvechurch	38	11	7	20	53	59	40
Hastings United	38	11	7	20	46	71	40
Witney Town	38	9	12	17	51	58	39
Gloucester City	38	10	6	22	49	74	36
Trowbridge	38	10	5	23	45	83	35
AP Leamington	38	2	5	31	22	112	11

Midland Division

Dudley Town	34	21	8	5	70	36	71
Aylesbury United	34	20	7	7	62	30	67
Hednesford Town	34	18	7	9	58	42	61
Moor Green	34	17	9	8	63	43	60
VS Rugby	34	17	9	8	59	41	60
Bromsgrove Rovers	34	16	10	8	53	42	58
Stourbridge	34	15	11	8	52	45	56
Redditch United	34	12	11	11	68	57	47
Sutton Coldfield Town	34	13	6	15	50	56	45
Bridgnorth Town	34	13	5	16	67	65	44
Coventry Sporting	34	11	9	14	45	52	42
Merthyr Tydfil	34	10	11	13	43	46	41
Rushden Town	34	10	7	17	42	52	37
Forest Green Rovers	34	9	10	15	49	65	37
Wellingborough Town	34	10	7	17	39	63	37
Oldbury United	34	10	6	18	52	66	36
Banbury United	34	9	5	20	33	59	32
Leicester United	34	3	6	25	17	62	15

Southern Division

Basingstoke Town	38	24	9	5	61	22	81
Gosport Borough	38	22	6	10	78	41	72
Poole Town	38	20	12	6	69	38	72
Hillingdon	38	19	10	9	51	23	67
Thanet United	38	19	9	10	63	47	66
Salisbury	38	19	5	14	55	54	62
Sheppey United	38	18	6	14	49	45	60
Addlestone & Weybridge	38	16	9	13	68	54	57
Waterlooville	38	15	10	13	71	63	55
Canterbury City	38	15	7	16	61	64	52
Woodford Town	38	13	13	12	46	53	52
Tonbridge AFC	38	16	3	19	59	62	51
Andover	38	15	5	18	42	54	50
Dorchester Town	38	13	7	18	45	60	46
Cambridge City	38	11	11	16	59	71	44
Chatham Town	38	12	8	18	44	66	44
Ashford Town	38	10	9	19	54	69	69
Dunstable	38	8	10	20	35	56	64
Dover Athletic	38	7	7	24	39	78	28
Erith & Belvedere	38	6	8	24	36	65	26

1985-86

Premier Division

Welling United	38	29	6	3	95	31	93
Chelmsford City	38	20	10	8	68	41	70
Fisher Athletic	38	20	7	11	67	45	67
Alvechurch	38	19	9	10	71	56	66
Worcester City	38	19	9	10	64	50	66
Crawley Town	38	18	5	15	76	59	59
Shepshed Charterhouse	38	19	1	18	51	52	58
Aylesbury United	38	14	10	14	52	49	52
Folkestone	38	14	10	14	56	56	52
Bedworth United	38	14	8	16	44	49	50
Willenhall Town	38	12	13	13	51	44	49
Dudley Town	38	15	4	19	58	62	49
Corby Town	38	14	7	17	61	67	49
King's Lynn	38	12	10	16	39	42	46
Basingstoke Town	38	13	4	21	36	67	43
RS Southampton	38	11	9	18	44	61	42
Witney Town	38	11	6	21	44	74	39
Gosport Borough	38	10	8	20	42	66	38
Fareham Town	38	8	13	17	40	62	37
Gravesend & Northfleet	38	9	9	20	29	55	36

Midland Division

Bromsgrove Rovers	40	29	5	6	95	44	92
Redditch United	40	23	6	11	70	42	75
Merthyr Tydfil	40	21	10	9	60	40	73
VS Rugby	40	17	14	9	41	31	65
Stourbridge	40	15	14	11	62	49	59
Rusden Town	40	17	7	16	69	74	58
Bilston Town	40	15	12	13	60	48	57
Bridgnorth Town	40	13	18	9	56	45	57
Gloucester City	40	15	12	13	61	57	57
Grantham	40	16	7	17	46	59	55
Wellingborough Town	40	15	9	16	56	56	54
Sutton Coldfield Town	40	13	14	13	60	45	53
Hednesford Town	40	14	9	17	67	70	51
Forest Green Rovers	40	14	9	17	52	56	51
Mile Oak Rovers	40	14	8	18	56	73	50
Leicester United	40	13	10	17	41	48	49
Banbury United	40	13	8	19	38	55	47
Coventry Sporting	40	10	15	15	42	48	45
Moor Green	40	12	6	22	63	91	42
Leamington	40	10	6	24	40	77	36
Oldbury United	40	8	7	25	50	87	31

Southern Division

Cambridge City	40	23	11	6	87	41	80
Salisbury	40	24	8	8	84	51	80
Hastings Town	40	23	9	8	83	51	78
Dover Athletic	40	23	6	11	89	53	75
Corinthian	40	20	9	11	79	45	69
Tonbridge AFC	40	17	13	10	65	51	64
Dunstable	40	17	11	12	70	61	62
Ruislip	40	17	6	17	67	66	57
Erith & Belvedere	40	14	12	14	35	40	54
Waterlooville	40	16	6	18	52	58	54
Burnham & Hillingdon	40	16	6	18	44	59	54
Canterbury City	40	13	13	14	58	58	52
Trowbridge Town	40	13	13	14	57	63	52
Sheppey United	40	14	10	16	43	53	52
Thanet United	40	13	7	20	58	63	46
Woodford Town	40	12	10	18	49	62	46
Poole Town	40	12	7	21	55	63	43
Ashford Town	40	10	12	18	45	65	42
Chatham Town	40	8	15	17	53	70	39
Andover	40	10	8	22	52	92	38
Dorchester Town	40	5	8	27	35	94	23

1986-87

Premier Division

Fisher Athletic	42	25	11	6	72	29	86
Bromsgrove Rovers	42	24	11	7	82	41	83
Aylesbury United	42	24	11	7	72	40	83
Dartford	42	19	12	11	76	43	69
Chelmsford City	42	17	13	12	48	45	64
Cambridge City	42	14	20	8	68	52	62
Redditch United	42	16	14	12	59	54	62
Alvechurch	42	18	8	16	66	62	62
Corby Town	42	14	17	11	65	51	59
Worcester City	42	16	11	15	62	55	59
Shepshed Charterhouse	42	16	10	16	59	59	58
Bedworth United	42	15	12	15	55	51	57
Crawley Town	42	14	11	17	59	60	53
Fareham Town	42	11	17	14	58	49	50
Willenhall Town	42	13	11	18	48	57	50
Basingstoke Town	42	12	12	18	53	78	48
Witney Town	42	12	12	18	29	56	48
Gosport Borough	42	11	13	18	42	57	46
Salisbury	42	12	7	23	52	82	43
King's Lynn	42	9	13	20	48	72	40
Dudley Town	42	9	9	24	39	76	36
Folkestone	42	8	11	23	36	79	35

Midland Division

VS Rugby	38	25	5	8	81	43	80
Leicester United	38	26	1	11	89	49	79
Merthyr Tydfil	38	23	6	9	95	54	75
Moor Green	38	22	6	10	73	55	72
Halesowen Town	38	19	12	7	72	50	69
Hednesford Town	38	21	5	12	84	56	68
Gloucester City	38	19	5	14	77	59	62
Coventry Sporting	38	17	8	13	55	54	59
Forest Green Rovers	38	16	9	13	65	53	57
Stourbridge	38	16	7	15	56	56	55
Grantham	38	15	9	14	74	54	54
Banbury United	38	14	7	17	55	65	49
Buckingham Town	38	13	9	16	55	59	48
Bridgnorth Town	38	12	9	17	59	63	45
Wellingborough Town	38	13	6	19	55	76	45
Mile Oak Rovers	38	11	10	17	50	63	43
Sutton Coldfield Town	38	8	10	20	56	78	34
Bilston Town	38	8	7	23	37	76	31
Leamington	38	4	13	21	37	80	25
Rushden Town	38	1	10	27	42	124	13

Southern Division

Dorchester Town	38	23	8	7	83	42	77
Ashford Town	38	23	7	8	63	32	76
Woodford Town	38	22	6	10	72	44	72
Hastings Town	38	20	10	8	74	54	70
Dover Athletic	38	20	6	12	66	43	66
Gravesend & Northfleet	38	18	7	13	67	46	61
Tonbridge AFC	38	16	10	12	73	67	58
Erith & Belvedere	38	15	12	11	57	50	57
Chatham Town	38	16	9	13	53	46	57
Thanet United	38	14	14	10	56	50	56
Waterlooville	38	16	8	14	66	65	56
Trowbridge Town	38	15	9	14	77	65	54
Dunstable	38	13	9	16	60	57	48
Corinthian	38	11	12	15	56	65	45
Sheppey United	38	9	12	17	43	65	39
Andover	38	9	9	20	51	80	36
Burnham & Hillingdon	38	7	11	20	32	62	32
Poole Town	38	8	6	24	50	90	30
Ruislip	38	6	12	20	35	75	30
Canterbury City	38	8	5	25	46	82	29

1987-88

Premier Division

Aylesbury United	42	27	8	7	79	35	89
Dartford	42	27	8	7	79	39	89
Cambridge City	42	24	8	10	84	43	80
Bromsgrove Rovers	42	22	11	9	65	39	77
Worcester City	42	22	6	14	58	48	72
Crawley Town	42	17	14	11	73	63	65
Alvechurch	42	17	13	12	54	52	64
Leicester United	42	15	14	13	68	59	59
Fareham Town	42	16	11	15	51	59	59
Corby Town	42	16	8	18	61	64	56
Dorchester Town	42	14	14	14	51	57	56
Ashford Town	42	12	16	14	45	54	52
Shepshed Charterhouse	42	13	11	18	53	62	50
Bedworth United	42	12	14	16	49	64	50
Gosport Borough	42	10	17	15	39	49	47
Burton Albion	42	11	14	17	62	74	47
VS Rugby	42	10	16	16	52	57	46
Redditch United	42	10	13	19	55	63	43
Chelmsford City	42	11	10	21	60	75	43
Willenhall Town	42	9	12	21	39	76	39
Nuneaton Borough	42	8	13	21	58	77	37
Witney Town	42	8	11	23	45	71	35

Midland Division

Merthyr Tydfil	42	30	4	8	102	40	94
Moor Green	42	26	8	8	91	49	86
Grantham Town	42	27	4	11	97	53	85
Atherstone United	42	22	10	10	93	56	76
Sutton Coldfield Town	42	22	6	14	71	47	72
Halesowen Town	42	18	15	9	75	59	69
Gloucester City	42	18	14	10	86	62	68
Dudley Town	42	20	5	17	64	55	65
Forest Green Rovers	42	14	16	12	67	54	58
Banbury United	42	17	7	18	48	46	58
Bridgnorth Town	42	16	7	19	59	75	55
Buckingham Town	42	15	9	18	74	75	54
King's Lynn	42	16	6	20	53	63	54
Wellingborough Town	42	14	10	18	67	70	52
Rushden Town	42	14	9	19	69	85	51
Trowbridge Town	42	14	3	25	53	82	45
Bilston Town	42	12	8	22	52	87	44
Hednesford Town	42	11	10	21	50	81	43
Mile Oak Rovers	42	9	14	19	43	65	41
Coventry Sporting	42	11	8	23	46	83	41
Stourbridge	42	10	10	22	46	79	40
Paget Rangers	42	10	9	23	49	89	39

Southern Division

Dover Athletic	40	28	10	2	81	28	94
Waterlooville	40	27	10	3	88	33	91
Salisbury	40	24	11	5	71	33	83
Gravesend & Northfleet	40	20	12	8	60	32	72
Thanet United	40	17	13	10	60	38	64
Andover	40	17	13	10	64	58	64
Dunstable	40	17	12	11	78	56	63
Burnham	40	17	10	13	61	45	61
Bury Town	40	17	7	16	80	67	58
Erith & Belvedere	40	16	9	15	52	56	57
Sheppey United	40	14	10	16	58	52	52
Hastings Town	40	14	10	16	62	70	52
Tonbridge AFC	40	14	8	18	51	56	50
Poole Town	40	13	10	17	69	70	49
Baldock Town	40	12	12	16	44	53	48
Hounslow	40	11	8	21	41	76	41
Folkestone	40	9	11	20	47	76	38
Corinthian	40	9	10	21	49	67	37
Ruislip	40	5	13	22	33	80	28
Canterbury City	40	7	6	27	33	87	27
Chatham Town	40	7	5	28	39	88	26

1988-89

Premier Division

Merthyr Tydfil	42	26	7	9	104	58	85
Dartford	42	25	7	10	79	33	82
VS Rugby	42	24	7	11	64	43	79
Worcester City	42	20	13	9	72	49	73
Cambridge City	42	20	10	12	72	51	70
Dover Athletic	42	19	12	11	65	47	69
Gosport Borough	42	18	12	12	73	57	66
Burton Albion	42	18	10	14	79	68	64
Bath City	42	15	13	14	66	51	59
Bromsgrove Rovers	42	14	16	12	68	56	59
Wealdstone	42	16	10	16	60	53	59
Crawley Town	42	14	16	12	61	56	59
Dorchester Town	42	14	16	12	56	61	59
Alvechurch	42	16	8	18	56	59	56
Moor Green	42	14	13	15	58	70	55
Corby Town	42	14	11	17	55	59	53
Waterlooville	42	13	13	16	61	63	52
Ashford Town	42	13	13	16	59	76	52
Fareham Town	42	15	6	21	43	68	51
Leicester United	42	6	11	25	46	84	29
Redditch United	42	5	7	30	36	105	22
Bedworth United	42	4	7	31	36	102	19

Midland Division

Gloucester City	42	28	8	6	95	37	92
Atherstone United	42	26	9	7	85	38	87
Tamworth	42	26	9	7	85	45	87
Halesowen Town	42	25	10	7	85	42	85
Grantham Town	42	23	11	8	66	37	80
Nuneaton Borough	42	19	9	14	71	58	66
Rushden Town	42	19	8	15	71	50	65
Spalding United	42	17	13	12	72	64	64
Dudley Town	42	16	13	13	73	62	61
Sutton Coldfield Town	42	18	7	17	56	56	61
Willenhall Town	42	16	12	14	65	71	60
Forest Green Rovers	42	12	16	14	64	67	52
Bilston Town	42	15	7	20	63	71	52
Ashtree Highfield	42	12	15	15	57	62	51
Hednesford Town	42	12	15	15	49	57	51
Banbury United	42	10	14	18	53	74	44
Bridgnorth Town	42	12	7	23	59	77	43
Stourbridge	42	11	10	21	37	65	43
King's Lynn	42	7	13	22	31	67	34
Coventry Sporting	42	6	13	23	39	91	31
Wellingborough Town	42	5	15	22	39	72	30
Mile Oak Rovers	42	5	10	27	46	98	25

Southern Division

Chelmsford City	42	30	5	7	106	38	95
Gravesend & Northfleet	42	27	6	9	70	40	87
Poole Town	42	24	11	7	98	48	83
Bury Town	42	25	7	10	75	34	82
Burnham	42	22	13	7	78	47	79
Baldock Town	42	23	5	14	69	40	74
Hastings Town	42	21	11	10	75	48	74
Hounslow	42	21	6	15	75	60	69
Salisbury	42	20	5	17	79	58	65
Trowbridge Town	42	19	7	16	59	52	64
Folkestone	42	17	8	17	62	65	59
Corinthian	42	13	13	16	59	69	52
Canterbury City	42	14	8	20	52	60	50
Witney Town	42	13	11	18	61	71	50
Dunstable	42	11	14	17	42	57	47
Buckingham Town	42	12	10	20	56	79	46
Erith & Belvedere	42	11	10	21	48	63	43
Andover	42	11	9	22	56	90	42
Sheppey United	42	10	8	24	50	90	38
Thanet United	42	7	15	20	47	95	36
Tonbridge AFC	42	7	6	29	50	98	27
Ruislip	42	6	8	28	47	112	26

1989-90

Premier Division

Dover Athletic	42	32	6	4	87	27	102
Bath City	42	30	8	4	81	28	98
Dartford	42	26	9	7	80	35	87
Burton Albion	42	20	12	10	64	40	72
VS Rugby	42	19	12	11	51	35	69
Atherstone United	42	19	10	13	60	52	67
Gravesend & Northfleet	42	18	12	12	44	50	66
Cambridge City	42	17	11	14	76	56	62
Gloucester City	42	17	11	14	80	68	62
Bromsgrove Rovers	42	17	10	15	56	48	61
Moor Green	42	18	7	17	62	59	61
Wealdstone	42	16	9	17	55	54	57
Dorchester Town	42	16	7	19	52	67	55
Worcester City	42	15	10	17	62	63	54
Crawley Town	42	13	12	17	53	57	51
Waterlooville	42	13	10	19	63	81	49
Weymouth	42	11	13	18	50	70	46
Chelmsford City	42	11	10	21	52	72	43
Ashford Town	42	10	7	25	43	75	37
Corby Town	42	10	6	26	57	77	36
Alvechurch	42	7	5	30	46	95	26
Gosport Borough	42	6	5	31	28	93	23

Midland Division

Halesowen Town	42	28	8	6	100	49	92
Rushden Town	42	28	5	9	82	39	89
Nuneaton Borough	42	26	7	9	81	47	85
Tamworth	42	22	8	12	82	70	74
Barry Town	42	21	8	13	67	53	71
Spalding United	42	20	7	15	73	63	67
Sutton Coldfield Town	42	18	10	14	72	69	64
Stourbridge	42	17	12	13	73	61	63
Dudley Town	42	18	9	15	69	64	63
Stroud	42	16	13	13	75	62	61
Leicester United	42	17	5	20	66	77	56
Bridgnorth Town	42	13	14	15	68	73	53
King's Lynn	42	16	5	21	57	69	53
Grantham Town	42	14	10	18	57	63	52
Bedworth United	42	14	9	19	50	60	51
Hednesford Town	42	11	14	17	50	62	47
Bilston Town	42	11	14	17	40	54	47
Redditch United	42	11	13	18	57	64	46
Racing Club Warwick	42	11	11	20	45	66	44
Willenhall Town	42	9	9	24	37	66	36
Banbury United	42	9	9	24	46	83	34
Sandwell Borough	42	6	12	24	46	79	30

Southern Division

Bashley	42	25	7	10	80	47	82
Poole Town	42	23	8	11	85	60	77
Buckingham Town	42	22	10	10	67	46	76
Dunstable	42	20	14	8	56	38	74
Salisbury	42	21	9	12	72	50	72
Hythe Town	42	20	12	10	69	48	72
Trowbridge Town	42	20	9	13	79	64	69
Hastings Town	42	20	9	13	64	54	69
Bury Town	42	18	12	12	76	62	66
Baldock Town	42	18	11	13	69	52	65
Burnham	42	17	11	14	77	52	62
Fareham Town	42	14	14	14	49	53	56
Yate Town	42	16	6	20	53	52	54
Witney Town	42	16	6	20	54	56	54
Canterbury City	42	14	10	18	52	52	52
Margate	42	12	15	15	46	45	51
Folkestone	42	14	9	19	61	83	51
Andover	42	13	11	18	54	70	50
Hounslow	42	11	5	26	39	82	38
Erith & Belvedere	42	8	11	23	34	73	35
Corinthian	42	6	10	26	44	93	28
Sheppey United	42	6	7	29	35	83	25

1990-91

Premier Division

Farnborough Town	42	26	7	9	79	43	85
Gloucester City	42	23	14	5	86	49	83
Cambridge City	42	21	14	7	63	43	77
Dover Athletic	42	21	11	10	56	37	74
Bromsgrove Rovers	42	20	11	11	68	49	71
Worcester City	42	18	12	12	55	42	66
Burton Albion	42	15	15	12	59	48	60
Halesowen Town	42	17	9	16	73	67	60
VS Rugby	42	16	11	15	56	46	59
Bashley	42	15	12	15	56	52	57
Dorchester Town	42	15	12	15	47	54	57
Wealdstone	42	16	8	18	57	58	56
Dartford	42	15	9	18	61	64	54
Rushden Town	42	14	11	17	64	66	53
Atherstone United	42	14	10	18	55	58	52
Moor Green	42	15	6	21	64	75	51
Poole Town	42	12	13	17	56	69	49
Chelmsford City	42	11	15	16	37	68	48
Crawley Town	42	12	12	18	45	67	48
Waterlooville	42	11	13	18	51	70	46
Gravesend & Northfleet	42	9	7	26	46	91	34
Weymouth	42	4	12	26	50	88	24

Midland Division

Stourbridge	42	28	6	8	80	48	90
Corby Town	42	27	4	11	99	48	85
Hednesford Town	42	25	7	10	79	47	82
Tamworth	42	25	5	12	84	45	80
Nuneaton Borough	42	21	11	10	74	51	70
Barry Town	42	20	7	15	61	48	67
Newport AFC	42	19	6	17	54	46	63
King's Lynn	42	17	9	16	53	62	60
Grantham Town	42	17	7	18	62	56	56
Redditch United	42	16	10	16	66	75	58
Hinckley Town	42	16	9	17	72	68	57
Sutton Coldfield Town	42	15	11	16	56	65	56
Bedworth United	42	15	9	18	57	73	54
Bilston Town	42	14	9	19	69	79	51
Leicester United	42	14	10	18	65	77	51
Racing Club Warwick	42	12	13	17	56	65	49
Bridgnorth Town	42	13	9	20	62	74	48
Stroud	42	11	14	17	51	64	47
Dudley Town	42	11	13	18	48	73	46
Alvechurch	42	10	8	24	54	92	38
Willenhall Town	42	10	10	22	58	69	37
Spalding United	42	8	9	25	35	70	33

Southern Division

Buckingham Town	40	25	8	7	73	38	83
Trowbridge Town	40	22	12	6	67	31	78
Salisbury	40	22	11	7	63	39	77
Baldock Town	40	21	9	10	66	52	72
Ashford Town	40	22	5	13	82	52	71
Yate Town	40	21	8	11	76	48	71
Hastings Town	40	18	11	11	66	46	65
Hythe Town	40	17	9	14	55	44	59
Andover	40	16	6	18	69	76	54
Margate	40	14	11	15	52	55	53
Burnham	40	12	16	12	57	49	52
Bury Town	40	15	5	20	58	74	50
Sudbury Town	40	13	0	17	60	68	49
Newport IOW	40	13	9	18	56	62	48
Gosport Borough	40	12	11	17	47	58	47
Witney Town	40	12	11	17	57	75	47
Dunstable	40	9	15	16	48	63	42
Canterbury City	40	12	6	22	60	83	42
Erith & Belvedere	40	10	0	24	46	73	36
Fareham Town	40	9	9	22	46	74	36
Corinthian	40	5	12	23	34	78	27

1991-92

Premier Division

Bromsgrove Rovers	42	27	9	6	78	34	90
Dover Athletic	42	23	15	4	66	30	84
VS Rugby	42	23	11	8	70	44	80
Bashley	42	22	8	12	70	44	74
Cambridge City	42	18	14	10	71	53	68
Dartford	42	17	15	10	62	45	66
Trowbridge Town	42	17	10	15	69	51	61
Halesowen Town	42	15	15	12	61	49	60
Moor Green	42	15	11	16	61	59	56
Burton Albion	42	15	10	17	59	61	55
Dorchester Town	42	14	13	15	66	73	55
Gloucester City	42	15	9	18	67	70	54
Atherstone United	42	15	8	19	54	66	53
Corby Town	42	13	12	17	66	81	51
Waterlooville	42	13	11	18	43	56	50
Worcester City	42	12	13	17	56	59	49
Crawley Town	42	12	12	18	62	67	48
Chelmsford City	42	12	12	18	49	56	48
Wealdstone	42	13	7	22	52	69	46
Poole Town	42	10	13	19	46	77	43
Fisher Athletic	42	9	11	22	53	89	38
Gravesend & Northfleet	42	8	9	25	39	87	33

Midland Division

Solihull Borough	42	29	10	3	92	40	97
Hednesford Town	42	26	13	3	81	37	91
Sutton Coldfield Town	42	21	11	10	71	51	74
Barry Town	42	21	6	15	88	56	69
Bedworth United	42	16	15	11	67	63	63
Nuneaton Borough	42	17	11	14	68	53	62
Tamworth	42	16	12	14	66	52	60
Rushden Town	42	16	12	14	69	63	60
Stourbridge	42	17	8	17	85	62	59
Newport AFC	42	15	13	14	72	60	58
Yate Town	42	14	15	13	65	64	57
Bilston Town	42	15	10	17	56	67	55
Grantham Town	42	11	17	14	59	55	50
King's Lynn	42	13	11	18	61	68	50
Hinckley Town	42	14	8	20	61	87	50
Leicester United	42	12	13	17	56	63	49
Bridgnorth Town	42	12	12	18	61	74	48
Racing Club Warwick	42	11	14	17	45	61	47
Stroud	42	14	4	24	66	88	46
Redditch United	42	12	8	22	52	92	44
Alvechurch	42	11	10	21	54	88	43
Dudley Town	42	8	9	25	41	92	33

Southern Division

Hastings Town	42	28	7	7	80	37	91
Weymouth	42	22	12	8	64	35	78
Havant Town	42	21	12	9	67	46	75
Braintree Town	42	21	8	13	77	58	71
Buckingham Town	42	19	15	8	57	26	69
Andover	42	18	10	14	73	68	64
Ashford Town	42	17	12	13	66	57	63
Sudbury Town	42	18	9	15	70	66	63
Sittingbourne	42	19	10	13	63	41	61
Burnham	42	15	14	13	57	55	59
Baldock Town	42	16	10	16	62	67	58
Salisbury	42	13	16	13	67	51	55
Hythe Town	42	15	10	17	61	62	55
Margate	42	13	16	13	49	56	55
Newport IOW	42	13	10	19	58	63	49
Dunstable	42	12	12	18	55	67	48
Bury Town	42	14	4	24	52	94	46
Witney Town	42	11	12	19	55	76	45
Fareham Town	42	12	8	22	45	71	44
Erith & Belvedere	42	11	10	21	44	67	43
Canterbury City	42	8	14	20	43	69	38
Gosport Borough	42	6	9	27	32	65	27

1992-93

Premier Division

Dover Athletic	40	25	11	4	65	23	86
Cheltenham Town	40	21	10	9	76	40	73
Corby Town	40	20	12	8	68	43	72
Hednesford Town	40	21	7	12	72	52	70
Trowbridge Town	40	18	8	14	70	66	62
Crawley Town	40	16	12	12	68	59	60
Solihull Borough	40	17	9	14	68	59	60
Burton Albion	40	16	11	13	53	50	59
Bashley	40	18	8	14	60	60	59
Halesowen Town	40	15	11	14	67	54	56
Waterlooville	40	15	9	16	59	62	54
Chelmsford City	40	15	9	16	59	69	54
Gloucester City	40	14	11	15	66	68	53
Cambridge City	40	14	10	16	62	73	52
Atherstone United	40	13	14	13	56	60	50
Hastings Town	40	13	11	16	50	55	50
Worcester City	40	12	9	19	45	62	45
Dorchester Town	40	12	6	22	52	74	42
Moor Green	40	10	6	24	58	79	36
VS Rugby	40	10	6	24	40	63	36
Weymouth	40	5	10	25	39	82	23

Bashley had 3 points deducted

Midland Division

Nuneaton Borough	42	29	5	8	102	45	92
Gresley Rovers	42	27	6	9	94	55	87
Rushden & Diamonds	42	25	10	7	85	41	85
Barri	42	26	5	11	82	49	83
Newport AFC	42	23	8	11	73	58	77
Bedworth United	42	22	8	12	72	55	74
Stourbridge	42	17	9	16	93	79	60
Sutton Coldfield Town	42	17	9	16	82	78	60
Redditch United	42	18	6	18	75	79	60
Tamworth	42	16	11	15	65	51	59
Weston-super-Mare	42	17	7	18	79	86	58
Leicester United	42	16	9	17	67	67	57
Grantham Town	42	16	9	17	60	73	57
Bilston Town	42	15	10	17	74	69	55
Evesham United	42	15	8	19	67	83	53
Bridgnorth Town	42	15	7	20	61	68	52
Dudley Town	42	14	8	20	60	75	50
Yate Town	42	15	5	22	63	81	50
Forest Green Rovers	42	12	6	24	61	97	42
Hinckley Athletic	42	9	11	22	56	89	37
King's Lynn	42	10	6	26	45	90	36
Racing Club Warwick	42	3	7	32	40	88	16

Southern Division

Sittingbourne	42	26	12	4	102	43	90
Salisbury	42	27	7	8	87	50	88
Witney Town	42	25	9	8	77	37	84
Gravesend & Northfleet	42	25	4	13	99	63	79
Havant Town	42	23	6	13	78	55	75
Sudbury Town	42	20	11	11	89	54	71
Erith & Belvedere	42	22	5	15	73	66	71
Ashford Town	42	20	8	14	91	66	68
Braintree Town	42	20	6	16	95	65	66
Margate	42	19	7	16	65	58	64
Wealdstone	42	18	7	17	75	69	61
Buckingham Town	42	16	11	15	61	58	59
Baldock Town	42	15	9	18	59	63	54
Poole Town	42	15	7	20	61	69	52
Fareham Town	42	14	8	20	67	65	50
Burnham	42	14	8	20	53	77	50
Canterbury City	42	12	10	20	54	76	46
Newport IOW	42	9	16	17	44	56	43
Fisher Athletic	42	8	9	25	38	98	33
Andover	42	7	9	26	42	99	30
Dunstable	42	5	14	23	42	92	29
Bury Town	42	8	5	29	46	119	29

1993-94

Premier Division

Farnborough Town	42	25	7	10	74	44	82
Cheltenham Town	42	21	12	9	67	38	75
Halesowen Town	42	21	11	10	69	46	74
Atherstone United	42	22	7	13	57	43	73
Crawley Town	42	21	10	11	56	42	73
Chelmsford City	42	21	7	14	74	59	70
Trowbridge Town	42	16	17	9	52	41	65
Sittingbourne	42	17	13	12	65	48	64
Corby Town	42	17	8	17	52	56	59
Gloucester City	42	17	6	19	55	60	57
Burton Albion	42	15	11	10	57	49	56
Hastings Town	42	16	7	19	51	60	55
Hednesford Town	42	15	9	18	67	66	54
Gresley Rovers	42	14	11	17	61	72	53
Worcester City	42	14	9	19	61	70	51
Solihull Borough	42	13	11	18	52	57	50
Cambridge City	42	13	11	18	50	60	50
Dorchester Town	42	12	11	19	38	51	47
Moor Green	42	11	10	21	49	66	43
Waterlooville	42	11	10	21	47	69	43
Bashley	42	11	10	21	47	80	43
Nuneaton Borough	42	11	8	23	42	66	41

Midland Division

Rushden & Diamonds	42	29	11	2	109	37	98
VS Rugby	42	28	8	6	98	41	92
Weston-super-Mare	42	27	10	5	94	39	91
Newport AFC	42	26	9	7	84	37	87
Clevedon Town	42	24	10	8	75	46	82
Redditch United	42	19	11	12	79	62	68
Tamworth	42	19	7	16	82	68	64
Bilston Town	42	16	10	16	65	73	58
Stourbridge	42	17	6	19	71	75	57
Evesham United	42	16	8	18	50	60	56
Grantham Town	42	16	6	20	77	73	54
Bridgnorth Town	42	15	6	21	56	68	51
Racing Club Warwick	42	13	12	17	53	66	51
Dudley Town	42	13	10	19	64	61	49
Forest Green Rangers	42	12	12	18	61	84	48
Sutton Coldfield Town	42	12	8	22	53	75	44
Bedworth United	42	12	7	23	62	81	43
Hinckley Town	42	11	10	21	44	71	43
Leicester United	42	11	9	22	34	73	42
King's Lynn	42	9	11	22	47	72	38
Yate Town	42	10	6	26	48	86	36
Armitage	42	8	11	23	45	103	35

Southern Division

Gravesend & Northfleet	42	27	11	4	87	24	92
Sudbury Town	42	27	8	7	98	47	89
Witney Town	42	27	8	7	69	36	89
Salisbury City	42	26	10	6	90	39	88
Havant Town	42	27	4	11	101	41	85
Ashford Town	42	24	13	5	93	46	85
Baldock Town	42	26	7	9	76	40	85
Newport IOW	42	22	8	12	74	51	74
Margate	42	20	8	14	76	58	68
Weymouth	42	18	9	15	71	65	63
Tonbridge	42	19	5	18	59	62	62
Buckingham Town	42	14	14	14	43	42	56
Braintree Town	42	16	7	19	72	84	55
Fareham Town	42	12	12	18	54	75	48
Poole Town	42	13	6	23	54	86	45
Burnham	42	10	9	23	53	92	39
Fisher 93	42	9	10	23	52	81	37
Dunstable	42	9	7	26	50	91	34
Erith & Belvedere	42	9	5	28	40	72	32
Canterbury City	42	8	7	27	35	80	31
Wealdstone	42	6	7	29	45	95	25
Bury Town	42	3	5	34	36	121	14

1994-95

Premier Division

Hednesford Town	42	28	9	5	99	49	93
Cheltenham Town	42	25	11	6	87	39	86
Burton Albion	42	20	15	7	55	39	75
Gloucester City	42	22	8	12	76	48	74
Rushden & Diamonds	42	19	11	12	99	65	68
Dorchester Town	42	19	10	13	84	61	67
Leek Town	42	19	10	13	72	60	67
Gresley Rovers	42	17	12	13	70	63	63
Cambridge City	42	18	8	16	60	55	62
Worcester City	42	14	15	13	46	34	57
Crawley Town	42	15	10	17	64	71	55
Hastings Town	42	13	14	15	55	57	53
Halesowen Town	42	14	10	18	81	80	52
Gravesend & Northfleet	42	16	13	16	38	55	52
Chelmsford City	42	14	6	22	56	60	48
Atherstone United	42	12	12	18	51	67	48
VS Rugby	42	11	14	17	49	61	47
Sudbury Town	42	12	10	20	50	77	46
Solihull Borough	42	10	15	17	39	65	45
Sittingbourne	42	11	10	21	51	73	43
Trowbridge Town	42	9	13	20	43	69	40
Corby Town	42	4	10	28	36	113	21

Corby Town had 1 point deducted for fielding ineligible players

Midland Division

Newport AFC	42	29	8	5	106	39	95
Ilkeston Town	42	25	6	11	101	75	81
Tamworth	42	24	8	10	98	70	80
Moor Green	42	23	8	11	105	63	77
Bridgnorth Town	42	22	10	10	75	49	76
Buckingham Town	42	20	14	8	55	37	74
Nuneaton Borough	42	19	11	12	76	55	68
Rothwell Town	42	19	7	16	71	71	64
King's Lynn	42	18	8	16	76	64	62
Racing Club Warwick	42	17	11	14	68	63	62
Dudley Town	42	17	10	15	65	69	61
Bilston Town	42	17	8	17	73	64	59
Bedworth United	42	17	7	18	64	68	58
Evesham United	42	14	10	18	57	56	52
Hinckley Town	42	14	0	18	61	76	52
Stourbridge	42	15	7	20	59	77	52
Sutton Coldfield Town	42	12	10	20	62	72	46
Forest Green Rovers	42	11	13	18	56	76	46
Redditch United	42	8	14	20	47	64	38
Leicester United	42	10	8	24	51	99	38
Grantham Town	42	8	9	25	55	93	33
Armitage	42	2	5	35	35	116	11

Southern Division

Salisbury City	42	30	7	5	88	37	97
Baldock Town	42	28	10	4	92	44	94
Havant Town	42	25	10	7	81	34	85
Waterlooville	42	24	8	10	77	36	80
Ashford Town	42	21	12	9	106	72	75
Weston-super-Mare	42	18	13	11	82	54	67
Bashley	42	18	11	13	62	49	65
Weymouth	42	16	13	13	60	55	61
Newporth IOW	42	17	10	15	67	67	61
Witney Town	42	14	14	14	57	57	56
Clevedon Town	42	14	13	15	73	64	55
Tonbridge Angels	42	14	12	16	74	87	54
Margate	42	15	7	20	60	72	52
Braintree Town	42	12	13	17	64	71	49
Wealdstone	42	13	8	21	76	94	47
Yate Town	42	11	13	18	57	75	46
Fisher 93	42	9	16	17	54	70	43
Bury Town	42	11	8	23	59	86	41
Erith & Belvedere	42	10	9	23	49	94	39
Poole Town	42	10	8	24	53	79	38
Fareham Town	42	10	8	24	46	91	38
Burnham	42	7	7	28	40	89	28

1995-96

Premier Division

Rushden & Diamonds	42	29	7	6	99	41	94
Halesowen Town	42	27	11	4	70	36	92
Cheltenham Town	42	21	11	10	76	57	74
Gloucester City	42	21	8	13	65	47	71
Gresley Rovers	42	20	10	12	70	58	70
Worcester City	42	19	12	11	61	43	69
Merthyr Tydfil	42	19	6	17	67	59	63
Hastings Town	42	16	13	13	68	56	61
Crawley Town	42	15	13	14	57	56	58
Sudbury Town	42	15	10	17	69	71	55
Gravesend & Northfleet	42	15	10	17	60	62	55
Chelmsford City	42	13	16	13	46	53	55
Dorchester Town	42	15	8	19	62	57	53
Newport AFC	42	13	13	16	53	59	52
Salisbury City	42	14	10	18	57	69	52
Burton Albion	42	13	12	17	55	56	51
Atherstone United	42	12	12	18	58	75	48
Baldock Town	42	11	14	17	51	56	47
Cambridge City	42	12	10	20	56	68	46
Ilkeston Town	42	11	10	21	53	87	43
Stafford Rangers	42	11	4	27	58	90	37
VS Rugby	42	5	10	27	37	92	25

Midland Division

Nuneaton Borough	42	30	5	7	82	35	95
King's Lynn	42	27	5	10	85	43	84
Bedworth United	42	24	10	8	76	42	81
Moor Green	42	22	8	12	81	47	74
Paget Rangers	42	21	9	12	70	45	72
Tamworth	42	22	3	17	97	64	69
Solihull Borough	42	19	9	14	77	64	66
Rothwell Town	42	17	14	11	79	62	65
Buckingham Town	42	18	9	15	74	62	63
Dudley Town	42	15	16	11	83	66	61
Stourbridge	42	17	8	17	60	63	59
Bilston Town	42	16	9	17	61	62	57
Sutton Coldfield Town	42	16	9	17	62	67	57
Grantham Town	42	17	5	20	71	83	56
Redditch United	42	14	11	17	57	77	53
Leicester United	42	13	13	16	58	72	52
Hinckley Town	42	14	7	21	62	83	49
Racing Club Warwick	42	10	13	19	67	90	43
Evesham United	42	11	6	25	59	94	39
Corby Town	42	9	7	26	52	95	34
Bury Town	42	8	8	26	57	95	32
Bridgnorth Town	42	7	6	29	53	112	27

Bedworth United 1 point deducted, King's Lynn had 2 points deducted

Southern Division

Sittingbourne	42	28	4	10	102	44	88
Ashford Town	42	25	9	8	75	44	84
Waterlooville	42	24	8	10	87	44	80
Newport IOW	42	24	6	12	75	58	78
Braintree Town	42	24	8	10	93	70	77
Weymouth	42	24	4	14	75	55	76
Havant Town	42	23	11	8	73	42	74
Forest Green Rovers	42	22	8	12	85	55	74
Trowbridge Town	42	18	8	16	86	51	62
Yate Town	42	17	8	17	85	71	59
Margate	42	18	5	19	68	62	59
Witney Town	42	16	11	15	60	54	59
Weston-super-Mare	42	16	9	17	78	68	57
Cinderford Town	42	16	8	18	74	77	56
Fisher 93	42	14	13	15	58	59	55
Bashley	42	14	11	17	63	61	53
Clevedon Town	42	15	6	21	70	80	51
Tonbridge Angels	42	13	10	19	58	79	49
Fleet Town	42	14	5	23	58	79	47
Fareham Town	42	12	5	25	71	97	41
Erith & Belvedere	42	4	4	34	38	111	16
Poole Town	42	0	1	41	17	188	1

Braintree Town 3 points deducted, Havant Town had 6 points deducted

1996-97

Premier Division

Gresley Rovers	42	25	10	7	75	40	85
Cheltenham Town	42	21	11	10	76	44	74
Gloucester City	42	21	10	11	81	56	73
Halesowen Town	42	21	10	11	77	54	73
King's Lynn	42	20	8	14	65	61	68
Burton Albion	42	18	12	12	70	53	66
Nuneaton Borough	42	19	9	14	61	52	66
Sittingbourne	42	19	7	16	76	65	64
Merthyr Tydfil	42	17	9	16	69	61	60
Worcester City	42	15	14	13	52	50	59
Atherstone United	42	15	13	14	46	47	58
Salisbury City	42	15	13	14	57	66	58
Sudbury Town	42	16	7	19	72	72	55
Gravesend & Northfleet	42	16	7	19	63	73	55
Dorchester Town	42	14	9	19	62	66	51
Hastings Town	42	12	15	15	49	60	51
Crawley Town	42	13	8	21	49	67	47
Cambridge City	42	11	13	18	57	65	46
Ashford Town	42	9	18	15	53	79	45
Baldock Town	42	11	8	23	52	90	41
Newport AFC	42	9	13	20	40	60	40
Chelmsford City	42	6	14	22	49	70	32

Midland Division

Tamworth	40	30	7	3	90	28	97
Rothwell Town	40	20	11	9	82	54	71
Ilkeston Town	40	19	13	8	76	50	70
Grantham Town	40	22	4	14	65	46	70
Bedworth United	40	18	11	11	77	41	65
Solihull Borough	40	19	8	13	84	62	65
Bilston Town	40	18	10	12	74	57	64
Moor Green	40	18	7	15	88	68	61
Stafford Rangers	40	17	9	14	68	62	60
Raunds Town	40	16	11	13	61	66	59
Racing Club Warwick	40	16	10	14	70	72	58
Shepshed Dynamo	40	14	12	14	64	65	54
Redditch United	40	15	8	17	56	59	53
Paget Rangers	40	13	9	18	42	55	48
Dudley Town	40	12	10	18	70	89	46
Hinckley Town	40	11	11	18	39	63	44
Stourbridge	40	10	9	21	61	81	39
Evesham United	40	9	12	19	55	77	39
VS Rugby	40	9	9	22	49	81	36
Corby Town	40	8	8	24	49	88	32
Sutton Coldfield Town	40	7	9	24	29	85	30

Leicester United FC closed down and their record was expunged from the League table.

Southern Division

Forest Green Rovers	42	27	10	5	87	40	91
St Leonards Stamcroft	42	26	9	7	95	48	87
Havant Town	42	23	10	9	81	49	79
Weston-super-Mare	42	21	13	8	82	43	76
Margate	42	21	9	12	70	47	72
Witney Town	42	20	11	11	71	42	71
Weymouth	42	20	10	12	82	51	70
Tonbridge Angels	42	17	15	10	56	44	66
Newport IOW	42	15	15	12	73	58	60
Fisher Athletic (London)	42	18	6	18	77	77	60
Clevedon Town	42	17	9	16	75	76	60
Fareham Town	42	14	12	16	53	70	54
Bashley	42	15	8	19	73	84	53
Dartford	42	14	10	18	59	64	52
Waterlooville	42	14	9	19	58	67	51
Cirencester Town	42	12	12	18	50	68	48
Cinderford Town	42	13	7	22	64	76	46
Trowbridge Town	42	11	11	20	50	61	44
Yate Town	42	12	8	22	55	87	44
Fleet Town	42	12	6	24	47	91	42
Erith & Belvedere	42	9	10	23	60	95	37
Buckingham Town	42	2	8	32	27	107	14

1997-98

Premier Division

Forest Green Rovers	42	27	8	7	93	55	89
Merthyr Tydfil	42	24	12	6	80	42	84
Burton Albion	42	21	8	13	64	43	71
Dorchester Town	42	19	13	10	63	38	70
Halesowen Town	42	18	15	9	70	38	69
Bath City	42	19	12	11	72	51	69
Worcester City	42	19	12	11	54	44	69
King's Lynn	42	18	11	13	64	65	65
Atherstone United	42	17	12	13	55	49	63
Crawley Town	42	17	8	17	63	60	59
Gloucester City	42	16	11	15	57	57	59
Nuneaton Borough	42	17	6	19	68	61	57
Cambridge City	42	16	8	18	62	70	56
Hastings Town	42	14	12	16	67	70	54
Tamworth	42	14	11	17	68	65	53
Rothwell Town	42	11	16	15	55	73	49
Gresley Rovers	42	14	6	22	59	77	48
Salisbury City	42	12	12	18	53	72	48
Bromsgrove Rovers	42	13	6	23	67	85	45
Sittingbourne	42	12	8	22	47	66	44
Ashford Town	42	8	5	29	34	85	29
St Leonards Stamcroft	42	5	10	27	48	97	25

Midland Division

Grantham Town	40	30	4	6	87	39	94
Ilkeston Town	40	29	6	5	123	39	93
Solihull Borough	40	22	9	9	81	48	75
Raunds Town	40	20	8	12	73	44	68
Wisbech Town	40	20	7	13	79	57	67
Moor Green	40	20	7	13	72	55	67
Bilston Town	40	20	5	15	69	57	65
Blakenall	40	17	13	10	66	55	64
Stafford Rangers	40	18	6	16	57	56	60
Redditch United	40	16	11	13	59	41	59
Stourbridge	40	16	9	15	57	55	57
Hinckley United	40	15	11	14	59	56	56
Brackley Town	40	15	7	18	45	57	52
Bedworth United	40	15	5	20	50	73	50
Racing Club Warwick	40	11	9	20	49	56	42
Shepshed Dynamo	40	9	14	17	55	74	41
Sutton Coldfield Town	40	9	12	19	42	68	39
Paget Rangers	40	9	12	19	40	75	39
VS Rugby	40	8	12	20	53	93	36
Evesham United	40	7	9	24	47	94	30
Corby Town	40	2	8	30	41	112	14

Southern Division

Weymouth	42	32	2	8	107	48	98
Chelmsford City	42	29	8	5	86	39	95
Bashley	42	29	4	9	101	59	91
Newport IOW	42	25	9	8	72	34	84
Fisher Athletic (London)	42	25	5	12	87	50	80
Margate	42	23	8	11	71	42	77
Newport AFC	42	21	6	15	83	65	69
Witney Town	42	20	9	13	74	58	69
Clevedon Town	42	20	7	15	57	55	67
Waterlooville	42	17	7	18	69	64	58
Dartford	42	17	7	18	60	60	58
Havant Town	42	13	14	16	65	70	53
Fleet Town	42	16	5	21	63	83	53
Tonbridge Angels	42	14	10	18	49	55	52
Trowbridge Town	42	14	6	22	55	69	48
Erith & Belvedere	42	11	13	18	47	68	46
Fareham Town	42	12	9	21	75	87	45
Cirencester Town	42	12	7	23	63	88	43
Weston-super-Mare	42	12	5	25	49	86	41
Baldock Town	42	10	5	27	53	81	35
Cinderford Town	42	6	5	31	40	112	23
Yate Town	42	5	7	30	44	97	22

1998-99

Premier Division

Nuneaton Borough	42	27	9	6	91	33	90
Boston United	42	17	16	9	69	51	67
Ilkeston Town	42	18	13	11	72	59	67
Bath City	42	18	11	13	70	44	65
Hastings Town	42	18	11	13	57	49	65
Gloucester City	42	18	11	13	57	52	65
Worcester City	42	18	9	15	58	54	63
Halesowen Town	42	17	11	14	72	60	62
Tamworth	42	19	5	18	62	67	62
King's Lynn	42	17	10	15	53	46	61
Crawley Town	42	17	10	15	57	58	61
Salisbury City	42	16	12	14	56	61	60
Burton Albion	42	17	7	18	58	52	58
Weymouth	42	14	14	14	56	55	56
Merthyr Tydfil	42	15	8	19	52	62	53
Atherstone United	42	12	14	16	47	52	50
Grantham Town	42	14	8	20	51	58	50
Dorchester Town	42	11	15	16	49	63	48
Rothwell Town	42	13	9	20	47	67	48
Cambridge City	42	11	12	19	47	68	45
Gresley Rovers	42	12	8	22	49	73	44
Bromsgrove Rovers	42	8	7	27	38	84	31

Hastings Town resigned from the League

Midland Division

Clevedon Town	42	28	8	6	83	35	92
Newport AFC	42	26	7	9	92	51	85
Redditch United	42	22	12	8	81	45	75
Hinckley United	42	20	12	10	58	40	72
Stafford Rangers	42	21	8	13	92	60	71
Bilston Town	42	20	11	11	79	69	71
Solihull Borough	42	19	12	11	76	53	69
Moor Green	42	20	7	15	71	61	67
Blakenall	42	17	14	11	65	54	65
Shepshed Dynamo	42	17	12	13	62	54	63
Sutton Coldfield Town	42	17	8	17	46	57	59
Stourbridge	42	16	10	16	60	55	58
Evesham United	42	16	9	17	63	63	57
Wisbech Town	42	16	9	17	59	66	57
Weston-super-Mare	42	15	10	17	59	56	55
Bedworth United	42	15	9	18	63	52	54
Cinderford Town	42	13	8	21	61	74	47
Stamford AFC	42	13	7	22	60	75	46
Paget Rangers	42	11	12	19	49	58	45
VS Rugby	42	12	9	21	53	74	45
Racing Club Warwick	42	5	8	29	38	93	23
Bloxwich Town	42	1	2	39	26	151	5

Southern Division

Havant & Waterlooville	42	29	7	6	86	32	94
Margate	42	27	8	7	84	33	89
Folkestone Invicta	42	26	8	8	92	47	86
Newport IOW	42	23	7	12	68	40	76
Chelmsford City	42	20	12	10	91	51	72
Raunds Town	42	19	13	10	87	50	70
Ashford Town	42	17	12	13	59	54	63
Baldock Town	42	17	9	16	60	59	60
Fisher Athletic (London)	42	16	11	15	58	54	59
Bashley	42	17	7	18	74	77	58
Witney Town	42	15	12	15	56	48	57
Cirencester Town	42	16	8	18	61	66	56
Sittingbourne	42	11	18	12	53	56	54
Dartford	42	14	10	18	48	53	52
Erith & Belvedere	42	15	7	20	48	64	52
Tonbridge Angels	42	12	15	15	48	59	51
St Leonards	42	14	8	20	57	72	50
Fleet Town	42	11	11	19	54	72	47
Corby Town	42	10	10	22	48	73	40
Yate Town	42	10	7	25	37	79	37
Andover	42	6	10	26	50	115	28
Brackley Town	42	6	8	28	41	105	26

1999-2000

Premier Division

Boston United	42	27	11	4	102	39	92
Burton Albion	42	23	9	10	73	43	78
Margate	42	23	8	11	64	43	77
Bath City	42	19	15	8	70	49	72
King's Lynn	42	19	14	9	59	43	71
Tamworth	42	20	10	12	80	51	70
Newport County	42	16	18	8	67	50	66
Clevedon Town	42	18	9	15	52	52	63
Ilkeston Town	42	16	12	14	77	69	60
Weymouth	42	14	16	12	60	51	58
Halesowen Town	42	14	14	14	52	54	56
Crawley Town	42	15	8	19	68	82	53
Havant & Waterlooville	42	13	13	16	63	68	52
Cambridge City	42	14	10	18	52	66	52
Worcester City	42	13	11	18	60	66	50
Salisbury City	42	14	8	20	70	84	50
Merthyr Tydfil	42	13	9	20	51	63	48
Dorchester Town	42	10	17	15	56	65	47
Grantham Town	42	14	5	23	63	76	47
Gloucester City	42	8	14	20	40	82	38
Rothwell Town	42	5	14	23	48	85	29
Atherstone United	42	5	13	24	30	76	28

Eastern Division

Fisher Athletic (London)	42	31	5	6	107	42	98
Folkestone Invicta	42	30	7	5	101	39	97
Newport IOW	42	25	7	10	74	40	82
Chelmsford City	42	24	8	10	74	38	80
Hastings Town	42	22	9	11	76	56	75
Ashford Town	42	21	9	12	70	49	72
Tonbridge Angels	42	20	10	12	82	60	70
Dartford	42	17	6	19	52	58	57
Burnham	42	15	9	18	55	64	54
Baldock Town	42	14	10	18	57	69	52
Erith & Belvedere	42	14	9	19	62	68	51
Witney Town	42	13	11	18	48	60	50
VS Rugby	42	13	11	18	58	79	50
Wisbech Town	42	14	7	21	58	66	49
Spalding United	42	14	6	22	52	71	48
Sittingbourne	42	13	7	22	48	75	46
Stamford	42	9	18	15	50	62	45
St Leonards	42	11	12	19	67	81	45
Raunds Town	42	11	12	19	44	63	45
Bashley	42	12	7	23	56	95	43
Corby Town	42	11	12	19	56	62	42
Fleet Town	42	8	8	26	54	104	32

Corby Town had 3 points deducted for fielding an ineligible player
Raunds Town gave notice to withdraw and take the place of the 2nd relegated Club. They then unsuccessfully sought re-election

Western Division

Stafford Rangers	42	29	6	7	107	47	93
Moor Green	42	26	12	4	85	33	90
Hinckley United	42	25	12	5	89	47	87
Tiverton Town	42	26	7	9	91	44	85
Solihull Borough	42	20	11	11	85	66	71
Blakenall	42	19	12	11	70	46	69
Cirencester Town	42	20	8	14	72	64	68
Bilston Town	42	16	18	8	66	52	66
Cinderford Town	42	17	11	14	62	64	62
Redditch United	42	17	10	15	73	65	61
Gresley Rovers	42	14	15	13	54	49	57
Weston-super-Mare	42	16	9	17	55	55	57
Sutton Coldfield Town	42	13	17	12	49	52	56
Evesham Town	42	13	12	17	69	61	51
Bedworth Town	42	13	10	19	52	71	49
Rocester	42	12	12	18	63	78	48
Bromsgrove Rovers	42	13	7	22	59	72	46
Shepshed Dynamo	42	12	7	23	46	66	43
Paget Rangers	42	11	4	27	44	82	37
Racing Club Warwick	42	7	14	21	41	82	35
Stourbridge	42	10	3	29	45	101	33
Yate Town	42	3	3	36	28	108	12

2000-2001

Premier Division

Margate	42	28	7	7	75	27	91
Burton Albion	42	25	13	4	76	36	88
King's Lynn	42	18	11	13	67	58	65
Welling United	42	17	13	12	59	55	64
Weymouth	42	17	12	13	69	51	63
Havant & Waterlooville	42	18	9	15	65	53	63
Stafford Rangers	42	18	9	15	70	59	63
Worcester City	42	18	8	16	52	53	62
Moor Green	42	18	8	16	49	53	62
Newport County	42	17	10	15	70	61	61
Crawley Town	42	17	10	15	61	54	61
Tamworth	42	17	8	17	58	55	59
Salisbury City	42	17	8	17	64	69	59
Ilkeston Town	42	16	11	15	51	61	59
Bath City	42	15	13	14	67	68	55
Cambridge City	42	13	11	18	56	59	50
Folkestone Invicta	42	14	6	22	49	74	48
Merthyr Tydfil	42	11	13	18	49	62	46
Clevedon Town	42	11	7	24	61	74	40
Fisher Athletic (London)	42	12	6	24	51	85	39
Dorchester Town	42	10	8	24	40	70	38
Halesowen Town	42	8	13	21	47	69	37

Bath City and Fisher Athletic (London) both had 3 points deducted

Eastern Division

Newport IOW	42	28	10	4	91	30	94
Chelmsford City	42	27	9	6	102	45	90
Grantham Town	42	25	11	6	100	47	86
Histon	42	23	11	8	84	53	80
Baldock Town	42	23	10	9	81	44	79
Hastings Town	42	22	10	10	72	50	76
Stamford	42	20	11	11	69	59	71
Tonbridge Angels	42	18	11	13	79	58	65
Langney Sports	42	19	8	15	75	55	65
Rothwell Town	42	20	5	17	86	74	62
Corby Town	42	14	10	18	64	92	52
Ashford Town	42	15	4	23	53	83	49
Banbury United	42	12	11	19	57	54	47
Witney Town	42	12	11	19	55	71	47
Bashley	42	10	14	18	57	71	44
Dartford	42	11	11	20	49	67	44
Burnham	42	10	14	18	39	65	43
Wisbech Town	42	10	9	23	45	89	39
St Leonards	42	9	10	23	55	87	37
Erith & Belvedere	42	10	7	25	49	92	37
Sittingbourne	42	8	9	25	41	79	33
Spalding United	42	7	12	23	35	73	33

Burnham had 1 point deducted, Rothwell Town had 3 points deducted

Western Division

Hinckley United	42	30	8	4	102	38	98
Tiverton Town	42	28	7	7	97	36	91
Bilston Town	42	27	9	6	88	48	90
Evesham United	42	27	5	10	86	46	86
Mangotsfield United	42	25	9	8	91	45	84
Solihull Borough	42	22	12	8	73	43	78
Redditch United	42	17	13	12	76	69	64
Weston-super-Mare	42	17	10	15	68	58	61
Atherstone United	42	16	11	15	64	58	59
Rochester	42	18	5	19	57	77	59
Cirencester Town	42	14	15	13	65	74	57
Rugby United	42	13	10	19	51	68	49
Gloucester City	42	12	11	19	76	86	47
Blakenall	42	13	10	19	54	64	46
Shepshed Dynamo	42	12	9	21	56	73	45
Bedworth United	42	12	9	21	38	60	45
Racing Club Warwick	42	13	6	23	46	77	45
Gresley Rovers	42	11	8	23	46	65	41
Cinderford Town	42	11	8	23	56	84	41
Sutton Coldfield Town	42	7	14	21	45	66	35
Paget Rovers	42	9	4	29	38	93	31
Bromsgrove Rovers	42	7	9	26	47	92	30

Blakenall had 3 points deducted

2001-2002

Premier Division							
Kettering Town	42	27	6	9	80	41	87
Tamworth	42	24	13	5	81	41	85
Havant & Waterlooville	42	22	9	11	74	50	75
Crawley Town	42	21	10	11	67	48	73
Newport County	42	19	9	14	61	48	66
Tiverton Town	42	17	10	15	70	63	61
Moor Green	42	18	7	17	64	62	61
Worcester City	42	16	12	14	65	54	60
Stafford Rangers	42	17	9	16	70	62	60
Ilkeston Town	42	14	16	12	58	61	58
Weymouth United	42	15	11	16	59	67	56
Hinckley Town	42	14	13	15	64	62	55
Folkestone Invicta	42	14	12	16	51	61	54
Cambridge City	42	12	16	14	60	70	52
Welling United	42	13	12	17	69	66	51
Hednesford Town	42	15	6	21	59	70	51
Bath City	42	13	11	18	56	65	50
Chelmsford City	42	13	11	18	63	75	50
Newport IOW	42	12	12	18	38	61	48
King's Lynn	42	11	13	18	44	57	46
Merthyr Tydfil	42	12	8	22	53	71	44
Salisbury City	42	6	8	28	36	87	26

Eastern Division							
Hastings Town	42	29	8	5	85	38	95
Grantham Town	42	29	6	7	99	43	93
Dorchester Town	42	26	10	6	81	36	88
Histon	42	23	8	11	83	49	77
Stamford	42	24	4	14	76	61	76
Fisher Athletic (London)	42	20	10	12	83	56	70
Eastbourne Borough	42	21	6	15	63	46	69
Dartford	42	18	5	19	62	66	59
Erith & Belvedere	42	18	3	21	75	79	57
Bashley	42	15	11	16	71	63	56
Burnham	42	15	10	17	52	54	55
Rugby United	42	16	6	20	55	67	54
Rothwell Town	42	14	8	20	46	66	50
Ashford Town	42	14	6	22	58	78	48
Banbury United	42	13	9	20	53	66	47
Chatham Town	42	13	8	21	56	87	47
Sittingbourne	42	14	4	24	46	69	46
Spalding	42	13	6	23	72	84	45
Tonbridge Angels	42	13	6	23	65	80	45
St Leonards	42	14	3	25	52	88	45
Corby Town	42	10	13	19	54	82	43
Wisbech Town	42	11	8	23	56	84	41

Western Division							
Halesowen Town	40	27	9	4	85	24	90
Chippenham Town	40	26	9	5	81	28	87
Weston-super-Mare	40	22	10	8	70	38	76
Solihull Borough	40	20	11	9	75	42	71
Gresley Rovers	40	19	9	12	59	50	66
Sutton Coldfield Town	40	17	11	12	53	46	62
Mangotsfield United	40	17	10	13	74	54	61
Stourport Swifts	40	18	6	16	59	59	60
Atherstone United	40	16	8	16	61	59	56
Clevedon Town	40	15	11	14	57	58	56
Bedworth United	40	16	7	17	59	63	55
Evesham United	40	16	7	17	54	70	55
Cirencester Town	40	17	3	20	64	69	54
Gloucester City	40	14	10	16	48	63	52
Cinderford Town	40	14	9	17	54	67	51
Shepshed Dynamo	40	10	10	20	64	84	40
Bilston Town	40	11	7	22	50	72	40
Redditch United	40	11	6	23	47	77	39
Swindon Supermarine	40	11	4	25	52	76	37
Racing Club Warwick	40	8	11	21	38	63	35
Rocester	40	5	12	23	33	75	27

2002-2003

Premier Division							
Tamworth	42	26	10	6	73	32	88
Stafford Rangers	42	21	12	9	76	40	75
Dover Athletic	42	19	14	9	42	35	71
Tiverton Town	42	19	12	11	60	43	69
Chippenham Town	42	17	17	8	59	37	68
Worcester City	42	18	13	11	60	39	67
Crawley Town	42	17	13	12	64	51	64
Havant & Waterlooville	42	15	15	12	67	64	60
Chelmsford City	42	15	12	15	65	63	57
Newport County	42	15	11	16	53	52	56
Hednesford Town	42	14	13	15	59	60	55
Moor Green	42	13	14	15	49	58	53
Hinckley Town	42	12	16	14	61	64	52
Bath City	42	13	13	16	50	61	52
Welling United	42	13	12	17	55	58	51
Grantham Town	42	14	9	19	59	65	51
Weymouth	42	12	15	15	44	62	51
Cambridge City	42	13	10	19	54	56	49
Halesowen Town	42	12	13	17	52	63	49
Hastings United	42	10	13	19	44	57	43
Ilkeston Town	42	10	10	22	54	92	40
Folkestone Invicta	42	7	7	28	57	105	28

Eastern Division							
Dorchester Town	42	28	9	5	114	40	93
Eastbourne Borough	42	29	6	7	92	33	93
Stamford	42	27	6	9	80	39	87
Salisbury City	42	27	8	7	81	42	86
Bashley	42	23	12	7	90	44	81
King's Lynn	42	24	7	11	98	62	79
Rothwell Town	42	22	10	10	77	52	76
Banbury United	42	21	11	10	75	50	74
Tonbridge Angels	42	20	11	11	71	55	71
Histon	42	20	7	15	99	62	67
Ashford Town	42	18	9	15	63	57	63
Sittingbourne	42	15	8	19	57	69	53
Burnham	42	15	7	20	62	79	52
Fisher Athletic	42	15	5	22	57	80	50
Chatham Town	42	14	5	23	54	84	47
Newport IOW	42	12	6	24	53	87	42
Dartford	42	11	8	23	48	78	41
Erith & Belvedere	42	11	6	25	65	96	39
Corby Town	42	9	11	22	49	84	38
Fleet Town	42	8	8	26	34	80	32
Spalding United	42	4	6	32	40	108	18
St. Leonards	42	4	4	34	38	116	16

Western Division							
Merthyr Tydfil	42	28	8	6	78	32	92
Weston-super-Mare	42	26	7	9	77	42	85
Bromsgrove Rovers	42	23	7	12	73	41	76
Solihull Borough	42	21	13	8	77	48	76
Gloucester City	42	22	9	11	87	58	75
Mangotsfield United	42	21	10	11	106	53	73
Redditch United	42	22	6	14	76	42	72
Rugby United	42	20	9	13	58	43	69
Gresley Rovers	42	19	10	13	63	54	67
Taunton Town	42	20	7	15	76	78	67
Sutton Coldfield Town	42	18	10	14	63	53	64
Evesham United	42	19	6	17	76	72	63
Clevedon Town	42	14	13	15	54	60	55
Cirencester Town	42	15	7	20	62	82	52
Cinderford Town	42	13	12	17	50	67	51
Shepshed Dynamo	42	12	6	24	48	76	42
Stourport Swifts	42	10	11	21	48	66	41
Bedworth United	42	11	7	24	46	74	40
Swindon Supermarine	42	11	5	26	52	85	38
Atherstone United	42	9	10	23	45	78	37
Rocester	42	9	10	23	34	74	37
Racing Club Warwick	42	3	9	30	33	104	18

2003-2004

Premier Division

Crawley Town	42	25	9	8	77	43	84
Weymouth	42	20	12	10	76	47	72
Stafford Rangers	42	19	11	12	55	43	68
Nuneaton Borough	42	17	15	10	65	49	66
Worcester City	42	18	9	15	71	50	63
Hinckley United	42	15	14	13	55	46	59
Newport County	42	15	14	13	52	50	59
Cambridge City	42	14	15	13	54	53	57
Welling United	42	16	8	18	56	58	56
Weston-super-Mare	42	14	13	15	52	52	55
Eastbourne Borough	42	14	13	15	48	56	55
Havant & Waterlooville	42	15	10	17	59	70	55
Moor Green	42	14	12	16	42	54	54
Merthyr Tydfil	42	13	14	15	60	66	53
Tiverton Town	42	12	15	15	63	64	51
Bath City	42	13	12	17	49	57	51
Dorchester Town	42	14	9	19	56	69	51
Chelmsford City	42	11	16	15	46	53	49
Dover Athletic	42	12	13	17	50	59	49
Hednesford Town	42	12	12	18	56	69	48
Chippenham Town	42	10	17	15	51	63	47
Grantham Town	42	10	15	17	45	67	45

Eastern Division

King's Lynn	42	28	7	7	90	35	91
Histon	42	26	10	6	96	41	88
Tonbridge Angels	42	27	7	8	82	46	88
* Eastleigh	42	27	4	11	88	40	82
Folkestone Invicta	42	20	15	7	91	45	75
Salisbury City	42	21	11	10	73	45	74
Stamford	42	20	11	11	63	45	71
Banbury United	42	19	10	13	65	57	67
Burgess Hill Town	42	19	7	16	67	54	64
Sittingbourne	42	18	8	16	61	55	62
Bashley	42	18	7	17	66	58	61
Ashford Town	42	15	9	18	51	53	54
Chatham Town	42	13	10	19	49	67	49
Fisher Athletic	42	13	10	19	61	81	49
Corby Town	42	12	9	21	44	75	45
Dartford	42	13	6	23	48	81	45
* Burnham	42	12	11	19	52	76	44
Hastings United	42	12	7	23	60	91	43
Newport IOW	42	11	7	24	42	69	40
Rothwell Town	42	9	11	22	30	47	38
Erith & Belvedere	42	7	10	25	45	84	31
Fleet Town	42	5	7	30	35	114	22

* Eastleigh and Burnham both had 3 points deducted.

Western Division

Redditch United	40	25	9	6	75	30	84
Gloucester City	40	24	7	9	77	46	79
Cirencester Town	40	24	4	12	73	40	76
Halesowen Town	40	20	13	7	64	40	73
Rugby United	40	21	8	11	57	40	71
Team Bath	40	21	6	13	62	41	69
Solihull Borough	40	19	9	12	50	31	66
Sutton Coldfield	40	16	15	9	52	38	63
Bromsgrove Rovers	40	16	11	13	60	48	59
Ilkeston Town	40	16	10	14	58	59	58
Clevedon Town	40	16	5	19	55	59	53
Gresley Rovers	40	15	7	18	52	60	52
Mangotsfield United	40	14	8	18	70	70	50
Evesham United	40	15	5	20	56	57	50
Taunton Town	40	14	8	18	50	55	50
Yate Town	40	11	9	20	51	79	42
Swindon Supermarine	40	10	9	21	41	69	39
Stourport Swifts	40	9	11	20	43	62	38
Bedworth United	40	8	12	20	39	61	36
Cinderford Town	40	7	9	24	50	94	30
Shepshed Dynamo	40	5	13	22	31	87	28

2004-2005

Premier Division

Histon	42	24	6	12	93	57	78
Chippenham Town	42	22	9	11	81	55	75
Merthyr Tydfil	42	19	14	9	62	47	71
Hednesford Town	42	20	10	12	68	40	70
Bedford Town	42	19	12	11	70	52	69
Bath City	42	19	12	11	57	43	69
Cirencester Town	42	19	11	12	63	52	68
Tiverton Town	42	18	13	11	70	55	67
Halesowen Town	42	19	9	14	64	52	66
Aylesbury United	42	20	3	19	67	66	63
King's Lynn	42	19	4	19	78	69	61
Chesham United	42	18	5	19	84	82	59
Grantham Town	42	17	7	18	57	55	58
Team Bath	42	14	12	16	54	68	54
Gloucester City	42	12	17	13	63	61	53
Rugby United	42	13	12	17	48	60	51
Banbury United	42	13	9	20	56	69	48
Hitchin Town	42	13	9	20	55	77	48
Hemel Hempstead Town	42	11	10	21	60	88	43
Dunstable Town	42	11	6	25	56	98	39
Stamford	42	6	18	18	40	60	36
Solihull Borough	42	10	4	28	45	85	34

Eastern Division

Fisher Athletic	42	30	6	6	96	41	96
East Thurrock United	42	25	12	5	92	38	87
Maldon Town	42	27	6	9	92	51	87
Uxbridge	42	26	7	9	87	37	85
Wivenhoe Town	42	21	11	10	74	49	74
Barking & East Ham United	42	20	10	12	63	37	70
Boreham Wood	42	19	9	14	80	61	66
Barton Rovers	42	20	4	18	76	72	64
Waltham Forest	42	16	9	17	68	61	57
Leighton Town	42	13	15	14	57	59	54
Chatham Town	42	15	9	18	53	63	54
Wingate & Finchley	42	15	8	19	60	75	53
Arlesey Town	42	14	10	18	53	67	52
Beaconsfield SYCOB	42	12	12	18	54	65	48
Harlow Town	42	13	8	21	53	65	47
Dartford	42	11	13	18	58	75	46
Aveley	42	12	9	21	57	69	45
Berkhamsted Town	42	15	7	20	66	101	45
Sittingbourne	42	10	12	20	53	70	42
Great Wakering Rovers	42	9	11	22	45	78	38
Erith & Belvedere	42	11	7	24	56	92	37
Tilbury	42	6	9	27	41	108	27

Berkhamsted Town had 7 points deducted.
Erith & Belvedere had 3 points deducted.

Western Division

Mangotsfield United	42	24	11	7	89	49	83
Yate Town	42	24	9	9	83	40	81
Evesham United	42	23	10	9	66	31	79
Clevedon Town	42	24	6	12	82	49	78
Bromsgrove Rovers	42	19	15	8	60	42	72
Ashford Town (Middlesex)	42	17	13	12	63	46	64
Brackley Town	42	18	10	14	69	53	64
Paulton Rovers	42	18	7	17	62	61	61
Burnham	42	17	7	18	64	64	58
Rothwell Town	42	16	10	16	57	57	58
Thame United	42	17	6	19	58	69	57
Corby Town	42	14	12	16	52	62	54
Marlow	42	13	14	15	58	67	53
Stourport Swifts	42	15	7	20	62	63	52
Bedworth United	42	15	7	20	51	60	52
Cinderford Town	42	13	12	17	50	64	51
Taunton Town	42	14	8	20	66	75	50
Sutton Coldfield	42	16	11	15	54	61	48
Swindon Supermarine	42	12	12	18	43	60	48
Bracknell Town	42	10	13	19	53	75	43
Oxford City	42	11	8	23	49	71	41
Egham Town	42	6	4	32	25	97	22

Sutton Coldfield had 11 points deducted.

2005-2006

Premier Division

Salisbury City	42	30	5	7	83	27	95
Bath City	42	25	8	9	66	33	83
King's Lynn	42	25	7	10	73	41	82
Chippenham Town	42	22	11	9	69	45	77
Bedford Town	42	22	10	10	69	53	76
Yate Town	42	21	5	16	78	74	68
Banbury United	42	17	11	14	66	61	62
Halesowen Town	42	15	15	12	54	45	60
Merthyr Tydfil	42	17	9	16	62	58	60
Mangotsfield United	42	15	13	14	67	67	58
Grantham Town	42	15	11	16	49	49	56
Tiverton Town	42	14	10	18	69	65	52
Gloucester City	42	14	10	18	57	60	52
Hitchin Town	42	13	12	17	59	76	51
Rugby Town	42	13	11	18	58	66	50
Cheshunt	42	13	9	20	57	70	48
Team Bath	42	14	6	22	55	68	48
Cirencester Town	42	14	4	24	49	68	46
Northwood	42	12	6	24	53	88	42
Evesham United	42	9	14	19	46	58	41
Aylesbury United	42	9	12	21	43	69	39
Chesham United	42	9	9	24	43	84	36

Eastern Division

Boreham Wood	42	24	12	6	84	41	84
Corby Town	42	25	9	8	63	33	84
Enfield Town	42	24	9	9	75	43	81
Stamford	42	20	10	12	73	53	70
Barking & East Ham United	42	20	10	12	63	47	70
Wivenhoe Town	42	17	11	14	56	54	62
Dartford	42	16	13	13	65	57	61
Waltham Forest	42	17	8	17	64	66	59
Harlow Town	42	14	16	12	57	56	58
Arlesey Town	42	15	11	16	58	65	56
Rothwell Town	42	13	14	15	48	53	53
Wingate & Finchley	42	13	14	15	57	64	53
Great Wakering Rovers	42	13	12	17	65	67	51
Uxbridge	42	13	11	18	62	64	50
Potters Bar Town	42	13	11	18	60	66	50
Enfield	42	13	11	18	52	64	50
Chatham Town	42	13	10	19	51	57	49
Sittingbourne	42	12	12	18	53	69	48
Barton Rovers	42	13	8	21	59	73	47
Aveley	42	11	13	18	51	70	46
Ilford	42	8	17	17	35	59	41
Berkhamsted Town	42	8	12	22	51	81	36

Western Division

Clevedon Town	42	28	6	8	86	45	90
Ashford Town (Middlesex)	42	24	8	10	84	50	80
Brackley Town	42	23	9	10	71	34	78
Hemel Hempstead Town	42	22	9	11	86	47	75
Swindon Supermarine	42	22	9	11	70	47	75
Marlow	42	22	6	14	62	59	72
Sutton Coldfield Town	42	21	6	15	91	62	69
Leighton Town	42	19	8	15	55	48	65
Willenhall Town	42	17	12	13	78	61	63
Rushall Olympic	42	17	11	14	73	57	62
Bromsgrove Rovers	42	17	11	14	65	50	62
Solihull Borough	42	15	13	14	50	51	58
Beaconsfield SYCOB	42	14	13	15	60	66	55
Burnham	42	16	5	21	58	71	53
Cinderford Town	42	14	9	19	71	79	51
Bedworth United	42	14	9	19	46	57	51
Paulton Rovers	42	12	10	20	55	76	46
Taunton Town	42	12	9	21	67	81	45
Bracknell Town	42	12	6	24	53	77	42
Stourport Swifts	42	9	14	19	55	80	41
Dunstable Town	42	8	12	22	45	91	36
Thame United	42	4	5	33	30	122	17

2006-2007

Premier Division

Bath City	42	27	10	5	84	29	91
Team Bath	42	23	9	10	66	42	78
King's Lynn	42	22	10	10	69	40	76
Maidenhead United	42	20	10	12	58	36	70
Hemel Hempstead Town	42	19	12	11	79	60	69
Halesowen Town	42	18	13	11	66	53	67
Chippenham Town	42	19	9	14	61	56	66
Stamford	42	16	11	15	65	62	59
Mangotsfield United	42	13	19	10	44	45	58
Gloucester City	42	15	13	14	67	70	58
Hitchin Town	42	16	9	17	55	68	57
Merthyr Tydfil	42	14	14	14	47	46	56
Banbury United	42	15	10	17	60	64	55
Yate Town	42	14	12	16	59	71	54
Tiverton Town	42	14	8	20	56	67	50
Cheshunt	42	14	7	21	56	71	49
Rugby Town	42	15	4	23	58	79	49
Clevedon Town	42	12	12	18	60	61	48
Wealdstone	42	13	9	20	69	82	48
Corby Town	42	10	9	23	52	69	39
Cirencester Town	42	9	12	21	46	76	39
Northwood	42	8	10	24	44	74	34

Division One Midlands

Brackley Town	42	29	4	9	95	53	91
Bromsgrove Rovers	42	23	7	12	86	62	76
Chasetown	42	23	6	13	59	39	75
Willenhall Town	42	20	12	10	67	47	72
Evesham United	42	19	15	8	66	51	72
Aylesbury United	42	20	11	11	58	42	71
Stourbridge	42	17	15	10	70	53	66
Woodford United	42	18	11	13	71	54	65
Cinderford Town	42	18	10	14	70	60	64
Rothwell Town	42	18	7	17	72	61	61
Dunstable Town	42	16	12	14	64	53	60
Sutton Coldfield Town	42	16	9	17	62	63	57
Bishops Cleeve	42	17	5	20	68	66	56
Solihull Borough	42	17	5	20	72	84	56
Rushall Olympic	42	15	9	18	56	55	54
Bedworth United	42	13	8	21	73	83	47
Malvern Town	42	12	11	19	46	66	47
Leighton Town	42	12	8	22	44	60	44
Spalding United	42	12	6	24	45	62	42
Barton Rovers	42	11	9	22	51	93	42
Berkhamsted Town	42	10	7	25	53	97	37
Stourport Swifts	42	9	7	26	43	87	34

Division One South & West

Bashley	42	32	6	4	111	35	102
Paulton Rovers	42	20	14	8	66	42	74
Burnham	42	23	4	15	74	60	73
Swindon Supermarine	42	20	11	11	68	40	71
Taunton Town	42	19	14	9	68	50	71
Thatcham Town	42	21	7	14	70	60	70
Marlow	42	19	12	11	74	49	69
Uxbridge	42	20	8	14	68	58	68
Andover	42	19	9	14	70	59	66
Didcot Town	42	16	13	13	86	67	61
Abingdon United	42	16	11	15	68	67	59
Oxford City	42	17	8	17	62	75	59
Winchester City	42	16	10	16	67	65	58
Windsor & Eton	42	16	10	16	76	75	58
Chesham United	42	17	6	19	68	79	57
Hillingdon Borough	42	13	13	16	80	85	52
Lymington & New Milton	42	16	3	23	81	79	51
Brook House	42	14	6	22	71	92	48
Bracknell Town	42	11	13	18	51	62	46
Newport IOW	42	9	3	30	44	106	30
Hanwell Town	42	6	7	29	52	102	24
Beaconsfield SYCOB	42	5	6	31	36	104	21

Hanwell Town had one point deducted.

2007-2008

Premier Division

King's Lynn	42	24	13	5	91	36	85
Team Bath	42	25	8	9	71	41	83
Halesowen Town	42	22	13	7	80	46	79
Chippenham Town	42	20	13	9	73	44	73
Bashley	42	19	12	11	60	46	69
Gloucester City	42	19	11	12	81	50	68
Hemel Hempstead Town	42	19	11	12	67	50	68
Brackley Town	42	16	12	14	57	53	60
Banbury United	42	14	16	12	55	57	58
Yate Town	42	16	10	16	71	76	58
Clevedon Town	42	13	18	11	49	46	57
Swindon Supermarine	42	14	12	16	51	67	54
Merthyr Tydfil	42	13	14	15	65	70	53
Mangotsfield United	42	12	16	14	38	42	52
Rugby Town	42	13	12	17	55	66	51
Corby Town	42	14	8	20	60	67	50
Tiverton Town	42	13	11	18	45	60	50
Hitchin Town	42	12	11	19	46	61	47
Bedford Town	42	12	9	21	54	73	45
Bromsgrove Rovers	42	10	12	20	46	67	42
Cirencester Town	42	8	8	26	44	80	32
Cheshunt	42	5	8	29	42	103	23

Division One Midlands

Evesham United	40	28	7	5	68	24	91
Leamington	40	27	8	5	74	27	89
Stourbridge	40	25	3	12	97	48	78
Sutton Coldfield Town	40	23	8	9	93	52	77
Rushall Olympic	40	23	7	10	68	23	76
Chesham United	40	23	7	10	78	40	76
Chasetown	40	23	6	11	71	38	75
Aylesbury United	40	19	9	12	64	49	66
Leighton Town	40	17	12	11	59	42	63
Romulus	40	18	8	14	60	53	62
Barton Rovers	40	14	16	10	54	45	58
Bishops Cleeve	40	17	7	16	63	61	58
Dunstable Town	40	14	5	21	63	65	47
Willenhall Town	40	12	13	15	53	58	46
Bedworth United	40	12	10	18	40	51	46
Cinderford Town	40	12	6	22	47	82	42
Stourport Swifts	40	10	8	22	40	81	38
Rothwell Town	40	9	5	26	34	69	32
Woodford United	40	7	6	27	30	88	27
Malvern Town	40	3	9	28	34	95	18
Berkhamsted Town	40	2	4	34	27	126	10

Willenhall Town had 3 points deducted.

Division One South & West

Farnborough	42	27	8	7	120	48	89
Fleet Town	42	26	7	9	78	48	85
Didcot Town	42	24	11	7	99	42	83
Oxford City	42	24	9	9	82	41	81
Uxbridge	42	22	9	11	72	50	75
Bridgwater Town	42	19	13	10	74	45	70
Paulton Rovers	42	20	10	12	77	57	70
Windsor & Eton	42	20	9	13	75	66	69
Marlow	42	20	6	16	74	54	66
Burnham	42	18	9	15	67	55	63
Gosport Borough	42	18	8	16	69	67	62
Godalming Town	42	17	9	16	70	70	60
Hillingdon Borough	42	16	8	18	68	70	56
AFC Hayes	42	17	4	21	75	99	55
Thatcham Town	42	13	10	19	59	62	49
Abingdon United	42	13	9	20	64	75	48
Winchester City	42	13	9	20	58	71	48
Taunton Town	42	12	11	19	66	79	47
Andover	42	11	7	24	62	101	40
Bracknell Town	42	8	10	24	45	93	34
Slough Town	42	9	5	28	44	87	32
Newport IOW	42	2	5	35	25	143	11

FOOTBALL CONFERENCE

1979-80

Altrincham	38	24	8	6	79	35	56
Weymouth	38	22	10	6	73	37	54
Worcester City	38	19	11	8	53	36	49
Boston United	38	16	13	9	52	43	45
Gravesend & Northfleet	38	17	10	11	49	44	44
Maidstone United	38	16	11	11	54	37	43
Kettering Town	38	15	13	10	55	50	43
Northwich Victoria	38	16	10	12	50	38	42
Bangor City	38	14	14	10	41	46	42
Nuneaton Borough	38	13	13	12	58	44	39
Scarborough	38	12	15	11	47	38	39
Yeovil Town	38	13	10	15	46	49	36
Telford United	38	13	8	17	52	60	34
Barrow	38	14	6	18	47	55	34
Wealdstone	38	9	15	14	42	54	33
Bath City	38	10	12	16	43	69	32
Barnet	38	10	10	18	32	48	30
AP Leamington	38	7	11	20	32	63	25
Stafford Rangers	38	6	10	22	41	57	22
Redditch United	38	5	8	25	26	69	18

1980-81

Altrincham	38	23	8	7	72	41	54
Kettering Town	38	21	9	8	66	37	51
Scarborough	38	17	13	8	49	29	47
Northwich Victoria	38	17	11	10	53	40	45
Weymouth	38	19	6	13	54	40	44
Bath City	38	16	10	12	51	32	42
Maidstone United	38	16	9	13	64	53	41
Boston United	38	16	9	13	63	58	41
Barrow	38	15	8	15	50	49	38
Frickley Athletic	38	15	8	15	61	62	38
Stafford Rangers	38	11	15	12	56	56	37
Worcester City	38	14	7	17	47	54	35
Telford United	38	13	9	16	47	59	35
Yeovil Town	38	14	6	18	60	64	34
Gravesend & Northfleet	38	13	8	17	48	55	34
AP Leamington	38	10	11	17	47	66	31
Barnet	38	12	7	19	39	64	31
Nuneaton Borough	38	10	9	19	49	65	29
Wealdstone	38	9	11	18	37	56	29
Bangor City	38	6	12	20	35	68	24

1981-82

Runcorn	42	28	9	5	75	37	93
Enfield	42	26	8	8	90	46	86
Telford United	42	23	8	11	70	51	77
Worcester City	42	21	8	13	70	60	71
Dagenham	42	19	12	11	69	51	69
Northwich Victoria	42	20	9	13	56	46	69
Scarborough	42	19	11	12	65	52	68
Barrow	42	18	11	13	59	50	65
Weymouth	42	18	9	15	56	47	63
Boston United	42	17	11	14	61	57	62
Altrincham	42	14	13	15	66	56	55
Bath City	42	15	10	17	50	57	55
Yeovil Town	42	14	11	17	56	68	53
Stafford Rangers	42	12	16	14	48	47	52
Frickley Athletic	42	14	10	18	47	60	52
Maidstone United	42	11	15	16	55	59	48
Trowbridge Town	42	12	11	19	38	54	47
Barnet	42	9	14	19	36	52	41
Kettering Town	42	9	13	20	64	76	40
Gravesend & Northfleet	42	10	10	22	51	69	40
Dartford	42	10	9	23	47	69	39
AP Leamington	42	4	10	28	40	105	22

1982-83

Enfield	42	25	9	8	95	48	84
Maidstone United	42	25	8	9	83	34	83
Wealdstone	42	22	13	7	80	41	79
Runcorn	42	22	8	12	73	53	74
Boston United	42	20	12	10	77	57	72
Telford United	42	20	11	11	69	48	71
Weymouth	42	20	10	12	63	48	70
Northwich Victoria	42	18	10	14	68	63	64
Scarborough	42	17	12	13	71	58	63
Bath City	42	17	9	16	58	55	60
Nuneaton Borough	42	15	13	14	57	60	58
Altrincham	42	15	10	17	62	56	55
Bangor City	42	14	13	15	71	77	55
Dagenham	42	12	15	15	60	65	51
Barnet	42	16	3	23	55	78	51
Frickley Athletic	42	12	13	17	66	77	49
Worcester City	42	12	10	20	58	87	46
Trowbridge Town	42	12	7	23	56	88	43
Kettering Town	42	11	7	24	69	99	40
Yeovil Town	42	11	7	24	63	99	40
Barrow	42	8	12	22	46	74	36
Stafford Rangers	42	5	14	23	40	75	29

1983-84

Maidstone United	42	23	13	6	71	34	70
Nuneaton Borough	42	24	11	7	70	40	69
Altrincham	42	23	9	10	64	39	65
Wealdstone	42	21	14	7	75	36	62
Runcorn	42	20	13	9	61	45	62
Bath City	42	17	12	13	60	48	53
Northwich Victoria	42	16	14	12	54	47	51
Worcester City	42	15	13	14	64	55	49
Barnet	42	16	10	16	55	58	49
Kidderminster Harriers	42	14	14	14	54	61	49
Telford United	42	17	11	14	50	58	49
Frickley Athletic	42	17	10	15	68	56	48
Scarborough	42	14	16	12	52	55	48
Enfield	42	14	9	19	61	58	43
Weymouth	42	13	8	21	54	65	42
Gateshead	42	12	13	17	59	73	42
Boston United	42	13	12	17	66	80	41
Dagenham	42	14	8	20	57	69	40
Kettering Town	42	12	9	21	53	67	37
Yeovil Town	42	12	8	22	55	77	35
Bangor City	42	10	6	26	54	82	29
Trowbridge Town	42	5	7	30	33	87	19

2 points awarded for a Home win, 3 points awarded for an Away win, 1 point awarded for any Draw

1984-85

Wealdstone	42	20	10	12	64	54	62
Nuneaton Borough	42	19	14	9	85	53	58
Dartford	42	17	13	12	57	48	57
Bath City	42	21	9	12	52	49	57
Altrincham	42	21	6	15	63	47	56
Scarborough	42	17	13	12	69	62	54
Enfield	42	17	13	12	84	61	53
Kidderminster Harriers	42	17	8	17	79	77	51
Northwich Victoria	42	16	11	15	50	46	50
Telford United	42	15	14	13	59	54	49
Frickley Athletic	42	18	7	17	65	71	49
Kettering Town	42	15	12	15	68	59	48
Maidstone United	42	15	13	14	58	51	48
Runcorn	42	13	15	14	48	47	48
Barnet	42	15	11	16	59	52	47
Weymouth	42	15	13	14	70	66	45
Boston United	42	15	10	17	69	69	45
Barrow	42	11	16	15	47	57	43
Dagenham	42	13	10	19	47	67	41
Worcester City	42	12	9	21	55	84	38
Gateshead	42	9	12	21	51	82	33
Yeovil Town	42	6	11	25	44	87	25

2 points awarded for a Home win, 3 points awarded for an Away win, 1 point awarded for any Draw. Gateshead had 1 point deducted

1985-86

Enfield	42	27	10	5	94	47	76
Frickley Athletic	42	25	10	7	78	50	69
Kidderminster Harriers	42	24	7	11	99	62	67
Altrincham	42	22	11	9	70	49	63
Weymouth	42	19	15	8	75	60	61
Runcorn	42	19	14	9	70	44	60
Stafford Rangers	42	19	13	10	61	54	60
Telford United	42	18	10	14	68	66	51
Kettering Town	42	15	15	12	55	53	49
Wealdstone	42	16	9	17	57	56	47
Cheltenham Town	42	16	11	15	69	69	46
Bath City	42	13	11	18	53	54	45
Boston United	42	16	7	19	66	76	44
Barnet	42	13	11	18	56	60	41
Scarborough	42	13	11	18	54	66	40
Northwich Victoria	42	10	12	20	42	54	37
Maidstone United	42	9	16	17	57	66	36
Nuneaton Borough	42	13	5	24	58	73	36
Dagenham	42	10	12	20	48	66	36
Wycombe Wanderers	42	10	13	19	55	84	36
Dartford	42	8	9	25	51	82	26
Barrow	42	7	8	27	41	86	24

2 points awarded for a Home win; 3 points awarded for an Away win; 1 point awarded for any Draw

1986-87

Scarborough	42	27	10	5	64	33	91
Barnet	42	25	10	7	86	39	85
Maidstone United	42	21	10	11	71	48	73
Enfield	42	21	7	14	66	47	70
Altrincham	42	18	15	9	66	53	69
Boston United	42	21	6	15	82	74	69
Sutton United	42	19	11	12	81	51	68
Runcorn	42	18	13	11	71	58	67
Telford United	42	18	10	14	69	59	64
Bath City	42	17	12	13	63	62	63
Cheltenham Town	42	16	13	13	64	50	61
Kidderminster Harriers	42	17	4	21	77	81	55
Stafford Rangers	42	14	11	17	58	60	53
Weymouth	42	13	12	17	68	77	51
Dagenham	42	14	7	21	56	72	49
Kettering Town	42	12	11	19	54	66	47
Northwich Victoria	42	10	14	18	53	69	44
Nuneaton Borough	42	10	14	18	48	73	44
Wealdstone	42	11	10	21	50	70	43
Welling United	42	10	10	22	61	84	40
Frickley Athletic	42	7	11	24	47	82	32
Gateshead	42	6	13	23	48	95	31

1987-88

Lincoln City	42	24	10	8	86	48	82
Barnet	42	23	11	8	93	45	80
Kettering Town	42	22	9	11	68	48	75
Runcorn	42	21	11	10	68	47	74
Telford United	42	20	10	12	65	50	70
Stafford Rangers	42	20	9	13	79	58	69
Kidderminster Harriers	42	18	15	9	75	66	69
Sutton United	42	16	18	8	77	54	66
Maidstone United	42	18	9	15	79	64	63
Weymouth	42	18	9	15	53	43	63
Macclesfield Town	42	18	9	15	64	62	63
Enfield	42	15	10	17	68	78	55
Cheltenham Town	42	11	20	11	64	67	53
Altrincham	42	14	10	18	59	59	52
Fisher Athletic	42	13	13	16	58	61	52
Boston United	42	14	7	21	60	75	49
Northwich Victoria	42	10	17	15	46	57	47
Wycombe Wanderers	42	11	13	18	50	76	46
Welling United	42	11	9	22	50	72	42
Bath City	42	9	10	23	48	76	37
Wealdstone	42	5	17	20	39	76	32
Dagenham	42	5	6	31	37	104	21

1988-89

Maidstone United	40	25	9	6	92	46	84
Kettering Town	40	23	7	10	56	39	76
Boston United	40	22	8	10	61	51	74
Wycombe Wanderers	40	20	11	9	68	52	71
Kidderminster Harriers	40	21	6	13	68	57	69
Runcorn	40	19	8	13	77	53	65
Macclesfield Town	40	17	10	13	63	57	61
Barnet	40	18	7	15	64	69	61
Yeovil Town	40	15	11	14	68	67	56
Northwich Victoria	40	14	11	15	64	65	53
Welling United	40	14	11	15	45	46	53
Sutton United	40	12	15	13	64	54	51
Enfield	40	14	8	18	62	67	50
Altrincham	40	13	10	17	51	61	49
Cheltenham Town	40	12	12	16	55	58	48
Telford United	40	13	9	18	37	43	48
Chorley	40	13	6	21	57	71	45
Fisher Athletic	40	10	11	19	55	65	41
Stafford Rangers	40	11	7	22	49	74	40
Aylesbury United	40	9	9	22	43	71	36
Weymouth	40	7	10	23	37	70	31
Newport County	29	4	7	18	31	62	19

Newport County expelled from League – their record was deleted.

1989-90

Darlington	42	26	9	7	76	25	87
Barnet	42	26	7	9	81	41	85
Runcorn	42	19	13	10	79	62	70
Macclesfield Town	42	17	15	10	56	41	66
Kettering Town	42	18	12	12	66	53	66
Welling United	42	18	10	14	62	50	64
Yeovil Town	42	17	12	13	62	54	63
Sutton United	42	19	6	17	68	64	63
Merthyr Tydfil	42	16	14	12	67	63	62
Wycombe Wanderers	42	17	10	15	64	56	61
Cheltenham Town	42	16	11	15	58	60	59
Telford United	42	15	13	14	56	63	58
Kidderminster Harriers	42	15	9	18	64	67	54
Barrow	42	12	16	14	51	67	52
Northwich Victoria	42	15	5	22	51	67	50
Altrincham	42	12	13	17	49	48	49
Stafford Rangers	42	12	12	18	50	62	48
Boston United	42	13	8	21	48	67	47
Fisher Athletic	42	13	7	22	55	78	46
Chorley	42	13	6	23	42	67	45
Farnborough Town	42	10	12	20	60	73	42
Enfield	42	10	6	26	52	89	36

1990-91

Barnet	42	26	9	7	103	52	87
Colchester United	42	25	10	7	68	35	85
Altrincham	42	23	13	6	87	46	82
Kettering Town	42	23	11	8	67	45	80
Wycombe Wanderers	42	21	11	10	75	46	74
Telford United	42	20	7	15	62	52	67
Macclesfield Town	42	17	12	13	63	52	63
Runcorn	42	16	10	16	69	67	58
Merthyr Tydfil	42	16	9	17	62	61	57
Barrow	42	15	12	15	59	65	57
Welling United	42	13	15	14	55	57	54
Northwich Victoria	42	13	13	16	65	75	52
Kidderminster Harrier	42	14	10	18	56	67	52
Yeovil Town	42	13	11	18	58	58	50
Stafford Rangers	42	12	14	16	48	51	50
Cheltenham Town	42	12	12	18	54	72	48
Gateshead	42	14	6	22	52	92	48
Boston United	42	12	11	19	55	69	47
Slough Town	42	13	6	23	51	80	45
Bath City	42	10	12	20	55	61	42
Sutton United	42	10	9	23	62	82	39
Fisher Athletic	42	5	15	22	38	79	30

1991-92

Colchester United	42	28	10	4	98	40	94
Wycombe Wanderers	42	30	4	8	84	35	94
Kettering Town	42	20	13	9	72	50	73
Merthyr Tydfil	42	18	14	10	59	56	68
Farnborough Town	42	18	12	12	68	53	66
Telford United	42	19	7	16	62	66	64
Redbridge Forest	42	18	9	15	69	56	63
Boston United	42	18	9	15	71	66	63
Bath City	42	16	12	14	54	51	60
Witton Albion	42	16	10	16	63	60	58
Northwich Victoria	42	16	6	20	63	58	54
Welling United	42	14	12	16	69	79	54
Macclesfield Town	42	13	13	16	50	50	52
Gateshead	42	12	12	18	49	57	48
Yeovil Town	42	11	14	17	40	49	47
Runcorn	42	11	13	18	50	63	46
Stafford Rangers	42	10	16	16	41	59	46
Altrincham	42	11	12	19	61	82	45
Kidderminster Harriers	42	12	9	21	56	77	45
Slough Town	42	13	6	23	56	82	45
Cheltenham Town	42	10	13	19	56	82	43
Barrow	42	8	14	20	52	72	38

1992-93

Wycombe Wanderers	42	24	11	7	84	37	83
Bromsgrove Rovers	42	18	14	10	67	49	68
Dagenham & Redbridge	42	19	11	12	75	47	67
Yeovil Town	42	18	12	12	59	49	66
Slough Town	42	18	11	13	60	55	65
Stafford Rangers	42	18	10	14	55	47	64
Bath City	42	15	14	13	53	46	59
Woking	42	17	8	17	58	62	59
Kidderminster Harriers	42	14	16	12	60	60	58
Altrincham	42	15	13	14	49	52	58
Northwich Victoria	42	16	8	18	68	55	56
Stalybridge Celtic	42	13	17	12	48	55	56
Kettering Town	42	14	13	15	61	63	55
Gateshead	42	14	10	18	53	56	52
Telford United	42	14	10	18	55	60	52
Merthyr Tydfil	42	14	10	18	51	79	52
Witton Albion	42	11	17	14	62	65	50
Macclesfield Town	42	12	13	17	40	50	49
Runcorn	42	13	10	19	58	76	49
Welling United	42	12	12	18	57	72	48
Farnborough Town	42	12	11	19	68	87	47
Boston United	42	9	13	20	50	69	40

Dagenham & Redbridge had 1 point deducted

1993-94

Kidderminster Harriers	42	22	9	11	63	35	75
Kettering Town	42	19	15	8	46	24	72
Woking	42	18	13	11	58	58	67
Southport	42	18	12	12	57	51	66
Runcorn	42	14	19	9	63	57	61
Dagenham & Redbridge	42	15	14	13	62	54	59
Macclesfield Town	42	16	11	15	48	49	59
Dover Athletic	42	17	7	18	48	49	58
Stafford Rangers	42	14	15	13	56	52	57
Altrincham	42	16	9	17	41	42	57
Gateshead	42	15	12	15	45	53	57
Bath City	42	13	17	12	47	38	56
Halifax Town	42	13	16	13	55	49	55
Stalybridge Celtic	42	14	12	16	54	55	54
Northwich Victoria	42	11	19	12	44	45	52
Welling United	42	13	12	17	47	49	51
Telford United	42	13	12	17	41	49	51
Bromsgrove Rovers	42	12	15	15	54	66	51
Yeovil Town	42	14	9	19	49	62	51
Merthyr Tydfil	42	12	15	15	60	61	49
Slough Town	42	11	14	17	44	58	47
Witton Albion	42	7	13	22	37	63	44

Merthyr Tydfil had 2 points deducted

1994-95

Macclesfield Town	42	24	8	10	70	40	80
Woking	42	21	12	9	76	54	75
Southport	42	21	9	12	68	50	72
Altrincham	42	20	8	14	77	60	68
Stevenage Borough	42	20	7	15	68	49	67
Kettering Town	42	19	10	13	73	56	67
Gateshead	42	19	10	13	61	53	67
Halifax Town	42	17	12	13	68	54	63
Runcorn	42	16	10	16	59	71	58
Northwich Victoria	42	14	15	13	77	66	57
Kidderminster Harriers	42	16	9	17	63	61	57
Bath City	42	15	12	15	55	56	57
Bromsgrove Rovers	42	14	13	15	66	69	55
Farnborough Town	42	15	10	17	45	64	55
Dagenham & Redbridge	42	13	13	16	56	69	52
Dover Athletic	42	11	16	15	48	55	49
Welling United	42	13	10	19	57	74	49
Stalybridge Celtic	42	11	14	17	52	72	47
Telford United	42	10	16	16	53	62	46
Merthyr Tydfil	42	11	11	20	53	63	44
Stafford Rangers	42	9	11	22	53	79	38
Yeovil Town	42	8	14	20	50	71	37

Yeovil Town had 1 point deducted for fielding an ineligible player

1995-96

Stevenage Borough	42	27	10	5	101	44	91
Woking	42	25	8	9	83	54	83
Hednesford Town	42	23	7	12	71	46	76
Macclesfield Town	42	22	9	11	66	49	75
Gateshead	42	18	13	11	58	46	67
Southport	42	18	12	12	77	64	66
Kidderminster Harriers	42	18	10	14	78	66	64
Northwich Victoria	42	16	12	14	72	64	60
Morecambe	42	17	8	17	78	72	59
Farnborough Town	42	15	14	13	63	58	59
Bromsgrove Rovers	42	15	14	13	59	57	59
Altrincham	42	15	13	14	59	64	58
Telford United	42	15	10	17	51	56	55
Stalybridge Celtic	42	16	7	19	59	68	55
Halifax Town	42	13	13	16	49	63	52
Kettering Town	42	13	9	20	68	84	48
Slough Town	42	13	8	21	63	76	47
Bath City	42	13	7	22	45	66	46
Welling United	42	10	15	17	42	53	45
Dover Athletic	42	11	7	24	51	74	40
Runcorn	42	9	8	25	48	87	35
Dagenham & Redbridge	42	7	12	23	43	73	33

1996-97

Macclesfield Town	42	27	9	6	80	30	90
Kidderminster Harriers	42	26	7	9	84	42	85
Stevenage Borough	42	24	10	8	87	53	82
Morecambe	42	19	9	14	69	56	66
Woking	42	18	10	14	71	63	64
Northwich Victoria	42	17	12	13	61	54	63
Farnborough Town	42	16	13	13	58	53	61
Hednesford Town	42	16	12	14	52	50	60
Telford United	42	16	10	16	46	56	58
Gateshead	42	15	11	16	59	63	56
Southport	42	15	10	17	51	61	55
Rushden & Diamonds	42	14	11	17	61	63	53
Stalybridge Celtic	42	14	10	18	53	58	52
Kettering Town	42	14	9	19	53	62	51
Hayes	42	12	14	16	54	55	50
Slough Town	42	12	14	16	62	65	50
Dover Athletic	42	12	14	16	57	68	50
Welling United	42	13	9	20	50	60	48
Halifax Town	42	12	12	18	55	74	48
Bath City	42	12	11	19	53	80	47
Bromsgrove Rovers	42	12	5	25	41	67	41
Altrincham	42	9	12	21	49	73	39

1997-98

Halifax Town	42	25	12	5	74	43	87
Cheltenham Town	42	23	9	10	63	43	78
Woking	42	22	8	12	72	46	74
Rushden & Diamonds	42	23	5	14	79	57	74
Morecambe	42	21	10	11	77	64	73
Hereford United	42	18	13	11	56	49	67
Hednesford Town	42	18	12	12	59	50	66
Slough Town	42	18	10	14	58	49	64
Northwich Victoria	42	15	15	12	63	59	60
Welling United	42	17	9	16	64	62	60
Yeovil Town	42	17	8	17	73	63	59
Hayes	42	16	10	16	62	52	58
Dover Athletic	42	15	10	17	60	70	55
Kettering Town	42	13	13	16	53	60	52
Stevenage Borough	42	13	12	17	59	63	51
Southport	42	13	11	18	56	58	50
Kidderminster Harriers	42	11	14	17	56	63	47
Farnborough Town	42	12	8	22	56	70	44
Leek Town	42	10	14	18	52	67	44
Telford United	42	10	12	20	53	76	42
Gateshead	42	8	11	23	51	87	35
Stalybridge Celtic	42	7	8	27	48	93	29

1998-99

Cheltenham Town	42	22	14	6	71	36	80
Kettering Town	42	22	10	10	58	37	76
Hayes	42	22	8	12	63	50	74
Rushden & Diamonds	42	20	12	10	71	42	72
Yeovil Town	42	20	11	11	68	54	71
Stevenage Borough	42	17	17	8	62	45	68
Northwich Victoria	42	19	9	14	60	51	66
Kingstonian	42	17	13	12	50	49	64
Woking	42	18	9	15	51	45	63
Hednesford Town	42	15	16	11	49	44	61
Dover Athletic	42	15	13	14	54	48	58
Forest Green Rovers	42	15	13	14	55	50	58
Hereford United	42	15	10	17	49	46	55
Morecambe	42	15	8	19	60	76	53
Kidderminster Harriers	42	14	9	19	56	52	51
Doncaster Rovers	42	12	12	18	51	55	48
Telford United	42	10	16	16	44	60	46
Southport	42	10	15	17	47	59	45
Barrow	42	11	10	21	40	63	43
Welling United	42	9	14	19	44	65	41
Leek Town	42	8	8	26	48	76	32
Farnborough Town	42	7	11	24	41	89	32

1999-2000

Kidderminster Harriers	42	26	7	9	75	40	85
Rushden & Diamonds	42	21	13	8	71	42	76
Morecambe	42	18	16	8	70	48	70
Scarborough	42	19	12	11	60	35	69
Kingstonian	42	20	7	15	58	44	67
Dover Athletic	42	18	12	12	65	56	66
Yeovil Town	42	18	10	14	60	63	64
Hereford United	42	15	14	13	61	52	59
Southport	42	15	13	14	55	56	58
Stevenage Borough	42	16	9	17	60	54	57
Hayes	42	16	8	18	57	58	56
Doncaster Rovers	42	15	9	18	46	48	54
Kettering Town	42	12	16	14	44	50	52
Woking	42	13	13	16	45	53	52
Nuneaton Borough	42	12	15	15	49	53	51
Telford United	42	14	9	19	56	66	51
Hednesford Town	42	15	6	21	45	68	51
Northwich Victoria	42	13	12	17	53	78	51
Forest Green Rovers	42	13	8	21	54	63	47
Welling United	42	13	8	21	54	66	47
Altrincham	42	9	19	14	51	60	46
Sutton United	42	8	10	24	39	75	34

2000-2001

Rushden & Diamonds	42	25	11	6	78	36	86
Yeovil Town	42	24	8	10	73	50	80
Dagenham & Redbridge	42	23	8	11	71	54	77
Southport	42	20	9	13	58	46	69
Leigh RMI	42	19	11	12	63	57	68
Telford United	42	19	8	15	51	51	65
Stevenage Borough	42	15	18	9	71	61	63
Chester City	42	16	14	12	49	43	62
Doncaster Rovers	42	15	13	14	47	43	58
Scarborough	42	14	16	12	56	54	58
Hereford United	42	14	15	13	60	46	57
Boston United	42	13	17	12	74	63	56
Nuneaton Borough	42	13	15	14	60	60	54
Woking	42	13	15	14	52	57	54
Dover Athletic	42	14	11	17	54	56	53
Forest Green Rovers	42	11	15	16	43	54	48
Northwich Victoria	42	11	13	18	49	67	46
Hayes	42	12	10	20	44	71	46
Morecambe	42	11	12	19	64	66	45
Kettering Town	42	11	10	21	46	62	43
Kingstonian	42	8	10	24	47	73	34
Hednesford Town	42	5	13	24	46	86	28

2001-2002

Boston United	42	25	9	8	84	42	84
Dagenham & Redbridge	42	24	12	6	70	47	84
Yeovil Town	42	19	13	10	66	53	70
Doncaster Rovers	42	18	13	11	68	46	67
Barnet	42	19	10	13	64	48	67
Morecambe	42	17	11	14	63	67	62
Farnborough Town	42	18	7	17	66	54	61
Margate	42	14	16	12	59	53	58
Telford United	42	14	15	13	63	58	57
Nuneaton Borough	42	16	9	17	57	57	57
Stevenage Borough	42	15	10	17	57	60	55
Scarborough	42	14	14	14	55	63	55
Northwich Victoria	42	16	7	19	57	70	55
Chester City	42	15	9	18	54	51	54
Southport	42	13	14	15	53	49	53
Leigh RMI	42	15	8	19	56	58	53
Hereford United	42	14	10	18	50	53	52
Forest Green Rovers	42	12	15	15	54	76	51
Woking	42	13	9	20	59	70	48
Hayes	42	13	5	24	53	80	44
Stalybridge Celtic	42	11	10	21	40	69	43
Dover Athletic	42	11	6	25	41	65	39

2002-2003

Yeovil Town	42	28	11	3	100	37	95
Morecambe	42	23	9	10	86	42	78
Doncaster Rovers	42	22	12	8	73	47	78
Chester City	42	21	12	9	59	31	75
Dagenham & Redbridge	42	21	9	12	71	59	72
Hereford United	42	19	7	16	64	51	64
Scarborough	42	18	10	14	63	54	64
Halifax Town	42	18	10	14	50	51	64
Forest Green Rovers	42	17	8	17	61	62	59
Margate	42	15	11	16	60	66	56
Barnet	42	13	14	15	65	68	53
Stevenage Borough	42	14	10	18	61	55	52
Farnborough Town	42	13	12	17	57	56	51
Northwich Victoria	42	13	12	17	66	72	51
Telford United	42	14	7	21	54	69	49
Burton Albion	42	13	10	19	52	77	49
Gravesend & Northfleet	42	12	12	18	62	73	48
Leigh RMI	42	14	6	22	44	71	48
Woking	42	11	14	17	52	81	47
Nuneaton Borough	42	13	7	22	51	78	46
Southport	42	11	12	19	54	69	45
Kettering Town	42	8	7	27	37	73	31

2003-2004

Chester City	42	27	11	4	85	34	92
Hereford United	42	28	7	7	103	44	91
Shrewsbury Town	42	20	14	8	67	42	74
Barnet	42	19	14	9	60	46	71
Aldershot Town	42	20	10	12	80	67	70
Exeter City	42	19	12	11	71	57	69
Morecambe	42	20	7	15	66	66	67
Stevenage Borough	42	18	9	15	58	52	63
Woking	42	15	16	11	65	52	61
Accrington Stanley	42	15	13	14	68	61	58
Gravesend & Northfleet	42	14	15	13	69	66	57
Telford United	42	15	10	17	49	51	55
Dagenham & Redbridge	42	15	9	18	59	64	54
Burton Albion	42	15	7	20	57	59	51
Scarborough	42	12	15	15	51	54	51
Margate	42	14	9	19	56	64	51
Tamworth	42	13	10	19	49	68	49
Forest Green Rovers	42	12	12	18	58	80	48
Halifax Town	42	12	8	22	43	65	44
Farnborough Town	42	10	9	23	53	74	39
Leigh RMI	42	7	8	27	46	97	29
Northwich Victoria	42	4	11	27	30	80	23

Burton Albion had 1 point deducted.

2004-2005

Conference National

Barnet	42	26	8	8	90	44	86
Hereford United	42	21	11	10	68	41	74
Carlisle United	42	20	13	9	74	37	73
Aldershot Town	42	21	10	11	68	52	73
Stevenage Borough	42	22	6	14	65	52	72
Exeter City	42	20	11	11	71	50	71
Morecambe	42	19	14	9	69	50	71
Woking	42	18	14	10	58	45	68
Halifax Town	42	19	9	14	74	56	66
Accrington Stanley	42	18	11	13	72	58	65
Dagenham & Redbridge	42	19	8	15	68	60	65
Crawley Town	42	16	9	17	50	50	57
Scarborough	42	14	14	14	60	46	56
Gravesend & Northfleet	42	13	11	18	58	64	50
Tamworth	42	14	11	17	53	63	50
Burton Albion	42	13	11	18	50	66	50
York City	42	11	10	21	39	66	43
Canvey Island	42	9	15	18	53	65	42
Northwich Victoria	42	14	10	18	58	72	42
Forest Green Rovers	42	6	15	21	41	81	33
Farnborough Town	42	6	11	25	35	89	29
Leigh RMI	42	4	6	32	31	98	18

Northwich Victoria had 10 points deducted.
Tamworth had 3 points deducted.

Conference North

Southport	42	25	9	8	83	45	84
Nuneaton Borough	42	25	6	11	68	45	81
Droylsden	42	24	7	11	82	52	79
Kettering Town	42	21	7	14	56	50	70
Altrincham	42	19	12	11	66	46	69
Harrogate Town	42	19	11	12	62	49	68
Worcester City	42	16	12	14	59	53	60
Stafford Rangers	42	14	17	11	52	44	59
Redditch United	42	18	8	16	65	59	59
Hucknall Town	42	15	14	13	59	57	59
Gainsborough Trinity	42	16	9	17	55	55	57
Hinckley United	42	15	11	16	55	62	56
Lancaster City	42	14	12	16	51	59	54
Alfreton Town	42	15	8	19	53	55	53
Vauxhall Motors	42	14	11	17	48	57	53
Barrow	42	14	10	18	50	64	52
Worksop Town	42	16	12	14	59	59	50
Moor Green	42	13	10	19	55	64	49
Stalybridge Celtic	42	12	12	18	52	70	48
Runcorn FC Halton	42	10	12	20	44	63	42
Ashton United	42	8	9	25	46	79	33
Bradford Park Avenue	42	5	9	28	37	70	24

Worksop Town had 10 points deducted.
Redditch United had 3 points deducted.

Conference South

Grays Athletic	42	30	8	4	118	31	98
Cambridge City	42	23	6	13	60	44	75
Thurrock	42	21	6	15	61	56	69
Lewes	42	18	11	13	73	64	65
Eastbourne Borough	42	18	10	14	65	47	64
Basingstoke Town	42	19	6	17	57	52	63
Weymouth	42	17	11	14	62	59	62
Dorchester Town	42	17	11	14	77	81	62
Bognor Regis Town	42	17	9	16	70	65	60
Bishop's Stortford	42	17	8	17	70	66	59
Weston-super-Mare	42	15	13	14	55	60	58
Hayes	42	15	11	16	55	57	56
Havant & Waterlooville	42	16	7	19	64	69	55
St. Albans City	42	16	6	20	64	76	54
Sutton United	42	14	11	17	60	71	53
Welling United	42	15	7	20	64	68	52
Hornchurch	42	17	10	15	71	63	51
Newport County	42	13	11	18	56	61	50
Carshalton Athletic	42	13	9	20	44	72	48
Maidenhead United	42	12	10	20	54	81	46
Margate	42	12	8	22	54	75	34
Redbridge	42	11	3	28	50	86	33

Horchurch and Margate had 10 points deducted.
Redbridge had 3 points deducted.

2005-2006

Conference National

Accrington Stanley	42	28	7	7	76	45	91
Hereford United	42	22	14	6	59	33	80
Grays Athletic	42	21	13	8	94	55	76
Halifax Town	42	21	12	9	55	40	75
Morecambe	42	22	8	12	68	41	74
Stevenage Borough	42	19	12	11	62	47	69
Exeter City	42	18	9	15	65	48	63
York City	42	17	12	13	63	48	63
Burton Albion	42	16	12	14	50	52	60
Dagenham & Redbridge	42	16	10	16	63	59	58
Woking	42	14	14	14	58	47	56
Cambridge United	42	15	10	17	51	57	55
Aldershot Town	42	16	6	20	61	74	54
Canvey Island	42	13	12	17	47	58	51
Kidderminster Harriers	42	13	11	18	39	55	50
Gravesend & Northfleet	42	13	10	19	45	57	49
Crawley Town	42	12	11	19	48	55	47
Southport	42	10	10	22	36	68	40
Forest Green Rovers	42	8	14	20	49	62	38
Tamworth	42	8	14	20	32	63	38
Scarborough	42	9	10	23	40	66	37
Altrincham	42	10	11	21	40	71	23

Altrincham had 18 points deducted for fielding an ineligible player but were not relegated after Canvey Island withdrew from the League and Scarborough were relegated for a breach of the rules.

Conference North

Northwich Victoria	42	29	5	8	97	49	92
Stafford Rangers	42	25	10	7	68	34	85
Nuneaton Borough	42	22	11	9	68	43	77
Droylsden	42	20	12	10	80	56	72
Harrogate Town	42	22	5	15	66	56	71
Kettering Town	42	19	10	13	63	49	67
Stalybridge Celtic	42	19	9	14	74	54	66
Worcester City	42	16	14	12	58	46	62
Moor Green	42	15	16	11	67	64	61
Hinckley United	42	14	16	12	60	55	58
Hyde United (P)	42	15	11	16	68	61	56
Hucknall Town	42	14	13	15	56	55	55
Workington (P)	42	14	13	15	60	62	55
Barrow	42	12	11	19	62	67	47
Lancaster City	42	12	11	19	52	66	47
Gainsborough Trinity	42	11	13	18	45	65	46
Alfreton Town	42	10	15	17	46	58	45
Vauxhall Motors	42	12	7	23	50	71	43
Worksop Town	42	10	11	21	46	71	41
Redditch United	42	9	12	21	53	78	39
Leigh RMI	42	9	13	20	45	79	39
Hednesford Town	42	7	14	21	42	87	35

Leigh RMI had 1 point deducted.

Conference South

Weymouth	42	30	4	8	80	34	90
St. Albans City	42	27	5	10	94	47	86
Farnborough Town	42	23	9	10	65	41	78
Lewes	42	21	10	11	78	57	73
Histon	42	21	8	13	70	56	71
Havant & Waterlooville	42	21	10	11	64	48	70
Cambridge City	42	20	10	12	78	46	67
Eastleigh	42	21	3	18	65	58	66
Welling United	42	16	17	9	58	44	65
Thurrock	42	16	10	16	60	60	58
Dorchester Town	42	16	7	19	60	72	55
Bognor Regis Town	42	12	13	17	54	55	49
Sutton United	42	13	10	19	48	61	49
Weston-super-Mare	42	14	7	21	57	88	49
Bishop's Stortford	42	11	15	16	55	63	48
Yeading	42	13	8	21	47	62	47
Eastbourne Borough	42	10	16	16	51	61	46
Newport County	42	12	8	22	50	67	44
Basingstoke Town	42	12	8	22	47	72	44
Hayes	42	11	9	22	47	60	42
Carshalton Athletic	42	8	16	18	42	68	40
Maidenhead United	42	8	9	25	49	99	31

Weymouth had 4 points deducted.
Havant & Waterlooville and Cambridge City had 3 points deducted.
Maidenhead United had 2 points deducted.

2006-2007

Conference National

Dagenham & Redbridge	46	28	11	7	93	48	95
Oxford United	46	22	15	9	66	33	81
Morecambe	46	23	12	11	64	46	81
York City	46	23	11	12	65	45	80
Exeter City	46	22	12	12	67	48	78
Burton Albion	46	22	9	15	52	47	75
Gravesend & Northfleet	46	21	11	14	63	56	74
Stevenage Borough	46	20	10	16	76	66	70
Aldershot Town	46	18	11	17	64	62	65
Kidderminster Harriers	46	17	12	17	43	50	63
Weymouth	46	18	9	19	56	73	63
Rushden & Diamonds	46	17	11	18	58	54	62
Northwich Victoria	46	18	4	24	51	69	58
Forest Green Rovers	46	13	18	15	59	64	57
Woking	46	15	12	19	56	61	57
Halifax Town	46	15	10	21	55	62	55
Cambridge United	46	15	10	21	57	66	55
Crawley Town	46	17	12	17	52	52	53
Grays Athletic	46	13	13	20	56	55	52
Stafford Rangers	46	14	10	22	49	71	52
Altrincham	46	13	12	21	53	67	51
Tamworth	46	13	9	24	43	61	48
Southport	46	11	14	21	57	67	47
St. Alban's City	46	10	10	26	57	89	40

Crawley Town had 10 points deducted.

Conference North

Droylsden	42	23	9	10	85	55	78
Kettering Town	42	20	13	9	75	58	73
Workington	42	20	10	12	61	46	70
Hinckley United	42	19	12	11	68	54	69
Farsley Celtic	42	19	11	12	58	51	68
Harrogate Town	42	18	13	11	58	41	67
Blyth Spartans	42	19	9	14	57	49	66
Hyde United	42	18	11	13	79	62	65
Worcester City	42	16	14	12	67	54	62
Nuneaton Borough	42	15	15	12	54	45	60
Moor Green	42	16	11	15	53	51	59
Gainsborough Trinity	42	15	11	16	51	57	56
Hucknall Town	42	15	9	18	69	69	54
Alfreton Town	42	14	12	16	44	50	54
Vauxhall Motors	42	12	15	15	62	64	51
Barrow	42	12	14	16	47	48	50
Leigh RMI	42	13	10	19	47	61	49
Stalybridge Celtic	42	13	10	19	64	81	49
Redditch United	42	11	15	16	61	68	48
Scarborough	42	13	16	13	50	45	45
Worksop Town	42	12	9	21	44	62	45
Lancaster City	42	2	5	35	27	110	1

Scarborough and Lancaster City each had 10 points deducted.

Conference South

Histon	42	30	4	8	85	44	94
Salisbury City	42	21	12	9	65	37	75
Braintree Town	42	21	11	10	51	38	74
Havant & Waterlooville	42	20	13	9	75	46	73
Bishop's Stortford	42	21	10	11	72	61	73
Newport County	42	21	7	14	83	57	70
Eastbourne Borough	42	18	15	9	58	42	69
Welling United	42	21	6	15	65	51	69
Lewes	42	15	17	10	67	52	62
Fisher Athletic	42	15	11	16	77	77	56
Farnborough Town	42	19	8	15	59	52	55
Bognor Regis Town	42	13	13	16	56	62	52
Cambridge City	42	15	7	20	44	52	52
Sutton United	42	14	9	19	58	63	51
Eastleigh	42	11	15	16	48	53	48
Yeading	42	12	9	21	56	78	45
Dorchester Town	42	11	12	19	49	77	45
Thurrock	42	11	11	20	58	79	44
Basingstoke Town	42	9	16	17	46	58	43
Hayes	42	11	10	21	47	73	43
Weston-super-Mare	42	8	11	23	49	77	35
Bedford Town	42	8	7	27	43	82	31

Farnborough Town had 10 points deducted.

Conference South (Blue Square South)

Lewes	42	27	8	7	81	39	89
Eastbourne Borough	42	23	11	8	83	38	80
Hampton & Richmond	42	21	14	7	87	49	77
Fisher Athletic	42	22	5	15	65	61	71
Braintree Town	42	19	12	11	52	42	69
Eastleigh	42	19	10	13	76	62	67
Havant & Waterlooville	42	19	10	13	59	53	67
Bath City	42	17	15	10	59	36	66
Newport County	42	18	12	12	64	49	66
Bishop's Stortford	42	18	10	14	72	60	64
Bromley	42	19	7	16	77	66	64
Thurrock	42	18	9	15	63	64	63
Hayes & Yeading United	42	14	12	16	67	73	54
Cambridge City	42	14	10	18	71	72	52
Basingstoke Town	42	12	14	16	54	75	50
Welling United	42	13	7	22	41	64	46
Maidenhead United	42	11	12	19	56	59	45
Bognor Regis Town	42	11	11	20	49	67	44
St. Alban's City	42	10	12	20	43	69	42
Weston Super Mare	42	9	10	23	52	85	37
Dorchester Town	42	8	10	24	36	70	34
Sutton United	42	5	9	28	32	86	24

2007-2008

Conference National (Blue Square Premier)

Aldershot Town	46	31	8	7	82	48	101
Cambridge United	46	25	11	10	68	41	86
Torquay United	46	26	8	12	83	57	86
Exeter City	46	22	17	7	83	58	83
Burton Albion	46	23	12	11	79	56	81
Stevenage Borough	46	24	7	15	82	55	79
Histon	46	20	12	14	76	67	72
Forest Green Rovers	46	19	14	13	76	59	71
Oxford United	46	20	11	15	56	48	71
Grays Athletic	46	19	13	14	58	47	70
Ebbsfleet United	46	19	12	15	65	61	69
Salisbury City	46	18	14	14	70	60	68
Kidderminster Harriers	46	19	10	17	74	57	67
York City	46	17	11	18	71	74	62
Crawley Town	46	19	9	18	73	67	60
Rushden & Diamonds	46	15	14	17	55	55	59
Woking	46	12	17	17	53	61	53
Weymouth	46	11	13	22	53	73	46
Northwich Victoria	46	11	11	24	52	78	44
Halifax Town	46	12	16	18	61	70	42
Altrincham	46	9	14	23	56	82	41
Farsley Celtic	46	10	9	27	48	86	39
Stafford Rangers	46	5	10	31	42	99	25
Droylsden	46	5	9	32	46	103	24

Halifax Town had 10 points deducted.
Crawley Town had 6 points deducted.

Conference North (Blue Square North)

Kettering Town	42	30	7	5	93	34	97
AFC Telford United	42	24	8	10	70	43	80
Stalybridge Celtic	42	25	4	13	88	51	79
Southport	42	22	11	9	77	50	77
Barrow	42	21	13	8	70	39	76
Harrogate Town	42	21	11	10	55	41	74
Nuneaton Borough	42	19	14	9	58	40	71
Burscough	42	19	8	15	62	58	65
Hyde United	42	20	3	19	84	66	63
Boston United	42	17	8	17	65	57	59
Gainsborough Trinity	42	15	12	15	62	65	57
Worcester City	42	14	12	16	48	68	54
Redditch United	42	15	8	19	41	58	53
Workington	42	13	11	18	52	56	50
Tamworth (R)	42	13	11	18	53	59	50
Alfreton Town	42	12	11	19	49	54	47
Solihull Moors	42	12	11	19	50	76	47
Blyth Spartans	42	12	10	20	52	62	46
Hinckley United	42	11	12	19	48	69	45
Hucknall Town	42	11	6	25	53	75	39
Vauxhall Motors	42	7	7	28	42	100	28
Leigh RMI	42	6	8	28	36	87	26

ISTHMIAN LEAGUE

1905-06

London Caledonians	10	7	1	2	25	8	15
Clapton	10	6	1	3	11	13	13
Casuals	10	3	4	3	14	14	10
Civil Service	10	4	1	5	16	20	9
Ealing Association	10	3	2	5	15	19	8
Ilford	10	1	3	6	5	12	5

1906-07

Ilford	10	8	2	0	26	9	18
London Caledonians	10	6	0	4	19	14	12
Clapton	10	4	3	3	18	11	11
Civil Service	10	3	1	6	11	19	7
Ealing Association	10	3	1	6	12	22	7
Casuals	10	2	1	7	15	26	5

1907-08

London Caledonians	10	5	2	3	20	15	12
Clapton	10	4	3	3	24	14	11
Ilford	10	5	1	4	28	22	11
Oxford City	10	5	1	4	20	20	11
Dulwich Hamlet	10	3	2	5	15	18	8
West Norwood	10	3	1	6	13	31	7

1908-09

Bromley	18	11	1	6	42	29	23
Leytonstone	18	9	4	5	43	31	22
Ilford	18	9	4	5	37	36	22
Dulwich Hamlet	18	9	2	7	39	30	20
Clapton	18	8	4	6	34	32	20
Oxford City	18	6	4	8	29	32	16
Nunhead	18	7	2	9	31	35	16
Shepherd's Bush	18	6	3	9	26	44	15
London Caledonians	18	4	6	8	25	34	14
West Norwood	18	5	2	11	40	43	12

1909-10

Bromley	18	11	4	3	32	10	26
Clapton	18	10	4	4	56	19	24
Nunhead	18	10	4	4	49	26	24
Ilford	18	10	3	5	31	17	23
Dulwich Hamlet	18	8	4	6	26	26	20
Leytonstone	18	7	3	8	44	46	17
Oxford City	18	5	4	9	28	45	14
London Caledonians	18	5	3	10	19	40	13
West Norwood	18	5	2	11	28	54	12
Shepherd's Bush	18	2	3	13	23	55	7

1910-11

Clapton	18	11	4	3	39	19	26
Leytonstone	18	12	1	5	47	30	25
Dulwich Hamlet	18	8	5	5	28	22	21
Oxford City	18	7	4	7	32	43	18
Ilford	18	8	1	9	41	32	17
Shepherd's Bush	18	7	3	8	31	27	17
Bromley	18	8	4	6	32	27	16
Nunhead	18	5	4	9	32	36	14
West Norwood	18	4	5	9	24	43	13
London Caledonians	18	3	3	12	18	45	9

Bromley had 4 points deducted

1911-12

London Caledonians	20	11	7	2	39	25	29
Ilford	20	11	3	6	37	24	25
Nunhead	20	10	5	5	36	30	25
Dulwich Hamlet	20	8	5	7	33	23	21
West Norwood	20	9	3	8	38	38	21
Clapton	20	7	5	8	37	37	19
Woking	20	7	5	8	38	41	19
Shepherd's Bush	20	5	6	9	39	49	16
Leytonstone	20	5	6	9	28	38	16
Oxford City	20	5	5	10	33	36	15
Tunbridge Wells	20	5	4	11	23	40	14

1912-13

London Caledonians	20	14	5	1	38	12	33
Leytonstone	20	12	3	5	45	20	27
Nunhead	20	12	3	5	36	23	27
Clapton	20	7	7	6	23	20	21
Dulwich Hamlet	20	8	4	8	34	28	20
Woking	20	7	5	8	33	40	19
Oxford City	20	6	6	8	23	39	18
Ilford	20	6	5	9	27	37	17
Shepherd's Bush	20	5	5	10	26	38	15
Tunbridge Wells	20	5	4	11	22	36	14
West Norwood	20	3	3	14	23	37	9

1913-14

London Caledonians	20	12	6	2	55	23	30
Nunhead	20	11	6	3	49	27	28
Ilford	20	11	4	5	52	35	26
Dulwich Hamlet	20	10	4	6	34	22	24
New Crusaders	20	10	3	7	40	30	23
Oxford City	20	10	0	10	42	42	20
Leytonstone	20	8	4	8	29	32	20
Clapton	20	8	3	9	29	27	19
Shepherd's Bush	20	7	2	11	24	46	16
West Norwood	20	4	3	13	27	47	11
Woking	20	1	1	18	11	61	3

1919

Leytonstone	8	5	1	2	21	7	11
Ilford	8	4	2	2	22	16	10
Dulwich Hamlet	8	3	2	3	19	17	8
Nunhead	8	3	2	3	18	19	8
Clapton	8	0	3	5	14	35	3

1919-20

Dulwich Hamlet	22	15	3	4	58	16	33
Nunhead	22	14	5	3	48	26	33
Tufnell Park	22	12	4	6	45	32	28
Ilford	22	13	1	8	63	42	27
Oxford City	22	12	3	7	63	51	27
London Caledonians	22	10	3	9	32	30	23
Leytonstone	22	8	3	11	50	43	19
Clapton	22	8	3	11	38	44	19
Civil Service	22	7	4	11	35	40	18
Woking	22	6	3	13	36	42	15
West Norwood	22	5	4	13	19	53	14
Casuals	22	3	2	17	20	88	8

1920-21

Ilford	22	16	4	2	70	24	36
London Caledonians	22	13	5	4	45	17	31
Tufnell Park	22	14	3	5	43	24	31
Nunhead	22	12	5	5	53	33	29
Dulwich Hamlet	22	11	6	5	60	30	28
Oxford City	22	12	3	7	56	38	27
Leytonstone	22	8	6	8	36	29	22
Clapton	22	7	7	8	33	52	21
Civil Service	22	3	7	12	28	45	13
Woking	22	3	5	14	16	43	11
Casuals	22	3	3	16	31	87	9
West Norwood	22	2	2	18	18	67	6

1921-22

Ilford	26	17	4	5	66	34	38
Dulwich Hamlet	26	14	8	4	65	24	36
London Caledonians	26	16	4	6	41	21	36
Nunhead	26	12	5	9	65	41	29
Clapton	26	13	3	10	51	46	29
Tufnell Park	26	10	7	9	44	39	27
Oxford City	26	18	2	12	48	47	26
Wycombe Wanderers	26	18	2	12	61	64	26
Civil Service	26	9	8	9	60	48	26
Woking	26	10	6	10	39	49	26
Leytonstone	26	9	6	11	41	48	24
West Norwood	26	8	5	13	43	57	21
Wimbledon	26	7	4	15	52	56	18
Casuals	26	0	2	24	25	107	2

1922-23

Clapton	26	15	7	4	51	33	37
Nunhead	26	15	5	6	52	32	35
London Caledonians	26	13	7	6	43	26	33
Ilford	26	11	7	8	57	38	29
Casuals	26	12	5	9	68	51	29
Civil Service	26	9	10	7	39	36	28
Wycombe Wanderers	26	11	4	11	61	61	26
Dulwich Hamlet	26	9	7	10	60	44	25
Leytonstone	26	9	7	10	45	56	25
Tufnell Park	26	9	5	12	41	45	23
Wimbledon	26	10	2	14	49	50	22
Woking	26	7	6	13	42	67	20
Oxford City	26	6	5	15	45	68	17
West Norwood	26	5	5	16	25	71	15

1923-24

St Albans City	26	17	5	4	72	38	39
Dulwich Hamlet	26	15	6	5	49	28	36
Clapton	26	14	5	7	73	50	33
Wycombe Wanderers	26	14	5	7	88	65	33
London Caledonians	26	14	3	9	53	49	31
Civil Service	26	12	5	9	52	47	29
Casuals	26	13	1	12	65	54	27
Ilford	26	9	6	11	56	59	24
Nunhead	26	8	8	10	41	46	24
Wimbledon	26	8	4	14	43	62	20
Tufnell Park	26	8	2	16	38	53	18
Woking	26	5	8	13	31	62	18
Oxford City	26	7	2	17	53	74	16
Leytonstone	26	6	4	16	41	68	16

1924-25

London Caledonians	26	18	5	3	76	36	41
Clapton	26	19	1	6	64	34	39
St Albans City	26	16	2	8	69	39	34
Tufnell Park	26	11	4	11	47	41	26
Ilford	26	11	4	11	46	42	26
Leytonstone	26	12	2	12	55	63	26
The Casuals	26	12	1	13	55	58	25
Wycombe Wanderers	26	11	2	13	58	61	24
Civil Service	26	10	4	12	52	64	24
Nunhead	26	9	5	12	45	43	23
Wimbledon	26	10	2	14	50	54	22
Dulwich Hamlet	26	8	5	13	42	57	21
Oxford City	26	9	2	15	38	71	20
Woking	26	5	3	18	33	67	13

1925-26

Dulwich Hamlet	26	20	1	5	80	49	41
London Caledonians	26	18	1	7	81	44	37
Clapton	26	14	4	8	64	50	32
Wycombe Wanderers	26	14	3	9	97	83	31
St Albans City	26	12	6	8	76	54	30
Nunhead	26	13	4	9	49	43	30
Ilford	26	13	2	11	81	70	28
Leytonstone	26	12	1	13	75	63	25
Woking	26	8	6	12	56	73	22
Tufnell Park	26	8	5	13	36	53	21
The Casuals	26	8	4	14	48	61	20
Wimbledon	26	9	1	16	61	77	19
Oxford City	26	8	1	17	48	76	17
Civil Service	26	5	1	20	43	99	11

1926-27

St Albans City	26	20	1	5	96	34	41
Ilford	26	18	0	9	76	57	34
Wimbledon	26	15	3	8	72	45	33
Nunhead	26	11	8	7	51	33	30
Woking	26	12	6	8	68	60	30
London Caledonians	26	11	7	8	58	47	29
Clapton	26	11	4	11	58	60	26
Leytonstone	26	11	1	14	54	78	23
Dulwich Hamlet	26	9	4	13	60	58	22
Wycombe Wanderers	26	10	2	14	59	86	22
Tufnell Park	26	8	4	14	45	55	20
Oxford City	26	7	5	14	46	72	19
The Casuals	26	8	3	15	37	78	19
Civil Service	26	6	4	16	48	65	16

1927-28

St Albans City	26	15	5	6	86	50	35
London Caledonians	26	12	9	5	63	38	33
Ilford	26	14	4	8	72	54	32
Woking	26	13	5	8	72	56	31
Nunhead	26	13	2	11	57	54	28
Wimbledon	26	12	3	11	57	48	27
Leytonstone	26	13	1	12	53	56	27
Clapton	26	8	10	8	52	47	26
Dulwich Hamlet	26	8	9	9	56	49	25
The Casuals	26	8	8	10	54	58	24
Wycombe Wanderers	26	9	5	12	60	69	23
Oxford City	26	7	7	12	36	57	21
Civil Service	26	8	4	14	38	76	20
Tufnell Park	26	4	4	18	38	82	12

1928-29

Nunhead	26	15	6	5	47	35	36
London Caledonians	26	15	4	7	65	33	34
Dulwich Hamlet	26	14	6	6	65	34	34
Wimbledon	26	9	10	7	66	54	28
Ilford	26	12	3	11	67	52	27
Clapton	26	11	5	10	60	53	27
Tufnell Park	26	11	5	10	58	55	27
St Albans City	26	12	3	11	63	69	27
Leytonstone	26	11	3	12	56	79	25
Wycombe Wanderers	26	10	3	13	58	60	23
Oxford City	26	10	3	13	61	71	23
The Casuals	26	8	5	13	49	60	21
Woking	26	8	3	15	39	65	19
Civil Service	26	4	5	17	39	71	13

1929-30

Nunhead	26	19	3	4	69	36	41
Dulwich Hamlet	26	15	6	5	74	39	36
Kingstonian	26	15	4	7	57	37	34
Ilford	26	16	1	9	84	60	33
Woking	26	11	5	10	66	65	27
Wimbledon	26	11	2	13	64	66	24
Wycombe Wanderers	26	10	4	12	49	52	24
The Casuals	26	8	7	11	50	51	23
Oxford City	26	10	3	13	45	60	23
St Albans City	26	9	4	13	54	77	22
Clapton	26	8	4	14	47	57	20
London Caledonians	26	8	3	15	49	69	19
Leytonstone	26	8	3	15	48	68	19
Tufnell Park	26	6	7	13	35	54	19

1930-31

Wimbledon	26	18	6	2	69	37	42
Dulwich Hamlet	26	12	9	5	51	39	33
Wycombe Wanderers	26	12	6	8	67	45	30
The Casuals	26	12	6	8	71	56	30
St Albans City	26	11	7	8	67	66	29
Ilford	26	10	6	10	70	62	26
Oxford City	26	10	5	11	43	48	25
London Caledonians	26	8	8	10	43	53	24
Kingstonian	26	10	4	12	49	64	24
Tufnell Park	26	9	5	12	45	61	23
Nunhead	26	9	4	13	49	54	22
Woking	26	9	4	13	56	63	22
Clapton	26	7	4	15	62	75	18
Leytonstone	26	6	4	16	46	65	16

1931-32

Wimbledon	26	17	2	7	60	35	36
Ilford	26	13	9	4	71	45	35
Dulwich Hamlet	26	15	3	8	69	43	33
Wycombe Wanderers	26	14	5	7	72	50	33
Oxford City	26	15	2	9	63	49	32
Kingstonian	26	13	3	10	71	50	29
Tufnell Park	26	9	7	10	50	48	25
Nunhead	26	9	7	10	54	61	25
The Casuals	26	10	4	12	59	65	24
Clapton	26	9	5	12	50	57	23
Leytonstone	26	9	3	14	36	61	21
St Albans City	26	8	4	14	57	78	20
Woking	26	6	5	15	44	64	17
London Caledonians	26	2	7	17	24	74	11

1932-33

Dulwich Hamlet	26	15	6	5	71	45	36
Leytonstone	26	16	4	6	66	43	36
Kingstonian	26	15	2	9	77	49	32
Ilford	26	14	0	12	60	58	28
The Casuals	26	12	2	12	48	36	26
Tufnell Park	26	11	3	12	51	51	25
St Albans City	26	12	1	13	57	63	25
Clapton	26	10	5	11	51	65	25
Oxford City	26	9	6	11	49	54	24
Woking	26	10	4	12	53	61	24
Wycombe Wanderers	26	10	4	12	47	56	24
Nunhead	26	8	6	12	42	50	22
Wimbledon	26	8	5	13	55	67	21
London Caledonians	26	5	6	15	35	64	16

1933-34

Kingstonian	26	15	7	4	80	42	37
Dulwich Hamlet	26	15	5	6	68	36	35
Wimbledon	26	13	7	6	62	35	33
Tufnell Park	26	14	5	7	55	50	33
Ilford	26	15	2	9	60	56	32
The Casuals	26	13	5	8	47	32	31
Leytonstone	26	13	3	10	55	48	29
Nunhead	26	10	5	11	48	44	25
London Caledonians	26	7	8	11	29	51	22
Wycombe Wanderers	26	9	2	15	57	60	20
St Albans City	26	8	4	14	44	75	20
Oxford City	26	7	4	15	45	57	18
Clapton	26	5	6	15	35	62	16
Woking	26	6	1	19	43	81	13

1934-35

Wimbledon	26	14	7	5	63	30	35
Oxford City	26	14	4	8	69	50	32
Leytonstone	26	15	2	9	49	36	32
Dulwich Hamlet	26	11	7	8	66	45	29
Tufnell Park	26	11	7	8	53	44	29
Kingstonian	26	11	6	9	44	40	28
Nunhead	26	10	7	9	35	34	27
London Caledonians	26	9	7	10	40	41	25
St Albans City	26	9	6	11	61	80	24
Ilford	26	9	6	11	40	56	24
Clapton	26	7	7	12	46	48	21
Woking	26	9	3	14	44	68	21
Wycombe Wanderers	26	7	6	13	51	69	20
The Casuals	26	6	5	15	37	57	17

1935-36

Wimbledon	26	19	2	5	82	29	40
The Casuals	26	14	5	7	60	45	33
Ilford	26	13	3	10	67	47	29
Dulwich Hamlet	26	10	8	8	64	47	28
Nunhead	26	11	6	9	51	40	28
Wycombe Wanderers	26	13	2	11	60	68	28
Clapton	26	11	5	10	42	46	27
Oxford City	26	11	4	11	60	58	26
St Albans City	26	11	2	13	59	64	24
Woking	26	9	4	13	43	62	22
Tufnell Park	26	9	3	14	42	61	21
London Caledonians	26	9	3	14	35	52	21
Kingstonian	26	9	2	15	43	56	20
Leytonstone	26	7	3	16	34	67	17

1936-37

Kingstonian	26	18	3	5	63	43	39
Nunhead	26	17	3	6	77	32	37
Leytonstone	26	16	4	6	71	42	36
Ilford	26	14	5	7	86	39	33
Dulwich Hamlet	26	12	6	8	64	48	30
Wycombe Wanderers	26	10	5	11	55	52	25
Wimbledon	26	9	7	10	52	53	25
Clapton	26	10	5	11	42	51	25
The Casuals	26	10	3	13	46	58	23
Woking	26	9	4	13	53	69	22
Oxford City	26	8	5	13	56	89	21
St Albans City	26	7	5	14	44	62	19
Tufnell Park	26	4	7	15	43	74	15
London Caledonians	26	5	4	17	26	66	14

1937-38

Leytonstone	26	17	6	3	72	34	40
Ilford	26	17	3	6	70	39	37
Tufnell Park	26	15	2	9	62	47	32
Nunhead	26	14	3	9	52	44	31
Wycombe Wanderers	26	12	5	9	69	55	29
Dulwich Hamlet	26	13	3	10	57	46	29
Kingstonian	26	12	4	10	51	48	28
Clapton	26	9	6	11	49	53	24
Wimbledon	26	10	3	13	62	49	23
London Caledonians	26	9	4	13	44	55	22
Oxford City	26	7	7	12	35	71	21
The Casuals	26	8	3	15	51	74	19
Woking	26	7	2	17	41	72	16
St Albans City	26	4	5	17	31	60	13

1938-39

Leytonstone	26	18	4	4	68	32	40
Ilford	26	17	4	5	68	32	38
Kingstonian	26	17	3	6	62	39	37
Dulwich Hamlet	26	15	5	6	60	32	35
Wimbledon	26	14	3	9	88	56	31
Nunhead	26	11	6	9	54	44	28
The Casuals	26	11	6	9	54	51	28
Clapton	26	12	2	12	69	61	26
Wycombe Wanderers	26	10	6	10	62	62	26
St Albans City	26	8	5	13	44	50	21
Woking	26	9	2	15	35	56	20
Oxford City	26	4	4	18	44	84	12
Tufnell Park	26	4	4	18	33	87	12
London Caledonians	26	3	4	19	26	81	10

1945-46

Walthamstow Avenue	26	21	0	5	100	31	42
Oxford City	26	17	6	3	91	40	40
Romford	26	15	3	8	83	59	33
Dulwich Hamlet	26	14	2	10	63	59	30
Tufnell Park	26	12	4	10	70	55	28
Woking	26	10	7	9	56	54	27
Ilford	26	12	2	12	56	71	26
Leytonstone	26	11	3	12	61	75	25
Wycombe Wanderers	26	9	3	14	80	88	21
Wimbledon	26	7	6	13	52	72	20
Corinthian Casuals	26	8	4	14	58	83	20
Clapton	26	8	3	15	51	62	19
St Albans City	26	6	6	14	48	85	18
Kingstonian	26	6	3	17	48	86	15

1946-47

Leytonstone	26	19	2	5	92	36	40
Dulwich Hamlet	26	17	3	6	78	46	37
Romford	26	13	8	5	76	52	34
Walthamstow Avenue	26	13	4	9	64	37	30
Oxford City	26	12	6	8	70	51	30
Kingstonian	26	12	4	10	54	57	28
Wycombe Wanderers	26	9	8	9	62	62	26
Wimbledon	26	10	5	11	68	64	25
Ilford	26	7	7	12	66	78	21
Tufnell Park	26	8	5	13	45	69	21
Woking	26	7	7	12	34	62	21
Clapton	26	6	8	12	41	59	20
St Albans City	26	7	5	14	47	79	19
Corinthian Casuals	26	4	4	18	36	80	12

1947-48

Leytonstone	26	19	1	6	87	38	39
Kingstonian	26	16	6	4	74	39	38
Walthamstow Avenue	26	17	3	6	61	37	37
Dulwich Hamlet	26	17	2	7	71	39	36
Wimbledon	26	13	6	7	66	40	32
Romford	26	14	1	11	53	47	29
Oxford City	26	10	5	11	50	68	25
Woking	26	10	3	13	63	55	23
Ilford	26	7	8	11	51	59	22
St Albans City	26	9	2	15	43	56	20
Wycombe Wanderers	26	7	5	14	51	65	19
Tufnell Park	26	7	4	15	38	83	18
Clapton	26	5	4	17	35	69	14
Corinthian Casuals	26	5	2	19	33	81	12

1948-49

Dulwich Hamlet	26	15	6	5	60	31	36
Walthamstow Avenue	26	16	4	6	65	38	36
Wimbledon	26	15	4	7	64	41	34
Ilford	26	14	3	9	56	36	31
Oxford City	26	13	5	8	48	34	31
Leytonstone	26	12	6	8	49	41	30
Woking	26	14	1	11	64	59	29
Romford	26	11	3	12	47	54	25
Kingstonian	26	10	4	12	43	47	24
Corinthian Casuals	26	11	2	13	47	59	24
Wycombe Wanderers	26	11	2	13	49	61	24
St Albans City	26	6	6	14	40	60	16
Clapton	26	5	5	16	32	61	15
Tufnell Park	26	1	5	20	28	70	7

St Albans City had 2 points deducted

1949-50

Leytonstone	26	17	5	4	77	31	39
Wimbledon	26	18	2	6	72	51	38
Kingstonian	26	16	3	7	59	39	35
Walthamstow Avenue	26	14	6	6	73	42	34
Dulwich Hamlet	26	14	3	9	60	47	31
St Albans City	26	12	3	11	59	45	27
Woking	26	10	6	10	60	71	26
Wycombe Wanderers	26	9	7	10	51	52	25
Romford	26	10	4	12	45	49	24
Ilford	26	10	4	12	46	53	24
Clapton	26	8	6	12	51	59	22
Oxford City	26	6	6	14	35	54	18
Corinthian Casuals	26	4	5	17	41	69	13
Tufnell Park	26	3	2	21	24	91	8

1950-51

Leytonstone	26	20	3	3	72	26	43
Walthamstow Avenue	26	15	4	7	57	37	34
Romford	26	15	3	8	58	49	33
Wimbledon	26	13	5	8	58	39	31
Dulwich Hamlet	26	14	2	10	54	43	30
Woking	26	11	6	9	65	55	28
Ilford	26	12	4	10	44	45	28
Corinthian Casuals	26	13	0	13	62	60	26
St Albans City	26	11	4	11	32	36	26
Kingstonian	26	9	4	13	46	54	22
Wycombe Wanderers	26	8	3	15	46	64	19
Oxford City	26	7	4	15	47	65	18
Clapton	26	6	5	15	29	50	17
Tufnell Park Edmonton	26	4	1	21	24	73	9

1951-52

Leytonstone	26	13	9	4	63	36	35
Wimbledon	26	16	3	7	65	44	35
Walthamstow Avenue	26	15	4	7	71	43	34
Romford	26	14	4	8	64	42	32
Kingstonian	26	11	7	8	62	48	29
Wycombe Wanderers	26	12	5	9	64	59	29
Woking	26	11	5	10	60	71	27
Dulwich Hamlet	26	11	4	11	60	53	26
Corinthian Casuals	26	11	4	11	55	66	26
St Albans City	26	9	7	10	48	53	25
Ilford	26	8	5	13	32	47	21
Clapton	26	9	2	15	50	59	20
Oxford City	26	6	3	17	50	72	15
Tufnell Park Edmonton	26	2	6	18	25	73	10

1952-53

Walthamstow Avenue	28	19	6	3	53	25	44
Bromley	28	17	4	7	71	35	38
Leytonstone	28	14	6	8	60	38	34
Wimbledon	28	14	5	9	68	37	33
Kingstonian	28	13	6	9	62	50	32
Dulwich Hamlet	28	15	2	11	62	52	32
Romford	28	12	8	8	62	52	32
Wycombe Wanderers	28	14	2	12	54	62	30
St Albans City	28	11	6	11	43	57	28
Barking	28	9	7	12	42	51	25
Ilford	28	10	4	14	59	57	24
Woking	28	10	4	14	57	72	24
Corinthian Casuals	28	7	9	12	45	56	23
Oxford City	28	5	2	21	37	87	12
Clapton	28	2	5	21	27	71	9

1953-54

Bromley	28	18	3	7	76	45	39
Walthamstow Avenue	28	13	7	8	55	30	33
Wycombe Wanderers	28	15	3	10	65	44	33
Ilford	28	11	10	7	48	44	32
Corinthian Casuals	28	12	7	9	59	44	31
Woking	28	13	4	11	54	58	30
Leytonstone	28	12	5	11	58	48	29
St Albans City	28	11	6	11	54	55	28
Dulwich Hamlet	28	11	6	11	55	57	28
Romford	28	11	5	12	57	54	27
Clapton	28	11	5	12	42	56	27
Barking	28	11	2	15	59	84	24
Kingstonian	28	8	7	13	59	71	23
Wimbledon	28	7	8	13	43	59	22
Oxford City	28	4	6	18	49	84	14

1954-55

Walthamstow Avenue	28	21	1	6	80	38	43
St Albans City	28	18	3	7	61	41	39
Bromley	28	18	2	8	66	34	38
Wycombe Wanderers	28	16	3	9	68	43	35
Ilford	28	13	5	10	61	46	31
Barking	28	15	1	12	55	51	31
Woking	28	12	3	13	75	79	27
Kingstonian	28	10	7	11	47	57	27
Leytonstone	28	10	4	14	35	51	24
Oxford City	28	10	3	15	43	74	23
Clapton	28	9	4	15	41	50	22
Wimbledon	28	10	2	16	48	62	22
Corinthian Casuals	28	9	3	16	50	65	21
Dulwich Hamlet	28	7	5	16	48	60	19
Romford	28	4	10	14	43	73	18

1955-56

Wycombe Wanderers	28	19	5	4	82	36	43
Bromley	28	12	7	9	54	43	31
Leytonstone	28	12	7	9	50	44	31
Woking	28	14	3	11	62	60	31
Barking	28	12	7	9	41	45	31
Kingstonian	28	12	6	10	67	64	30
Walthamstow Avenue	28	13	3	12	61	45	29
Ilford	28	10	8	10	44	52	28
Oxford City	28	10	7	11	48	55	27
Clapton	28	9	8	11	45	48	26
Wimbledon	28	12	2	14	51	62	26
Corinthian Casuals	28	9	7	12	56	56	25
Dulwich Hamlet	28	9	6	13	55	67	24
Romford	28	9	6	13	42	55	24
St Albans City	28	2	10	16	36	62	14

1956-57

Wycombe Wanderers	30	18	6	6	86	53	42
Woking	30	20	1	9	104	47	41
Bromley	30	16	5	9	78	60	37
Oxford City	30	16	3	11	65	57	35
Ilford	30	12	8	10	59	65	32
Tooting & Mitcham United	30	10	11	9	53	48	31
Kingstonian	30	11	9	10	72	77	31
Walthamstow Avenue	30	11	8	11	48	46	30
Dulwich Hamlet	30	13	3	14	65	54	29
St Albans City	30	13	3	14	62	71	29
Leytonstone	30	11	6	13	50	50	28
Clapton	30	9	9	12	48	59	27
Wimbledon	30	10	5	15	47	66	25
Romford	30	10	5	15	53	81	25
Barking	30	7	6	17	48	72	20
Corinthian Casuals	30	7	4	19	46	78	18

1957-58

Tooting & Mitcham United	30	20	6	4	79	33	46
Wycombe Wanderers	30	19	4	7	78	42	42
Walthamstow Avenue	30	17	5	8	63	35	39
Bromley	30	13	9	8	66	51	35
Oxford City	30	13	6	11	59	48	32
Leytonstone	30	13	6	11	49	48	32
Wimbledon	30	15	2	13	64	66	32
Corinthian Casuals	30	12	8	10	62	68	32
Woking	30	12	7	11	70	58	31
Barking	30	10	6	14	49	61	26
St Albans City	30	11	3	16	56	76	25
Clapton	30	8	9	13	42	65	25
Kingstonian	30	7	8	15	45	66	22
Dulwich Hamlet	30	7	7	16	49	64	21
Ilford	30	8	4	18	46	70	20
Romford	30	6	8	16	45	71	20

1958-59

Wimbledon	30	22	3	5	91	38	47
Dulwich Hamlet	30	18	5	7	68	44	41
Wycombe Wanderers	30	18	4	8	93	50	40
Oxford City	30	17	4	9	87	58	38
Walthamstow Avenue	30	16	5	9	59	40	37
Tooting & Mitcham United	30	15	4	11	84	55	34
Barking	30	14	2	14	59	53	30
Woking	30	12	6	12	66	66	30
Bromley	30	11	7	12	56	55	29
Clapton	30	10	6	14	55	67	26
Ilford	30	10	6	14	46	67	26
Kingstonian	30	9	4	17	54	72	22
St Albans City	30	8	6	16	53	89	22
Leytonstone	30	7	6	17	40	87	20
Romford	30	7	5	18	54	76	19
Corinthian Casuals	30	7	5	18	44	92	19

1959-60

Tooting & Mitcham United	30	17	8	5	75	43	42
Wycombe Wanderers	30	19	3	8	84	46	41
Wimbledon	30	18	3	9	66	36	39
Kingstonian	30	18	3	9	76	51	39
Corinthian Casuals	30	18	1	11	69	61	37
Bromley	30	15	6	9	75	46	36
Dulwich Hamlet	30	14	6	10	65	47	34
Walthamstow Avenue	30	11	11	8	48	38	33
Oxford City	30	10	10	10	57	57	30
Leytonstone	30	10	8	12	43	46	28
Woking	30	10	6	14	54	61	26
St Albans City	30	10	6	14	50	65	26
Maidstone United	30	10	5	15	53	60	25
Barking	30	7	4	19	30	75	18
Ilford	30	5	6	19	34	86	16
Clapton	30	3	4	23	32	92	10

1960-61

Bromley	30	20	6	4	89	42	46
Walthamstow Avenue	30	20	5	5	87	38	45
Wimbledon	30	18	6	6	72	43	42
Dulwich Hamlet	30	17	4	9	71	59	35
Maidstone United	30	14	8	8	63	39	36
Leytonstone	30	15	6	9	46	34	36
Tooting & Mitcham United	30	14	3	13	69	51	31
Wycombe Wanderers	30	12	5	13	63	61	29
St Albans City	30	12	4	14	45	72	28
Oxford City	30	10	7	13	59	59	27
Corinthian Casuals	30	9	9	12	49	59	27
Kingstonian	30	10	6	14	55	61	26
Woking	30	10	6	14	58	71	26
Ilford	30	5	8	17	30	69	18
Barking	30	3	8	19	30	76	14
Clapton	30	3	5	22	25	77	11

1961-62

Wimbledon	30	19	6	5	68	24	44
Leytonstone	30	17	7	6	61	44	41
Walthamstow Avenue	30	14	8	8	51	31	36
Kingstonian	30	15	5	10	65	48	35
Tooting & Mitcham United	30	12	10	8	62	47	34
Oxford City	30	12	9	9	56	49	33
Wycombe Wanderers	30	12	7	11	57	51	31
Corinthian Casuals	30	12	7	11	45	51	31
St Albans City	30	10	9	11	55	55	29
Woking	30	9	9	12	51	60	27
Dulwich Hamlet	30	11	4	15	55	66	26
Barking	30	9	8	13	40	64	26
Ilford	30	7	10	13	50	59	24
Bromley	30	10	4	16	49	69	24
Clapton	30	6	8	16	45	67	20
Maidstone United	30	6	7	17	34	59	19

1962-63

Wimbledon	30	19	8	3	84	33	46
Kingstonian	30	18	8	4	79	37	44
Tooting & Mitcham United	30	17	8	5	65	37	42
Ilford	30	19	3	8	70	44	41
Walthamstow Avenue	30	14	7	9	51	44	35
Maidstone United	30	13	8	9	56	45	34
Bromley	30	12	10	8	57	51	34
Leytonstone	30	12	7	11	48	50	31
Wycombe Wanderers	30	10	10	10	56	61	30
St Albans City	30	11	5	14	54	49	27
Barking	30	8	10	12	39	50	26
Oxford City	30	8	9	13	55	64	25
Woking	30	8	6	16	42	66	22
Clapton	30	7	4	19	30	71	18
Dulwich Hamlet	30	4	5	21	30	71	13
Corinthian Casuals	30	4	4	22	28	71	12

1963-64

Wimbledon	38	27	6	5	87	44	60
Hendon	38	25	4	9	124	38	54
Kingstonian	38	24	4	10	100	62	52
Sutton United	38	23	5	10	99	64	51
Enfield	38	20	10	8	96	56	50
Oxford City	38	20	8	10	90	55	48
Tooting & Mitcham United	38	19	8	11	78	51	46
St Albans City	38	14	12	12	62	63	40
Ilford	38	16	8	14	75	79	40
Maidstone United	38	15	8	15	65	71	38
Walthamstow Avenue	38	15	6	17	70	66	36
Leytonstone	38	14	8	16	66	71	36
Wycombe Wanderers	38	13	6	19	74	80	32
Hitchin Town	38	14	4	20	67	100	32
Bromley	38	11	8	19	64	75	30
Barking	38	10	9	19	46	69	29
Woking	38	10	9	19	48	88	29
Corinthian Casuals	38	10	4	24	52	92	24
Dulwich Hamlet	38	6	12	20	47	97	24
Clapton	38	2	5	31	31	120	9

1964-65

Hendon	38	28	7	3	123	49	63
Enfield	38	29	5	4	98	35	63
Kingstonian	38	24	8	6	86	44	56
Leytonstone	38	24	5	9	115	62	53
Oxford City	38	20	7	11	76	51	47
St Albans City	38	18	9	11	63	43	45
Sutton United	38	17	11	10	74	57	45
Wealdstone	38	19	6	13	93	68	44
Bromley	38	14	11	13	71	80	39
Tooting & Mitcham United	38	15	7	16	71	66	37
Hitchin Town	38	13	9	16	61	66	35
Walthamstow Avenue	38	15	5	18	63	82	35
Wycombe Wanderers	38	13	7	18	70	85	33
Corinthian Casuals	38	13	7	18	56	77	33
Barking	38	10	8	20	58	80	28
Ilford	38	8	8	22	43	89	24
Maidstone United	38	8	6	24	49	86	22
Dulwich Hamlet	38	8	5	25	45	79	21
Clapton	38	8	3	27	43	91	19
Woking	38	7	4	27	45	113	18

Hendon beat Enfield in a play-off to decide the Championship

1965-66

Leytonstone	38	27	7	4	98	33	63
Hendon	38	27	5	6	111	55	59
Enfield	38	24	8	6	104	54	56
Wycombe Wanderers	38	25	6	7	100	65	56
Kingstonian	38	24	5	9	94	55	53
Wealdstone	38	20	6	12	90	64	46
Maidstone United	38	19	6	13	74	61	44
St Albans City	38	19	5	14	57	56	43
Sutton United	38	17	7	14	83	72	41
Tooting & Mitcham United	38	16	7	15	65	58	39
Corinthian Casuals	38	17	5	16	74	67	39
Woking	38	12	10	16	60	83	34
Walthamstow Avenue	38	12	9	17	81	75	33
Oxford City	38	10	9	19	49	72	29
Barking	38	10	7	21	51	72	27
Bromley	38	10	5	23	69	101	25
Ilford	38	7	10	21	50	84	24
Hitchin Town	38	6	8	24	57	118	20
Clapton	38	5	6	27	46	103	16
Dulwich Hamlet	38	5	5	28	30	95	15

1966-67

Sutton United	38	26	7	5	89	33	59
Walthamstow Avenue	38	22	12	4	89	47	56
Wycombe Wanderers	38	23	8	7	92	54	54
Enfield	38	25	2	11	87	33	52
Hendon	38	20	9	9	64	37	49
Tooting & Mitcham United	38	19	10	9	76	60	48
Leytonstone	38	19	9	10	67	38	47
St Albans City	38	16	12	10	59	45	44
Kingstonian	38	18	8	12	60	49	44
Oxford City	38	15	9	14	74	61	39
Woking	38	13	10	15	65	71	36
Wealdstone	38	13	8	17	72	73	34
Barking	38	11	12	15	56	61	34
Bromley	38	12	7	19	50	67	31
Clapton	38	10	8	20	49	92	28
Ilford	38	8	10	20	43	77	26
Corinthian Casuals	38	9	7	22	45	68	25
Maidstone United	38	6	10	22	43	90	22
Hitchin Town	38	8	6	24	39	89	22
Dulwich Hamlet	38	3	4	31	33	107	10

1967-68

Enfield	38	28	8	2	85	22	64
Sutton United	38	22	11	5	89	27	55
Hendon	38	23	6	9	90	36	52
Leytonstone	38	21	10	7	78	41	52
St Albans City	38	20	8	10	78	41	48
Walthamstow Avenue	38	19	9	10	81	64	47
Wealdstone	38	19	8	11	80	45	46
Tooting & Mitcham United	38	19	5	14	57	45	43
Barking	38	17	8	13	75	57	42
Oxford City	38	17	4	17	59	58	38
Kingstonian	38	14	10	14	56	61	38
Hitchin Town	38	14	9	15	61	73	37
Bromley	38	12	10	16	58	80	34
Wycombe Wanderers	38	13	5	20	73	85	31
Dulwich Hamlet	38	10	7	21	39	66	27
Clapton	38	10	7	21	51	88	27
Woking	38	8	8	22	50	90	24
Corinthian Casuals	38	7	10	21	40	80	24
Ilford	38	7	7	24	41	77	21
Maidstone United	38	3	4	31	26	131	10

1968-69

Enfield	38	27	7	4	103	28	61
Hitchin Town	38	23	10	5	67	41	56
Sutton United	38	22	9	7	83	29	53
Wycombe Wanderers	38	23	6	9	70	37	52
Wealdstone	38	20	11	7	73	48	51
Hendon	38	22	5	11	69	47	49
St Albans City	38	17	13	8	75	44	47
Barking	38	20	7	11	69	46	47
Oxford City	38	18	8	12	76	64	44
Tooting & Mitcham United	38	16	10	12	68	55	42
Leytonstone	38	18	4	16	71	53	40
Kingstonian	38	15	8	15	62	56	38
Walthamstow Avenue	38	10	10	18	47	71	30
Maidstone United	38	10	8	20	47	75	28
Clapton	38	10	7	21	52	76	27
Woking	38	8	7	23	45	77	23
Bromley	38	8	7	23	52	95	23
Dulwich Hamlet	38	6	9	23	31	77	21
Ilford	38	6	8	24	33	77	20
Corinthian Casuals	38	2	4	32	23	120	8

1969-70

Enfield	38	27	8	3	91	26	62
Wycombe Wanderers	38	25	11	2	85	24	61
Sutton United	38	24	9	5	75	35	57
Barking	38	21	9	8	93	47	51
Hendon	38	19	12	7	77	44	50
St Albans City	38	21	8	9	69	40	50
Hitchin Town	38	19	10	9	71	40	48
Tooting & Mitcham United	38	19	5	14	88	62	43
Leytonstone	38	17	7	14	57	41	41
Wealdstone	38	15	10	13	53	48	40
Oxford City	38	15	7	16	61	78	37
Kingstonian	38	13	9	16	55	57	35
Ilford	38	8	15	15	42	73	31
Dulwich Hamlet	38	8	12	18	46	66	28
Woking	38	10	7	21	46	69	27
Walthamstow Avenue	38	11	5	22	52	81	27
Clapton	38	9	7	22	45	87	25
Maidstone United	38	7	8	23	48	84	22
Corinthian Casuals	38	6	3	29	30	99	15
Bromley	38	3	4	31	28	111	10

1970-71

Wycombe Wanderers	38	28	6	4	93	32	62
Sutton United	38	29	3	6	76	35	61
St Albans City	38	23	10	5	87	26	56
Enfield	38	24	7	7	67	24	55
Ilford	38	21	7	10	74	51	49
Hendon	38	18	11	9	81	37	47
Barking	38	20	4	14	89	59	44
Leytonstone	38	17	10	11	68	50	44
Woking	38	18	6	14	57	50	42
Walthamstow Avenue	38	14	11	13	63	52	39
Oxford City	38	13	10	15	51	48	36
Hitchin Town	38	12	9	17	46	60	33
Wealdstone	38	12	8	18	45	64	32
Tooting & Mitcham United	38	11	9	18	44	66	31
Kingstonian	38	11	8	19	53	71	30
Bromley	38	10	6	22	34	77	26
Dulwich Hamlet	38	7	10	21	30	66	24
Maidstone United	38	7	6	25	42	84	20
Clapton	38	5	7	26	33	101	17
Corinthian Casuals	38	2	8	28	23	103	12

1971-72

Wycombe Wanderers	40	31	3	6	102	20	65
Enfield	40	26	8	6	90	41	60
Walton & Hersham	40	24	8	8	69	25	56
Hendon	40	23	10	7	79	35	56
Bishop's Stortford	40	24	5	11	61	37	53
Sutton United	40	21	10	9	77	43	52
St Albans City	40	23	4	13	74	47	50
Ilford	40	17	11	12	62	52	45
Barking	40	20	4	16	65	61	44
Hitchin Town	40	17	10	13	68	66	44
Bromley	40	16	10	14	67	64	42
Hayes	40	14	12	14	50	48	40
Oxford City	40	13	9	18	67	74	35
Woking	40	11	10	19	52	58	32
Kingstonian	40	10	12	18	49	59	32
Walthamstow Avenue	40	12	8	20	58	71	32
Leytonstone	40	11	8	21	48	68	30
Tooting & Mitcham United	40	6	9	25	38	93	21
Clapton	40	7	7	26	45	118	21
Dulwich Hamlet	40	4	12	24	35	81	20
Corinthian Casuals	40	3	4	33	21	116	10

1972-73

Hendon	42	34	6	2	88	18	74
Walton & Hersham	42	25	11	6	60	25	61
Leatherhead	42	23	10	9	76	32	56
Wycombe Wanderers	42	25	6	11	66	32	56
Walthamstow Avenue	42	20	12	10	66	48	52
Tooting & Mitcham United	42	20	11	11	73	39	51
Sutton United	42	21	9	12	69	48	51
Kingstonian	42	20	10	12	60	49	50
Enfield	42	20	8	14	90	54	48
Bishop's Stortford	42	18	12	12	58	51	48
Hayes	42	19	8	15	69	42	46
Dulwich Hamlet	42	18	9	15	59	52	45
Ilford	42	18	9	15	61	59	45
Leytonstone	42	17	11	14	55	54	45
Woking	42	18	8	16	61	56	44
Hitchin Town	42	15	9	18	52	64	39
Barking	42	8	7	27	45	88	23
St Albans City	42	5	12	25	34	76	22
Oxford City	42	6	7	29	30	101	19
Bromley	42	4	10	28	31	70	18
Clapton	42	3	11	28	31	100	17
Corinthian Casuals	42	3	8	31	30	106	14

1973-74

First Division

Wycombe Wanderers	42	27	9	6	96	34	90
Hendon	42	25	13	4	63	20	88
Bishop's Stortford	42	26	9	7	78	26	87
Dulwich Hamlet	42	22	11	9	71	38	77
Leatherhead	42	23	6	13	81	44	75
Walton & Hersham	42	20	12	10	68	50	72
Woking	42	22	6	14	63	55	72
Leytonstone	42	20	9	13	63	44	69
Ilford	42	20	8	14	60	44	68
Hayes	42	17	14	11	65	43	65
Oxford City	42	15	16	11	45	47	61
Sutton United	42	13	16	13	51	52	55
Hitchin Town	42	15	10	17	68	73	55
Barking	42	14	12	16	57	58	54
Kingstonian	42	12	15	15	47	46	51
Tooting & Mitcham United	42	14	9	19	57	62	51
Enfield	42	13	11	18	50	57	50
Walthamstow Avenue	42	11	13	18	46	62	46
Bromley	42	7	9	26	37	81	30
Clapton	42	8	3	31	36	128	27
St Albans City	42	4	7	31	30	92	19
Corinthian Casuals	42	3	4	35	31	107	13

Second Division

Dagenham	30	22	4	4	68	23	70
Slough Town	30	18	6	6	46	23	60
Hertford Town	30	17	5	8	46	29	56
Chesham Town	30	16	6	8	61	43	54
Aveley	30	16	5	9	50	28	53
Tilbury	30	14	5	11	47	36	47
Maidenhead United	30	12	11	7	36	30	47
Horsham	30	12	9	9	47	35	45
Harwich & Parkeston	30	11	9	10	46	41	42
Staines Town	30	10	8	12	34	41	38
Carshalton Athletic	30	8	8	14	34	51	32
Hampton	30	6	10	14	33	51	28
Harlow Town	30	6	9	15	33	48	27
Finchley	30	6	7	17	29	52	25
Southall	30	3	10	17	17	52	19
Wokingham Town	30	3	8	19	30	74	17

1974-75

First Division

Wycombe Wanderers	42	28	11	3	93	30	95
Enfield	42	29	8	5	78	26	95
Dagenham	42	28	5	9	95	44	89
Tooting & Mitcham United	42	25	9	8	78	46	84
Dulwich Hamlet	42	24	10	8	75	38	82
Leatherhead	42	23	10	9	83	42	79
Ilford	42	23	10	9	98	51	79
Oxford City	42	17	9	16	63	56	60
Slough Town	42	17	6	19	68	52	57
Sutton United	42	17	6	19	68	63	57
Bishop's Stortford	42	17	6	19	56	64	57
Hitchin Town	42	15	10	17	57	71	55
Hendon	42	15	7	20	59	74	52
Walthamstow Avenue	42	13	9	20	56	62	48
Woking	42	12	10	20	53	73	46
Hayes	42	10	14	18	52	66	44
Barking	42	12	8	22	57	81	44
Leytonstone	42	12	7	23	42	61	43
Kingstonian	42	13	4	25	48	73	43
Clapton	42	12	4	26	46	96	40
Walton & Hersham	42	9	4	29	37	108	31
Bromley	42	6	3	33	25	110	21

Second Division

Staines Town	34	23	2	9	65	23	71
Southall	34	20	3	11	55	41	63
Tilbury	34	19	5	10	64	36	60
Harwich & Parkeston	34	18	4	12	52	44	58
Chesham United	34	17	6	11	59	39	57
St Albans City	34	15	11	8	42	37	56
Harlow Town	34	16	6	12	53	47	54
Horsham	34	16	5	13	59	49	53
Maidenhead United	34	13	7	14	38	40	46
Hampton	34	12	7	15	44	42	43
Croydon	34	11	10	13	48	55	43
Hertford Town	34	10	7	17	35	52	37
Boreham Wood	34	7	15	12	41	49	36
Wokingham Town	34	10	6	18	32	43	36
Finchley	34	9	9	16	36	53	36
Carshalton Athletic	34	9	9	16	38	58	36
Aveley	34	9	7	18	34	63	34
Corinthian Casuals	34	8	9	17	35	59	33

Tilbury had 2 points deducted

1975-76

First Division

Enfield	42	26	9	7	83	38	87
Wycombe Wanderers	42	24	10	8	71	41	82
Dagenham	42	25	6	11	89	55	81
Ilford	42	22	10	10	58	39	76
Dulwich Hamlet	42	22	5	15	67	41	71
Hendon	42	20	11	11	60	41	71
Tooting & Mitcham United	42	19	11	12	73	49	68
Leatherhead	42	19	10	13	63	53	67
Staines Town	42	19	9	14	46	37	66
Slough Town	42	17	12	13	58	45	63
Sutton United	42	17	11	14	71	60	62
Bishop's Stortford	42	15	12	15	51	47	57
Walthamstow Avenue	42	14	11	17	47	60	53
Woking	42	14	9	19	58	62	51
Barking	42	15	6	21	57	70	51
Hitchin Town	42	13	11	18	45	57	50
Hayes	42	10	19	13	44	48	49
Kingstonian	42	13	8	21	53	87	47
Southall & Ealing Borough	42	11	9	22	56	69	42
Leytonstone	42	10	10	22	41	63	40
Oxford City	42	9	8	25	29	65	35
Clapton	42	3	3	36	19	112	12

Second Division

Tilbury	42	32	6	4	97	30	102
Croydon	42	28	14	0	81	27	98
Carshalton Athletic	42	28	6	8	75	37	90
Chesham United	42	21	12	9	91	51	75
Harwich & Parkeston	42	21	11	10	78	56	74
Hampton	42	21	9	12	72	52	72
St Albans City	42	18	12	12	59	48	66
Boreham Wood	42	17	12	13	68	50	63
Harrow Borough	42	15	12	15	71	74	57
Hornchurch	42	15	11	16	61	61	56
Horsham	42	14	13	15	60	55	55
Wembley	42	14	13	15	51	54	55
Wokingham Town	42	13	16	13	45	52	55
Walton & Hersham	42	14	12	16	61	56	54
Finchley	42	14	11	17	52	53	53
Bromley	42	11	11	20	64	86	44
Aveley	42	11	9	22	34	51	42
Harlow Town	42	11	9	22	50	73	42
Maidenhead United	42	6	17	19	32	65	35
Ware	42	7	12	23	50	95	33
Hertford Town	42	5	9	28	32	87	24
Corinthian Casuals	42	4	7	31	42	113	19

1976-77

First Division

Enfield	42	24	12	6	63	34	84
Wycombe Wanderers	42	25	8	9	71	34	83
Dagenham	42	23	10	9	80	39	79
Hendon	42	19	10	13	60	48	67
Tilbury	42	18	13	11	57	49	67
Tooting & Mitcham	42	18	10	14	85	72	64
Walthamstow Avenue	42	19	7	16	61	55	64
Slough Town	42	18	9	15	51	46	63
Hitchin Town	42	19	6	17	60	66	63
Leatherhead	42	18	7	17	61	47	61
Staines Town	42	16	13	13	52	48	61
Leytonstone	42	16	11	15	59	57	59
Barking	42	16	9	17	63	61	57
Southall & Ealing Borough	42	15	8	19	52	64	53
Croydon	42	13	10	19	38	52	49
Sutton United	42	14	7	21	40	55	49
Kingstonian	42	13	7	22	45	60	46
Hayes	42	12	10	20	49	69	46
Woking	42	11	12	19	47	61	45
Bishop's Stortford	42	11	11	20	51	71	44
Dulwich Hamlet	42	11	8	23	52	68	41
Ilford	42	10	8	24	32	73	38

Second Division

Boreham Wood	42	35	4	5	80	26	103
Carshalton Athletic	42	25	12	5	80	33	87
Harwich & Parkeston	42	23	8	11	93	61	77
Wembley	42	23	8	11	82	58	77
Harrow Borough	42	21	12	9	78	44	75
Horsham	42	23	5	14	67	56	74
Bromley	42	20	10	12	71	46	70
Oxford City	42	20	8	14	73	55	68
Hampton	42	20	8	14	62	45	68
Wokingham Town	42	16	14	12	60	44	62
Hornchurch	42	18	7	17	62	53	61
Chesham United	42	17	10	15	63	66	61
St Albans City	42	16	12	14	59	53	60
Walton & Hersham	42	17	9	16	57	56	60
Aveley	42	14	8	20	49	62	50
Corinthian Casuals	42	13	6	23	52	75	45
Harlow Town	42	11	8	23	39	77	41
Hertford Town	42	9	9	24	45	80	36
Maidenhead United	42	8	8	26	36	73	32
Clapton	42	7	9	28	43	87	30
Finchley	42	5	13	24	36	82	28
Ware	42	5	8	29	43	98	23

1977-78

Premier Division

Enfield	42	35	5	2	96	27	110
Dagenham	42	24	7	11	78	55	79
Wycombe Wanderers	42	22	9	11	66	41	75
Tooting & Mitcham United	42	22	8	12	64	49	74
Hitchin Town	42	20	9	13	69	53	69
Sutton United	42	18	12	12	66	57	66
Leatherhead	42	18	11	13	62	48	65
Croydon	42	18	10	14	61	52	64
Walthamstow Avenue	42	17	12	13	64	61	63
Barking	42	17	7	18	76	66	58
Carshalton Athletic	42	15	11	16	60	62	56
Hayes	42	15	11	16	46	53	56
Hendon	42	16	7	19	57	55	55
Woking	42	14	11	17	62	62	53
Boreham Wood	42	15	8	19	48	65	53
Slough Town	42	14	8	20	52	69	0
Staines Town	42	12	13	17	46	60	49
Tilbury	42	11	12	19	57	68	45
Kingstonian	42	8	13	21	43	65	37
Leytonstone	42	7	15	20	44	71	36
Southall & Ealing Borough	42	6	15	21	43	74	33
Bishop's Stortford	42	7	8	27	36	83	29

First Division

Dulwich Hamlet	42	28	9	5	91	25	93
Oxford City	42	26	5	11	85	44	83
Bromley	42	23	13	6	74	41	82
Walton & Hersham	42	22	11	9	69	41	77
Ilford	42	21	14	7	57	47	77
St Albans City	42	22	10	10	83	46	76
Wokingham Town	42	19	12	11	69	48	69
Harlow Town	42	19	8	15	63	49	65
Harrow Borough	42	17	10	15	59	54	61
Maidenhead United	42	16	13	13	55	54	61
Hertford Town	42	15	14	13	57	51	59
Chesham United	42	14	13	15	69	70	55
Hampton	42	13	13	16	49	53	52
Harwich & Parkeston	42	12	13	17	68	79	49
Wembley	42	15	3	24	56	82	48
Horsham	42	12	10	20	41	57	46
Finchley	42	11	13	18	41	68	46
Aveley	42	13	7	22	47	75	46
Ware	42	8	13	21	61	95	37
Clapton	42	10	6	26	46	78	36
Hornchurch	42	8	10	24	47	81	34
Corinthian Casuals	42	3	10	29	40	88	19

Second Division

Epsom & Ewell	32	21	5	6	65	34	68
Metropolitan Police	32	19	6	7	53	30	63
Farnborough Town	32	19	4	9	68	40	61
Molesey	32	17	8	7	47	27	59
Egham Town	32	15	9	8	52	34	54
Tring Town	32	14	11	7	62	32	53
Letchworth Garden City	32	14	11	7	67	48	53
Lewes	32	13	7	12	52	51	46
Rainham Town	32	13	6	13	42	50	45
Worthing	32	11	9	12	40	45	42
Eastbourne United	32	10	8	14	40	50	38
Cheshunt	32	9	6	17	43	60	33
Feltham	32	7	9	16	30	49	30
Camberley Town	32	6	11	15	32	49	29
Hemel Hempstead	32	6	9	17	33	50	27
Epping Town	32	7	6	19	37	64	27
Willesden	32	7	3	22	38	88	24

1978-79

Premier Division

Barking	42	28	9	5	92	50	93
Dagenham	42	25	6	11	83	63	81
Enfield	42	22	11	9	69	37	77
Dulwich Hamlet	42	21	13	8	69	39	76
Slough Town	42	20	12	10	61	44	72
Wycombe Wanderers	42	20	9	13	59	44	69
Woking	42	18	14	10	79	59	68
Croydon	42	19	9	14	61	51	66
Hendon	42	16	14	12	55	48	62
Leatherhead	42	17	9	16	57	45	60
Sutton United	42	17	9	16	62	51	60
Tooting & Mitcham United	42	15	14	13	52	52	59
Walthamstow Avenue	42	15	6	21	61	69	51
Tilbury	42	13	1	18	60	76	50
Boreham Wood	42	13	10	19	50	67	49
Hitchin Town	42	12	11	19	59	71	47
Carshalton Athletic	42	10	16	16	49	69	46
Hayes	42	9	18	15	45	58	45
Oxford City	42	12	7	23	50	80	43
Staines Town	42	6	16	20	40	64	34
Leytonstone	42	8	7	27	36	75	31
Kingstonian	42	3	15	24	35	72	24

First Division

Harlow Town	42	31	7	4	93	32	100
Harrow Borough	42	26	8	8	85	49	86
Maidenhead United	42	25	6	11	72	50	81
Bishop's Stortford	42	22	11	9	68	40	77
Horsham	42	23	7	12	63	47	76
Hertford Town	42	21	11	10	62	41	74
Harwich & Parkeston	42	22	5	15	90	57	71
Bromley	42	18	12	12	76	50	66
Hampton	42	17	11	14	59	47	62
Epsom & Ewell	42	18	7	17	69	41	61
Wembley	42	15	14	13	57	57	59
Aveley	42	17	6	19	57	67	57
Wokingham Town	42	17	8	17	64	68	56
Clapton	42	15	8	19	67	80	53
Metropolitan Police	42	12	13	17	58	55	49
Walton & Hersham	42	12	9	21	47	71	45
Ilford	42	13	5	24	48	80	44
Ware	42	11	10	21	46	69	43
Chesham United	42	11	9	22	46	66	42
Finchley	42	7	15	20	43	75	36
St Albans City	42	7	7	28	43	90	28
Southall & Ealing Borough	42	5	5	32	41	114	20

Wokingham Town had 3 points deducted

Second Division

Farnborough Town	34	26	3	5	77	34	81
Camberley Town	34	21	8	5	71	32	71
Molesey	34	19	11	4	55	33	68
Lewes	34	19	6	9	66	50	63
Feltham	34	16	7	11	47	36	55
Letchworth Garden City	34	14	10	10	56	48	52
Eastbourne United	34	16	4	14	47	45	52
Hemel Hempstead	34	13	11	10	46	37	50
Epping Town	34	14	7	13	49	44	49
Rainham Town	34	13	10	11	42	41	49
Cheshunt	34	11	8	15	43	49	41
Hungerford Town	34	11	8	15	48	58	41
Worthing	34	9	8	17	40	50	35
Hornchurch	34	9	8	17	39	62	35
Egham Town	34	7	12	15	48	54	33
Tring Town	34	6	8	20	33	56	26
Willesden	34	6	8	20	41	77	26
Corinthian Casuals	34	4	7	23	23	65	19

1979-80

Premier Division

Enfield	42	25	9	8	74	32	84
Walthamstow Avenue	42	24	9	9	87	48	81
Dulwich Hamlet	42	21	16	5	66	37	79
Sutton United	42	20	13	9	67	40	73
Dagenham	42	20	13	9	82	56	73
Tooting & Mitcham United	42	21	6	15	62	59	69
Barking	42	19	10	13	72	51	67
Harrow Borough	42	17	15	10	64	51	66
Woking	42	17	13	12	78	59	64
Wycombe Wanderers	42	17	13	12	72	53	64
Harlow Town	42	14	12	16	55	61	54
Hitchin Town	42	13	15	14	55	69	54
Hendon	42	12	13	17	50	57	49
Slough Town	42	13	10	19	54	71	49
Boreham Wood	42	13	10	19	50	69	49
Staines Town	42	14	6	22	46	67	48
Hayes	42	12	9	21	48	68	45
Leatherhead	42	11	11	20	51	60	44
Carshalton Athletic	42	12	7	23	48	78	43
Croydon	42	10	10	22	51	59	40
Oxford City	42	10	9	23	49	87	39
Tilbury	42	7	11	24	41	90	30

Tilbury had 2 points deducted

First Division

Leytonstone & Ilford	42	31	6	5	83	35	99
Bromley	42	24	10	8	93	44	82
Maidenhead United	42	24	8	10	81	46	80
Bishop's Stortford	42	24	8	10	74	47	80
Kingstonian	42	22	8	12	59	44	74
Chesham United	42	18	13	11	68	56	67
St Albans City	42	17	13	12	65	47	64
Farnborough Town	42	19	7	16	70	57	64
Epsom & Ewell	42	18	7	17	62	57	61
Camberley Town	42	16	10	16	43	38	58
Walton & Hersham	42	15	12	15	61	50	57
Wembley	42	16	8	18	46	52	56
Wokingham Town	42	14	11	17	45	49	53
Hertford Town	42	13	11	18	71	74	50
Aveley	42	12	13	17	45	55	49
Hampton	42	14	7	21	57	74	49
Finchley	42	13	9	20	44	59	48
Metropolitan Police	42	13	8	21	46	67	47
Ware	42	11	12	19	45	61	45
Clapton	42	14	3	25	48	77	45
Harwich & Parkeston	42	11	6	25	51	84	38
Horsham	42	6	4	32	29	113	22

Harwich & Parkeston had 1 point deducted

Second Division

Billericay Town	36	31	3	2	100	18	96
Lewes	36	24	7	5	82	33	79
Hungerford Town	36	21	8	7	78	36	71
Eastbourne United	36	21	6	9	77	45	69
Letchworth Garden City	36	21	6	9	63	32	69
Hornchurch	36	21	6	9	66	39	69
Molesey	36	15	9	12	67	60	54
Barton Rovers	36	15	7	14	49	49	52
Worthing	36	14	9	13	58	54	51
Cheshunt	36	13	7	16	47	52	46
Rainham Town	36	12	7	17	54	65	43
Egham Town	36	11	9	16	47	53	42
Southall & Ealing Borough	36	11	6	19	43	69	39
Feltham	36	8	11	17	23	49	35
Tring Town	36	7	13	16	38	55	34
Epping Town	36	10	4	22	44	69	34
Willesden	36	9	6	21	32	83	33
Hemel Hempstead	36	4	9	23	33	72	21
Corinthian Casuals	36	6	3	27	24	92	21

1980-81

Premier Division

Slough Town	42	23	13	6	73	34	82
Enfield	42	23	11	8	81	43	80
Wycombe Wanderers	42	22	9	11	76	49	75
Leytonstone & Ilford	42	19	12	11	78	57	69
Sutton United	42	19	12	11	82	65	69
Hendon	42	18	10	14	66	58	64
Dagenham	42	17	11	14	79	66	62
Hayes	42	18	8	16	45	50	62
Harrow Borough	42	16	11	15	57	52	59
Bromley	42	16	9	17	63	69	57
Staines Town	42	15	9	18	60	61	54
Tooting & Mitcham United	42	15	8	19	49	53	53
Hitchin Town	42	14	10	18	64	62	52
Croydon	42	12	15	15	51	51	51
Dulwich Hamlet	42	13	12	17	62	67	51
Leatherhead	42	12	14	16	36	50	50
Carshalton Athletic	42	14	8	20	57	82	50
Barking	42	13	12	17	58	72	49
Harlow Town	42	11	15	16	53	66	48
Walthamstow Avenue	42	13	7	22	50	81	46
Boreham Wood	42	10	13	19	46	69	43
Woking	42	11	7	24	40	69	37

Barking had 1 point deducted
Woking had 3 points deducted

First Division

Bishop's Stortford	42	30	6	6	84	28	96
Billericay Town	42	29	6	7	67	34	93
Epsom & Ewell	42	24	12	6	80	36	84
Farnborough Town	42	23	11	8	75	39	80
St Albans City	42	24	5	13	85	61	77
Kingstonian	42	20	9	13	63	52	66
Oxford City	42	18	9	15	71	48	63
Wokingham Town	42	16	15	11	70	56	63
Metropolitan Police	42	18	7	17	61	58	61
Chesham United	42	17	7	18	64	64	58
Lewes	42	17	7	18	72	83	58
Maidenhead United	42	16	7	19	58	62	55
Walton & Hersham	42	12	15	15	46	53	51
Hertford Town	42	13	11	18	46	65	50
Hampton	42	12	13	17	46	53	49
Aveley	42	13	9	20	54	55	48
Wembley	42	13	8	21	47	61	47
Clapton	42	12	8	22	53	86	44
Ware	42	9	13	20	50	69	40
Tilbury	42	10	8	24	42	84	35
Camberley Town	42	8	7	27	42	88	31
Finchley	42	6	11	25	36	77	29

Kingstonian and Tilbury both had 3 points deducted

Second Division

Feltham	38	24	10	4	65	30	82
Hornchurch	38	25	6	7	74	35	81
Hungerford Town	38	23	10	5	84	29	79
Barton Rovers	38	19	11	8	61	25	68
Worthing	38	19	11	8	74	43	68
Cheshunt	38	19	11	8	57	33	68
Letchworth Garden City	38	18	7	13	49	40	61
Southall	38	14	11	13	48	52	53
Dorking Town	38	13	12	13	47	45	51
Horsham	38	16	3	19	47	47	51
Hemel Hempstead	38	14	7	17	47	54	49
Egham Town	38	13	9	16	45	62	48
Harwich & Parkeston	38	12	11	15	57	58	47
Rainham Town	38	11	13	14	44	45	46
Epping Town	38	12	7	19	37	50	43
Eastbourne United	38	11	10	17	59	75	43
Willesden	38	11	8	19	57	68	41
Tring Town	38	11	6	21	40	71	39
Molesey	38	4	9	25	31	83	21
Corinthian Casuals	38	1	8	29	17	95	11

1981-82

Premier Division

Leytonstone & Ilford	42	26	5	11	91	52	83
Sutton United	42	22	9	11	72	49	75
Wycombe Wanderers	42	21	10	11	63	48	73
Staines Town	42	21	9	12	58	45	72
Walthamstow Avenue	42	21	7	14	81	62	70
Harrow Borough	42	18	13	11	77	55	67
Tooting & Mitcham United	42	19	10	13	58	47	67
Slough Town	42	17	13	12	64	54	64
Leatherhead	42	16	12	14	57	52	60
Hayes	42	16	10	16	58	52	58
Croydon	42	16	9	17	59	57	57
Barking	42	14	14	14	53	51	56
Hendon	42	13	13	16	56	65	52
Dulwich Hamlet	42	14	10	18	47	59	52
Bishop's Stortford	42	15	5	22	50	70	50
Carshalton Athletic	42	14	8	20	58	86	50
Billericay Town	42	11	16	15	41	50	49
Hitchin Town	42	12	11	19	56	77	47
Bromley	42	13	7	22	63	79	46
Woking	42	11	13	18	57	75	46
Harlow Town	42	10	11	21	50	73	41
Boreham Wood	42	8	13	21	47	58	37

First Division

Wokingham Town	40	29	5	6	86	30	92
Bognor Regis Town	40	23	10	7	65	34	79
Metropolitan Police	40	22	11	7	75	48	77
Oxford City	40	21	11	8	82	47	74
Feltham	40	20	8	12	65	49	68
Lewes	40	19	7	14	73	66	64
Hertford Town	40	16	10	14	62	54	58
Wembley	40	14	15	11	69	55	57
Farnborough Town	40	15	11	14	71	57	56
Epsom & Ewell	40	16	8	16	52	44	56
Kingstonian	40	16	7	17	57	56	55
Hampton	40	15	9	16	52	52	54
Hornchurch	40	13	15	12	42	50	54
Aveley	40	14	10	16	46	58	54
St Albans City	40	14	9	17	55	55	51
Maidenhead United	40	11	10	19	49	70	43
Tilbury	40	9	15	16	49	66	42
Walton & Hersham	40	10	11	19	43	65	41
Chesham United	40	9	9	22	41	71	36
Clapton	40	9	7	24	44	75	34
Ware	40	5	2	33	29	105	17

Second Division

Worthing	40	29	6	5	95	25	93
Cheshunt	40	25	7	8	79	33	82
Hungerford Town	40	22	10	8	89	42	74
Barton Rovers	40	22	8	10	65	32	74
Windsor & Eton	40	22	6	12	69	49	72
Corinthian Casuals	40	19	12	9	67	50	69
Harwich & Parkeston	40	19	12	9	64	47	69
Letchworth Garden City	40	15	11	14	67	55	56
Dorking Town	40	13	17	10	52	44	56
Hemel Hempstead	40	15	9	16	54	49	54
Basildon United	40	16	5	19	64	51	53
Finchley	40	14	9	17	57	68	51
Southall	40	12	14	14	36	42	50
Epping Town	40	12	11	17	48	62	47
Molesey	40	13	7	20	61	73	46
Egham Town	40	11	9	20	56	64	42
Rainham Town	40	11	9	20	53	83	42
Tring Town	40	9	13	18	49	78	40
Eastbourne United	40	9	12	19	51	73	39
Horsham	40	10	9	21	42	79	39
Camberley Town	40	3	2	35	21	140	11

Hungerford Town had 2 points deducted

1982-83

Premier Division

Wycombe Wanderers	42	26	7	9	79	47	85
Leytonstone & Ilford	42	24	9	9	71	39	81
Harrow Borough	42	24	7	11	91	58	79
Hayes	42	23	9	10	63	41	78
Sutton United	42	20	8	14	96	71	68
Dulwich Hamlet	42	18	14	10	59	52	68
Slough Town	42	18	13	11	73	36	67
Bognor Regis Town	42	19	8	15	53	48	65
Tooting & Mitcham United	42	18	9	15	65	62	63
Billericay Town	42	17	10	15	54	51	61
Croydon	42	17	9	16	68	58	60
Hendon	42	18	6	18	68	61	60
Bishop's Stortford	42	17	9	16	61	58	60
Barking	42	14	14	14	47	55	56
Bromley	42	14	12	16	51	50	54
Carshalton Athletic	42	15	9	18	58	60	54
Wokingham Town	42	13	9	20	37	51	48
Walthamstow Avenue	42	12	11	19	48	64	47
Staines Town	42	12	11	19	62	79	47
Hitchin Town	42	11	9	22	49	77	42
Woking	42	6	6	30	30	79	24
Leatherhead	42	4	5	33	35	121	17

First Division

Worthing	40	25	6	9	76	39	81
Harlow Town	40	21	11	8	84	55	74
Farnborough Town	40	20	13	7	69	39	73
Hertford Town	40	20	11	9	70	61	71
Oxford City	40	19	13	8	70	49	70
Boreham Wood	40	21	6	13	62	42	69
Metropolitan Police	40	19	9	12	77	57	66
Walton & Hersham	40	17	6	17	65	59	57
Hampton	40	15	10	15	62	60	55
Wembley	40	14	10	16	62	61	52
Aveley	40	15	7	18	52	62	52
Kingstonian	40	13	12	15	53	53	51
Tilbury	40	12	10	18	41	47	46
Feltham	40	11	12	17	45	54	45
Chesham United	40	13	6	21	43	70	45
Epsom & Ewell	40	10	14	16	44	49	44
Lewes	40	12	8	20	47	71	44
Cheshunt	40	10	13	17	41	49	43
Hornchurch	40	11	8	21	45	74	41
Maidenhead United	40	10	10	20	57	87	40
St Albans City	40	10	9	21	52	79	37

St Albans City had 2 points deducted

Second Division

Clapton	42	30	4	8	96	46	94
Windsor & Eton	42	27	7	8	98	43	88
Barton Rovers	42	26	6	10	86	48	84
Leyton Wingate	42	25	8	9	111	41	83
Basildon United	42	23	13	6	92	42	82
Uxbridge	42	22	12	8	80	42	78
Hungerford Town	42	22	10	10	82	39	76
Corinthian Casuals	42	23	6	13	95	48	75
Egham Town	42	21	8	13	77	67	71
Tring Town	42	20	10	12	86	59	70
Letchworth Garden City	42	18	13	11	68	53	66
Southall	42	18	7	17	81	80	61
Molesey	42	17	9	16	73	56	60
Dorking Town	42	15	9	18	56	75	54
Hemel Hempstead	42	12	14	16	53	59	50
Rainham Town	42	14	4	24	57	94	46
Eastbourne United	42	10	6	26	54	104	36
Epping Town	42	6	8	28	29	89	26
Ware	42	6	6	30	34	97	24
Finchley	42	4	12	26	28	92	24
Horsham	42	5	7	30	32	106	22
Harwich & Parkeston	42	5	7	30	42	130	22

Letchworth Garden City had 1 point deducted

1983-84

Premier Division

Harrow Borough	42	25	13	4	73	42	88
Worthing	42	20	11	11	89	72	71
Slough Town	42	20	9	13	73	56	69
Sutton United	42	18	12	12	67	45	66
Hayes	42	17	13	12	56	41	64
Hitchin Town	42	16	15	11	58	57	63
Wycombe Wanderers	42	16	14	12	63	52	62
Wokingham Town	42	18	10	14	78	55	61
Hendon	42	17	10	15	62	51	61
Dulwich Hamlet	42	16	11	15	61	64	59
Bishop's Stortford	42	15	13	14	56	57	58
Harlow Town	42	15	11	16	64	70	56
Bognor Regis Town	42	14	13	15	62	69	55
Staines Town	42	15	9	18	63	72	54
Billericay Town	42	15	8	19	53	73	53
Barking	42	13	13	16	60	64	52
Croydon	42	14	10	18	52	58	52
Walthamstow Avenue	42	13	10	19	53	67	49
Leytonstone & Ilford	42	13	9	20	54	67	48
Carshalton Athletic	42	11	10	21	59	72	43
Tooting & Mitcham United	42	10	13	19	50	63	43
Bromley	42	7	11	24	33	72	32

Wokingham Town had 3 points deducted

First Division

Windsor & Eton	42	26	7	9	89	44	85
Epsom & Ewell	42	23	9	10	73	51	78
Wembley	42	21	11	10	65	32	74
Maidenhead United	42	22	8	12	67	42	74
Boreham Wood	42	22	7	13	74	43	73
Farnborough Town	42	18	12	12	78	60	66
Hampton	42	18	12	12	65	49	66
Metropolitan Police	42	20	5	17	79	64	65
Chesham United	42	18	8	16	64	57	62
Tilbury	42	17	10	15	54	64	61
Leatherhead	42	15	10	17	67	56	55
Aveley	42	15	10	17	49	53	55
Woking	42	16	7	19	66	73	55
Hertford Town	42	15	9	18	56	73	54
Oxford City	42	14	9	19	57	56	51
Lewes	42	13	12	17	49	65	51
Walton & Hersham	42	13	10	19	52	70	49
Hornchurch	42	13	10	19	43	65	49
Kingstonian	42	13	9	20	47	67	48
Clapton	42	12	11	19	49	67	47
Cheshunt	42	12	8	22	45	64	44
Feltham	42	7	4	31	31	106	25

Second Division

Basildon United	42	30	7	5	88	27	97
St Albans City	42	29	9	5	100	46	96
Leyton Wingate	42	29	4	9	97	41	91
Tring Town	42	23	11	8	89	44	80
Corinthian Casuals	42	23	11	8	75	47	80
Hungerford Town	42	21	12	9	94	47	75
Uxbridge	42	18	15	9	61	36	69
Grays Athletic	42	20	9	13	72	57	69
Dorking	42	21	5	16	66	54	68
Southall	42	20	8	14	79	60	65
Egham Town	42	16	15	11	59	49	63
Epping Town	42	15	16	11	61	50	61
Molesey	42	13	14	15	59	68	53
Barton Rovers	42	15	8	19	54	64	53
Letchworth Garden City	42	15	7	20	48	66	52
Newbury Town	42	14	5	23	60	82	47
Hemel Hempstead	42	12	9	21	63	69	45
Rainham Town	42	7	5	30	38	114	26
Finchley	42	5	9	28	28	78	24
Eastbourne United	42	7	3	32	36	98	24
Ware	42	6	6	30	48	114	24
Horsham	42	7	4	31	40	104	23

Southall had 2 points deducted
Horsham had 3 points deducted

1984-85

Premier Division

Sutton United	42	23	15	4	115	55	84
Worthing	42	24	8	10	89	59	80
Wycombe Wanderers	42	24	6	12	68	46	78
Wokingham Town	42	20	13	9	74	54	73
Windsor & Eton	42	19	10	13	65	55	67
Bognor Regis Town	42	20	6	16	67	58	66
Dulwich Hamlet	42	16	17	9	82	57	65
Harrow Borough	42	18	8	16	70	56	62
Hayes	42	17	8	17	60	56	59
Tooting & Mitcham United	42	16	11	15	64	66	59
Walthamstow Avenue	42	15	11	16	64	65	56
Croydon	42	15	12	15	62	63	54
Epsom & Ewell	42	13	14	15	65	62	53
Slough Town	42	13	12	17	69	74	51
Carshalton Athletic	42	14	8	20	55	68	50
Bishop's Stortford	42	12	12	18	48	67	48
Hendon	42	9	19	14	62	65	46
Billericay Town	42	11	14	17	53	74	46
Barking	42	13	7	22	43	75	46
Hitchin Town	42	10	15	17	55	70	45
Leytonstone & Ilford	42	11	10	21	37	72	43
Harlow Town	42	5	12	25	45	95	27

Billercay Town had 1 point deducted
Croydon had 3 points deducted

First Division

Farnborough Town	42	26	8	8	101	45	86
Kingstonian	42	23	10	9	67	39	79
Leatherhead	42	23	10	9	109	61	76
Chesham United	42	22	8	12	78	46	74
Wembley	42	20	10	12	59	40	70
St Albans City	42	19	10	13	79	60	67
Tilbury	42	18	13	11	86	68	67
Bromley	42	18	9	15	71	64	63
Hampton	42	17	11	14	75	62	62
Staines Town	42	16	11	15	59	53	59
Maidenhead United	42	17	8	17	65	64	59
Walton & Hersham	42	16	8	18	60	69	55
Aveley	42	16	7	19	62	78	55
Oxford City	42	14	12	16	62	53	54
Lewes	42	15	9	18	70	72	54
Basildon United	42	15	8	19	55	61	53
Boreham Wood	42	15	7	20	72	83	52
Hornchurch	42	15	6	21	55	74	51
Woking	42	15	6	21	60	91	51
Metropolitan Police	42	10	12	20	65	92	42
Clapton	42	5	11	26	50	124	26
Hertford Town	42	5	10	27	36	97	25

Walton & Hersham had 1 point deducted
Leatherhead had 3 points deducted

Second Division North

Leyton Wingate	38	24	9	5	98	50	81
Finchley	38	24	8	6	66	31	79
Heybridge Swifts	38	22	9	7	71	33	75
Stevenage Borough	38	23	6	9	79	49	75
Saffron Walden Town	38	22	8	8	73	31	74
Tring Town	38	19	11	8	76	41	68
Chalfont St Peter	38	17	10	11	72	41	61
Flackwell Heath	38	16	11	11	54	40	59
Berkhamsted Town	38	15	12	11	50	42	57
Letchworth Garden City	38	17	6	15	66	69	57
Royston Town	38	13	9	16	47	77	48
Cheshunt	38	14	5	19	52	57	47
Marlow	38	13	6	19	64	81	45
Hemel Hempstead	38	11	7	20	49	65	40
Barton Rovers	38	9	8	21	40	62	35
Wolverton Town	38	9	8	21	38	77	35
Kingsbury Town	38	9	7	22	53	72	34
Harefield United	38	7	9	22	51	81	30
Haringey Borough	38	6	12	20	38	79	30
Ware	38	7	5	26	40	100	26

Finchley had 1 point deducted
The record of Epping Town was expunged

Second Division South

Grays Athletic	36	24	9	3	84	25	81
Uxbridge	36	22	10	4	81	20	76
Molesey	36	20	5	11	62	42	65
Hungerford Town	36	18	9	9	71	49	63
Whyteleafe	36	17	10	9	66	34	61
Egham Town	36	17	7	12	54	42	58
Southall	36	18	3	15	54	57	57
Bracknell Town	36	15	7	14	54	48	52
Banstead Athletic	36	14	8	14	63	70	50
Horsham	36	13	10	13	44	39	49
Ruislip Manor	36	13	10	13	48	49	49
Dorking	36	12	11	13	45	50	47
Rainham Town	36	12	8	16	58	61	44
Feltham	36	10	13	13	44	58	43
Camberley Town	36	10	12	14	44	54	42
Eastbourne United	36	10	9	17	66	72	39
Petersfield Town	36	9	5	22	41	80	32
Newbury Town	36	8	7	21	35	69	16
Chertsey Town	36	2	3	31	23	118	6

Chertsey Town had 3 points deducted
Newbury Town had 15 points deducted

1985-86

Premier Division

Sutton United	42	29	8	5	109	39	95
Yeovil Town	42	28	7	7	92	48	91
Farnborough Town	42	23	8	11	90	50	77
Croydon	42	23	7	12	70	50	76
Harrow Borough	42	21	8	13	76	66	71
Slough Town	42	18	8	16	66	68	62
Bishop's Stortford	42	17	10	15	55	61	61
Kingstonian	42	15	15	12	57	56	60
Dulwich Hamlet	42	17	9	16	64	79	60
Wokingham Town	42	16	10	16	67	64	58
Windsor & Eton	42	17	7	18	58	75	58
Tooting & Mitcham United	42	14	11	17	65	76	53
Walthamstow Avenue	42	12	14	16	69	70	50
Worthing	42	13	10	19	72	82	49
Bognor Regis Town	42	15	6	21	63	70	48
Hayes	42	10	17	15	36	42	47
Hitchin Town	42	11	14	17	53	69	47
Barking	42	11	13	18	45	55	46
Hendon	42	10	13	19	59	77	43
Carshalton Athletic	42	9	13	20	56	79	40
Billericay Town	42	9	12	21	59	78	39
Epsom & Ewell	42	8	12	22	63	90	36

Bognor Regis Town had 3 points deducted

First Division

St Albans City	42	23	11	8	92	61	80
Bromley	42	24	8	10	68	41	80
Wembley	42	22	12	8	59	30	78
Oxford City	42	22	11	9	75	51	77
Hampton	42	21	11	10	63	45	74
Leyton Wingate	42	21	10	11	77	56	73
Uxbridge	42	20	8	14	64	49	68
Staines Town	42	18	10	14	69	66	64
Boreham Wood	42	15	16	11	62	54	61
Walton & Hersham	42	16	10	16	68	71	58
Lewes	42	16	8	18	61	75	56
Leytonstone & Ilford	42	13	15	14	57	67	54
Finchley	42	12	17	13	61	59	53
Grays Athletic	42	13	11	18	69	75	50
Leatherhead	42	14	8	20	62	68	50
Tilbury	42	13	11	18	60	66	50
Maidenhead United	42	13	7	22	61	67	46
Basildon United	42	12	9	21	52	72	45
Hornchurch	42	11	11	20	44	59	44
Chesham United	42	12	6	24	51	87	42
Harlow Town	42	8	14	20	53	70	38
Aveley	42	8	6	28	59	98	30

Second Division North

Stevenage Borough	38	26	6	6	71	24	84
Kingsbury Town	38	25	8	5	84	35	83
Heybridge Swifts	38	20	8	10	65	46	68
Cheshunt	38	18	10	10	60	40	64
Hertford Town	38	17	7	14	60	50	58
Chalfont St Peter	38	15	11	12	53	50	56
Tring Town	38	14	13	11	58	46	55
Royston Town	38	13	13	12	59	57	52
Saffron Walden Town	38	13	12	13	61	65	51
Berkhamsted Town	38	14	8	16	45	52	50
Haringey Borough	38	14	7	17	49	51	49
Letchworth Garden City	38	13	8	17	46	52	47
Rainham Town	38	14	4	20	54	91	46
Hemel Hempstead	38	12	9	17	50	66	45
Ware	38	11	11	16	56	61	44
Vauxhall Motors	38	11	10	17	58	62	43
Barton Rovers	38	12	7	19	50	60	43
Harefield United	38	9	12	17	56	72	39
Clapton	38	10	7	21	51	90	37
Wolverton Town	38	8	11	19	42	58	35

Second Division South

Southwick	38	25	8	5	86	34	83
Bracknell Town	38	24	9	5	80	23	81
Woking	38	23	9	6	94	45	78
Newbury Town	38	22	7	9	86	53	73
Whyteleafe	38	21	10	7	61	41	73
Molesey	38	21	8	9	59	39	71
Metropolitan Police	38	20	6	12	72	48	66
Southall	38	19	7	12	76	58	64
Dorking	38	18	10	10	70	57	64
Feltham	38	16	7	15	65	60	55
Banstead Athletic	38	15	8	15	60	66	53
Petersfield United	38	12	9	17	61	71	45
Hungerford Town	38	11	6	21	57	78	39
Flackwell Heath	38	11	6	21	46	72	39
Eastbourne United	38	9	8	21	51	81	35
Camberley Town	38	9	7	22	53	64	34
Egham Town	38	7	8	23	41	83	29
Horsham	38	6	10	22	33	74	28
Ruislip Manor	38	5	12	21	44	87	27
Marlow	38	6	5	27	47	108	23

1986-87

Premier Division

Wycombe Wanderers	42	32	5	5	103	32	101
Yeovil Town	42	28	8	6	71	27	92
Slough Town	42	23	8	11	70	44	77
Hendon	42	22	7	13	67	53	73
Bognor Regis Town	42	20	10	12	85	61	70
Harrow Borough	42	20	10	12	68	44	70
Croydon	42	18	10	14	51	48	64
Barking	42	16	14	12	76	56	62
Farnborough Town	42	17	11	14	66	72	62
Bishop's Stortford	42	15	15	12	62	57	60
Bromley	42	16	11	15	63	72	59
Kingstonian	42	16	9	17	58	50	57
Windsor & Eton	42	13	15	14	47	52	54
St Albans City	42	14	9	19	61	70	51
Carshalton Athletic	42	13	9	20	55	68	48
Wokingham Town	42	14	6	22	47	61	48
Hayes	42	12	12	18	45	68	48
Dulwich Hamlet	42	12	10	20	62	71	46
Tooting & Mitcham United	42	12	9	21	51	53	45
Hitchin Town	42	13	5	24	56	69	44
Worthing	42	8	9	25	58	107	33
Walthamstow Avenue	42	4	6	32	36	113	18

First Division

Leytonstone & Ilford	42	30	5	7	78	29	95
Leyton Wingate	42	23	13	6	68	31	82
Bracknell Town	42	24	9	9	92	48	81
Southwick	42	23	7	12	80	66	76
Wembley	42	21	9	12	61	47	72
Grays Athletic	42	19	10	13	76	64	67
Kingsbury Town	42	20	7	15	69	67	67
Boreham Wood	42	20	6	16	59	52	66
Uxbridge	42	18	9	15	60	59	63
Leatherhead	42	17	11	14	45	48	62
Hampton	42	18	5	19	57	55	59
Basildon United	42	16	10	16	58	60	58
Billericay Town	42	14	12	16	57	52	54
Staines Town	42	13	13	16	40	51	52
Lewes	42	15	6	21	55	65	51
Stevenage Borough	42	12	11	19	61	67	47
Oxford City	42	11	10	21	64	72	43
Walton & Hersham	42	11	10	21	53	74	43
Tilbury	42	12	7	23	46	70	43
Epsom & Ewell	42	12	7	23	44	68	43
Maidenhead United	42	11	4	27	44	76	37
Finchley	42	6	11	25	44	90	29

Second Division North

Chesham United	42	28	6	8	81	48	90
Wolverton Town	42	23	14	5	74	32	83
Haringey Borough	42	22	13	7	86	40	79
Heybridge Swifts	42	21	11	10	81	54	74
Aveley	42	19	13	10	68	50	70
Letchworth Garden City	42	19	11	12	77	62	68
Barton Rovers	42	18	11	13	49	39	65
Tring Town	42	19	7	16	69	49	64
Collier Row	42	19	5	18	67	65	62
Ware	42	17	8	17	51	50	59
Saffron Walden Town	42	14	14	14	56	54	56
Wivenhoe Town	42	15	11	16	61	61	56
Vauxhall Motors	42	15	10	17	61	57	55
Hornchurch	42	13	16	13	60	60	55
Hertford Town	42	14	13	15	52	53	55
Berkhamsted Town	42	12	16	14	62	64	52
Harlow Town	42	13	11	18	45	55	50
Rainham Town	42	12	11	19	53	70	47
Clapton	42	10	11	21	45	63	41
Hemel Hempstead	42	9	12	21	48	77	39
Royston Town	42	4	12	26	37	109	24
Cheshunt	42	5	6	31	43	114	21

Second Division South

Woking	40	27	7	6	110	32	88
Marlow	40	28	4	8	78	36	88
Dorking	40	24	12	4	78	30	84
Feltham	40	25	3	12	79	34	78
Ruislip Manor	40	22	10	8	85	47	76
Chertsey Town	40	18	11	11	58	44	65
Metropolitan Police	40	16	13	11	70	61	61
Chalfont St Peter	40	17	10	13	60	55	61
Hungerford Town	40	14	14	12	55	48	56
Harefield United	40	14	14	12	53	47	56
Eastbourne United	40	15	10	15	72	59	55
Whyteleafe	40	12	15	13	52	63	51
Horsham	40	14	8	18	54	61	50
Egham Town	40	14	6	20	45	77	48
Camberley Town	40	13	3	24	62	89	42
Flackwell Heath	40	9	11	20	34	63	38
Banstead Athletic	40	7	15	18	44	61	36
Petersfield United	40	9	8	23	45	84	34
Molesey	40	7	12	21	37	89	33
Newbury Town	40	6	14	20	51	83	32
Southall	40	6	6	28	28	85	24

1987-88

Premier Division

Yeovil Town	42	24	9	9	66	34	81
Bromley	42	23	7	12	68	40	76
Slough Town	42	21	9	12	67	41	72
Leytonstone & Ilford	42	20	11	11	59	43	71
Wokingham Town	42	21	7	14	62	52	70
Hayes	42	20	9	13	62	48	69
Windsor & Eton	42	16	17	9	59	43	65
Farnborough Town	42	17	11	14	63	60	62
Carshalton Athletic	42	16	13	13	49	41	61
Hendon	42	16	12	14	62	58	60
Tooting & Mitcham United	42	15	14	13	57	59	59
Harrow Borough	42	15	11	16	53	58	56
Bishop's Stortford	42	15	10	17	55	58	55
Kingstonian	42	14	12	16	47	53	54
St Albans City	42	15	6	21	60	69	51
Bognor Regis Town	42	14	9	19	41	57	51
Leyton Wingate	42	14	8	20	58	64	50
Croydon	42	11	13	18	40	52	46
Barking	42	11	12	19	44	57	45
Dulwich Hamlet	42	10	11	21	46	64	41
Hitchin Town	42	10	8	24	46	79	38
Basingstoke Town	42	6	17	19	37	71	35

First Division

Marlow	42	32	5	5	100	44	101
Grays Athletic	42	30	10	2	74	25	100
Woking	42	25	7	10	91	52	82
Boreham Wood	42	21	9	12	65	45	72
Staines Town	42	19	11	12	71	48	68
Wembley	42	18	11	13	54	46	65
Basildon United	42	18	9	15	65	58	63
Walton & Hersham	42	15	16	11	53	44	61
Hampton	42	17	10	15	59	54	61
Leatherhead	42	16	11	15	64	53	59
Southwick	42	13	12	17	59	63	51
Oxford City	42	13	12	17	70	77	51
Worthing	42	14	8	20	67	73	50
Kingsbury Town	42	11	17	14	62	69	50
Walthamstow Avenue	42	13	11	18	53	63	50
Lewes	42	12	13	17	83	77	49
Uxbridge	42	11	16	15	41	47	49
Chesham United	42	12	10	20	69	77	46
Bracknell Town	42	12	9	21	54	80	45
Billericay Town	42	11	11	20	58	88	44
Stevenage Borough	42	11	9	22	36	64	42
Wolverton Town	42	3	3	36	23	124	12

Second Division North

Wivenhoe Town	42	26	10	6	105	42	88
Collier Row	42	22	13	7	71	39	79
Tilbury	42	18	15	9	61	40	69
Berkhamsted Town	42	19	12	11	71	53	69
Harlow Town	42	17	16	9	67	36	67
Ware	42	17	15	10	63	58	66
Witham Town	42	17	14	11	69	47	65
Vauxhall Motors	42	16	17	9	56	42	65
Heybridge Swifts	42	17	13	12	56	50	64
Tring Town	42	18	6	18	69	67	60
Letchworth Garden City	42	18	5	19	59	64	59
Finchley	42	16	10	16	67	54	58
Clapton	42	14	15	13	50	62	57
Hornchurch	42	13	15	14	56	65	54
Barton Rovers	42	13	10	19	43	60	49
Rainham Town	42	12	12	18	63	66	48
Royston Town	42	13	8	21	49	70	47
Saffron Waldon Town	42	13	7	22	34	67	46
Hemel Hempstead	42	11	12	19	38	71	45
Haringey Borough	42	11	8	23	54	78	41
Aveley	42	8	13	21	42	65	37
Hertford Town	42	8	4	30	45	92	28

Second Division South

Chalfont St Peter	42	26	9	7	81	35	87
Metropolitan Police	42	23	17	2	80	32	86
Dorking	42	25	11	6	86	39	86
Feltham	42	21	12	9	74	41	75
Epsom & Ewell	42	21	11	10	71	49	74
Chertsey Town	42	22	7	13	63	47	73
Whyteleafe	42	20	11	11	84	55	71
Hungerford Town	42	21	7	14	66	54	70
Ruislip Manor	42	21	5	16	74	57	68
Yeading	42	19	10	13	83	56	67
Maidenhead United	42	18	12	12	69	54	66
Eastbourne United	42	18	10	14	67	57	64
Harefield Town	42	18	6	18	59	60	60
Egham Town	42	12	12	18	45	55	48
Horsham	42	12	10	20	45	66	46
Southall	42	13	7	22	45	72	46
Molesey	42	11	11	20	42	63	44
Newbury Town	42	8	13	21	40	81	37
Camberley Town	42	9	9	24	51	94	36
Flackwell Heath	42	6	8	28	42	96	26
Banstead Athletic	42	6	7	29	34	81	25
Petersfield United	42	6	7	29	45	102	25

1988-89

Premier Division

Leytonstone & Ilford	42	26	11	5	76	36	89
Farnborough Town	42	24	9	9	85	61	81
Slough Town	42	24	6	12	72	42	78
Carshalton Athletic	42	19	15	8	59	36	72
Grays Athletic	42	19	13	10	62	47	70
Kingstonian	42	19	11	12	54	37	68
Bishop's Stortford	42	20	6	16	70	56	66
Hayes	42	18	12	12	6	47	66
Bognor Regis Town	42	17	11	14	38	49	62
Barking	42	16	13	13	49	45	61
Wokingham Town	42	15	11	16	60	54	56
Hendon	42	13	17	12	51	68	56
Windsor & Eton	42	14	13	15	52	50	55
Bromley	42	13	15	14	61	48	54
Leyton Wingate	42	13	15	14	55	56	54
Dulwich Hamlet	42	12	12	18	58	57	48
St Albans City	42	12	9	21	51	59	45
Dagenham	42	11	12	19	53	68	45
Harrow Borough	42	9	13	20	53	75	40
Marlow	42	9	11	22	48	83	38
Tooting & Mitcham United	42	10	6	26	41	81	36
Croydon	42	4	9	29	27	81	21

First Division

Staines Town	40	26	9	5	79	29	87
Basingstoke Town	40	25	8	7	85	36	83
Woking	40	24	10	6	72	30	82
Hitchin Town	40	21	11	8	60	32	74
Wivenhoe Town	40	22	6	12	62	44	72
Lewes	40	21	8	11	72	54	71
Walton & Hersham	40	21	7	12	56	36	70
Kingsbury Town	40	20	7	13	65	41	67
Uxbridge	40	19	7	14	60	54	64
Wembley	40	18	6	16	45	58	60
Boreham Wood	40	16	9	15	57	52	57
Leatherhead	40	14	8	18	56	58	50
Metropolitan Police	40	13	9	18	52	68	48
Chesham United	40	12	9	19	54	67	45
Southwick	40	9	15	16	44	58	42
Chalfont St Peter	40	11	9	20	56	82	42
Hampton	40	7	14	19	37	62	35
Worthing	40	8	10	22	49	80	32
Collier Row	40	8	7	25	37	82	31
Bracknell Town	40	8	6	26	38	70	30
Basildon Town	40	6	7	27	34	77	25

Worthing had 2 points deducted.

Second Division North

Harlow Town	42	27	9	6	83	38	90
Purfleet	42	22	12	8	60	42	78
Tring Town	42	22	10	10	65	44	76
Stevenage Borough	42	20	13	9	84	55	73
Heybridge Swifts	42	21	9	12	64	43	72
Billericay Town	42	19	11	12	65	52	68
Clapton	42	18	11	13	65	56	65
Barton Rovers	42	18	11	13	58	50	65
Aveley	42	18	10	14	54	52	64
Hertford Town	42	16	13	13	62	49	59
Ware	42	17	8	17	60	65	59
Hemel Hempstead	42	16	10	16	55	58	58
Witham Town	42	16	7	19	69	67	55
Vauxhall Motors	42	15	9	18	53	57	54
Berkhamsted Town	42	14	10	18	57	70	52
Hornchurch	42	11	16	15	59	61	49
Tilbury	42	13	10	19	53	60	49
Royston Town	42	12	7	23	46	72	43
Rainham Town	42	9	15	18	49	62	42
Saffron Walden Town	42	8	16	18	54	72	40
Letchworth Garden City	42	4	18	20	34	71	30
Wolverton Town	42	5	7	30	42	95	13

Hertford Town 2 points deducted, Wolverton Town 9 points deducted.

Second Division South

Dorking	40	32	4	4	109	35	100
Whyteleafe	40	25	9	6	86	41	84
Finchley	40	21	9	10	70	45	72
Molesey	40	19	13	8	58	42	70
Harefield United	40	19	7	14	56	45	64
Hungerford Town	40	17	13	10	55	45	64
Ruislip Manor	40	16	9	15	56	43	57
Feltham	40	16	9	15	58	53	57
Epsom & Ewell	40	16	8	16	55	55	56
Egham Town	40	16	7	17	54	58	55
Eastbourne United	40	15	9	16	68	61	54
Chertsey Town	40	13	14	13	55	58	53
Flackwell Heath	40	13	11	16	51	49	50
Camberley Town	40	15	5	20	51	71	50
Yeading	40	13	9	18	47	63	46
Banstead Athletic	40	12	8	20	50	65	44
Maidenhead United	40	10	13	17	44	61	43
Southall	40	11	10	19	41	73	43
Newbury Town	40	11	8	21	47	65	41
Horsham	40	7	14	19	36	68	35
Petersfield United	40	5	7	28	36	87	22

Yeading had 2 points deducted.

1989-90

Premier Division

Slough Town	42	27	11	4	85	38	92
Wokingham Town	42	26	11	5	67	34	89
Aylesbury United	42	25	9	8	86	30	84
Kingstonian	42	24	9	9	87	51	81
Grays Athletic	42	19	13	10	59	44	70
Dagenham	42	17	15	10	54	43	66
Leyton Wingate	42	20	6	16	54	48	66
Basingstoke Town	42	18	9	15	65	55	63
Bishop's Stortford	42	19	6	17	60	59	63
Carshalton Athletic	42	19	5	18	63	59	59
Redbridge Forest	42	16	11	15	65	62	59
Hendon	42	15	10	17	54	63	55
Windsor & Eton	42	13	15	14	51	47	54
Hayes	42	14	11	17	61	59	53
St Albans City	42	13	10	19	49	59	49
Staines Town	42	14	6	22	53	69	48
Marlow	42	11	13	18	42	59	46
Harrow Borough	42	11	10	21	51	79	43
Bognor Regis Town	42	9	14	19	37	67	41
Barking	42	7	11	24	53	86	32
Bromley	42	7	11	24	32	69	32
Dulwich Hamlet	42	6	8	28	32	80	26

Carshalton Athletic had 3 points deducted.

First Division

Wivenhoe Town	42	31	7	4	94	36	100
Woking	42	30	8	4	102	29	98
Southwick	42	23	15	4	68	30	84
Hitchin Town	42	22	13	7	60	30	79
Walton & Hersham	42	20	10	12	68	50	70
Dorking	42	19	12	11	66	41	69
Boreham Wood	42	17	13	12	60	59	64
Harlow Town	42	16	13	13	60	53	61
Metropolitan Police	42	16	11	15	54	59	59
Chesham United	42	15	12	15	46	49	57
Chalfont St Peter	42	14	13	15	50	59	55
Tooting & Mitcham United	42	14	13	15	42	51	55
Worthing	42	15	8	19	56	63	53
Whyteleafe	42	11	16	15	50	65	49
Lewes	42	12	11	19	55	65	47
Wembley	42	11	10	21	57	68	43
Croydon	42	9	16	17	43	57	43
Uxbridge	42	11	10	21	52	75	43
Hampton	42	8	13	21	28	51	37
Leatherhead	42	7	10	25	34	77	31
Purfleet	42	7	8	27	33	78	29
Kingsbury Town	42	8	10	24	45	78	25

Kingsbury Town had 9 points deducted

Second Division North

Heybridge Swifts	42	26	9	7	79	29	87
Aveley	42	23	16	3	68	24	85
Hertford Town	42	24	11	7	92	51	83
Stevenage Borough	42	21	16	5	70	31	79
Barton Rovers	42	22	6	14	60	45	72
Tilbury	42	20	9	13	68	54	69
Basildon United	42	13	20	9	50	44	59
Collier Row	42	15	13	14	43	45	58
Royston Town	42	15	11	16	63	72	56
Saffron Walden Town	42	15	11	16	60	73	56
Vauxhall Motors	42	14	13	15	55	54	55
Clapton	42	13	16	13	50	46	54
Ware	42	14	11	17	53	59	53
Hemel Hempstead	42	12	15	15	58	70	51
Billericay Town	42	13	11	18	49	58	50
Hornchurch	42	12	12	18	49	64	48
Berkhamsted Town	42	9	16	17	44	68	43
Finchley	42	11	10	21	50	75	43
Tring Town	42	10	9	23	48	70	39
Witham Town	42	8	14	20	44	56	38
Rainham Town	42	9	11	22	48	75	38
Letchworth Garden City	42	7	12	23	30	68	33

Clapton had 1 point deducted

Second Division South

Yeading	40	29	4	7	86	37	91
Molesey	40	24	11	5	76	30	83
Abingdon Town	40	22	9	9	64	39	75
Ruislip Manor	40	20	12	8	60	32	72
Maidenhead United	40	20	12	8	66	39	72
Southall	40	22	5	13	56	33	71
Newbury Town	40	21	7	12	50	36	70
Flackwell Heath	40	16	11	13	69	65	59
Hungerford Town	40	14	16	10	54	51	58
Egham Town	40	12	14	14	39	38	50
Banstead Athletic	40	14	8	18	46	47	50
Harefield United	40	13	9	18	44	46	48
Chertsey Town	40	13	9	18	53	58	48
Epsom & Ewell	40	13	9	18	49	54	48
Malden Vale	40	13	7	20	36	67	46
Eastbourne United	40	11	10	19	47	65	43
Camberley Town	40	11	9	20	44	66	42
Feltham	40	11	7	22	47	80	40
Bracknell Town	40	10	9	21	40	57	39
Petersfield United	40	10	8	22	48	93	38
Horsham	40	4	8	28	29	70	20

Second Division North

Stevenage Borough	42	34	5	3	122	29	107
Vauxhall Motors	42	24	10	8	82	50	82
Billericay Town	42	22	8	12	70	41	74
Ware	42	22	8	12	78	51	74
Berkhamsted Town	42	19	11	12	60	51	68
Witham Town	42	19	10	13	70	59	67
Purfleet	42	17	14	11	68	57	65
Rainham Town	42	19	7	16	57	46	64
Hemel Hempstead	42	16	14	12	62	56	62
Barton Rovers	42	17	10	15	61	58	61
Saffron Walden Town	42	16	13	13	72	77	61
Collier Row	42	16	11	15	63	63	59
Kingsbury Town	42	17	8	17	64	72	59
Edgware Town	42	17	7	18	73	65	58
Hertford Town	42	16	10	16	69	70	58
Royston Town	42	14	15	13	78	62	57
Tilbury	42	14	6	22	70	79	48
Basildon United	42	11	10	21	61	90	43
Hornchurch	42	10	9	23	53	87	39
Clapton	42	9	10	23	54	93	34
Finchley	42	6	7	29	50	112	24
Tring Town	42	1	9	32	30	99	12

Finchley had 1 point deducted
Clapton had 3 points deducted

1990-91

Premier Division

Redbridge Forest	42	29	6	7	74	43	93
Enfield	42	26	11	5	83	30	89
Aylesbury United	42	24	11	7	90	47	83
Woking	42	24	10	8	84	39	82
Kingstonian	42	21	12	9	86	57	75
Grays Athletic	42	20	8	14	66	53	68
Marlow	42	18	13	11	72	49	67
Hayes	42	20	5	17	60	57	65
Carshalton Athletic	42	19	7	16	80	67	64
Wivenhoe Town	42	16	11	15	69	66	59
Wokingham Town	42	15	13	14	58	54	58
Windsor & Eton	42	15	10	17	48	63	55
Bishop's Stortford	42	14	12	16	54	49	54
Dagenham	42	13	11	18	62	68	50
Hendon	42	12	10	20	48	62	46
St Albans City	42	11	12	19	60	74	45
Bognor Regis Town	42	12	8	22	44	71	44
Basingstoke Town	42	12	7	23	57	95	43
Staines Town	42	10	10	22	46	79	39
Harrow Borough	42	10	8	24	57	84	38
Barking	42	8	10	24	41	85	34
Leyton Wingate	42	7	7	28	44	91	28

Staines Town had 1 point deducted

First Division

Chesham United	42	27	8	7	102	37	89
Bromley	42	22	14	6	62	37	80
Yeading	42	23	8	11	75	45	77
Aveley	42	21	9	12	76	43	72
Hitchin Town	42	21	9	12	78	50	72
Tooting & Mitcham United	42	20	12	10	71	48	72
Walton & Hersham	42	21	8	13	73	48	71
Molesey	42	22	5	15	65	46	71
Whyteleafe	42	21	6	15	62	53	69
Dorking	42	20	5	17	78	67	65
Chalfont St Peter	42	19	5	18	56	63	62
Dulwich Hamlet	42	16	11	15	67	54	59
Harlow Town	42	17	8	17	73	64	59
Boreham Wood	42	15	8	19	46	53	53
Wembley	42	13	12	17	62	59	51
Uxbridge	42	15	5	22	45	61	50
Croydon	42	15	5	22	44	85	50
Heybridge Swifts	42	13	10	19	46	59	49
Southwick	42	13	8	21	49	75	47
Lewes	42	10	8	24	49	82	38
Metropolitan Police	42	9	6	27	55	76	33
Worthing	42	2	4	36	28	157	10

Second Division South

Abingdon Town	42	29	7	6	95	28	94
Maidenhead United	42	28	8	6	85	33	92
Egham Town	42	27	6	9	100	46	87
Malden Vale	42	26	5	11	72	44	83
Ruislip Manor	42	25	5	12	93	44	80
Southall	42	23	10	9	84	43	79
Harefield United	42	23	10	9	81	56	79
Newbury Town	42	23	8	11	71	45	77
Hungerford Town	42	16	13	13	84	69	61
Leatherhead	42	17	9	16	82	55	60
Banstead Athletic	42	15	13	14	58	62	58
Hampton	42	14	15	13	62	43	57
Epsom & Ewell	42	15	12	15	49	50	57
Chertsey Town	42	15	9	18	76	72	54
Horsham	42	14	7	21	58	67	49
Flackwell Heath	42	11	11	20	56	78	44
Bracknell Town	42	11	7	24	60	97	40
Feltham	42	10	8	24	45	80	38
Cove	42	10	7	25	51	94	37
Eastbourne United	42	10	7	25	53	109	37
Petersfield United	42	6	3	33	35	119	21
Camberley Town	42	1	6	35	27	143	9

1991-92

Premier Division

Woking	42	30	7	5	96	25	97
Enfield	42	24	7	11	59	45	79
Sutton United	42	19	13	10	88	51	70
Chesham United	42	20	10	12	67	48	70
Wokingham Town	42	19	10	13	73	58	67
Marlow	42	20	7	15	56	50	67
Ayelsbury United	42	16	17	9	69	46	65
Carshalton Athletic	42	18	8	16	64	67	62
Dagenham	42	15	16	11	70	59	61
Kingstonian	42	17	8	17	71	65	59
Windsor & Eton	42	15	11	16	56	56	56
Bromley	42	14	12	16	51	57	54
St Albans City	42	14	11	17	66	70	53
Basingstoke Town	42	14	11	17	56	65	53
Grays Athletic	42	14	11	17	53	68	53
Wivenhoe Town	42	16	4	22	56	81	52
Hendon	42	13	9	20	59	73	48
Harrow Borough	42	11	13	18	58	78	46
Hayes	42	10	14	18	52	63	44
Staines Town	42	11	10	21	43	73	43
Bognor Regis Town	42	9	11	22	51	89	38
Bishop's Stortford	42	7	12	23	41	68	33

First Division

Stevenage Borough	40	30	6	4	95	37	96
Yeading	40	24	10	6	83	34	82
Dulwich Hamlet	40	22	9	9	71	40	75
Boreham Wood	40	22	7	11	65	40	73
Wembley	40	21	6	13	54	43	69
Abingdon Town	40	19	8	13	60	47	65
Tooting & Mitcham United	40	16	13	11	57	45	61
Hitchin Town	40	17	10	13	55	45	61
Walton & Hersham	40	15	13	12	62	50	58
Molesey	40	16	9	15	55	61	57
Dorking	40	16	7	17	68	65	55
Barking	40	14	11	15	51	54	53
Chalfont St Peter	40	15	6	19	62	70	51
Leyton Wingate	40	13	11	16	53	56	50
Uxbridge	40	13	8	19	47	62	47
Maidenhead United	40	13	7	20	52	61	46
Harlow Town	40	11	9	20	50	70	42
Croydon	40	11	6	23	44	68	39
Heybridge Swifts	40	8	9	23	33	71	33
Whyteleafe	40	7	10	23	42	78	31
Aveley	40	8	3	29	33	95	27

Second Division

Purfleet	42	27	8	7	97	48	89
Lewes	42	23	14	5	74	36	83
Billericay Town	42	24	8	10	75	44	80
Leatherhead	42	23	6	13	68	40	75
Ruislip Manor	42	20	9	13	74	51	69
Egham Town	42	19	12	11	81	62	69
Metropolitan Police	42	20	9	13	76	58	69
Saffron Walden Town	42	19	11	12	86	67	68
Hemel Hempstead	42	18	10	14	63	50	64
Hungerford Town	42	18	7	17	53	58	61
Barton Rovers	42	17	8	17	61	64	59
Worthing	42	17	8	17	67	72	59
Witham Town	42	16	11	15	56	61	59
Banstead Athletic	42	16	10	16	69	58	58
Malden Vale	42	15	12	15	63	48	57
Rainham Town	42	14	13	15	53	48	55
Ware	42	14	9	19	58	62	51
Berkhamsted Town	42	13	11	18	56	57	50
Harefield United	42	11	7	24	47	66	40
Southall	42	8	7	27	39	93	31
Southwick	42	6	2	34	29	115	20
Newbury Town	42	4	8	30	30	117	20

Third Division

Edgware Town	40	30	3	7	106	44	93
Chertsey Town	40	29	4	7	115	44	91
Tilbury	40	26	9	5	84	40	87
Hampton	40	26	5	9	93	35	83
Horsham	40	23	8	9	92	51	77
Cove	40	21	9	10	74	49	72
Flackwell Heath	40	19	12	9	78	50	69
Thame United	40	19	7	14	73	46	64
Epsom & Ewell	40	17	11	12	55	50	62
Collier Row	40	17	9	14	67	59	60
Royston Town	40	17	7	16	59	58	58
Kingsbury Town	40	12	10	18	54	61	46
Hertford Town	40	12	10	18	55	73	46
Petersfield United	40	12	9	19	45	67	45
Camberley Town	40	11	8	21	52	69	41
Feltham & Hounslow	40	11	2	22	53	78	40
Bracknell Town	40	10	7	23	48	90	37
Hornchurch	40	8	7	25	40	87	31
Tring Town	40	9	4	27	35	94	31
Clapton	40	9	3	28	47	92	30
Eastbourne United	40	5	5	30	34	121	20

1992-93

Premier Division

Chesham United	42	30	8	4	104	34	98
St Albans City	42	28	9	5	103	50	93
Enfield	42	25	6	11	94	48	81
Carshalton Athletic	42	22	10	10	96	56	76
Sutton United	42	18	14	10	74	57	68
Grays Athletic	42	18	11	13	61	64	65
Stevenage Borough	42	8	8	16	62	60	62
Harrow Borough	42	16	14	12	59	60	62
Hayes	42	16	13	13	64	59	61
Aylesbury United	42	18	6	18	70	77	60
Hendon	42	12	18	12	52	54	54
Basingstoke Town	42	12	17	13	49	45	53
Kingstonian	42	14	10	18	59	58	52
Dulwich Hamlet	42	12	14	16	52	66	50
Marlow	42	12	11	19	72	73	47
Wokingham Town	42	11	13	18	62	81	46
Bromley	42	11	13	18	51	72	46
Wivenhoe Town	42	13	7	22	41	75	46
Yeading	42	11	12	19	58	66	45
Staines Town	42	10	13	19	59	77	43
Windsor & Eton	42	8	7	27	40	90	31
Bognor Regis Town	42	5	10	27	46	106	25

First Division

Hitchin Town	40	25	7	8	67	29	82
Molesey	40	23	11	6	81	38	80
Dorking	40	23	9	8	73	40	78
Purfleet	40	19	12	9	67	42	69
Bishop's Stortford	40	19	10	11	63	42	67
Abingdon Town	40	17	13	10	65	47	64
Tooting & Mitcham United	40	17	12	11	68	46	63
Billericay Town	40	18	6	16	67	61	60
Wembley	40	14	15	11	44	34	57
Walton & Hersham	40	14	12	14	58	54	54
Boreham Wood	40	12	14	14	44	43	50
Maidenhead United	40	10	18	12	45	50	48
Leyton	40	11	14	15	56	61	47
Whyteleafe	40	12	10	18	63	71	46
Uxbridge	40	11	13	16	50	59	46
Heybridge Swifts	40	11	9	20	47	65	42
Croydon	40	11	9	20	54	82	42
Chalfont St Peter	40	7	17	16	48	70	38
Barking	40	10	8	22	42	80	38
Lewes	40	9	10	21	34	80	37
Aveley	40	9	7	24	45	87	34

Second Division

Worthing	42	28	7	7	105	50	91
Ruislip Manor	42	25	12	5	78	33	87
Berkhamsted Town	42	24	8	10	77	55	80
Hemel Hempstead	42	22	12	8	84	52	78
Metropolitan Police	42	22	6	14	84	51	72
Malden Vale	42	20	9	13	78	54	69
Chertsey Town	42	20	7	15	84	60	67
Saffron Walden Town	42	19	10	13	63	49	67
Newbury Town	42	14	18	10	53	51	60
Hampton	42	16	11	15	59	59	59
Edgware Town	42	16	10	16	84	75	58
Egham Town	42	16	9	17	60	71	57
Banstead Athletic	42	14	13	15	67	52	55
Leatherhead	42	14	11	17	66	61	53
Ware	42	12	11	19	68	76	47
Witham Town	42	10	16	16	54	65	46
Tilbury	42	12	8	22	55	101	44
Barton Rovers	42	9	14	19	40	66	41
Hungerford Town	42	11	8	23	37	93	41
Rainham Town	42	9	10	23	56	80	37
Harefield United	42	10	7	25	37	72	37
Southall	42	7	7	28	43	106	28

Third Division

Aldershot Town	38	28	8	2	90	35	92
Thame United	38	21	11	6	84	38	74
Collier Row	38	21	11	6	68	30	74
Leighton Town	38	21	10	7	89	47	73
Cove	38	21	8	9	69	42	71
Northwood	38	19	11	8	84	68	68
Royston Town	38	17	8	13	59	42	59
East Thurrock United	38	17	7	14	69	58	58
Kingsbury Town	38	15	9	14	62	59	54
Hertford Town	38	14	10	14	61	64	52
Flackwell Heath	38	15	6	17	82	76	51
Tring Town	38	12	11	15	59	63	47
Hornchurch	38	11	13	14	53	52	46
Horsham	38	12	7	19	63	72	43
Epsom & Ewell	38	10	11	17	52	67	41
Bracknell Town	38	7	13	18	52	94	34
Clapton	38	8	7	23	46	74	31
Camberley Town	38	8	7	23	37	72	31
Petersfield United	38	6	12	20	36	90	30
Feltham & Hounslow	38	5	4	29	47	119	19

1993-94

Premier Division

Stevenage Borough	42	31	4	7	88	39	97
Enfield	42	28	8	6	80	28	92
Marlow	42	25	7	10	90	67	82
Chesham United	42	24	8	10	73	45	80
Sutton United	42	23	10	9	77	31	79
Carshalton Athletic	42	22	7	13	81	53	73
St Albans City	42	21	10	11	81	54	73
Hitchin Town	42	21	7	14	81	56	70
Harrow Borough	42	18	11	13	54	56	65
Kingstonian	42	18	9	15	101	64	63
Hendon	42	18	9	15	61	51	63
Aylesbury United	42	17	7	18	64	67	58
Hayes	42	15	8	19	63	72	53
Grays Athletic	42	15	5	22	56	69	50
Bromley	42	14	7	21	56	69	49
Dulwich Hamlet	42	13	8	21	52	74	47
Yeading	42	11	13	18	58	66	46
Molesey	42	11	11	20	44	62	44
Wokingham Town	42	11	6	25	38	67	39
Dorking	42	9	4	29	58	104	31
Basingstoke Town	42	5	12	25	38	86	27
Wivenhoe Town	42	5	3	34	38	152	18

First Division

Bishop's Stortford	42	24	13	5	83	31	85
Purfleet	42	22	12	8	70	44	78
Walton & Hersham	42	22	11	9	81	53	77
Tooting & Mitcham United	42	21	12	9	66	37	75
Heybridge Swifts	42	20	11	11	72	45	71
Billericay Town	42	20	11	11	70	51	71
Abingdon Town	42	20	10	12	61	50	70
Worthing	42	19	11	12	79	46	68
Leyton	42	20	8	14	88	66	68
Boreham Wood	42	17	15	10	69	50	66
Staines Town	42	18	9	15	85	56	63
Bognor Regis Town	42	15	14	13	57	48	59
Wembley	42	16	10	16	66	52	58
Barking	42	15	11	16	63	69	56
Uxbridge	42	15	8	19	57	58	53
Whyteleafe	42	15	6	21	71	90	51
Maidenhead United	42	12	13	17	52	48	49
Berkhamsted Town	42	12	9	21	65	77	45
Ruislip Manor	42	10	8	24	42	79	38
Chalfont St Peter	42	7	10	25	40	79	31
Windsor & Eton	42	8	7	27	47	94	31
Croydon	42	3	3	36	37	198	12

Second Division

Newbury Town	42	32	7	3	115	36	103
Chertsey Town	42	33	3	6	121	48	102
Aldershot Town	42	30	7	5	78	27	97
Barton Rovers	42	25	8	9	68	37	83
Witham Town	42	21	10	11	68	51	73
Malden Vale	42	20	10	12	70	49	70
Thame United	42	19	12	11	87	51	69
Metropolitan Police	42	20	9	13	75	54	69
Banstead Athletic	42	19	9	14	56	53	66
Aveley	42	19	5	18	60	66	62
Edgware Town	42	16	10	16	88	75	58
Saffron Walden Town	42	17	7	18	61	62	58
Hemel Hempstead	42	14	11	17	47	43	53
Egham Town	42	14	8	20	48	65	50
Ware	42	14	7	21	48	76	49
Hungerford Town	42	13	7	22	56	66	46
Tilbury	42	13	3	26	59	81	42
Hampton	42	12	5	25	42	70	41
Leatherhead	42	10	6	26	46	92	36
Lewes	42	8	11	24	38	85	34
Collier Row	42	7	8	27	37	88	29
Rainham Town	42	4	2	36	24	116	14

Third Division

Bracknell Town	40	25	8	7	78	29	83
Cheshunt	40	23	12	5	62	34	81
Oxford City	40	24	6	10	94	55	78
Harlow Town	40	22	11	7	61	36	77
Southall	40	17	12	11	66	53	63
Camberley Town	40	18	7	15	56	50	61
Hertford Town	40	18	6	16	67	65	60
Royston Town	40	15	11	14	44	41	56
Northwood	40	15	11	14	78	77	56
Epsom & Ewell	40	15	9	16	63	62	54
Harefield United	40	12	15	13	45	55	51
Cove	40	15	6	19	59	74	51
Kingsbury Town	40	12	14	14	57	54	50
Feltham & Hounslow	40	14	7	19	60	63	49
Leighton Town	40	12	11	17	51	64	47
East Thurrock Town	40	10	15	15	65	64	45
Clapton	40	12	9	19	51	65	45
Hornchurch	40	12	8	20	42	60	44
Tring Town	40	10	11	19	48	64	41
Flackwell Heath	40	9	11	20	44	83	38
Horsham	40	6	8	26	43	86	26

1994-95

Premier Division

Enfield	42	26	9	5	106	43	93
Slough Town	42	22	13	7	82	56	79
Hayes	42	20	14	8	66	47	74
Aylesbury United	42	21	6	15	86	59	69
Hitchin Town	42	18	12	12	68	59	66
Bromley	42	18	11	13	76	67	65
St Albans City	42	17	13	12	96	81	64
Molesey	42	18	8	16	65	61	62
Yeading	42	14	15	13	60	59	57
Harrow Borough	42	17	6	19	64	67	57
Dulwich Hamlet	42	16	9	17	70	82	57
Carshalton Athletic	42	16	9	17	69	84	57
Kingstonian	42	16	8	18	62	57	56
Walton & Hersham	42	14	11	17	75	73	53
Sutton United	42	13	12	17	74	69	51
Purfleet	42	13	12	17	76	90	51
Hendon	42	12	14	16	57	65	50
Grays Athletic	42	11	16	15	57	61	49
Bishop's Stortford	42	12	11	19	53	76	47
Chesham United	42	12	9	21	60	87	45
Marlow	42	10	9	23	52	84	39
Wokingham Town	42	6	9	27	39	86	27

First Division

Boreham Wood	42	31	5	6	90	38	98
Worthing	42	21	13	8	93	49	76
Chertsey Town	42	21	11	10	109	57	74
Aldershot Town	42	23	5	14	80	53	74
Billericay Town	42	20	9	13	68	52	69
Staines Town	42	17	12	13	83	65	63
Basingstoke Town	42	17	10	15	81	71	61
Tooting & Mitcham United	42	15	14	13	58	48	59
Wembley	42	16	11	15	70	61	59
Abingdon Town	42	16	11	15	67	69	59
Whyteleafe	42	17	7	18	70	78	58
Maidenhead United	42	15	12	15	73	76	57
Uxbridge	42	15	11	16	54	62	56
Leyton	42	15	10	17	67	66	55
Barking	42	16	7	19	74	77	55
Heybridge Swifts	42	16	6	20	73	78	54
Ruislip Manor	42	14	11	17	70	75	53
Bognor Regis Town	42	13	14	15	57	63	53
Berkhamsted Town	42	14	10	18	54	70	52
Newbury Town	42	12	15	15	58	71	51
Wivenhoe Town	42	8	7	27	47	94	31
Dorking	42	3	3	36	40	163	12

Second Division

Thame United	42	30	3	9	97	49	93
Barton Rovers	42	25	7	10	93	51	82
Oxford City	42	24	8	10	86	47	80
Bracknell Town	42	23	9	10	86	47	78
Metropolitan Police	42	19	12	11	81	65	69
Hampton	42	20	9	13	79	74	69
Croydon	42	20	5	17	85	65	65
Banstead Athletic	42	18	10	14	73	59	64
Saffron Walden Town	42	17	13	12	64	59	64
Chalfont St Peter	42	17	12	13	67	54	63
Witham Town	42	18	9	15	75	64	63
Leatherhead	42	16	12	14	71	75	60
Edgware Town	42	16	10	16	70	66	58
Tilbury	42	15	9	18	62	82	54
Cheshunt	42	13	13	16	66	81	52
Ware	42	14	7	21	61	81	49
Egham Town	42	11	14	17	60	65	47
Hemel Hempstead	42	10	11	21	45	76	41
Hungerford Town	42	11	7	24	55	81	40
Windsor & Eton	42	10	8	24	58	84	38
Aveley	42	9	5	28	48	95	32
Malden Vale	42	5	9	28	46	108	24

Third Division

Collier Row	40	30	5	5	86	23	95
Canvey Island	40	28	4	8	88	42	88
Bedford Town	40	22	11	7	90	50	77
Northwood	40	22	8	10	80	47	74
Horsham	40	22	6	12	84	61	72
Southall	40	21	8	11	87	59	71
Leighton Town	40	20	8	12	66	43	68
Camberley Town	40	19	8	13	59	39	65
Kingsbury Town	40	18	11	1	72	54	65
Hornchurch	40	17	8	15	64	63	59
Clapton	40	14	11	15	69	61	53
Tring Town	40	13	12	15	68	69	51
East Thurrock United	40	14	8	18	60	79	50
Epsom & Ewell	40	13	10	17	58	62	49
Harlow Town	40	13	8	19	53	83	47
Harefield United	40	12	8	20	51	79	44
Hertford Town	40	11	10	19	56	78	43
Feltham & Hounslow	40	13	4	23	64	87	43
Flackwell Heath	40	8	4	28	50	99	28
Lewes	40	6	5	29	34	104	23
Cove	40	3	5	32	37	94	14

1995-96

Premier Division

Hayes	42	24	14	4	76	32	86
Enfield	42	26	8	8	78	35	86
Boreham Wood	42	24	1	7	69	29	83
Yeovil Town	42	23	11	8	83	51	80
Dulwich Hamlet	42	23	11	8	85	59	80
Carshalton Athletic	42	22	8	12	68	49	74
St Albans City	42	20	12	10	70	41	72
Kingstonian	42	20	11	11	62	38	71
Harrow Borough	42	19	10	13	70	56	67
Sutton United	42	17	14	11	71	56	65
Aylesbury United	42	17	12	13	71	58	63
Bishop's Stortford	42	16	9	17	61	62	57
Yeading	42	11	14	17	48	60	47
Hendon	42	12	10	20	52	65	46
Chertsey Town	42	13	6	23	45	71	45
Purfleet	42	12	8	22	48	67	44
Grays Athletic	42	11	11	20	43	63	44
Hitchin Town	42	10	10	22	41	74	40
Bromley	42	10	7	25	52	91	37
Molesey	42	9	9	24	46	81	36
Walton & Hersham	42	9	7	26	42	79	34
Worthing	42	4	7	31	42	106	19

First Division

Oxford City	42	28	7	7	98	60	91
Heybridge Swifts	42	27	7	8	97	43	88
Staines Town	42	23	11	8	82	59	80
Leyton Pennant	42	22	7	13	77	57	73
Aldershot Town	42	21	9	12	81	46	72
Billericay Town	42	19	9	14	58	58	66
Bognor Regis Town	42	18	11	13	71	53	65
Marlow	42	19	5	18	72	75	62
Basingstoke Town	42	16	13	13	70	60	61
Uxbridge	42	16	12	14	46	49	60
Wokingham Town	42	16	10	16	62	65	58
Chesham United	42	15	12	15	51	44	57
Thame United	42	14	13	15	64	73	55
Maidenhead United	42	12	14	16	50	63	50
Whyteleafe	42	12	13	17	71	81	49
Abingdon Town	42	13	9	20	63	80	48
Barton Rovers	42	12	10	20	69	87	46
Berkhamsted Town	42	11	11	20	52	68	44
Tooting & Mitcham United	42	11	10	21	45	64	43
Ruislip Manor	42	11	9	22	55	77	42
Wembley	42	11	8	23	49	66	41
Barking	42	4	12	26	35	90	24

Second Division

Canvey Island	40	25	12	3	91	36	87
Croydon	40	25	6	9	78	42	81
Hampton	40	23	10	7	74	44	79
Banstead Athletic	40	21	11	8	72	36	74
Collier Row	40	21	11	8	73	41	74
Wivenhoe Town	40	21	8	11	82	57	71
Metropolitan Police	40	18	10	12	57	45	64
Bedford Town	40	18	10	12	69	59	64
Bracknell Town	40	18	8	14	69	50	62
Edgware Town	40	16	9	15	72	67	57
Tilbury	40	12	11	17	52	62	47
Ware	40	13	8	19	55	80	47
Chalfont St Peter	40	11	13	16	58	63	46
Leatherhead	40	12	10	18	71	77	46
Saffron Walden Town	40	11	12	17	56	58	45
Cheshunt	40	10	12	18	56	90	42
Hemel Hempstead	40	10	10	20	46	62	40
Egham Town	40	12	3	25	42	74	39
Witham Town	40	8	10	22	35	68	34
Hungerford Town	40	9	7	24	44	79	34
Dorking	40	8	5	27	44	104	29

Third Division

Horsham	40	29	5	6	95	40	92
Leighton Town	40	28	5	7	95	34	89
Windsor & Eton	40	27	6	7	117	46	87
Wealdstone	40	23	8	9	104	39	77
Harlow Town	40	22	10	8	85	62	76
Northwood	40	20	9	11	76	56	69
Epsom & Ewell	40	18	14	8	95	57	68
Kingsbury Town	40	15	16	9	61	48	61
East Thurrock United	40	17	8	15	61	50	59
Aveley	40	16	10	14	62	53	58
Wingate & Finchley	40	16	7	17	74	70	55
Lewes	40	14	7	19	56	72	49
Flackwell Heath	40	14	5	21	60	84	47
Hornchurch	40	11	8	21	55	77	41
Harefield United	40	11	7	22	49	89	40
Tring Town	40	10	8	22	40	78	38
Camberley Town	40	9	9	22	45	81	36
Hertford Town	40	10	5	25	72	103	35
Cove	40	8	10	22	37	89	34
Clapton	40	9	6	25	48	89	33
Southall	40	9	5	26	34	104	32

1996-97

Premier Division

Yeovil Town	42	31	8	3	83	34	101
Enfield	42	28	11	3	91	29	98
Sutton United	42	18	13	11	87	70	67
Dagenham & Redbridge	42	18	11	13	57	43	65
Yeading	42	17	14	11	58	47	65
St Albans City	42	18	11	13	65	55	65
Aylesbury United	42	18	11	13	64	54	65
Purfleet	42	17	11	14	67	63	62
Heybridge Swifts	42	16	14	12	62	62	62
Boreham Wood	42	15	13	14	56	52	58
Kingstonian	42	16	8	18	79	79	56
Dulwich Hamlet	42	14	13	15	57	57	55
Carshalton Athletic	42	14	11	17	51	56	53
Hitchin Town	42	15	7	20	67	73	52
Oxford City	42	14	10	18	67	83	52
Hendon	42	13	12	17	53	59	51
Harrow Borough	42	12	14	16	58	62	50
Bromley	42	13	9	20	67	72	48
Bishop's Stortford	42	10	13	19	43	64	43
Staines Town	42	10	8	24	46	71	38
Grays Athletic	42	8	9	25	43	78	33
Chertsey Town	42	8	7	27	40	98	31

First Division

Chesham United	42	27	6	9	80	46	87
Basingstoke Town	42	22	13	7	81	38	79
Walton & Hersham	42	21	13	8	67	41	76
Hampton	42	21	12	9	62	39	75
Billericay Town	42	21	12	9	69	49	75
Bognor Regis Town	42	21	9	12	63	44	72
Aldershot Town	42	19	14	9	67	45	71
Uxbridge	42	15	17	10	65	48	62
Whyteleafe	42	18	7	17	71	68	61
Molesey	42	17	9	16	50	53	60
Abingdon Town	42	15	11	16	44	42	56
Leyton Pennant	42	14	12	16	71	72	54
Maidenhead United	42	15	10	17	57	57	52
Wokingham Town	42	14	10	18	41	45	52
Thame United	42	13	10	19	57	69	49
Worthing	42	11	11	20	58	77	44
Barton Rovers	42	11	11	20	61	58	44
Croydon	42	11	10	21	40	57	43
Berkhamsted Town	42	11	9	22	47	66	42
Canvey Island	42	9	14	19	52	71	41
Marlow	42	11	6	25	41	84	39
Tooting & Mitcham United	42	8	8	26	40	85	32

Maidenhead United had 3 points deducted

Second Division

Collier Row & Romford	42	28	12	2	93	33	96
Leatherhead	42	30	5	7	116	45	95
Wembley	42	23	11	8	92	45	80
Barking	42	22	13	7	69	40	79
Horsham	42	22	11	9	78	48	77
Edgware Town	42	20	14	8	74	50	74
Bedford Town	42	21	8	13	77	43	71
Banstead Athletic	42	21	5	16	75	52	68
Windsor & Eton	42	17	13	12	65	62	64
Leighton Town	42	17	12	13	64	52	63
Bracknell Town	42	17	9	16	78	71	60
Wivenhoe Town	42	17	9	16	69	62	60
Chalfont St Peter	42	14	13	15	53	61	55
Hungerford Town	42	14	13	15	68	77	55
Metropolitan Police	42	14	7	21	72	75	49
Tilbury	42	14	7	21	68	77	49
Witham Town	42	11	10	21	39	67	43
Egham Town	42	10	9	23	47	86	39
Cheshunt	42	9	3	30	37	101	30
Ware	42	7	8	27	44	80	29
Dorking	42	7	6	29	40	100	27
Hemel Hempstead	42	5	6	31	34	125	21

Third Division

Wealdstone	32	24	3	5	72	24	75
Braintree Town	32	23	5	4	99	29	74
Northwood	32	18	10	4	60	31	64
Harlow Town	32	19	4	9	60	41	61
Aveley	32	17	6	9	64	39	57
East Thurrock United	32	16	6	10	58	51	54
Camberley Town	32	15	6	11	55	44	51
Wingate & Finchley	32	11	7	14	52	63	40
Hornchurch	32	11	6	15	35	51	39
Clapton	32	11	6	15	31	49	39
Lewes	32	10	8	14	45	53	38
Kingsbury Town	32	11	4	17	41	54	37
Hertford Town	32	10	6	16	55	65	36
Epsom & Ewell	32	8	5	19	62	78	29
Flackwell Heath	32	8	5	19	36	71	29
Tring Town	32	7	3	22	33	74	24
Southall	32	6	4	22	28	69	22

1997-98

Premier Division

Kingstonian	42	25	12	5	84	35	87
Boreham Wood	42	23	11	8	81	42	80
Sutton United	42	22	12	8	83	56	78
Dagenham & Redbridge	42	21	10	11	73	50	73
Hendon	42	21	10	11	69	50	73
Heybridge Swifts	42	18	11	13	74	62	65
Enfield	42	18	8	16	66	58	62
Basingstoke Town	42	17	11	14	56	60	62
Walton & Hersham	42	18	6	18	50	70	60
Purfleet	42	15	13	14	57	58	58
St Albans City	42	17	7	18	54	59	58
Harrow Borough	42	15	10	17	60	67	55
Gravesend & Northfleet	42	15	8	19	65	67	53
Chesham United	42	14	10	18	71	70	52
Bromley	42	13	13	16	53	53	52
Dulwich Hamlet	42	13	11	18	56	67	50
Carshalton Athletic	42	13	9	20	54	77	48
Aylesbury United	42	13	8	21	55	70	47
Bishop's Stortford	42	14	5	23	53	69	47
Yeading	42	12	11	19	49	65	47
Hitchin Town	42	8	15	19	45	62	39
Oxford City	42	7	9	26	35	76	30

First Division

First Division							
Aldershot Town	42	28	8	6	89	36	92
Billericay Town	42	25	6	11	78	44	81
Hampton	42	22	15	5	75	47	81
Maidenhead United	42	25	5	12	76	37	80
Uxbridge	42	23	6	13	66	59	75
Grays Athletic	42	21	10	11	79	49	73
Romford	42	21	8	13	92	59	71
Bognor Regis Town	42	20	9	13	77	45	69
Leatherhead	42	18	11	13	70	51	65
Leyton Pennant	42	17	11	14	66	58	62
Chertsey Town	42	16	13	13	83	70	61
Worthing	42	17	6	19	64	71	57
Berkhamsted Town	42	15	8	19	59	69	53
Staines Town	42	13	10	19	54	74	49
Croydon	42	13	10	19	47	64	49
Barton Rovers	42	11	13	18	53	72	46
Wembley	42	10	15	17	38	61	45
Molesey	42	10	11	21	47	65	41
Whyteleafe	42	10	10	22	48	83	40
Wokingham Town	42	7	10	25	41	74	31
Abingdon Town	42	9	4	29	47	101	31
Thame United	42	7	9	25	33	96	30

Second Division

Second Division							
Canvey Island	42	30	8	4	116	41	98
Braintree Town	42	29	11	2	117	45	98
Wealdstone	42	24	11	7	81	46	83
Bedford Town	42	22	12	8	55	25	78
Metropolitan Police	42	21	8	13	80	65	71
Wivenhoe Town	42	18	12	12	84	66	66
Edgware Town	42	18	10	14	81	65	64
Chalfont St Peter	42	17	13	12	63	60	64
Northwood	42	17	11	14	65	69	62
Windsor & Eton	42	17	7	18	75	72	58
Tooting & Mitcham United	42	16	9	17	58	56	57
Barking	42	15	12	15	62	75	57
Banstead Athletic	42	15	9	18	60	63	54
Marlow	42	16	5	21	64	78	53
Horsham	42	13	9	20	67	75	48
Bracknell Town	42	13	8	21	68	93	47
Leighton Town	42	13	6	23	45	78	45
Hungerford Town	42	11	11	20	66	77	44
Witham Town	42	9	13	20	55	68	40
Tilbury	42	9	12	21	57	88	39
Egham Town	42	9	5	28	47	101	32
Cheshunt	42	4	10	28	31	90	32

Third Division

Third Division							
Hemel Hempstead	38	27	6	5	86	28	87
Hertford Town	38	26	5	7	77	31	83
Harlow Town	38	24	11	3	81	43	83
Camberley Town	38	24	7	7	93	43	79
Ford United	38	23	9	6	90	34	78
East Thurrock United	38	23	7	8	70	40	76
Epsom & Ewell	38	17	6	15	69	57	57
Ware	38	17	6	15	69	57	57
Aveley	38	16	7	15	65	57	55
Corinthian Casuals	38	16	6	16	59	57	54
Hornchurch	38	12	9	17	55	68	45
Clapton	38	13	6	19	46	61	45
Flackwell Heath	38	12	9	17	50	76	45
Croydon Athletic	38	12	7	19	58	63	43
Tring Town	38	12	7	19	51	69	43
Southall	38	10	6	22	41	85	46
Dorking	38	9	6	23	49	94	33
Wingate & Finchley	38	7	8	23	46	80	29
Lewes	38	7	5	26	34	88	26
Kingsbury Town	38	5	3	30	35	93	18

1998-99

Premier Division

Premier Division							
Sutton United	42	27	7	8	89	39	88
Aylesbury United	42	23	8	11	67	38	77
Dagenham & Redbridge	42	20	13	9	71	44	73
Purfleet	42	22	7	13	71	54	73
Enfield	42	21	9	12	73	49	72
St Albans City	42	17	17	8	71	52	68
Aldershot Town	42	16	14	12	83	48	62
Basingstoke Town	42	17	10	15	63	53	61
Harrow Borough	42	17	9	16	72	66	60
Gravesend & Northfleet	42	18	6	18	54	53	60
Slough Town	42	16	11	15	60	53	59
Billericay Town	42	15	13	14	54	56	58
Hendon	42	16	9	17	70	71	57
Boreham Wood	42	14	15	13	59	63	57
Chesham United	42	15	9	18	58	79	54
Dulwich Hamlet	42	14	8	20	53	63	50
Heybridge Swifts	42	13	9	20	51	85	48
Walton & Hersham	42	12	7	23	50	77	43
Hampton	42	10	12	20	41	71	42
Carshalton Athletic	42	10	10	22	47	82	40
Bishops Stortford	42	9	10	23	49	90	37
Bromley	42	8	11	23	50	72	35

First Division

First Division							
Canvey Island	42	28	6	8	76	41	90
Hitchin Town	42	25	10	7	75	38	85
Wealdstone	42	26	6	10	75	48	84
Braintree Town	42	20	10	12	75	48	70
Bognor Regis Town	42	20	8	14	63	44	68
Grays Athletic	42	19	11	12	56	42	68
Oxford City	42	16	14	12	58	51	62
Croydon	42	16	13	13	53	53	61
Chertsey Town	42	14	16	12	57	57	58
Romford	42	14	15	13	58	63	57
Maidenhead United	42	13	15	14	50	46	54
Worthing	42	13	13	16	47	61	52
Leyton Pennant	42	13	12	17	62	70	51
Uxbridge	42	13	11	18	54	51	50
Barton Rovers	42	11	15	16	43	49	48
Yeading	42	12	10	20	51	55	46
Leatherhead	42	12	9	21	48	59	45
Whyteleafe	42	13	6	23	51	72	45
Staines Town	42	10	15	17	33	57	45
Molesey	42	8	20	14	35	52	44
Wembley	42	10	10	22	36	71	40
Berkhamsted Town	42	10	7	25	53	81	37

Second Division

Second Division							
Bedford Town	42	29	7	6	89	31	94
Harlow Town	42	27	8	7	100	47	89
Thame United	42	26	8	8	89	50	86
Hemel Hempstead	42	21	12	9	90	50	75
Windsor & Eton	42	22	6	14	87	55	72
Banstead Athletic	42	21	8	13	83	62	71
Northwood	42	20	7	15	67	68	67
Tooting & Mitcham United	42	19	9	14	63	62	66
Chalfont St Peter	42	16	12	14	70	71	60
Metropolitan Police	42	17	8	17	61	58	59
Leighton Town	42	16	10	16	60	64	58
Horsham	42	17	6	19	74	67	57
Marlow	42	16	9	17	72	68	57
Edgware Town	42	14	10	18	65	68	52
Witham Town	42	12	15	15	64	64	51
Hungerford Town	42	13	12	17	59	61	51
Wivenhoe Town	42	14	8	20	71	83	50
Wokingham Town	42	14	4	24	44	79	46
Barking	42	10	11	21	50	75	41
Hertford Town	42	11	2	29	44	96	35
Bracknell Town	42	7	10	25	48	92	31
Abingdon Town	42	6	6	30	48	124	24

Third Division

Ford United	38	27	5	6	110	42	86
Wingate & Finchley	38	25	5	8	79	38	80
Cheshunt	38	23	10	5	70	41	79
Lewes	38	25	3	10	86	45	78
Epsom & Ewell	38	19	5	14	61	51	62
Ware	38	19	4	15	79	60	61
Tilbury	38	17	8	13	74	52	59
Croydon Athletic	38	16	10	12	82	59	58
East Thurrock United	38	15	13	10	74	56	58
Egham Town	38	16	8	14	65	58	56
Corinthian Casuals	38	16	7	15	70	71	55
Southall	38	14	9	15	68	66	51
Camberley Town	38	14	8	16	66	77	50
Aveley	38	12	7	19	50	67	43
Flackwell Heath	38	11	9	18	59	70	42
Hornchurch	38	10	9	19	48	73	39
Clapton	38	11	6	21	48	89	39
Dorking	38	8	7	23	52	98	31
Kingsbury Town	38	6	3	29	40	98	21
Tring Town	38	5	6	27	38	108	21

1999-2000

Premier Division

Dagenham & Redbridge	42	32	5	5	97	35	101
Aldershot Town	42	24	5	13	71	51	77
Chesham United	42	20	10	12	64	50	70
Purfleet	42	18	15	9	70	48	69
Canvey Island	42	21	6	15	70	53	69
St Albans City	42	19	10	13	75	55	67
Billericay Town	42	18	12	12	62	62	66
Hendon	42	18	8	16	61	64	62
Slough Town	42	17	9	16	61	59	60
Dulwich Hamlet	42	17	5	20	62	68	56
Gravesend & Northfleet	42	15	10	17	66	67	55
Farnborough Town	42	14	11	17	52	55	53
Hampton & Richmond Borough	42	13	13	16	49	57	52
Enfield	42	13	11	18	64	68	50
Heybridge Swifts	42	13	11	18	57	65	50
Hitchin Town	42	13	11	18	59	72	50
Carshalton Athletic	42	12	12	18	55	65	48
Basingstoke Town	42	13	9	20	56	71	48
Harrow Borough	42	14	6	22	54	70	48
Aylesbury United	42	13	9	20	64	81	48
Boreham Wood	42	11	10	21	44	71	43
Walton & Hersham	42	11	8	23	44	70	41

First Division

Croydon	42	25	9	8	85	47	84
Grays Athletic	42	21	12	9	80	44	75
Maidenhead United	42	20	15	7	72	45	75
Thame United	42	20	13	9	61	38	73
Worthing	42	19	12	11	80	60	69
Staines Town	42	19	12	11	63	52	69
Whyteleafe	42	20	9	13	60	49	69
Bedford Town	42	17	12	13	59	52	63
Bromley	42	17	9	16	63	65	60
Uxbridge	42	15	13	14	60	44	58
Bishop's Stortford	42	16	10	16	57	62	58
Barton Rovers	42	16	8	18	64	83	56
Oxford City	42	17	4	21	57	55	55
Braintree Town	42	15	10	17	65	74	55
Yeading	42	12	18	12	53	54	54
Wealdstone	42	13	12	17	51	58	51
Bognor Regis Town	42	12	13	17	47	53	49
Harlow Town	42	11	13	18	62	76	46
Romford	42	12	9	21	51	70	45
Leatherhead	42	9	13	20	47	70	40
Chertsey Town	42	9	5	28	50	84	32
Leyton Pennant	42	7	9	26	34	85	30

Second Division

Hemel Hempstead	42	31	8	3	98	27	101
Northwood	42	29	9	4	109	40	96
Ford United	42	28	8	6	108	41	92
Berkhamsted Town	42	22	8	12	75	52	74
Windsor & Eton	42	20	13	9	73	53	73
Wivenhoe Town	42	20	9	13	61	47	69
Barking	42	18	13	11	70	51	67
Marlow	42	20	4	18	86	66	64
Metropolitan Police	42	18	7	17	75	71	61
Banstead Athletic	42	16	11	15	55	56	59
Tooting & Mitcham United	42	16	7	19	72	74	55
Wokingham Town	42	15	9	18	58	80	54
Wembley	42	14	11	17	47	53	53
Edgware Town	42	13	11	18	72	71	50
Hungerford Town	42	13	10	19	61	78	49
Cheshunt	42	12	12	18	53	65	48
Horsham	42	13	8	21	66	81	47
Leighton Town	42	13	8	21	65	84	47
Molesey	42	10	12	20	54	69	42
Wingate & Finchley	42	11	7	24	54	97	40
Witham Town	42	7	9	26	39	110	30
Chalfont St Peter	42	2	8	32	39	124	14

Third Division

East Thurrock United	40	26	7	7	89	42	85
Great Wakering Rovers	40	25	7	8	81	41	82
Tilbury	40	21	12	7	67	39	75
Hornchurch	40	19	12	9	72	57	69
Croydon Athletic	40	19	11	10	85	52	68
Epsom & Ewell	40	18	12	10	67	46	66
Lewes	40	18	10	12	73	51	64
Bracknell Town	40	15	16	9	81	64	61
Aveley	40	17	10	13	73	64	61
Corinthian Casuals	40	16	10	14	59	51	58
Flackwell Heath	40	17	6	17	74	76	57
Ware	40	16	8	16	74	62	56
Egham Town	40	14	13	13	48	43	55
Hertford Town	40	15	10	15	63	60	55
Abingdon Town	40	10	12	18	48	64	42
Kingsbury Town	40	11	8	21	55	86	41
Camberley Town	40	11	7	22	44	79	40
Tring Town	40	10	9	21	37	64	39
Dorking	40	9	10	21	53	69	37
Clapton	40	9	7	24	50	93	34
Southall	40	3	5	32	33	123	14

2000-2001

Premier Division

Farnborough Town	42	31	6	5	86	27	99
Canvey Island	42	27	8	7	79	41	89
Basingstoke Town	42	22	13	7	73	40	79
Aldershot Town	41	21	11	9	73	39	74
Chesham United	42	22	6	14	78	52	72
Gravesend & Northfleet	42	22	5	15	62	45	71
Heybridge Swifts	42	18	13	11	74	60	67
Billericay Town	41	18	13	10	62	54	67
Hampton & Richmond Borough	42	18	12	12	73	60	66
Hitchin Town	42	18	5	19	72	69	59
Purfleet	42	14	13	15	55	55	55
Hendon	42	16	6	18	62	62	54
Sutton United	41	14	11	16	74	70	53
St Albans City	42	15	5	22	50	69	50
Grays Athletic	42	14	8	20	49	68	50
Maidenhead United	42	15	2	25	47	63	47
Croydon	42	12	10	20	55	77	46
Enfield	42	12	9	21	48	74	45
Harrow Borough	41	10	11	20	61	90	41
Slough Town	42	10	9	23	40	62	39
Carshalton Athletic	42	10	6	26	40	85	36
Dulwich Hamlet	42	4	10	28	33	84	22

First Division

Boreham Wood	42	26	7	9	82	49	85
Bedford Town	42	22	16	4	81	40	82
Braintree Town	42	25	6	11	112	60	81
Bishop's Stortford	42	24	6	12	103	76	78
Thame United	42	22	8	12	86	54	74
Ford United	42	19	12	11	70	58	69
Uxbridge	42	21	5	16	73	55	68
Northwood	42	20	8	14	89	81	68
Whyteleafe	42	20	6	16	62	69	66
Oxford City	42	16	13	13	64	49	61
Harlow Town	42	15	16	11	70	66	61
Worthing	42	16	9	17	69	69	57
Staines Town	42	16	8	18	60	66	56
Aylesbury United	42	17	4	21	65	55	55
Yeading	42	15	9	18	72	74	54
Bognor Regis Town	42	13	11	18	71	71	50
Walton & Hersham	42	14	8	20	59	80	50
Bromley	42	14	6	22	63	86	48
Wealdstone	42	12	9	21	54	73	45
Leatherhead	42	12	4	26	37	87	40
Romford	42	9	4	29	53	113	31
Barton Rovers	42	2	9	31	30	94	15

Second Division

Tooting & Mitcham United	42	26	11	5	92	35	89
Windsor	42	24	10	8	70	40	82
Barking	42	23	13	6	82	54	82
Berkhamsted Town	42	24	8	10	99	49	80
Wivenhoe Town	42	23	11	8	78	52	80
Hemel Hempstead	42	22	10	10	74	44	76
Horsham	42	19	9	14	84	61	66
Chertsey Town	42	18	9	15	59	59	63
Great Wakering Rovers	42	16	13	13	69	59	61
Tilbury	42	18	6	18	61	67	60
Banstead Athletic	42	17	8	17	69	58	59
East Thurrock United	42	16	11	15	72	64	59
Metropolitan Police	42	18	4	20	64	77	58
Marlow	42	15	11	16	62	61	56
Molesey	42	14	9	19	53	61	51
Wembley	42	12	10	20	39	63	46
Hungerford Town	42	11	9	22	40	73	42
Leyton Pennant	42	10	11	21	47	74	41
Cheshunt	42	11	6	25	48	77	39
Edgware Town	42	9	9	24	41	77	36
Leighton Town	42	8	10	24	44	87	34
Wokingham Town	42	3	12	27	39	94	20

Wokingham Town had 1 point deducted

Third Division

Arlesey Town	42	34	6	2	138	37	108
Lewes	41	25	11	5	104	34	86
Ashford Town	42	26	7	9	102	49	85
Flackwell Heath	42	24	10	8	93	51	82
Corinthian Casuals	42	24	10	8	83	50	82
Aveley	42	24	3	15	85	61	75
Epsom & Ewell	42	23	4	15	76	52	73
Witham Town	42	21	9	12	76	57	72
Bracknell Town	41	19	10	12	90	70	67
Croydon Athletic	41	15	12	14	78	63	57
Ware	42	17	6	19	75	76	57
Tring Town	42	16	9	17	60	71	57
Egham Town	42	15	11	16	60	60	56
Hornchurch	42	14	13	15	73	60	55
Wingate & Finchley	42	15	7	20	75	75	52
Kingsbury Town	42	11	8	23	74	100	41
Abingdon Town	42	12	7	23	53	102	40
Dorking	42	10	9	23	59	99	39
Hertford Town	41	9	8	24	57	97	35
Camberley Town	42	8	8	26	53	107	32
Clapton	42	5	9	28	48	121	24
Chalfont St Peter	42	4	1	37	30	150	13

Abingdon Town had 3 points deducted

2001-2002

Premier Division

Gravesend & Northfleet	42	31	6	5	90	33	99
Canvey Island	42	30	5	7	107	41	95
Aldershot Town	42	22	7	13	76	51	73
Braintree Town	42	23	4	15	66	61	73
Purfleet	42	19	15	8	67	44	72
Grays Athletic	42	20	10	12	65	55	70
Chesham United	42	19	10	13	69	53	67
Hendon Town	42	19	5	18	66	54	62
Billericay Town	42	16	13	13	59	60	61
St Albans City	42	16	9	17	71	60	57
Hitchin Town	42	15	10	17	73	81	55
Sutton Albion	42	13	15	14	62	62	54
Heybridge Swifts	42	15	9	18	68	85	54
Kingstonian	42	13	13	16	50	56	52
Boreham Wood	42	15	6	21	49	62	51
Maidenhead United	42	15	5	22	51	63	50
Bedford Town	42	12	12	18	64	69	48
Basingstoke Town	42	11	15	16	50	68	48
Enfield	42	11	9	22	48	77	42
Hampton & Richmond Borough	42	9	13	20	51	71	40
Harrow Borough	42	8	10	24	50	89	34
Croydon	42	7	5	30	36	93	26

First Division

Ford United	42	27	7	8	92	56	88
Bishop's Stortford	42	26	9	7	104	51	87
Aylesbury United	42	23	10	9	96	64	79
Bognor Regis Town	42	20	13	9	74	55	73
Northwood	42	19	11	12	92	64	68
Carshalton Athletic	42	17	16	9	64	53	67
Harlow Town	42	19	9	14	77	65	66
Slough Town	42	17	11	14	68	51	62
Uxbridge	42	18	6	18	68	65	60
Oxford City	42	17	9	16	59	66	60
Thame United	42	15	14	13	75	61	59
Tooting & Mitcham United	42	16	11	15	70	70	59
Walton & Hersham	42	16	10	16	75	70	58
Yeading	42	16	10	16	84	90	58
Worthing	42	15	8	19	69	65	53
Staines Town	42	12	11	19	45	60	47
Dulwich Hamlet	42	11	13	18	64	76	46
Wealdstone	42	11	12	19	60	82	45
Bromley	42	10	11	21	44	74	41
Whyteleafe	42	10	11	21	46	86	41
Barking & East Ham United	42	8	7	27	61	123	31
Windsor & Eton	42	7	5	30	53	93	26

Second Division

Lewes	42	29	9	4	108	31	96
Horsham	42	27	9	6	104	44	90
Berkhamstead Town	42	23	10	9	82	51	79
Arlesey Town	42	23	6	13	89	55	75
Banstead Athletic	42	22	8	12	83	54	74
Leyton Pennant	42	22	8	12	84	60	74
Great Wakering Rovers	42	21	8	13	64	37	71
East Thurrock United	42	21	8	13	67	59	71
Marlow	42	18	13	11	73	63	67
Hemel Hempstead Town	42	18	10	14	82	66	64
Leatherhead	42	17	6	19	72	62	57
Ashford Town	42	15	11	16	58	71	56
Metropolitan Police	42	16	7	19	84	84	55
Barton Rovers	42	15	9	18	54	60	54
Hungerford Town	42	14	9	19	56	75	51
Tilbury	42	15	6	21	55	74	51
Chertsey Town	42	10	14	18	79	112	44
Wembley	42	9	10	23	51	82	37
Molesey	42	10	6	26	40	93	36
Cheshunt	42	7	13	22	51	84	34
Wivenhoe Town	42	8	9	25	55	111	33
Romford	42	4	7	31	42	105	19

Third Division

Croydon Athletic	42	30	5	7	138	41	95
Hornchurch	42	25	11	6	96	46	86
Aveley	42	26	6	10	109	55	84
Bracknell Town	42	25	8	9	96	54	83
Epsom & Ewell	42	20	15	7	79	51	75
Egham Town	42	21	11	10	72	59	74
Wingate & Finchley	42	20	9	13	80	60	69
Dorking	42	18	14	10	77	66	68
Tring Town	42	19	11	12	64	62	68
Corinthian-Casuals	42	18	13	11	69	44	67
Hertford Town	42	20	7	15	88	74	67
Witham Town	42	15	10	17	66	72	55
Ware	42	14	10	18	74	76	52
Chalfont St Peter	42	15	4	23	69	92	49
Wokingham Town	42	14	6	22	79	105	48
Abingdon Town	42	13	7	22	61	75	46
Leighton Town	42	8	12	22	56	95	36
Kingsbury Town	42	8	11	23	58	91	35
Edgware Town	42	9	7	26	65	101	34
Flackwell Heath	42	9	8	25	53	99	32
Clapton	42	9	4	29	45	118	31
Camberley Town	42	7	9	26	37	95	30

2002-2003

Premier Division

Aldershot Town	46	33	6	7	81	36	105
Canvey Island	46	28	8	10	112	56	92
Hendon	46	22	13	11	70	56	79
St. Albans City	46	23	8	15	73	65	77
Basingstoke Town	46	23	7	16	80	60	76
Sutton United	46	22	9	15	77	62	75
Hayes	46	20	13	13	67	54	73
Purfleet	46	19	15	12	68	48	72
Bedford Town	46	21	9	16	66	58	72
Maidenhead United	46	16	17	13	75	63	65
Kingstonian	46	16	17	13	71	64	65
Billericay Town	46	17	11	18	46	44	62
Bishop's Stortford	46	16	11	19	74	72	59
Hitchin Town	46	15	13	18	69	67	58
Ford United	46	15	12	19	78	84	57
Braintree Town	46	14	12	20	59	71	54
Aylesbury United	46	13	15	18	62	75	54
Harrow Borough	46	15	9	22	54	75	54
Grays Athletic	46	14	11	21	53	59	53
Heybridge Swifts	46	13	14	19	52	80	53
Chesham United	46	14	10	22	56	81	52
Boreham Wood	46	11	15	20	50	58	48
Enfield	46	9	11	26	47	101	38
Hampton & Richmond Borough	46	3	14	29	35	86	23

Division One (North)

Northwood	46	28	7	11	109	56	91
Hornchurch	46	25	15	6	85	48	90
Hemel Hempstead Town	46	26	7	13	70	55	85
Slough Town	46	22	14	10	86	59	80
Uxbridge	46	23	10	13	62	41	79
Aveley	46	21	14	11	66	48	77
Berkhamsted Town	46	21	13	12	92	68	76
Thame United	46	20	12	14	84	51	72
Wealdstone	46	21	9	16	85	69	72
Harlow Town	46	20	12	14	66	53	72
Marlow	46	19	10	17	74	63	67
Barking & East Ham United	46	19	9	18	73	76	66
Yeading	46	18	11	17	77	69	65
Great Wakering Rovers	46	17	14	15	64	70	65
Oxford City	46	17	13	16	55	51	64
Arlesey Town	46	17	12	17	69	71	63
East Thurrock United	46	17	10	19	75	79	61
Wingate & Finchley	46	15	11	20	70	74	56
Barton Rovers	46	15	7	24	53	65	52
Tilbury	46	14	7	25	55	96	49
Wivenhoe Town	46	9	11	26	56	94	38
Leyton Pennant	46	9	7	30	38	81	34
Wembley	46	7	11	28	57	111	32
Hertford Town	46	6	6	34	46	119	24

Division One (South)

Carshalton Athletic	46	28	8	10	73	44	92
Bognor Regis Town	46	26	10	10	92	34	88
Lewes	46	24	16	6	106	50	88
Dulwich Hamlet	46	23	12	11	73	49	81
Whyteleafe	46	21	13	12	74	51	76
Bromley	46	21	13	12	70	53	76
Walton & Hersham	46	20	13	13	87	63	73
Horsham	46	21	9	16	80	58	72
Epsom & Ewell	46	19	12	15	67	66	69
Egham Town	46	19	10	17	62	71	67
Tooting & Mitcham United	46	18	9	19	83	78	63
Worthing	46	17	12	17	78	75	63
Windsor & Eton	46	18	9	19	66	65	63
Leatherhead	46	16	13	17	71	66	61
Staines Town	46	14	16	16	57	63	58
Banstead Athletic	46	14	15	17	58	59	57
Ashford Town (Middlesex)	46	14	11	21	47	70	53
Croydon	46	15	8	23	56	87	53
Croydon Athletic	46	13	13	20	52	66	52
Bracknell Town	46	12	16	18	57	74	52
Corinthian Casuals	46	12	14	20	50	68	50
Molesey	46	13	9	24	52	79	48
Metropolitan Police	46	12	10	24	50	76	46
Chertsey Town	46	3	7	36	43	139	16

Division Two

Cheshunt	30	25	3	2	91	29	78
Leyton	30	21	5	4	77	22	68
Flackwell Heath	30	17	3	10	52	44	54
Abingdon Town	30	14	11	5	65	42	53
Hungerford Town	30	12	12	6	49	36	48
Leighton Town	30	14	3	13	61	43	45
Witham Town	30	12	8	10	40	43	44
Ware	30	12	5	13	47	53	41
Clapton	30	12	5	13	40	47	41
Tring Town	30	11	5	14	49	58	38
Kingsbury Town	30	9	11	10	38	48	38
Edgware Town	30	10	3	17	49	65	33
Wokingham Town	30	7	7	16	34	81	28
Dorking	30	6	6	18	49	63	24
Chalfont St. Peter	30	6	5	19	34	63	23
Camberley Town	30	4	4	22	23	61	16

2003-2004

Premier Division

Canvey Island	46	32	8	6	106	42	104
Sutton United	46	25	10	11	94	56	85
Thurrock	46	24	11	11	87	45	83
Hendon	46	25	8	13	68	47	83
* Hornchurch	46	24	11	11	63	35	82
Grays Athletic	46	22	15	9	82	39	81
Carshalton Athletic	46	24	9	13	66	55	81
Hayes	46	21	11	14	56	46	74
Kettering Town	46	20	11	15	63	63	71
Bognor Regis Town	46	20	10	16	69	67	70
Bishop's Stortford	46	20	9	17	78	61	69
Maidenhead United	46	18	9	19	60	68	63
Ford United	46	16	14	16	69	63	62
Basingstoke Town	46	17	9	20	58	64	60
Bedford Town	46	14	13	19	62	63	55
Heybridge Swifts	46	14	11	21	57	78	53
Harrow Borough	46	12	14	20	47	63	50
Kingstonian	46	12	13	21	40	56	49
St. Albans City	46	12	12	22	55	83	48
Hitchin Town	46	13	8	25	55	89	47
Northwood	46	12	9	25	65	95	45
Billericay Town	46	11	11	24	51	66	44
Braintree Town	46	11	6	29	41	88	39
Aylesbury United	46	5	14	27	41	101	29

* Hornchurch had 1 point deducted

Division One (North)

Yeading	46	32	7	7	112	54	103
Leyton	46	29	9	8	90	53	96
Cheshunt	46	27	10	9	119	54	91
Chesham United	46	24	9	13	104	60	81
Dunstable Town	46	23	9	14	86	61	78
Hemel Hempstead Town	46	22	12	12	75	72	78
Wealdstone	46	23	7	16	81	51	76
Arlesey Town	46	23	7	16	95	70	76
Boreham Wood	46	20	13	13	82	59	73
Harlow Town	46	20	10	16	75	51	70
Wingate & Finchley	46	19	13	14	68	63	70
East Thurrock United	46	19	11	16	62	54	68
Uxbridge	46	15	14	17	59	57	59
Aveley	46	15	14	17	67	71	59
Thame United	46	16	9	21	72	83	57
* Waltham Forest	46	15	13	18	62	60	55
Wivenhoe Town	46	15	10	21	79	104	55
Barton Rovers	46	16	6	24	52	80	54
Oxford City	46	14	11	21	55	65	53
Berkhamstead Town	46	12	10	24	66	88	46
Great Wakering Rovers	46	10	13	23	47	97	43
Tilbury	46	10	9	27	56	100	39
Barking & East Ham United	46	8	7	31	37	100	31
Enfield	46	5	7	34	44	138	22

* Waltham Forest had 3 points deducted.

Division One (South)

Lewes	46	29	7	10	113	61	94
Worthing	46	26	14	6	87	46	92
Windsor & Eton	46	26	13	7	75	39	91
Slough Town	46	28	6	12	103	63	90
Hampton & Richmond Borough	46	26	11	9	82	45	89
Staines Town	46	26	9	11	85	52	87
Dulwich Hamlet	46	23	15	8	77	57	84
Bromley	46	22	10	14	80	58	76
Walton & Hersham	46	20	14	12	76	55	74
Croydon Athletic	46	20	10	16	70	54	70
Tooting & Mitcham United	46	20	9	17	82	68	69
Ashford Town (Middlesex)	46	18	13	15	69	62	67
Leatherhead	46	19	9	18	83	88	66
Bracknell Town	46	19	6	21	81	87	63
Horsham	46	16	11	19	71	69	59
Marlow	46	16	11	19	50	64	59
Whyteleafe	46	17	4	25	66	93	55
Banstead Athletic	46	15	8	23	56	73	53
Molesey	46	12	6	28	45	84	42
Metropolitan Police	46	9	14	23	58	84	41
Croydon	46	10	10	26	57	88	40
Egham Town	46	8	8	30	55	92	32
Corinthian Casuals	46	6	6	34	48	110	24
Epsom & Ewell	46	5	8	33	40	117	23

Division Two

Leighton Town	42	28	7	7	111	36	91
Dorking	42	27	8	7	87	47	89
Hertford Town	42	24	9	9	74	35	81
Chertsey Town	42	22	9	11	75	53	75
Flackwell Heath	42	22	5	15	71	53	71
Witham Town	42	20	10	12	75	54	70
Kingsbury Town	42	14	11	17	60	64	53
Ware	42	14	10	18	67	60	52
Abingdon Town	42	15	6	21	83	81	51
Camberley Town	42	15	6	21	51	71	51
Wembley	42	13	9	20	46	67	48
Wokingham Town	42	12	7	23	55	94	43
Edgware Town	42	12	6	24	62	88	42
Chalfont St. Peter	42	12	6	24	57	89	42
Clapton	42	8	5	29	47	129	29

2004-2005

Premier Division

Yeading	42	25	11	6	74	48	86
Billericay Town	42	23	11	8	78	40	80
Eastleigh	42	22	13	7	84	49	79
Braintree Town	42	19	17	6	67	33	74
Leyton	42	21	8	13	71	57	71
Hampton & Richmond	42	21	8	13	64	53	71
Heybridge Swifts	42	18	9	15	76	65	63
Chelmsford City	42	17	11	14	63	58	62
Staines Town	42	17	9	16	59	53	60
Worthing	42	16	11	15	50	45	59
Hendon	42	17	7	18	48	60	58
Salisbury City	42	16	9	17	60	64	57
Slough Town	42	15	10	17	61	66	55
Folkestone Invicta	42	14	10	18	51	53	52
Windsor & Eton	42	12	14	16	48	62	50
Harrow Borough	42	13	10	19	41	54	49
Northwood	42	14	7	21	49	66	49
Wealdstone	42	13	8	21	60	73	47
Cheshunt	42	12	11	19	58	71	47
Tonbridge Angels	42	11	10	21	47	73	43
Dover Athletic	42	10	9	23	50	66	39
Kingstonian	42	7	5	30	43	93	26

Division One

AFC Wimbledon	42	29	10	3	91	33	97
Walton & Hersham	42	28	4	10	69	34	88
Horsham	42	24	6	12	90	61	78
Bromley	42	22	9	11	69	44	75
Metropolitan Police	42	22	8	12	72	51	74
Cray Wanderers	42	19	16	7	95	54	73
Leatherhead	42	20	13	9	73	55	73
Tooting & Mitcham United	42	18	15	9	92	60	69
Whyteleafe	42	20	6	16	60	59	66
Burgess Hill Town	42	19	6	17	73	62	63
Hastings United	42	15	11	16	55	57	56
Croydon Athletic	42	13	16	13	66	65	55
Corinthian-Casuals	42	15	9	18	56	64	54
Bashley	42	13	13	16	68	74	52
Dulwich Hamlet	42	10	14	18	61	64	44
Molesey	42	12	8	22	46	70	44
Banstead Athletic	42	10	10	22	50	64	40
Newport IOW	42	10	10	22	50	88	40
Fleet Town	42	11	5	26	47	86	38
Ashford Town	42	8	12	22	47	85	36
Dorking	42	8	11	23	43	89	35
Croydon	42	5	10	27	37	91	25

Division Two

Ilford	30	22	3	5	62	23	69
Enfield	30	21	3	6	64	33	66
Brook House	30	20	4	6	65	25	64
Hertford Town	30	17	7	6	65	40	58
Witham Town	30	16	3	11	67	53	51
Chertsey Town	30	15	6	9	55	48	51
Abingdon Town	30	13	9	8	65	42	48
Edgware Town	30	12	3	15	40	41	39
Flackwell Heath	30	11	5	14	50	55	38
Ware	30	9	10	11	41	55	37
Chalfont St Peter	30	9	7	14	41	52	34
Camberley Town	30	9	5	16	36	44	32
Wembley	30	8	5	17	41	55	29
Epsom & Ewell	30	8	4	18	41	64	28
Kingsbury Town	30	5	4	21	35	76	19
Clapton	30	3	6	21	20	82	15

2005-2006

Premier Division

Braintree Town	42	28	10	4	74	32	94
Heybridge Swifts	42	28	3	11	70	46	87
Fisher Athletic	42	26	7	9	84	46	85
AFC Wimbledon	42	22	11	9	67	36	77
Hampton & Richmond	42	24	3	15	73	54	75
Staines Town	42	20	10	12	74	56	70
Billericay Town	42	19	12	11	69	45	69
Worthing	42	19	10	13	71	60	67
Walton & Hersham	42	19	7	16	55	50	64
Chelmsford City	42	18	10	14	57	62	64
Bromley	42	16	14	12	57	49	62
East Thurrock United	42	18	5	19	60	60	59
Folkestone Invicta	42	16	10	16	47	51	58
Margate	42	11	17	14	49	55	50
Leyton	42	13	9	20	58	61	48
Harrow Borough	42	13	9	20	56	73	48
Slough Town	42	13	8	21	63	75	47
Wealdstone	42	13	5	24	68	82	44
Hendon	42	9	12	21	44	64	39
Maldon Town	42	8	11	23	41	73	35
Windsor & Eton	42	8	8	26	37	75	32
Redbridge	42	3	5	34	28	97	14

Division One

Ramsgate	44	24	14	6	84	38	86
Horsham	44	25	11	8	94	55	86
Tonbridge Angels	44	24	8	12	71	48	80
Metropolitan Police	44	24	7	13	72	46	79
Dover Athletic	44	21	14	9	69	46	77
Tooting & Mitcham United	44	22	9	13	93	62	75
Kingstonian	44	20	14	10	82	56	74
Croydon Athletic	44	20	13	11	56	41	73
Bashley	44	20	10	14	63	61	70
Leatherhead	44	18	14	12	64	50	68
Cray Wanderers	44	20	8	16	80	74	68
Hastings United	44	19	10	15	65	58	67
Dulwich Hamlet	44	19	8	17	55	43	65
Fleet Town	44	13	19	12	50	56	58
Walton Casuals	44	16	10	18	68	75	58
Lymington & New Milton	44	12	11	21	61	80	47
Molesey	44	12	10	22	56	79	46
Whyteleafe	44	10	14	20	50	66	44
Burgess Hill Town	44	10	10	24	57	83	40
Banstead Athletic	44	8	13	23	43	71	37
Ashford Town	44	8	11	25	41	81	35
Newport IOW	44	6	11	27	38	97	29
Corinthian Casuals	44	6	9	29	39	85	27

Division Two

Ware	30	19	4	7	77	36	61
Witham Town	30	17	7	6	61	30	58
Brook House	30	17	7	6	63	33	58
Flackwell Heath	30	15	7	8	54	49	52
Egham Town	30	15	5	10	39	36	50
Chertsey Town	30	14	7	9	47	37	49
Edgware Town	30	13	5	12	46	41	44
Chalfont St Peter	30	13	2	15	50	53	41
Dorking	30	11	8	11	48	51	41
Croydon	30	11	7	12	43	43	40
Wembley	30	11	6	13	44	43	39
Kingsbury Town	30	9	10	11	32	37	37
Hertford Town	30	7	10	13	35	54	31
Camberley Town	30	5	8	17	31	57	23
Epsom & Ewell	30	5	6	19	32	64	21
Clapton	30	4	9	17	33	71	16

Clapton had 5 points deducted.

2006-2007

Premier Division

Hampton & Richmond	42	24	10	8	77	53	82
Bromley	42	23	11	8	83	43	80
Chelmsford City	42	23	8	11	96	51	77
Billericay Town	42	22	11	9	71	42	77
AFC Wimbledon	42	21	15	6	76	37	75
Margate	42	20	11	11	79	48	71
Boreham Wood	42	19	12	11	71	49	69
Horsham	42	18	14	10	70	57	68
Ramsgate	42	20	5	17	63	63	65
Heybridge Swifts	42	17	13	12	57	40	64
Tonbridge Angels	42	20	4	18	74	72	64
Staines Town	42	15	12	15	64	64	57
Carshalton Athletic	42	14	12	16	54	59	54
Hendon	42	16	6	20	53	64	54
Leyton	42	13	10	19	55	77	49
East Thurrock United	42	14	6	22	56	70	48
Ashford Town (Middlesex)	42	11	13	18	59	71	46
Folkestone Invicta	42	12	10	20	45	66	46
Harrow Borough	42	13	6	23	61	71	45
Worthing	42	8	11	23	57	82	35
Walton & Hersham	42	9	6	27	38	83	33
Slough Town	42	4	6	32	26	123	18

AFC Wimbledon had 3 points deducted.

Division One North

AFC Hornchurch	42	32	7	3	96	27	103
Harlow Town	42	24	10	8	71	31	82
Enfield Town	42	24	7	11	74	39	79
Maldon Town	42	20	11	11	50	42	71
AFC Sudbury	42	19	13	10	67	41	70
Canvey Island	42	19	10	13	65	47	67
Ware	42	19	10	13	70	56	67
Waltham Forest	42	17	14	11	60	56	65
Wingate & Finchley	42	16	11	15	58	49	59
Waltham Abbey	42	15	13	14	65	51	58
Wivenhoe Town	42	16	9	17	50	52	57
Great Wakering Rovers	42	16	9	17	57	64	57
Enfield	42	16	6	20	65	63	54
Potters Bar Town	42	14	9	19	60	62	51
Aveley	42	14	9	19	47	57	51
Redbridge	42	15	5	22	42	48	50
Bury Town	42	13	11	18	57	69	50
Arlesey Town	42	13	11	18	44	63	50
Tilbury	42	11	10	21	43	72	43
Witham Town	42	10	7	25	52	90	37
Ilford	42	9	5	28	36	97	32
Flackwell Heath	42	7	9	26	37	90	30

Division One South

Maidstone United	42	23	11	8	79	47	80
Tooting & Mitcham	42	22	13	7	70	41	79
Dover Athletic	42	22	11	9	77	41	77
Hastings United	42	22	10	10	79	56	76
Fleet Town	42	21	12	9	65	52	75
Metropolitan Police	42	18	15	9	65	48	69
Dartford	42	19	11	12	86	65	68
Dulwich Hamlet	42	18	13	11	83	56	67
Horsham YMCA	42	17	7	18	59	69	58
Sittingbourne	42	14	15	13	68	63	57
Leatherhead	42	15	10	17	58	63	55
Cray Wanderers	42	14	12	16	67	69	54
Kingstonian	42	13	13	16	60	63	52
Burgess Hill Town	42	13	12	17	58	81	51
Molesey	42	12	13	17	52	63	49
Chatham Town	42	12	11	19	52	62	47
Walton Casuals	42	11	13	18	57	71	46
Ashford Town	42	10	14	18	52	65	44
Croydon Athletic	42	12	8	22	44	77	44
Whyteleafe	42	9	15	18	52	65	42
Corinthian-Casuals	42	8	10	24	53	88	34
Godalming Town	42	8	9	25	45	76	33

2007-2008

Premier Division

Chelmsford City	42	26	9	7	84	39	87
Staines Town	42	22	12	8	85	54	78
AFC Wimbledon	42	22	9	11	81	47	75
AFC Hornchurch	42	20	10	12	68	44	70
Ramsgate	42	19	11	12	67	53	68
Ashford Town (Middlesex)	42	20	6	16	79	65	66
Hendon	42	18	11	13	79	67	65
Tonbridge Angels	42	17	12	13	77	57	63
Margate	42	17	11	14	71	68	62
Billericay Town	42	16	12	14	66	57	60
Horsham	42	18	5	19	63	63	59
Heybridge Swifts	42	14	13	15	64	64	55
Wealdstone	42	15	9	18	68	75	54
Hastings United	42	15	8	19	58	67	53
Harlow Town	42	13	13	16	56	52	52
Harrow Borough	42	15	7	20	61	74	52
Maidstone United	42	16	4	22	56	79	52
Carshalton Athletic	42	14	8	20	52	65	50
Boreham Wood	42	15	5	22	56	73	50
East Thurrock United	42	14	9	19	48	67	50
Folkestone Invicta	42	13	10	19	49	70	49
Leyton	42	4	4	34	35	123	16

East Thurrock United had one point deducted.

Division One North

Dartford	42	27	8	7	107	42	89
AFC Sudbury	42	24	8	10	86	40	80
Redbridge	42	24	9	9	70	43	80
Ware	42	23	10	9	110	58	79
Canvey Island	42	23	10	9	82	39	79
Brentwood Town	42	22	11	9	70	49	77
Bury Town	42	22	9	11	76	53	75
Edgware Town	42	20	14	8	53	39	74
Maldon Town	42	19	10	13	78	63	67
Northwood	42	18	12	12	71	61	66
Aveley	42	18	12	12	68	65	66
Enfield Town	42	18	9	15	60	63	63
Great Wakering Rovers	42	13	9	20	64	66	48
Waltham Abbey	42	12	10	20	42	78	46
Arlesey Town	42	12	9	21	64	84	45
Witham Town	42	12	5	25	75	109	41
Potters Bar Town	42	10	9	23	45	77	39
Wingate & Finchley	42	8	11	23	45	72	35
Waltham Forest	42	7	12	23	44	74	33
Tilbury	42	7	12	23	49	96	32
Ilford	42	8	8	26	47	95	32
Wivenhoe Town	42	8	7	27	46	86	31

Redbridge and Tilbury both had one point deducted.

Division One South

Dover Athletic	42	30	8	4	84	29	98
Tooting & Mitcham	42	26	8	8	88	41	86
Cray Wanderers	42	25	11	6	87	42	86
Metropolitan Police	42	24	3	15	69	47	75
Worthing	42	22	7	13	77	49	73
Dulwich Hamlet	42	20	10	12	68	47	70
Kingstonian	42	20	10	12	66	52	70
Ashford Town	42	19	10	13	64	51	67
Sittingbourne	42	20	7	15	56	58	67
Walton & Hersham	42	15	12	15	65	62	57
Whyteleafe	42	17	5	20	57	62	56
Burgess Hill Town	42	18	8	16	61	57	54
Croydon Athletic	42	14	9	19	65	76	51
Whitstable Town	42	14	8	20	69	84	50
Chipstead	42	15	5	22	58	76	50
Walton Casuals	42	11	15	16	55	68	48
Leatherhead	42	13	7	22	52	63	46
Chatham Town	42	12	10	20	58	70	46
Eastbourne Town	42	11	11	20	58	84	44
Corinthian-Casuals	42	11	11	20	51	77	44
Horsham YMCA	42	7	6	29	36	85	27
Molesey	42	3	9	30	36	100	18

Burgess Hill Town had 8 points deducted.

NORTHERN PREMIER LEAGUE

1968-69

Macclesfield Town	38	27	6	5	82	38	60
Wigan Athletic	38	18	12	8	59	41	48
Morecambe	38	16	14	8	64	37	46
Gainsborough Trinity	38	19	8	11	64	43	46
South Shields	38	19	8	11	78	56	46
Bangor City	38	18	9	11	102	64	45
Hyde United	38	16	10	12	71	65	42
Goole Town	38	15	10	13	80	78	40
Altrincham	38	14	10	14	69	52	38
Fleetwood	38	16	6	16	58	58	38
Gateshead	38	14	9	15	42	48	37
South Liverpool	38	12	13	13	56	66	37
Northwich Victoria	38	16	5	17	59	82	37
Boston United	38	14	8	16	59	65	36
Runcorn	38	12	11	15	59	63	35
Netherfield	38	12	4	22	51	69	28
Scarborough	38	9	10	19	49	68	28
Ashington	38	10	8	20	48	74	28
Chorley	38	8	9	21	46	75	25
Worksop Town	38	6	8	24	34	88	20

1969-70

Macclesfield Town	38	22	8	8	72	41	52
Wigan Athletic	38	20	12	6	56	32	52
Boston United	38	21	8	9	65	33	50
Scarborough	38	20	10	8	74	39	50
South Shields	38	19	7	12	66	43	45
Gainsborough Trinity	38	16	11	11	64	49	43
Stafford Rangers	38	16	7	15	59	52	39
Bangor City	38	15	9	14	68	63	39
Northwich Victoria	38	15	8	15	60	66	38
Netherfield	38	14	9	15	56	54	37
Hyde United	38	15	7	16	59	59	37
Altincham	38	14	8	16	62	65	36
Fleetwood	38	13	10	15	53	60	36
Runcorn	38	11	13	14	57	72	35
Morecambe	38	10	13	15	41	51	33
South Liverpool	38	11	11	16	44	55	33
Great Harwood	38	10	9	19	63	92	29
Matlock Town	38	8	12	18	52	67	28
Goole Town	38	10	6	22	50	71	26
Gateshead	38	5	12	21	37	94	22

1970-71

Wigan Athletic	42	27	13	2	91	32	67
Stafford Rangers	42	27	7	8	87	51	61
Scarborough	42	23	12	7	83	40	58
Boston United	42	22	12	8	69	31	56
Macclesfield Town	42	23	10	9	84	45	56
Northwich Victoria	42	22	5	15	71	55	49
Bangor City	42	19	10	13	72	61	48
Altrincham	42	19	10	13	80	76	48
South Liverpool	42	15	15	12	67	57	45
Chorley	42	14	14	14	58	61	42
Gainsborough Trinity	42	15	11	16	65	63	41
Morecambe	42	14	11	17	67	79	39
South Shields	42	12	14	16	67	66	38
Bradford Park Avenue	42	15	8	19	54	73	38
Lancaster City	42	12	12	18	53	76	36
Netherfield	42	13	9	20	59	57	35
Matlock Town	42	10	13	19	58	80	33
Fleetwood	42	10	11	21	56	90	31
Great Harwood	42	8	13	21	66	98	29
Runcorn	42	10	5	27	58	84	25
Kirkby Town	42	6	13	23	57	93	25
Goole Town	42	10	4	28	44	98	24

1971-72

Stafford Rangers	46	30	11	5	91	32	71
Boston United	46	28	13	5	87	37	69
Wigan Athletic	46	27	10	9	70	43	64
Scarborough	46	21	15	10	75	46	57
Northwich Victoria	46	20	14	12	65	59	54
Macclesfield Town	46	18	15	13	61	50	51
Gainsborough Trinity	46	21	9	16	93	79	51
South Shields	46	18	14	14	75	57	50
Bangor City	46	20	8	18	93	74	48
Altrincham	46	18	11	17	72	58	47
Skelmersdale United	46	19	9	18	61	58	47
Matlock Town	46	20	7	19	67	75	47
Chorley	46	17	12	17	66	59	46
Lancaster City	46	15	14	17	84	84	44
Great Harwood	46	15	14	17	60	74	44
Ellesmere Port Town	46	17	9	20	67	71	43
Morecambe	46	15	10	21	51	64	40
Bradford Park Avenue	46	13	13	20	54	71	39
Netherfield	46	16	5	25	51	73	37
Fleetwood	46	11	15	20	43	67	37
South Liverpool	46	12	12	22	61	73	36
Runcorn	46	8	14	24	48	80	30
Goole Town	46	9	10	27	51	97	28
Kirkby Town	46	6	12	28	38	104	24

1972-73

Boston United	46	27	16	3	88	34	70
Scarborough	46	26	9	11	72	39	61
Wigan Athletic	46	23	14	9	69	38	60
Altrincham	46	22	16	8	75	55	60
Bradford Park Avenue	46	19	17	10	63	50	55
Stafford Rangers	46	20	11	15	63	46	51
Gainsborough Trinity	46	18	13	15	70	50	49
Northwich Victoria	46	17	15	14	74	62	49
Netherfield	46	20	9	17	68	65	49
Macclesfield Town	46	16	16	14	58	47	48
Ellesmere Port Town	46	18	11	17	52	56	47
Skelmersdale United	46	15	16	15	58	59	46
Bangor City	46	16	13	17	70	60	45
Mossley	46	17	11	18	70	73	45
Morecambe	46	17	11	18	62	70	45
Great Harwood	46	14	15	17	63	74	43
South Liverpool	46	12	19	15	47	57	43
Runcorn	46	15	12	19	75	78	42
Goole Town	46	13	13	20	64	73	39
South Shields	46	17	4	25	64	81	38
Matlock Town	46	11	11	24	42	80	33
Lancaster City	46	10	11	25	53	78	31
Barrow	46	12	6	28	52	101	30
Fleetwood	46	5	15	26	31	77	25

1973-74

Boston United	46	27	11	8	69	32	65
Wigan Athletic	46	28	8	10	96	39	64
Altrincham	46	26	11	9	77	34	63
Stafford Rangers	46	27	9	10	101	45	63
Scarborough	46	22	14	10	62	43	58
South Shields	46	25	6	15	87	48	56
Runcorn	46	21	14	11	72	47	56
Macclesfield Town	46	18	15	13	48	47	51
Bangor City	46	19	11	16	65	56	49
Gainsborough Trinity	46	18	11	17	77	64	47
South Liverpool	46	16	15	15	55	47	47
Skelmersdale United	46	16	13	17	50	59	45
Goole Town	46	14	15	17	60	69	43
Fleetwood	46	14	15	17	48	68	43
Mossley	46	15	11	20	53	65	41
Northwich Victoria	46	14	13	19	68	75	41
Morecambe	46	13	13	20	62	84	39
Buxton	46	14	10	22	45	71	38
Matlock Town	46	11	14	21	50	79	36
Great Harwood	46	10	14	22	52	74	34
Bradford Park Avenue	46	9	15	22	42	84	33
Barrow	46	13	7	26	46	94	33
Lancaster City	46	10	12	24	52	67	32
Netherfield	46	11	5	30	42	88	27

1974-75

Wigan Athletic	46	33	6	7	94	38	72
Runcorn	46	30	8	8	102	42	68
Altrincham	46	26	12	8	87	43	64
Stafford Rangers	46	25	13	8	81	39	63
Scarborough	46	24	12	10	73	45	60
Mossley	46	23	11	12	78	52	57
Gateshead United	46	22	12	12	74	48	56
Goole Town	46	19	12	15	75	71	50
Northwich Victoria	46	18	12	16	83	71	48
Great Harwood	46	17	14	15	69	66	48
Matlock Town	46	19	8	19	87	79	46
Boston United	46	16	14	16	64	63	46
Morecambe	46	14	15	17	71	87	43
Worksop Town	46	14	14	18	69	66	42
South Liverpool	46	14	14	18	59	71	42
Buxton	46	11	17	18	50	77	39
Macclesfield Town	46	11	14	21	46	62	36
Lancaster City	46	13	10	23	53	76	36
Bangor City	46	13	9	24	56	67	35
Gainsborough Trinity	46	10	15	21	46	79	35
Skelmersdale United	46	13	7	26	63	93	33
Barrow	46	9	15	22	45	72	33
Netherfield	46	12	8	26	42	91	32
Fleetwood	46	5	10	31	26	97	20

1975-76

Runcorn	46	29	10	7	95	42	68
Stafford Rangers	46	26	15	5	81	41	67
Scarborough	46	26	10	10	84	43	62
Matlock Town	46	26	9	11	96	63	61
Boston United	46	27	6	13	95	58	60
Wigan Athletic	46	21	15	10	81	42	57
Altrincham	46	20	14	12	77	57	54
Bangor City	46	21	12	13	80	70	54
Mossley	46	21	11	14	70	58	53
Goole Town	46	20	13	13	58	49	53
Northwich Victoria	46	17	17	12	79	59	51
Lancaster City	46	18	9	19	61	70	45
Worksop Town	46	17	10	19	63	56	44
Gainsborough Trinity	46	13	17	16	58	69	43
Macclesfield Town	46	15	12	19	50	64	42
Gateshead United	46	17	7	22	64	63	41
Buxton	46	11	13	22	37	62	35
Skelmersdale United	46	12	10	24	45	74	34
Netherfield	46	11	11	24	55	76	33
Morecambe	46	11	11	24	47	67	33
Great Harwood	46	13	7	26	58	86	33
South Liverpool	46	12	9	25	45	78	33
Barrow	46	12	9	25	47	84	33
Fleetwood	46	3	9	34	36	131	15

1976-77

Boston United	44	27	11	6	82	35	65
Northwich Victoria	44	27	11	6	85	43	65
Matlock Town	44	26	11	7	108	57	63
Bangor City	44	22	11	11	87	52	55
Scarborough	44	21	12	11	77	66	54
Goole Town	44	23	6	15	64	50	52
Lancaster City	44	21	9	14	71	58	51
Gateshead United	44	18	12	14	80	64	48
Mossley	44	17	14	13	74	59	48
Altrincham	44	19	9	16	60	53	47
Stafford Rangers	44	16	14	14	60	55	46
Runcorn	44	15	14	15	57	49	44
Worksop Town	44	16	12	16	50	58	44
Wigan Athletic	44	14	15	15	62	54	43
Morecambe	44	13	11	20	59	75	37
Gainsborough Trinity	44	13	10	21	58	74	36
Great Harwood	44	11	14	19	63	84	36
Buxton	44	11	13	20	48	63	35
Macclesfield Town	44	8	15	21	41	68	31
Frickley Athletic	44	11	8	25	53	93	30
Barrow	44	11	6	27	56	87	28
South Liverpool	44	10	8	26	51	104	28
Netherfield	44	9	8	27	47	92	26

1977-78

Boston United	46	31	9	6	85	35	71
Wigan Athletic	46	25	15	6	83	45	65
Bangor City	46	26	10	10	92	50	62
Scarborough	46	26	10	10	80	39	62
Altrincham	46	22	15	9	84	49	59
Northwich Victoria	46	22	14	10	83	55	50
Stafford Rangers	46	22	13	11	71	41	57
Runcorn	46	19	18	9	70	44	56
Mossley	46	22	11	13	85	73	55
Matlock Town	46	21	12	13	79	60	54
Lancaster City	46	15	14	17	66	82	44
Frickley Athletic	46	15	12	19	77	81	42
Barrow	46	14	12	20	50	61	40
Goole Town	46	15	9	22	60	68	39
Great Harwood	46	13	13	20	66	83	39
Gainsborough Trinity	46	14	10	22	61	74	38
Gateshead	46	16	5	25	65	74	37
Netherfield	46	11	13	22	50	80	35
Workington	46	13	8	25	48	80	34
Worksop Town	46	12	10	24	45	84	34
Morecambe	46	11	11	24	67	92	33
Macclesfield Town	46	12	9	25	60	92	33
Buxton	46	13	6	27	60	95	32
South Liverpool	46	9	7	30	53	111	25

1978-79

Mossley	44	32	5	7	117	48	69
Altrincham	44	25	11	8	93	39	61
Matlock Town	44	24	8	12	100	59	56
Scarborough	44	19	14	11	61	44	52
Southport	44	19	14	11	62	49	52
Boston United	44	17	18	9	40	33	52
Runcorn	44	21	9	14	79	54	51
Stafford Rangers	44	18	14	12	67	41	50
Goole Town	44	17	15	12	56	61	49
Northwich Victoria	44	18	11	15	64	52	47
Lancaster City	44	17	12	15	62	54	46
Bangor City	44	15	14	15	65	66	44
Worksop Town	44	13	14	17	55	67	40
Workington	44	16	7	21	62	74	39
Netherfield	44	13	11	20	39	69	37
Barrow	44	14	9	21	47	78	37
Gainsborough Trinity	44	12	12	20	52	67	36
Morecambe	44	11	13	20	55	65	35
Frickley Athletic	44	13	9	22	58	70	35
South Liverpool	44	12	10	22	48	85	34
Gateshead	44	11	11	22	42	63	33
Buxton	44	11	9	24	50	84	31
Macclesfield Town	44	8	10	26	40	92	26

1979-80

Mossley	42	28	9	5	96	41	65
Witton Albion	42	28	8	6	89	30	64
Frickley Athletic	42	24	13	5	93	48	61
Burton Albion	42	25	6	11	83	42	56
Matlock Town	42	18	17	7	87	53	53
Buxton	42	21	9	12	61	48	51
Worksop Town	42	20	10	12	65	52	50
Macclesfield Town	42	18	11	13	67	53	47
Grantham	42	18	8	16	71	65	44
Marine	42	16	10	16	65	57	42
Goole Town	42	14	13	15	61	63	41
Lancaster City	42	13	13	16	74	77	39
Oswestry Town	42	12	14	16	44	60	38
Gainsborough Trinity	42	14	8	20	64	75	36
Runcorn	42	11	11	20	46	63	33
Gateshead	42	11	11	20	50	77	33
Morecambe	42	10	12	20	40	59	32
Netherfield	42	7	15	20	37	66	29
Southport	42	8	13	21	30	75	29
South Liverpool	42	7	14	21	51	84	28
Workington	42	8	12	22	50	85	28
Tamworth	42	8	9	25	26	77	25

1980-81

Runcorn	42	32	7	3	99	22	71
Mossley	42	24	7	11	95	55	55
Marine	42	22	10	10	60	41	54
Buxton	42	21	7	14	64	50	49
Gainsborough Trinity	42	17	13	12	50	57	47
Burton Albion	42	19	8	15	63	54	46
Witton Albion	42	19	8	15	70	62	46
Goole Town	42	14	16	12	56	50	44
South Liverpool	42	19	6	17	59	64	44
Workington	42	15	13	14	57	48	43
Gateshead	42	12	18	12	65	61	42
Worksop Town	42	15	11	16	66	61	41
Macclesfield Town	42	13	13	16	52	69	39
Grantham	42	14	9	19	57	74	37
Matlock Town	42	12	12	18	57	80	36
Lancaster City	42	13	9	20	48	70	35
Netherfield	42	11	12	19	73	81	34
Oswestry Town	42	13	8	21	54	67	34
King's Lynn	42	8	18	16	46	65	34
Southport	42	11	11	26	42	68	33
Morecambe	42	11	8	23	42	74	30
Tamworth	42	9	12	21	38	76	30

1981-82

Bangor City	42	27	8	7	108	60	62
Mossley	42	24	11	7	76	43	59
Witton Albion	42	22	10	10	75	44	54
Gateshead	42	19	14	9	65	49	52
King's Lynn	42	19	12	11	61	36	50
Grantham	42	18	13	11	65	53	49
Burton Albion	42	19	9	14	71	62	47
Southport	42	16	14	12	63	55	46
Marine	42	17	12	13	64	57	46
Macclesfield Town	42	17	9	16	67	58	43
Workington	42	18	7	17	62	60	43
Worksop Town	42	15	13	14	52	60	43
South Liverpool	42	13	13	16	55	57	39
Goole Town	42	13	13	16	56	60	39
Oswestry Town	42	14	11	17	55	59	39
Buxton	42	14	11	17	48	56	39
Lancaster City	42	13	12	17	47	50	38
Gainsborough Trinity	42	10	13	19	60	69	33
Tamworth	42	10	9	23	31	56	29
Morecambe	42	9	11	22	43	86	29
Matlock Town	42	7	12	23	38	72	26
Netherfield	42	5	9	28	31	91	19

1982-83

Gateshead	42	32	4	6	114	43	100
Mossley	42	25	9	8	77	42	84
Burton Albion	42	24	9	9	81	53	81
Chorley	42	23	11	8	77	49	80
Macclesfield Town	42	24	8	10	71	49	80
Marine	42	17	17	8	81	57	68
Workington	42	19	10	13	71	55	67
Hyde United	42	18	12	12	91	63	66
King's Lynn	42	17	13	12	62	44	64
Matlock Town	42	18	10	14	70	65	64
Witton Albion	42	17	12	13	82	52	63
Buxton	42	17	9	16	60	62	60
Morecambe	42	16	11	15	75	66	59
Grantham	42	15	13	14	49	50	58
Southport	42	11	14	17	58	65	47
Goole Town	42	13	7	22	52	66	46
Gainsborough Trinity	42	11	9	22	60	71	42
Oswestry Town	42	10	8	24	56	99	38
South Liverpool	42	7	15	20	57	91	36
Tamworth	42	7	8	27	44	97	29
Worksop Town	42	5	10	27	50	98	25
Netherfield	42	2	9	31	28	129	15

1983-84

Barrow	42	29	10	3	92	38	97
Matlock Town	42	23	8	11	72	48	77
South Liverpool	42	22	11	9	55	44	77
Grantham	42	20	8	14	64	51	68
Burton Albion	42	17	13	12	61	47	64
Macclesfield Town	42	18	10	14	63	55	64
Rhyl	42	19	6	17	64	55	63
Horwich	42	18	9	15	64	59	63
Gainsborough Trinity	42	17	11	14	82	66	62
Stafford Rangers	42	15	17	10	65	52	62
Hyde United	42	17	8	17	61	63	59
Marine	42	16	10	16	63	68	58
Witton Albion	42	14	14	14	64	57	56
Chorley	42	14	11	17	68	65	53
Workington	42	14	9	19	53	57	51
Southport	42	14	8	20	57	74	50
Worksop Town	42	13	8	21	57	74	47
Goole Town	42	12	10	20	59	80	46
Morecambe	42	11	12	19	59	75	45
Oswestry Town	42	11	8	23	66	97	41
Buxton	42	11	6	25	52	91	39
Mossley	42	9	9	24	47	74	33

Mossley had 3 points deducted

1984-85

Stafford Rangers	42	26	8	8	81	40	86
Macclesfield Town	42	23	13	6	67	39	82
Witton Albion	42	22	8	12	57	39	74
Hyde United	42	21	8	13	68	52	71
Marine	42	18	15	9	59	34	69
Burton Albion	42	18	15	9	70	49	69
Worksop Town	42	19	10	13	68	56	67
Workington	42	18	9	15	59	53	53
Horwich	42	16	14	12	67	50	62
Bangor City	42	17	9	16	70	61	60
Gainsborough Trinity	42	14	14	14	72	73	56
Southport	42	15	9	18	65	66	54
Matlock Town	42	14	9	19	56	66	51
Oswestry Town	42	14	9	19	59	75	51
Mossley	42	14	9	19	45	65	51
Goole Town	42	13	11	18	60	65	50
Rhyl	42	11	14	17	52	63	47
Morecambe	42	11	14	17	51	67	47
Chorley	42	12	10	20	47	63	46
South Liverpool	42	9	15	18	43	71	42
Grantham	42	8	13	21	41	69	36
Buxton	42	8	6	28	38	79	30

Grantham had 1 point deducted

1985-86

Gateshead	42	24	10	8	85	51	82
Marine	42	23	11	8	63	35	80
Morecambe	42	17	17	8	59	39	68
Gainsborough Trinity	42	18	14	10	66	52	68
Burton Albion	42	18	12	12	64	47	66
Southport	42	17	11	14	70	66	62
Worksop Town	42	17	10	15	51	48	61
Workington	42	14	18	10	54	46	59
Macclesfield Town	42	17	8	17	67	65	59
Hyde United	42	14	15	13	63	62	57
Witton Albion	42	15	13	14	56	59	57
Mossley	42	13	16	13	56	60	55
Bangor City	42	13	15	14	51	51	54
Rhyl	42	14	10	18	65	71	52
South Liverpool	42	11	17	14	43	44	50
Horwich	42	15	6	21	53	63	50
Caernarfon Town	42	11	17	14	51	63	50
Oswestry Town	42	12	13	17	51	60	49
Buxton	42	11	12	19	55	76	45
Chorley	42	9	15	18	56	64	42
Matlock Town	42	9	15	18	59	75	42
Goole Town	42	7	11	24	37	78	31

Workington, Witton Albion, Horwich and Goole Town all had 1 point deducted.

1986-87

Macclesfield Town	42	26	10	6	80	47	88
Bangor City	42	25	12	5	74	35	87
Caernarfon Town	42	20	16	6	67	40	76
Marine	42	21	10	11	70	43	73
South Liverpool	42	21	10	11	58	40	73
Morecambe	42	20	12	10	68	49	72
Matlock Town	42	20	10	12	81	67	70
Southport	42	19	11	12	67	49	68
Chorley	42	16	12	14	58	59	60
Mossley	42	15	12	15	57	52	57
Hyde United	42	15	10	17	81	70	55
Burton Albion	42	16	6	20	56	68	54
Buxton	42	13	14	15	71	68	53
Witton Albion	42	15	8	19	68	79	53
Barrow	42	15	7	20	42	57	52
Goole Town	42	13	12	17	58	62	51
Oswestry Town	42	14	8	20	55	83	50
Rhyl	42	10	15	17	56	74	45
Worksop Town	42	9	13	20	56	74	40
Gainsborough Trinity	42	9	10	23	53	77	37
Workington	42	5	14	23	38	70	28
Horwich RMI	42	3	12	27	36	85	20

Workington and Horwich RMI both had 1 point deducted.

1987-88

Premier Division

Chorley	42	26	10	6	78	35	88
Hyde United	42	25	10	7	91	52	85
Caernarfon Town	42	22	10	10	56	34	76
Morecambe	42	19	15	8	61	41	72
Barrow	42	21	8	13	70	41	71
Worksop Town	42	20	11	11	74	55	71
Bangor City	42	20	10	12	71	55	70
Rhyl	42	18	13	11	70	42	67
Marine	42	19	10	13	67	45	67
Frickley Athletic	42	18	11	13	61	55	65
Witton Albion	42	16	12	14	61	47	60
Goole Town	42	17	9	16	71	61	60
Horwich	42	17	9	16	46	42	60
Southport	42	15	12	15	43	48	57
South Liverpool	42	10	19	13	56	64	49
Buxton	42	11	14	17	72	76	47
Mossley	42	11	11	20	54	75	44
Gateshead	42	11	7	24	52	71	40
Matlock Town	42	10	8	24	58	89	38
Gainsborough Trinity	42	8	10	24	38	81	34
Oswestry Town	42	6	10	26	44	101	28
Workington	42	6	3	33	28	113	21

First Division

Fleetwood Town	36	22	7	7	85	45	73
Stalybridge Celtic	36	22	6	8	72	42	72
Leek Town	36	20	10	6	63	38	70
Accrington Stanley	36	21	6	9	71	39	69
Farsley Celtic	36	18	9	9	64	48	60
Droylsden	36	16	10	10	63	48	58
Eastwood Hanley	36	14	12	10	50	37	54
Winsford United	36	15	6	15	59	47	51
Congleton Town	36	12	16	8	43	39	51
Harrogate Town	36	13	9	14	51	50	48
Alfreton Town	36	13	8	15	53	54	47
Radcliffe Borough	36	11	13	12	66	62	46
Irlam Town	36	12	10	14	39	45	46
Penrith	36	11	11	14	46	51	44
Sutton Town	36	11	5	20	51	96	38
Lancaster City	36	10	6	20	45	72	36
Eastwood Town	36	8	10	18	45	65	34
Curzon Ashton	36	8	4	24	43	73	28
Netherfield	36	4	4	28	35	93	16

Congleton Town had 1 point deducted
Farsley Celtic had 3 points deducted

1988-89

Premier Division

Barrow	42	26	9	7	89	35	87
Hyde United	42	24	8	10	77	44	80
Witton Albion	42	22	13	7	67	39	79
Bangor City	42	22	10	10	77	48	76
Marine	42	23	7	12	69	48	76
Goole Town	42	22	7	13	75	60	73
Fleetwood Town	42	19	16	7	53	44	73
Rhyl	42	18	10	14	75	65	64
Frickley Athletic	42	17	10	15	64	53	61
Mossley	42	17	9	16	56	58	60
South Liverpool	42	15	13	14	65	57	58
Caernarfon Town	42	15	10	17	49	53	55
Matlock Town	42	16	5	21	65	73	53
Southport	42	13	12	17	66	52	51
Buxton	42	12	14	16	61	63	50
Morecambe	42	13	9	20	55	60	47
Gainsborough Trinity	42	12	11	19	56	73	47
Shepshed Charterhouse	42	14	8	20	19	80	44
Stalybridge Celtic	42	9	13	20	16	81	40
Horwich	42	7	14	21	12	70	35
Gateshead	42	7	13	22	36	70	34
Worksop Town	42	6	5	31	42	103	23

Morecambe had 1 point deducted
Shepshed Charterhouse had 6 points deducted

First Division

Colne Dynamo	42	30	11	1	102	21	98
Bishop Auckland	42	28	5	9	78	28	89
Leek Town	42	25	11	6	74	41	85
Droylsden	42	25	9	8	84	48	84
Whitley Bay	42	23	6	13	77	49	75
Accrington Stanley	42	21	10	11	81	60	73
Lancaster City	42	21	8	13	76	54	71
Harrogate Town	42	19	7	16	68	61	64
Newtown	42	15	12	15	65	59	57
Congleton Town	42	15	11	16	62	66	56
Workington	42	17	3	22	59	74	54
Eastwood Town	42	14	10	13	55	61	52
Curzon Ashton	42	13	11	18	74	72	50
Farsley Celtic	42	12	13	17	52	73	49
Irlam Town	42	11	14	17	53	63	47
Penrith	42	14	5	23	61	91	47
Radcliffe Borough	42	12	10	20	62	86	46
Eastwood Hanley	42	11	12	10	46	67	45
Winsford United	42	13	6	23	58	93	35
Alfreton Town	42	8	11	23	44	92	35
Netherfield	42	8	9	25	57	90	32
Sutton Town	42	7	6	29	70	109	23

Leek Town and Netherfield both had 1 point deducted
Colne Dynamo had 3 points deducted
Sutton Town had 4 points deducted

1989-90

Premier Division

Colne Dynamoes	42	32	6	4	86	40	102
Gateshead	42	22	10	10	78	58	76
Witton Albion	42	22	7	13	67	39	73
Hyde United	42	21	8	13	73	50	71
South Liverpool	42	20	9	13	89	79	69
Matlock Town	42	18	12	12	61	42	66
Southport	42	17	14	11	54	48	65
Fleetwood Town	42	17	12	13	73	66	63
Marine	42	16	14	12	59	55	62
Bangor City	42	15	15	12	64	58	60
Bishop Auckland	42	17	8	17	72	64	59
Frickley Athletic	42	16	8	18	56	61	56
Horwich	42	15	13	14	66	69	55
Morecambe	42	15	9	18	58	70	54
Gainsborough Trinity	42	16	8	18	59	55	53
Buxton	42	15	8	19	59	72	53
Stalybridge Celtic	42	12	9	21	48	61	45
Mossley	42	11	10	21	61	82	43
Goole Town	42	12	5	25	54	77	41
Shepshed	42	11	7	24	55	82	40
Caernarfon Town	42	10	8	24	56	86	38
Rhyl	42	7	10	25	43	77	30

Rhyl had 1 point deducted
Horwich and Gainsborough Trinity both had 3 points deducted

First Division

Leek Town	42	26	8	8	70	31	86
Droylsden	42	27	6	9	81	46	80
Accrington Stanley	42	22	10	10	80	53	76
Whitley Bay	42	21	11	10	93	59	74
Emley	42	20	9	13	70	42	69
Congleton Town	42	20	12	10	65	53	69
Winsford United	42	18	10	14	65	53	64
Curzon Ashton	42	17	11	14	66	60	62
Harrogate Town	42	17	9	16	68	62	60
Lancaster City	42	15	14	13	73	54	59
Eastwood Town	42	16	11	15	61	64	59
Farsley Celtic	42	17	6	19	71	75	57
Rossendale United	42	15	9	18	73	69	54
Newtown	42	14	12	16	49	62	54
Irlam Town	42	14	11	17	61	66	53
Workington	42	14	8	20	56	64	50
Radcliffe Borough	42	14	7	21	47	63	49
Alfreton Town	42	13	8	21	59	85	47
Worksop Town	42	13	5	24	56	95	44
Netherfield	42	11	6	25	56	89	39
Eastwood Hanley	42	10	6	26	45	76	36
Penrith	42	9	9	24	44	88	36

Congleton Town 3 points deducted. Droylsden 7 points deducted.

1990-91

Premier Division

Witton Albion	40	28	9	3	81	31	93
Stalybridge Celtic	40	22	11	7	44	26	77
Morecambe	40	19	16	5	72	44	73
Fleetwood Town	40	20	9	11	69	44	69
Southport	40	18	14	8	66	48	68
Marine	40	18	11	11	56	39	65
Bishop Auckland	40	17	10	13	62	56	61
Buxton	40	17	11	12	66	61	59
Leek Town	40	15	11	14	48	44	56
Frickley Athletic	40	16	6	18	64	62	54
Hyde United	40	14	11	15	73	63	53
Goole Town	40	14	10	16	68	74	52
Droylsden	40	12	11	17	67	70	47
Chorley	40	12	10	18	55	55	46
Mossley	40	13	10	17	55	68	45
Horwich	40	13	6	21	62	81	45
Matlock Town	40	12	7	21	52	70	43
Bangor City	40	9	12	19	52	70	39
South Liverpool	40	10	9	21	58	92	39
Gainsborough Trinity	40	9	11	20	57	84	38
Shepshed Charterhouse	40	6	7	27	38	83	25

First Division

Whitley Bay	42	25	10	7	95	38	85
Emley	42	24	12	6	78	37	84
Worksop Town	42	25	7	10	85	56	82
Accrington Stanley	42	21	13	8	83	57	76
Rhyl	42	21	7	14	62	63	70
Eastwood Town	42	17	11	14	70	60	62
Warrington Town	42	17	10	15	68	52	61
Lancaster City	42	19	8	15	58	56	61
Bridlington Town	42	15	15	12	72	52	60
Curzon Ashton	42	14	14	14	49	57	56
Congleton Town	42	14	12	16	57	71	54
Netherfield	42	14	11	17	67	66	53
Newtown	42	13	12	17	68	75	51
Caernarfon Town	42	13	10	19	51	64	49
Rossendale United	42	12	13	17	66	67	48
Radcliffe Borough	42	12	12	18	50	69	48
Irlam Town	42	12	11	19	55	76	47
Winsford United	42	11	13	18	51	66	46
Harrogate Town	42	11	13	18	55	73	46
Workington	42	11	11	20	54	67	41
Farsley Celtic	42	11	9	22	49	78	39
Alfreton Town	42	7	12	23	41	84	33

1991-92

Premier Division

Stalybridge Celtic	42	26	14	2	84	33	92
Marine	42	23	9	10	64	32	78
Morecambe	42	21	13	8	70	44	76
Leek Town	42	21	10	11	62	49	73
Buxton	42	21	9	12	65	47	72
Emley	42	18	11	13	69	47	65
Southport	42	16	17	9	57	48	65
Accrington Stanley	42	17	12	13	78	62	63
Hyde United	42	17	9	16	69	67	60
Fleetwood United	42	17	8	17	67	64	59
Bishop Auckland	42	16	9	17	48	58	57
Goole Town	42	15	9	18	60	72	54
Horwich	42	13	14	15	44	52	53
Frickley Athletic	42	12	16	14	61	57	52
Droylsden	42	12	14	16	62	72	50
Mossley	42	15	4	23	51	73	49
Whitley Bay	42	13	9	20	53	79	48
Gainsborough Trinity	42	11	13	18	48	63	46
Matlock Town	42	12	9	21	59	87	45
Bangor City	42	11	10	21	46	57	43
Chorley	42	11	9	22	61	82	42
Shepshed Albion	42	6	8	28	46	79	26

First Division

Colwyn Bay	42	30	4	8	99	49	94
Winsford United	42	29	6	7	96	41	93
Worksop Town	42	25	5	12	101	54	80
Guiseley	42	22	12	8	93	56	78
Caernarfon Town	42	23	9	10	78	47	78
Bridlington Town	42	22	9	11	86	46	75
Warrington Town	42	20	8	14	79	64	68
Knowsley United	42	18	10	14	69	52	64
Netherfield	42	18	7	17	54	61	61
Harrogate Town	42	14	16	12	73	69	58
Curzon Ashton	42	15	9	18	71	83	54
Farsley Celtic	42	15	9	18	79	101	53
Radcliffe Borough	42	15	9	18	67	72	51
Newtown	42	15	6	21	60	95	51
Eastwood Town	42	13	11	18	59	70	50
Lancaster City	42	10	19	13	55	62	49
Congleton Town	42	14	5	23	59	81	47
Rhyl	42	11	10	21	59	69	43
Rossendale United	42	9	11	22	61	90	38
Alfreton Town	42	12	2	28	63	98	38
Irlam Town	42	9	7	26	45	95	33
Workington	42	7	8	27	45	99	28

Farsley Celtic 1 point deducted. Radcliffe Borough 3 points deducted.

1992-93

Premier Division

Southport	42	29	9	4	103	31	96
Winsford United	42	27	9	6	91	43	90
Morecambe	42	25	11	6	93	51	86
Marine	42	26	8	8	83	47	86
Leek Town	42	21	11	10	86	51	74
Accrington Stanley	42	20	13	9	79	45	73
Frickley Athletic	42	21	6	15	62	52	69
Barrow	42	18	11	13	71	55	65
Hyde United	42	17	13	12	87	71	64
Bishop Auckland	42	17	11	14	63	52	62
Gainsborough Trinity	42	17	8	17	63	66	59
Colwyn Bay	42	16	6	20	80	79	54
Horwich	42	14	10	18	72	79	52
Buxton	42	13	10	19	60	75	49
Matlock Town	42	13	11	18	56	79	47
Emley	42	13	6	23	62	91	45
Whitley Bay	42	11	8	23	57	96	41
Chorley	42	10	10	22	52	93	40
Fleetwood Town	42	10	7	25	50	77	37
Droylsden	42	10	7	25	47	84	37
Mossley	42	7	8	27	53	95	29
Goole Town	42	6	9	27	47	105	27

Matlock Town had 3 points deducted

First Division

Bridlington Town	40	25	11	4	84	35	86
Knowsley United	40	23	7	10	86	48	76
Ashton United	40	22	8	10	81	54	74
Guiseley	40	20	10	10	90	64	70
Warrington Town	40	19	10	11	85	57	67
Gretna	40	17	12	11	64	47	63
Curzon Ashton	40	16	15	9	69	63	63
Great Harwood Town	40	17	9	14	66	57	60
Alfreton Town	40	15	9	16	80	80	54
Harrogate Town	40	14	12	14	77	81	54
Worksop Town	40	15	9	16	66	70	54
Radcliffe Borough	40	13	14	13	66	69	53
Workington	40	13	13	14	51	61	52
Eastwood Town	40	3	11	16	49	52	50
Netherfield	40	11	14	15	68	63	47
Caernarfon Town	40	13	8	19	66	74	47
Farsley Celtic	40	12	8	20	64	77	44
Lancaster City	40	10	12	18	49	76	42
Shepshed Albion	40	9	12	19	46	66	39
Congleton Town	40	10	7	23	58	95	37
Rossendale United	40	5	5	30	50	126	20

1993-94

Premier Division

Marine	42	27	9	6	106	62	90
Leek Town	42	27	8	7	79	50	89
Boston United	42	23	9	10	90	43	78
Bishop Auckland	42	23	9	10	73	58	78
Frickley Athletic	42	21	12	9	90	51	75
Colwyn Bay	42	18	14	10	74	51	68
Morecambe	42	20	7	15	90	56	67
Barrow	42	18	10	14	59	51	64
Hyde United	42	17	10	15	80	71	61
Chorley	42	17	10	15	70	67	61
Whitley Bay	42	17	9	16	61	72	60
Gainsborough Trinity	42	15	11	16	64	66	56
Emley	42	12	16	14	63	71	52
Matlock Town	42	13	12	17	71	76	51
Buxton	42	13	10	19	67	73	49
Accrington Stanley	42	14	7	21	63	85	49
Droylsden	42	11	14	17	57	82	47
Knowsley United	42	11	11	20	52	66	44
Winsford United	42	9	11	22	50	74	38
Horwich RMI	42	8	12	22	50	75	35
Bridlington Town	42	7	10	25	41	91	28
Fleetwood Town	42	7	7	28	55	114	28

Horwich RMI 1 point deducted. Bridlington Town 3 points deducted

First Division

Guiseley	40	29	6	5	87	37	93
Spennymoor United	40	25	6	9	95	50	81
Ashton United	40	24	7	9	85	41	79
Lancaster City	40	20	10	10	74	46	70
Netherfield	40	20	6	14	68	60	66
Alfreton Town	40	18	10	12	83	70	64
Warrington Town	40	17	11	12	52	48	62
Goole Town	40	16	11	13	72	58	59
Great Harwood Town	40	15	14	11	56	60	59
Gretna	40	16	7	17	64	65	55
Workington	40	14	10	16	70	74	52
Worksop Town	40	14	9	17	79	87	51
Bamber Bridge	40	13	11	16	62	59	50
Curzon Ashton	40	13	8	19	62	71	47
Congleton Town	40	12	9	19	53	68	45
Radcliffe Borough	40	10	14	16	62	75	44
Mossley	40	10	12	18	44	68	39
Caernarfon Town	40	9	11	20	54	88	38
Farsley Celtic	40	6	16	18	42	77	34
Harrogate Town	40	8	9	23	40	86	33
Eastwood Town	40	7	11	22	47	63	32

Mossley had 3 points deducted

1994-95

Premier Division

Marine	42	29	11	2	83	27	98
Morecambe	42	28	10	4	99	34	94
Guiseley	42	28	9	5	96	50	93
Hyde United	42	22	10	10	89	59	76
Boston United	42	20	11	11	80	43	71
Spennymoor United	42	20	11	11	66	52	71
Buxton	42	18	9	15	65	62	63
Gainsborough Trinity	42	16	13	13	69	61	61
Bishop Auckland	42	16	12	14	68	55	57
Witton Albion	42	14	14	14	54	56	56
Barrow	42	17	5	20	68	71	56
Colwyn Bay	42	16	8	18	71	80	56
Emley	42	14	13	15	62	68	55
Matlock Town	42	15	5	22	62	72	50
Accrington Stanley	42	12	13	17	55	77	49
Knowsley United	42	11	14	17	64	83	47
Winsford United	42	10	11	21	56	75	41
Chorley	42	11	7	24	64	87	40
Frickley Athletic	42	10	10	22	53	79	40
Droylsden	42	10	8	24	56	93	38
Whitley Bay	42	8	8	26	46	97	32
Horwich RMI	42	9	4	29	49	94	31

Bishop Auckland had 3 points deducted

First Division

Blyth Spartans	42	26	9	7	95	55	87
Bamber Bridge	42	25	10	7	101	51	85
Warrington Town	42	25	9	8	74	40	84
Alfreton Town	42	25	7	10	94	49	82
Lancaster City	42	23	10	9	81	44	79
Worksop Town	42	19	14	9	95	68	71
Radcliffe Borough	42	18	10	14	76	70	64
Ashton United	42	18	8	16	80	70	62
Netherfield	42	17	7	118	54	56	58
Eastwood Town	42	14	13	15	67	61	55
Gretna	42	14	13	15	64	66	55
Atherton Laburnum Rovers	42	14	8	20	60	67	50
Harrogate Town	42	14	8	20	57	78	50
Caernarfon Town	42	13	10	19	59	62	49
Curzon Ashton	42	10	16	16	64	80	46
Great Harwood Town	42	11	13	18	66	87	46
Congleton Town	42	11	13	18	52	75	46
Fleetwood	42	12	11	19	51	74	44
Farsley Celtic	42	12	7	23	66	100	43
Workington	42	12	6	24	61	91	42
Goole Town	42	11	7	24	46	81	40
Mossley	42	11	5	26	52	90	37

Mossley had 1 point deducted. Fleetwood had 3 points deducted

1995-96

Premier Division

Bamber Bridge	42	20	16	6	81	49	76
Boston United	42	23	6	13	86	59	75
Hyde United	42	21	11	10	86	51	74
Barrow	42	20	13	9	69	42	73
Gainsborough Trinity	42	20	13	9	60	41	73
Blyth Spartans	42	17	13	12	75	61	64
Accrington Stanley	42	17	14	11	62	54	62
Emley	42	17	10	15	57	53	61
Spennymoor United	42	14	18	10	67	61	60
Guiseley	42	15	14	13	62	57	59
Bishop Auckland	42	16	11	15	60	55	59
Marine	42	15	14	13	59	54	59
Witton Albion	42	17	8	17	60	62	59
Chorley	42	14	9	19	67	74	48
Knowsley United	42	14	6	22	61	89	48
Winsford United	42	10	16	16	56	79	46
Leek Town	42	10	15	17	52	55	45
Colwyn Bay	42	8	21	13	43	57	45
Frickley Athletic	42	11	14	17	63	87	44
Buxton	42	9	11	22	43	72	38
Droylsden	42	10	8	24	58	100	38
Matlock Town	42	8	11	23	71	86	35

Accrington Stanley, Chorley & Frickley Town all had 3 points deducted

First Division

Lancaster City	40	24	11	5	79	38	83
Alfreton Town	40	23	9	8	79	47	78
Lincoln United	40	22	7	11	80	56	73
Curzon Ashton	40	20	7	13	73	53	67
Farsley Celtic	40	19	9	12	66	61	66
Radcliffe Borough	40	17	13	10	70	48	64
Eastwood Town	40	18	9	13	60	47	63
Whitley Bay	40	18	8	14	72	62	62
Ashton United	40	19	7	14	73	65	60
Atherton Laburnum Rovers	40	15	12	13	60	61	57
Worksop Town	40	16	8	16	84	90	56
Gretna	40	13	13	14	75	65	52
Warrington Town	40	13	10	17	75	72	49
Leigh	40	14	7	19	53	59	49
Netherfield	40	13	10	17	64	73	49
Workington	40	11	12	17	50	62	45
Bradford Park Avenue	40	9	14	17	57	72	41
Congleton Town	40	11	11	18	36	59	41
Great Harwood Town	40	9	7	24	44	78	33
Fleetwood	40	7	10	23	41	81	31
Harrogate Town	40	7	10	23	54	96	31

Great Harwood Town had 1 point deducted, Congleton Town had 3 points deducted and Ashton United had 4 points deducted

1996-97

Premier Division

Leek Town	44	28	9	7	71	35	93
Bishop Auckland	44	23	14	7	88	43	83
Hyde United	44	22	16	6	93	46	82
Emley	44	23	12	9	89	54	81
Barrow	44	23	11	10	71	45	80
Boston United	44	22	13	9	74	47	79
Blyth Spartans	44	22	11	11	74	49	77
Marine	44	20	15	9	53	37	75
Guiseley	44	20	11	13	63	54	71
Gainsborough Trinity	44	18	12	14	65	46	66
Accrington Stanley	44	18	12	14	77	70	66
Runcorn	44	15	15	14	63	62	60
Chorley	44	16	9	19	69	66	57
Winsford United	44	13	14	17	50	56	53
Knowsley United	44	12	14	18	58	79	49
Colwyn Bay	44	11	13	20	60	76	46
Lancaster City	44	12	9	23	48	75	45
Frickley Athletic	44	12	8	24	62	91	44
Spennymoor United	44	10	10	24	52	68	40
Bamber Bridge	44	11	7	26	59	99	40
Alfreton Town	44	8	13	23	45	83	37
Witton Albion	44	5	14	25	41	91	39
Buxton	44	5	12	27	33	86	27

Knowsley United had 1 point deducted

First Division

Radcliffe Borough	42	26	7	9	77	33	85
Leigh	42	24	11	7	65	33	83
Lincoln United	42	25	8	9	78	47	83
Farsley Celtic	42	23	8	11	75	48	77
Worksop Town	42	20	12	10	68	38	69
Stocksbridge Park Steels	42	19	11	12	66	54	60
Bradford Park Avenue	42	20	8	14	58	50	68
Ashton United	42	17	14	11	73	52	65
Great Harwood Town	42	16	12	14	56	46	60
Droylsden	42	15	14	13	69	67	59
Matlock Town	42	16	10	16	61	69	58
Whitley Bay	42	14	12	16	47	54	54
Flixton	42	15	7	20	57	72	52
Netherfield	42	12	14	16	54	56	50
Eastwood Town	42	12	14	16	42	50	50
Gretna	42	10	18	14	55	68	48
Harrogate Town	42	13	8	21	55	76	47
Congleton Town	42	12	9	21	47	64	45
Workington	42	10	12	20	45	63	42
Curzon Ashton	42	8	10	24	48	79	34
Warrington Town	42	5	18	19	42	79	33
Atherton Laburnum Rovers	42	7	9	26	45	85	30

Worksop Town had 3 points deducted

1997-98

Premier Division

Barrow	42	25	8	9	61	29	83
Boston United	42	22	12	8	55	40	78
Leigh RMI	42	21	13	8	63	41	76
Runcorn	42	22	9	11	80	50	75
Gainsborough Trinity	42	22	9	11	60	39	75
Emley	42	22	8	12	81	61	74
Winsford United	42	19	12	11	54	43	69
Altrincham	42	18	11	13	76	44	65
Guiseley	42	16	16	10	61	53	64
Bishop Auckland	42	17	12	13	78	60	63
Marine	42	15	11	16	56	59	56
Hyde United	42	13	16	13	60	55	55
Colwyn Bay	42	15	9	18	53	57	54
Spennymoor United	42	14	11	17	58	72	52
Chorley	42	14	7	21	51	70	49
Frickley Athletic	42	12	12	18	45	62	48
Lancaster City	42	13	8	21	55	74	47
Blyth Spartans	42	12	13	17	52	63	39
Bamber Bridge	42	9	12	21	51	74	39
Accrington Stanley	42	8	14	20	49	68	38
Radcliffe Borough	42	6	12	24	39	70	30
Alfreton Town	42	3	13	26	32	86	22

Spennymoor United had 1 point deducted
Blyth Spartans had 10 points deducted

First Division

Whitby Town	42	30	8	4	99	48	98
Worksop Town	42	28	7	7	93	44	91
Ashton Town	42	26	9	7	93	43	87
Droylsden	42	24	8	10	70	49	80
Lincoln United	42	20	11	11	76	62	71
Farsley Celtic	42	20	10	12	72	66	70
Witton Albion	42	19	9	14	77	55	66
Eastwood Town	42	18	12	12	68	51	66
Bradford Park Avenue	42	18	11	13	62	46	65
Belper Town	42	18	7	17	68	66	61
Stocksbridge Park Steels	42	17	9	16	68	63	60
Trafford	42	16	6	20	59	61	54
Whitley Bay	42	14	12	16	60	63	54
Matlock Town	42	14	11	17	68	65	53
Gretna	42	13	9	20	58	64	48
Netherfield	42	12	11	19	55	75	47
Flixton	42	10	12	20	45	73	42
Congleton Town	42	11	8	23	65	101	41
Harrogate Town	42	8	14	20	57	80	38
Great Harwood Town	42	8	12	22	42	88	36
Workington	42	8	7	27	38	84	31
Buxton	42	7	3	32	41	87	24

1998-99

Premier Division

Altrincham	42	23	11	8	67	33	80
Worksop Town	42	22	10	10	66	48	76
Guiseley	42	21	9	12	64	47	72
Bamber Bridge	42	18	15	9	63	40	69
Gateshead	42	18	11	13	69	58	65
Gainsborough Trinity	42	19	8	15	65	59	65
Whitby Town	42	17	13	12	77	62	64
Leigh	42	16	15	11	63	54	63
Hyde United	42	16	11	15	61	48	59
Stalybridge Celtic	42	16	11	15	71	63	59
Winsford United	42	14	15	13	56	52	57
Runcorn	42	12	19	11	46	49	55
Emley	42	12	17	13	47	49	53
Blyth Spartans	42	14	9	19	56	64	51
Colwyn Bay	42	12	13	17	60	71	49
Frickley Athletic	42	11	15	16	55	71	48
Marine	42	10	17	15	61	69	47
Spennymoor United	42	12	11	19	52	71	47
Lancaster City	42	11	13	18	50	62	46
Bishop Auckland	42	10	15	17	49	67	45
Chorley	42	8	15	19	45	68	39
Accrington Stanley	42	9	9	24	47	77	36

First Division

Droylsden	42	26	8	8	97	55	86
Hucknall Town	42	26	11	5	80	38	86
Ashton United	42	22	12	8	79	46	78
Lincoln United	42	20	12	10	94	65	72
Eastwood Town	42	20	8	14	65	69	68
Radcliffe Borough	42	19	8	15	78	62	65
Burscough	42	19	8	15	67	61	65
Witton Albion	42	18	9	15	70	63	63
Bradford Park Avenue	42	17	11	14	64	55	62
Stocksbridge Park Steels	42	16	13	13	64	60	61
Harrogate Town	42	17	7	18	75	77	58
Gretna	42	16	10	16	73	80	58
Belper Town	42	15	11	16	58	57	56
Trafford	42	14	11	17	50	58	53
Netherfield Kendal	42	13	10	19	51	64	49
Flixton	42	12	12	18	50	64	48
Matlock Town	42	14	6	22	53	72	48
Farsley Celtic	42	11	13	18	56	73	46
Whitley Bay	42	10	9	23	53	77	39
Congleton Town	42	8	15	19	65	91	39
Great Harwood Town	42	10	8	24	51	73	38
Alfreton Town	42	9	8	25	53	86	35

Hucknall Town had 3 points deducted

1999-2000

Premier Division

Leigh	44	28	8	8	91	45	92
Hyde United	44	24	13	7	77	44	85
Gateshead	44	23	13	8	79	41	82
Marine	44	21	16	7	78	46	79
Emley	44	20	12	12	54	41	72
Lancaster City	44	20	11	13	65	55	71
Stalybridge Celtic	44	18	12	14	64	54	66
Bishop Auckland	44	18	11	15	63	61	65
Runcorn	44	18	10	16	64	55	64
Worksop Town	44	19	6	19	78	65	63
Gainsborough Trinity	44	16	15	13	59	49	63
Whitby Town	44	15	13	16	66	66	58
Barrow	44	14	15	15	65	59	57
Blyth Spartans	44	15	9	20	62	67	54
Droylsden	44	14	12	18	53	60	54
Frickley Athletic	44	15	9	20	64	85	54
Bamber Bridge	44	14	11	19	70	67	53
Hucknall Town	44	14	11	19	55	61	53
Leek Town	44	14	10	20	58	79	52
Colwyn Bay	44	12	12	20	46	85	48
Spennymoor United	44	10	13	21	41	71	42
Guiseley	44	8	17	19	52	72	41
Winsford United	44	3	7	34	40	116	16

Spennymoor United had 1 point deducted

First Division

Accrington Stanley	42	25	9	8	96	43	84
Burscough	42	22	18	2	81	35	84
Witton Albion	42	23	15	4	88	46	84
Bradford Park Avenue	42	23	9	10	77	48	78
Radcliffe Borough	42	22	12	8	71	48	78
Farsley Celtic	42	19	11	12	66	52	68
Matlock Town	42	17	16	9	72	55	67
Ossett Town	42	17	8	17	77	55	59
Stocksbridge Park Steels	42	16	8	18	55	70	56
Eastwood Town	42	15	11	16	64	65	55
Harrogate Town	42	14	12	16	65	67	54
Congleton Town	42	14	12	16	63	73	54
Chorley	42	13	15	14	53	64	54
Ashton United	42	12	16	14	65	67	52
Workington	42	13	13	16	49	55	52
Lincoln United	42	13	12	17	52	80	51
Belper Town	42	13	11	18	59	72	50
Trafford	42	11	12	19	55	63	45
Gretna	42	11	7	24	48	78	40
Netherfield Kendal	42	8	9	25	46	82	33
Flixton	42	7	9	26	47	85	30
Whitley Bay	42	7	9	26	41	87	30

Eastwood Town had 1 point deducted

2000-2001

Premier Division

Stalybridge Celtic	44	31	9	4	96	32	102
Emley	44	31	8	5	86	42	101
Bishop Auckland	44	26	7	11	89	53	85
Lancaster City	44	24	9	11	84	60	81
Worksop Town	44	20	13	11	102	60	73
Barrow	44	21	9	14	83	53	72
Altrincham	44	20	10	14	80	59	70
Gainsborough Trinity	44	17	14	13	59	56	65
Accrington Stanley	44	18	10	16	72	65	64
Hucknall Town	44	17	12	15	57	63	63
Gateshead	44	16	12	16	67	61	60
Bamber Bridge	44	17	8	19	63	65	59
Runcorn	44	15	10	19	56	71	55
Blyth Spartans	44	15	9	20	61	64	54
Burscough	44	14	10	20	59	68	52
Hyde United	44	13	12	19	72	79	51
Whitby Town	44	13	11	20	60	76	50
Marine	44	12	13	19	62	78	49
Colwyn Bay	44	12	10	22	68	102	46
Frickley Athletic	44	10	15	19	50	79	45
Droylsden	44	13	6	25	50	80	45
Leek Town	44	12	8	24	45	70	44
Spennymoor United	44	4	5	35	32	108	17

First Division

Bradford Park Avenue	42	28	5	9	83	40	89
Vauxhall Motors	42	23	10	9	95	50	79
Ashton United	42	23	9	10	91	49	78
Stocksbridge Park Steels	42	19	13	10	80	60	70
Trafford	42	20	9	13	70	62	68
Belper Town	42	18	11	13	71	62	65
Witton Albion	42	15	16	11	51	50	61
Ossett Town	42	16	12	14	66	58	60
Radcliffe Borough	42	17	8	17	72	71	59
Chorley	42	15	14	13	71	70	59
Harrogate Town	42	15	10	17	60	70	55
Matlock Town	42	14	10	18	70	74	52
North Ferriby United	42	14	10	18	64	73	52
Workington	42	13	12	17	53	60	51
Lincoln United	42	13	12	17	60	75	51
Gretna	42	12	12	18	72	82	48
Guiseley	42	11	15	16	37	50	48
Kendal Town	42	12	12	18	60	69	47
Farsley Celtic	42	12	11	19	53	71	47
Eastwood Town	42	12	8	21	40	63	47
Winsford United	42	13	11	18	61	70	44
Congleton Town	42	13	6	28	43	94	30

Trafford and Kendal Town both had 1 point deducted
Winsford United had 6 points deducted

2001-2002

Premier Division

Burton Albion	44	31	11	2	106	30	104
Vauxhall Motors	44	27	8	9	86	55	89
Lancaster City	44	23	9	12	80	57	78
Worksop Town	44	23	9	12	74	51	78
Emley	44	22	9	13	69	55	75
Accrington Stanley	44	21	9	14	89	64	72
Runcorn FC Halton	44	21	8	15	76	53	71
Barrow	44	19	10	15	75	59	67
Altrincham	44	19	9	16	66	58	66
Bradford Park Avenue	44	18	5	21	77	76	59
Droylsden	44	17	8	19	65	78	59
Blyth Spartans	44	14	16	14	59	62	58
Frickley Athletic	44	16	11	17	63	69	58
Gateshead	44	14	14	16	58	71	56
Whitby Town	44	15	8	21	61	76	53
Hucknall Town	44	14	9	21	50	68	51
Marine	44	11	17	16	62	71	50
Burscough	44	15	5	24	69	86	50
Gainsborough Trinity	44	13	10	21	61	76	49
Colwyn Bay	44	12	11	21	49	82	47
Bishop Auckland	44	12	8	24	46	68	44
Hyde United	44	10	10	24	61	87	40
Bamber Bridge	44	7	10	27	38	88	30

First Division

Harrogate Town	42	25	11	6	80	35	86
Ossett Town	42	21	13	8	73	44	76
Ashton United	42	21	12	9	90	63	75
Spennymoor United	42	22	6	14	75	73	72
Radcliffe Borough	42	20	8	14	73	51	68
Leek Town	42	20	8	14	67	51	68
Gretna	42	19	7	16	66	66	63
Eastwood Town	42	17	11	14	61	59	62
Rossendale United	42	17	10	15	69	58	61
Witton Albion	42	17	10	15	72	68	61
Guiseley	42	18	7	17	60	67	61
North Ferriby United	42	14	16	12	71	60	58
Chorley	42	16	9	17	59	57	57
Matlock Town	42	15	9	18	49	48	54
Trafford	42	14	9	19	64	80	51
Workington	42	12	12	18	51	57	48
Farsley Celtic	42	12	11	19	64	78	47
Belper Town	42	12	11	19	49	66	47
Lincoln United	42	11	14	17	62	80	47
Stocksbridge Park Steels	42	12	9	21	55	76	45
Kendal Town	42	9	9	24	52	76	36
Ossett Albion	42	8	8	26	43	92	32

2002-2003

Premier Division

Accrington Stanley	44	30	10	4	97	44	100
Barrow	44	24	12	8	84	52	84
Vauxhall Motors	44	22	10	12	81	46	76
Stalybridge Celtic	44	21	13	10	77	51	76
Worksop Town	44	21	9	14	82	67	72
Harrogate Town	44	21	8	15	75	63	71
Bradford Park Avenue	44	20	10	14	73	70	70
Hucknall Town	44	17	15	12	72	62	66
Droylsden	44	18	10	16	62	52	64
Whitby Town	44	17	12	15	80	69	63
Marine	44	17	10	17	63	60	61
Wakefield & Emley	44	14	18	12	46	49	60
Runcorn FC Halton	44	15	15	14	69	74	60
Altrincham	44	17	9	18	58	63	60
Gainsborough Trinity	44	16	11	17	67	66	59
Ashton United	44	15	13	16	71	79	58
Lancaster City	44	16	9	19	71	75	57
Burscough	44	14	9	21	44	51	51
Blyth Spartans	44	14	9	21	67	87	51
Frickley Athletic	44	13	8	23	45	78	47
Gateshead	44	10	11	23	60	81	41
Colwyn Bay	44	5	9	30	52	99	24
Hyde United	44	5	8	31	40	98	23

Division One

Alfreton Town	42	26	9	7	106	59	87
Spennymoor United	42	27	6	9	81	42	87
Radcliffe Borough	42	25	10	7	90	46	85
North Ferriby United	42	23	9	10	78	45	78
Chorley	42	21	10	11	80	51	73
Belper Town	42	20	13	9	53	42	73
Witton Albion	42	19	15	8	67	50	72
Matlock Town	42	20	10	12	67	48	70
Leek Town	42	20	9	13	63	46	69
Workington	42	19	10	13	73	60	67
Farsley Celtic	42	17	11	14	66	67	62
Kendal Town	42	18	7	17	68	58	61
Bamber Bridge	42	15	9	18	55	59	54
Guiseley	42	14	11	17	68	63	53
Bishop Auckland	42	13	10	19	58	83	49
Lincoln United	42	12	9	21	67	77	45
Stocksbridge PS	42	11	9	22	54	81	42
Rossendale United	42	12	5	25	58	88	41
Kidsgrove Athletic	42	9	11	22	49	71	38
Ossett Town	42	8	9	25	39	80	33
Eastwood Town	42	5	8	29	33	92	23
Trafford	42	5	6	31	34	99	21

2003-2004

Premier Division

Hucknall Town	44	29	8	7	83	38	95
Droylsden	44	26	8	10	96	64	86
Barrow	44	22	14	8	82	52	80
Alfreton Town	44	23	9	12	73	43	78
Harrogate Town	44	24	5	15	79	63	77
Southport	44	20	10	14	71	52	70
Worksop Town	44	19	13	12	69	50	70
Lancaster City	44	20	9	15	62	49	69
Vauxhall Motors	44	19	10	15	78	75	67
Gainsborough Trinity	44	17	13	14	70	52	64
Stalybridge Celtic	44	18	10	16	72	66	64
Altrincham	44	16	15	13	66	51	63
Runcorn FC Halton	44	16	13	15	67	63	61
Ashton United	44	17	8	19	59	79	59
Whitby Town	44	14	11	19	55	70	53
Marine	44	13	12	19	62	74	51
Bradford Park Avenue	44	12	14	18	48	62	50
Spennymoor United	44	14	6	24	55	93	48
Burscough	44	10	15	19	47	67	45
Radcliffe Borough	44	12	6	26	74	99	42
Blyth Spartans	44	10	10	24	54	74	40
Frickley Athletic	44	11	7	26	51	83	40
Wakefield & Emley	44	8	6	30	45	99	30

Division One

Hyde United	42	24	8	10	79	49	80
Matlock Town	42	23	7	12	78	51	76
Farsley Celtic	42	20	14	8	78	56	74
Lincoln United	42	20	11	11	73	53	71
Witton Albion	42	17	12	13	61	56	63
Gateshead	42	21	4	17	65	68	63
Workington	42	17	11	14	70	58	62
Leek Town	42	16	13	13	56	47	61
Guiseley	42	16	12	14	66	54	60
Bamber Bridge	42	16	12	14	64	53	60
Bridlington Town	42	16	10	16	70	68	58
Prescot Cables	42	16	10	16	63	65	58
Bishop Auckland	42	14	13	15	61	64	55
Ossett Town	42	15	10	17	62	73	52
Rossendale United	42	13	12	17	53	62	51
Colwyn Bay	42	14	9	19	56	82	51
North Ferriby United	42	13	11	18	64	70	50
Chorley	42	13	10	19	54	70	49
Stocksbridge Park Steels	42	12	12	18	57	69	48
Belper Town	42	9	15	18	44	58	42
Kendal Town	42	11	7	24	53	79	40
Kidsgrove Athletic	42	10	9	23	45	67	39

2004-2005

Premier Division

Hyde United	42	25	13	4	80	43	88
Workington	42	26	7	9	73	30	85
Farsley Celtic	42	25	8	9	81	41	83
Whitby Town	42	23	11	8	65	49	80
Prescot Cables	42	21	8	13	63	54	71
Burscough	42	21	7	14	93	74	70
Leek Town	42	16	15	11	63	52	63
Witton Albion	42	15	17	10	56	44	62
Radcliffe Borough	42	16	14	12	60	60	62
Guiseley	42	16	13	13	70	64	61
Matlock Town	42	14	13	15	59	67	55
Blyth Spartans	42	13	13	16	53	55	52
Wakefield & Emley	42	14	10	18	60	67	52
Lincoln United	42	15	4	23	53	66	49
Marine	42	10	18	14	53	60	48
Ossett Town	42	11	13	18	53	62	46
Gateshead	42	11	12	19	61	84	45
Frickley Athletic	42	10	14	18	44	57	44
Bishop Auckland	42	11	7	24	51	74	40
Bridlington Town	42	7	14	21	43	66	35
Bamber Bridge	42	9	7	26	48	92	34
Spennymoor United	42	9	10	23	44	65	25

Spennymoor United had 12 points deducted.

Division One

North Ferriby United	42	25	8	9	83	49	83
Ilkeston Town	42	24	9	9	64	40	81
AFC Telford United	42	23	11	8	78	44	80
Willenhall Town	42	22	12	8	71	46	78
Kendal Town	42	21	8	13	89	69	71
Eastwood Town	42	20	9	13	73	54	69
Mossley	42	20	6	16	81	56	66
Brigg Town	42	15	19	8	59	46	64
Gresley Rovers	42	17	12	13	57	53	63
Kidsgrove Athletic	42	15	15	12	60	55	60
Woodley Sports	42	16	11	15	68	74	59
Ossett Albion	42	15	13	14	83	74	58
Colwyn Bay	42	14	13	15	54	62	55
Stocksbridge Park Steels	42	15	9	18	58	58	51
Shepshed Dynamo	42	13	11	18	53	75	50
Chorley	42	13	9	20	62	69	48
Belper Town	42	13	8	21	57	66	47
Spalding United	42	13	8	21	57	69	47
Clitheroe	42	12	10	20	47	57	46
Warrington Town	42	11	13	18	45	59	46
Rossendale United	42	10	10	22	64	87	40
Rocester	42	0	6	36	31	132	6

Stocksbridge Park Steels had 3 points deducted.

2005-2006

Premier Division

Blyth Spartans	42	26	11	5	79	32	89
Frickley Athletic	42	26	8	8	72	36	86
Marine	42	23	12	7	61	25	81
Farsley Celtic	42	23	10	9	84	34	79
North Ferriby United	42	21	10	11	77	54	73
Whitby Town	42	18	10	14	60	59	64
Burscough	42	19	6	17	64	64	63
Witton Albion	42	17	9	16	68	55	60
Matlock Town	42	16	11	15	60	55	59
AFC Telford United	42	14	17	11	54	52	59
Ossett Town	42	17	7	18	57	61	58
Leek Town	42	14	14	14	50	53	56
Prescot Cables	42	15	8	19	49	60	53
Guiseley	42	14	9	19	45	58	51
Ashton United	42	13	10	19	62	63	49
Ilkeston Town	42	12	13	17	48	51	49
Gateshead	42	12	10	20	52	77	46
Radcliffe Borough	42	12	8	22	54	62	44
Lincoln United	42	10	14	18	44	64	44
Wakefield Emley	42	11	9	22	38	69	42
Bradford Park Avenue	42	10	9	23	64	86	39
Runcorn FC Halton	42	6	11	25	36	108	29

Division One

Mossley	42	23	9	10	83	55	78
Fleetwood Town	42	22	10	10	72	48	76
Kendal Town	42	22	10	10	81	58	76
Woodley Sports	42	22	8	12	85	53	74
Gresley Rovers	42	20	10	12	79	64	70
Stocksbridge PS	42	17	16	9	66	43	67
Eastwood Town	42	16	14	12	66	58	62
Brigg Town	42	16	14	12	70	64	62
Belper Town	42	17	8	17	53	56	59
Shepshed Dynamo	42	15	13	14	57	56	58
Bridlington Town	42	16	10	16	61	68	58
Colwyn Bay	42	15	11	16	56	53	56
Bamber Bridge	42	13	15	14	65	59	54
Ossett Albion	42	15	9	18	54	64	54
Rossendale United	42	12	17	13	58	61	53
Clitheroe	42	15	8	19	54	73	53
Kidsgrove Athletic	42	14	9	19	66	69	51
Chorley	42	14	8	20	58	59	50
Warrington Town	42	11	15	16	62	74	48
Spalding United	42	10	15	17	49	70	45
Goole	42	11	11	20	55	85	43
Bishop Auckland	42	3	6	33	39	99	15

Goole had 1 point deducted.

2006-2007

Premier Division

Burscough	42	23	12	7	80	37	80
Witton Albion	42	24	8	10	90	48	80
AFC Telford United	42	21	15	6	72	40	78
Marine	42	22	8	12	70	53	74
Matlock Town	42	21	9	12	70	43	72
Guiseley	42	19	12	11	71	49	69
Hednesford Town	42	18	14	10	49	41	68
Fleetwood Town	42	19	10	13	71	60	67
Gateshead	42	17	14	11	75	57	65
Ossett Town	42	18	10	14	61	52	64
Whitby Town	42	18	6	18	63	78	60
Ilkeston Town	42	16	11	15	66	62	59
North Ferriby United	42	15	9	18	54	61	54
Prescot Cables	42	13	14	15	52	56	53
Lincoln United	42	12	15	15	40	58	51
Frickley Athletic	42	13	10	19	50	69	49
Leek Town	42	13	9	20	49	61	48
Ashton United	42	13	9	20	52	72	48
Kendal Town	42	12	11	19	59	79	47
Mossley	42	10	5	27	48	79	35
Radcliffe Borough	42	7	11	24	39	71	32
Grantham Town	42	3	8	31	39	94	17

Burscough had one point deducted.

Division One

Buxton	46	30	11	5	94	37	101
Cammell Laird	46	28	10	8	105	56	94
Eastwood Town	46	26	9	11	89	43	87
Bradford Park Avenue	46	24	10	12	77	47	82
Colwyn Bay	46	22	11	13	74	65	77
Stocksbridge Park Steels	46	22	10	14	82	49	76
Goole	46	21	9	16	80	84	72
Kidsgrove Athletic	46	21	7	18	91	80	70
Rossendale United	46	21	7	18	64	59	70
Woodley Sports	46	19	11	16	89	71	68
Ossett Albion	46	19	11	16	71	66	68
Harrogate Railway	46	21	5	20	72	78	68
Bamber Bridge	46	18	8	20	78	75	62
Alsager Town	46	18	7	21	72	75	61
Skelmersdale United	46	17	10	19	72	77	61
Clitheroe	46	18	6	22	78	75	60
Brigg Town	46	16	10	20	57	72	58
Gresley Rovers	46	16	7	23	59	75	55
Belper Town	46	17	4	25	58	86	55
Shepshed Dynamo	46	15	7	24	62	96	52
Wakefield	46	13	10	23	48	71	49
Warrington Town	46	13	8	25	64	84	47
Chorley	46	10	6	30	52	99	36
Bridlington Town	46	3	14	29	33	101	23

2007-2008

Premier Division

Fleetwood Town	40	28	7	5	81	39	91
Witton Albion	40	27	8	5	84	28	89
Gateshead	40	26	7	7	93	42	85
Eastwood Town	40	20	9	11	61	45	69
Buxton	40	20	8	12	60	50	68
Guiseley	40	19	10	11	65	43	67
Marine	40	19	4	17	70	65	61
Hednesford Town	40	15	8	17	62	65	53
Worksop Town	40	13	12	15	59	62	51
Ashton United	40	11	15	14	63	73	48
Kendal Town	40	12	11	17	61	70	47
Whitby Town	40	13	7	20	68	75	46
Prescot Cables	40	13	8	19	48	62	46
Frickley Athletic	40	11	13	16	50	68	46
North Ferriby United	40	13	7	20	53	76	46
Matlock Town	40	12	9	19	55	68	45
Ilkeston Town	40	10	14	16	64	72	44
Ossett Town	40	12	8	20	48	60	44
Leek Town	40	11	11	18	54	68	44
Stamford	40	11	10	19	59	86	43
Lincoln United	40	7	8	25	44	85	29

Prescot Cables had one point deducted.

Division One North

Bradford Park Avenue	42	25	7	10	91	43	82
FC United of Manchester	42	24	9	9	91	49	81
Skelmersdale United	42	23	9	10	94	46	78
Curzon Ashton	42	23	9	10	78	48	78
Bamber Bridge	42	22	8	12	70	54	74
Ossett Albion	42	20	10	12	77	65	70
Wakefield	42	19	7	16	58	49	64
Newcastle Blue Star	42	17	12	13	71	58	63
Rossendale United	42	16	11	15	66	74	59
Garforth Town	42	16	8	18	60	63	56
Lancaster City	42	15	9	18	54	70	54
Harrogate Railway	42	13	12	17	51	58	51
Clitheroe	42	13	11	18	63	77	50
Chorley	42	10	12	20	56	80	42
Mossley	42	12	6	24	60	100	42
Radcliffe Borough	42	9	11	22	53	75	38
Woodley Sports	42	7	13	22	38	65	33
Bridlington Town	42	8	8	26	42	99	32

Woodley Sports had one point deducted.

NORTH-WEST COUNTIES LEAGUE

FORMATION

The North-West Counties League was previously featured in the 2003 edition of 'Non-League tables'. Tables have now been updated, transposition errors from that edition corrected and additional information included.

For almost 50 years the best non-League clubs in the north-west played in either the Cheshire League or the Lancashire Combination. There were few transfers between the two leagues, only 10 clubs moving from Lancashire to Cheshire between 1920 and 1968 with 5 going in the opposite direction. Generally speaking, the two competitions were of roughly equal status although the Cheshire League probably became slightly the stronger after the Second World War. However the formation of the Northern Premier League (NPL) in 1968 not only added an extra layer above the two older leagues, it also fundamentally changed the relationship between them. Instead of being roughly equal, the Cheshire League very quickly became the more senior as the Lancashire Combination rapidly declined in strength, as the movements of its clubs shows very clearly.

In 1968 the Lancashire Combination lost 5 of its 22 clubs to the new NPL, theoretically still leaving 17 strong clubs to continue in the competition. Yet by the start of the 1970-71 season, 12 of those 17 had left, 3 more to the NPL and 7 to the Cheshire League. After 1970, no Lancashire Combination club was good enough to be promoted to the NPL but the Cheshire League had another 8 clubs good enough to be promoted. To a large extent the Cheshire League made up its losses in this period by recruiting from the Lancashire Combination, taking 5 clubs between 1970 and 1977 and 8 more to help to form its new Second Division in 1978. The very fact that 8 Lancashire Combination clubs preferred Division Two of the Cheshire League shows that they recognised that in effect their own competition had now become a feeder to its neighbour.

It therefore made perfect sense when in 1982, the management committees of the Cheshire League and the Lancashire Combination decided to recognise the position formally and merge the two competitions. A three division structure was put in place and 57 of the 58 clubs in the two leagues applied to join the new North-West Counties League, the exception being Middlewich Athletic of Division Two of the Cheshire League who applied initially but then withdrew their application and rejoined the Mid-Cheshire League instead. A points system was devised to decide which division of the new league the 57 clubs should play in and the results of this were recorded on 3rd June, 1982.

The scoring system was as follows. The previous two seasons, that is 1980-81 and 1981-82, were considered and for each of those two seasons the top team in Division One of the Cheshire League was awarded 40 points, the second team 39, and so on down the league table. The top teams of the Lancashire Combination and Cheshire League Division Two were each awarded 20 points, the second team 19 and so on down the league tables. Champions and runners-up in the Lancashire Combination and Cheshire League Division Two were awarded 5 bonus points each.

Having calculated the points the three Divisions were split as follows:

Division One – Included all clubs with ground grades of A to C with 35 points or more. The number of clubs was made up to 20 by adding the necessary number of D graded clubs with the most points.

Division Two – Included all remaining A to D clubs, all E clubs and the number of clubs was made up to 20 by adding the necessary number of F graded clubs with the most points.

Division Three – Included all remaining F graded clubs and all G graded clubs. The number was made even by electing new applicants.

The exceptions were that any club whose pitch size failed to meet the standards laid down was not considered for Division One and any club not playing on their own ground (i.e. ground-sharing) was also not considered for Division One. The results of all these deliberations are shown below.

However Hyde United and Chorley did not take up their places in the North-West Counties League as they were later elected to the NPL. Their places were taken by Lancaster City who dropped down from the NPL due to financial difficulties and Penrith who were elected from the Northern League. Division Three was made up to 18 clubs by the election of Newton from the Mid-Cheshire League where they had been known as HB & H Newton.

Meanwhile across the Pennines, the Midland League and Yorkshire League were also merging to form the Northern Counties (East) League and thus the second layer of the non-League pyramid covering most of the northern half of the country was then in place.

Grading System for North-West Counties League

Club	Ground Grade	Points Awarded				Previous League	NWLC Division	See Notes
		1980-81	1981-82	Bonus	Total			
Hyde United	A	39	40		79	CL – 1	1	N
Chorley	A	35	39		74	CL – 1	1	N
Stalybridge Celtic	A	36	31		67	CL – 1	1	
Horwich RMI	A	32	25		57	CL – 1	1	
Winsford United	B	38	37		75	CL – 1	1	
Prescot Cables	B	33	32		65	CL – 1	1	
Burscough	B	25	38		63	CL – 1	1	
Leek Town	B	31	26		57	CL – 1	1	
Accrington Stanley	B	20	28	5	53	CL – 1	1	
Rhyl	B	14	19	5	38	CL – 2	1	
Kirkby Town	B	22	14		36	CL – 2	2	G
Curzon Ashton	C	29	33		62	CL – 1	1	
Ashton United	C	30	22		52	CL – 1	1	
St. Helens Town	C	28	23		51	CL – 1	1	
Droylsden	C	23	21		44	CL – 1	2	P
Congleton Town	C	11	20	5	36	CL – 2	1	
Leyland Motors	C	18	17		35	CL – 2	1	
Nantwich Town	D	40	27		67	CL – 1	1	
Formby	D	37	29		66	CL – 1	1	
Glossop	D	19	35	5	59	CL – 1	1	
Bootle	D	34	24		58	CL – 1	1	
Darwen	D	24	34		58	CL – 1	1	

Club	Ground Grade	Points Awarded 1980-81	1981-82	Bonus	Total	Previous League	NWLC Division	See Notes
Fleetwood Town	D	27	30		57	CL – 1	2	
Ellesmere Port & Neston	A	0	7		7	CL – 2	2	
Great Harwood Town	B	18	15		33	Lancs.	2	P
Ford Motors	C	12	9		21	CL – 2	2	
Salford	C	6	5		11	CL – 2	2	
Skelmersdale United	C	4	6		10	CL – 2	2	
Padiham	D	17	11		28	Lancs.	2	
Atherton Laburnum Rovers	D	16	10		26	CL – 2	2	
Chadderton	D	11	14		25	Lancs.	2	
Radcliffe Borough	D	10	15		25	CL – 2	2	
Eastwood Hanley	D	5	12		17	CL – 2	2	
Rossendale United	E	26	36		62	CL – 1	2	
Caernarfon Town	E	15	20	5	40	Lancs.	2	
Irlam Town	E	9	18		27	CL – 2	2	
Lytham	E	13	10		23	Lancs.	2	
New Mills	E	21	2		23	CL – 2	2	
Prescot BI	E	15	8		23	CL – 2	2	
Wren Rovers	F	20	17	5	42	Lancs.	2	
Maghull	F	13	16		29	CL – 2	3	
Clitheroe	F	12	16		28	Lancs.	3	
Vulcan Newton	F	14	12		26	Lancs.	3	
Nelson	F	4	18		22	Lancs.	3	
Warrington Town	F	8	13		21	CL – 2	3	
Bacup Borough	F	7	7		14	Lancs.	3	
Oldham Dew	F	0	9		9	Lancs.	3	
Atherton Collieries	F	3	4		7	CL – 2	3	
Ashton Town	F	2	3		5	CL – 2	3	
Colne Dynamoes	G	19	19	10	48	Lancs.	3	
Blackpool Mechanics	G	5	13		18	Lancs.	3	
Wigan Rovers	G	9	8		17	Lancs.	3	
Whitworth Valley	G	10	6		16	Lancs.	3	
Daisy Hill	G	8	5		13	Lancs.	3	
Ashton Athletic	G	6	3		9	Lancs.	3	
Prestwich Heys	G	7	1		8	CL – 2	3	
Bolton ST	G	0	4		4	Lancs.	3	

Notes

N – Subsequently elected to the Northern Premier League.

G – Ground-sharing at Prescot Cables.

P – Under-sized pitch.

NORTH-WEST COUNTIES LEAGUE

1982-83

Division One

Burscough	38	26	7	5	93	45	59
Rhyl	38	23	11	4	76	30	57
Horwich RMI	38	22	10	6	77	35	54
Stalybridge Celtic	38	17	15	6	60	32	49
Winsford United	38	18	10	10	72	48	46
Darwen	38	17	12	9	68	46	46
Lancaster City	38	17	11	10	69	54	45
Congleton Town	38	13	14	11	52	35	40
Penrith	38	17	6	15	68	61	40
Accrington Stanley	38	13	12	13	56	55	38
Leek Town	38	14	9	15	42	44	37
Curzon Ashton	38	14	8	16	46	47	36
Ashton United	38	13	10	15	55	69	36
Bootle	38	14	6	18	55	79	32
Prescot Cables	38	9	13	16	50	60	31
Formby	38	10	8	20	48	68	28
Leyland Motors	38	7	10	21	34	74	24
Glossop	38	6	11	21	29	67	23
St. Helens Town	38	5	10	23	29	80	20
Nantwich Town	38	6	5	27	43	93	17

Bootle had 2 points deducted.
Netherfield joined after relegation from the Northern Premier League.

Division Two

Radcliffe Borough	38	33	4	1	110	25	70
Caernarfon Town	38	28	7	3	85	27	63
Wren Rovers	38	23	7	8	84	38	53
Eastwood Hanley	38	23	7	8	81	42	53
Kirkby Town	38	22	3	13	80	60	47
Irlam Town	38	17	8	13	79	52	42
Chadderton	38	18	6	14	55	51	42
Rossendale United	38	15	10	13	75	68	40
Ford Motors	38	18	4	16	61	59	40
Ellesmere Port & Neston	38	17	5	16	56	68	39
Skelmersdale United	38	13	11	14	70	63	37
Fleetwood Town	38	12	8	18	54	80	32
Atherton Laburnum Rovers	38	11	9	18	52	70	31
Lytham	38	11	5	22	54	71	27
Great Harwood Town	38	8	10	20	54	76	26
Salford	38	10	6	22	43	86	26
Droylsden	38	11	5	22	49	71	25
Prescot BI	38	10	5	23	46	81	25
Padiham	38	8	6	24	41	74	22
New Mills	38	7	4	27	39	106	18

Droylsden had 2 points deducted.
Kirkby Town disbanded and New Mills also left.

Division Three

Colne Dynamoes	34	25	5	4	95	37	55
Warrington Town	34	24	6	4	83	33	54
Clitheroe	34	22	7	5	87	35	51
Prestwich Heys	34	18	11	5	70	37	47
Vulcan Newton	34	13	10	11	70	65	36
Blackpool Mechanics	34	11	13	10	67	56	35
Bacup Borough	34	14	7	13	53	45	35
Atherton Collieries	34	12	11	11	55	57	35
Whitworth Valley	34	13	9	12	54	65	35
Nelson	34	7	16	11	49	56	30
Daisy Hill	34	10	10	14	47	58	30
Maghull	34	10	9	15	56	61	29
Ashton Town	34	12	5	17	53	73	29
Newton	34	8	12	14	59	62	28
Oldham Dew	34	10	8	16	48	61	28
Bolton ST	34	9	6	19	50	84	24
Wigan Rovers	34	5	7	22	35	72	17
Ashton Athletic	34	3	8	23	18	92	14

Wigan Rovers left to join Division Two of the West Lancashire League.
Urmston Town joined from the Manchester League and Cheadle Town also joined.

1983-84

Division One

Stalybridge Celtic	38	26	8	4	81	30	60
Penrith	38	23	9	6	88	39	55
Radcliffe Borough	38	26	3	9	79	41	55
Burscough	38	22	8	8	87	47	52
Curzon Ashton	38	21	5	12	74	51	47
Lancaster City	38	21	3	14	76	56	43
Accrington Stanley	38	17	8	13	67	60	42
St. Helens Town	38	17	7	14	69	55	41
Congleton Town	38	18	5	15	64	50	41
Prescot Cables	38	17	6	15	72	45	40
Leek Town	38	14	10	14	56	64	38
Winsford United	38	12	12	14	49	54	36
Formby	38	14	7	17	48	61	35
Caernarfon Town	38	11	12	15	46	55	34
Glossop	38	11	11	16	38	61	33
Bootle	38	11	7	20	46	69	27
Leyland Motors	38	9	9	20	44	79	27
Netherfield	38	5	11	22	27	73	21
Ashton United	38	7	9	22	47	86	19
Darwen	38	2	2	34	29	111	6

Bootle and Lancaster City both had 2 points deducted.
Ashton United had 4 points deducted.

Division Two

Fleetwood Town	34	24	8	2	73	24	56
Eastwood Hanley	34	21	6	7	69	35	48
Irlam Town	34	19	8	7	67	41	46
Warrington Town	34	18	7	9	65	45	43
Droylsden	34	19	5	10	59	42	43
Colne Dynamoes	34	16	9	9	55	37	41
Ellesmere Port & Neston	34	12	10	12	49	38	34
Chadderton	34	14	6	14	56	46	34
Atherton Laburnum Rovers	34	11	11	12	37	41	33
Wren Rovers	34	11	10	13	45	47	32
Skelmersdale United	34	13	6	15	60	63	32
Ford Motors	34	9	9	16	38	53	27
Prescot BI	34	9	9	16	50	66	27
Lytham	34	13	3	18	56	81	27
Rossendale United	34	10	6	18	53	84	26
Great Harwood Town	34	5	12	17	36	60	22
Salford	34	5	11	18	24	60	21
Nantwich Town	34	8	2	24	44	73	18

Lytham had 2 points deducted.
Prescot BI left the league.

Division Three

Clitheroe	34	22	7	5	79	29	51
Padiham	34	19	8	7	58	34	46
Ashton Town	34	19	7	8	54	42	45
Oldham Dew	34	17	9	8	63	37	43
Daisy Hill	34	19	3	12	54	40	41
Maghull	34	16	8	10	60	50	40
Blackpool Mechanics	34	17	5	12	70	49	39
Atherton Collieries	34	14	9	11	54	50	37
Vulcan Newton	34	15	8	11	64	54	36
Prestwich Heys	34	15	5	14	61	59	33
Whitworth Valley	34	11	8	15	45	53	30
Bolton ST	34	10	10	14	49	64	30
Bacup Borough	34	11	9	14	65	60	27
Nelson	34	8	10	16	49	55	26
Cheadle Town	34	9	8	17	39	67	26
Urmston Town	34	7	9	18	35	67	23
Newton	34	8	4	22	33	63	20
Ashton Athletic	34	4	3	27	30	89	11

Prestwich Heys and Vulcan Newton both had 2 points deducted.
Bacup Borough had 4 points deducted.
Colwyn Bay joined from the Welsh League (North) and Kirkby Town also joined. Vulcan Newton left the league.

1984-85

Division One

Radcliffe Borough	38	24	10	4	67	33	58
Caernarfon Town	38	23	9	6	73	40	55
Burscough	38	23	7	8	81	46	53
Stalybridge Celtic	38	21	10	7	89	40	52
Eastwood Hanley	38	20	12	6	72	42	52
Curzon Ashton	38	21	6	11	85	60	48
Winsford United	38	20	7	11	58	37	47
Fleetwood Town	38	18	8	12	84	57	44
Leek Town	38	16	11	11	52	38	43
Congleton Town	38	13	11	14	43	46	37
Leyland Motors	38	13	8	17	52	67	34
St. Helens Town	38	12	9	17	64	75	33
Prescot Cables	38	13	7	18	64	68	31
Bootle	38	10	11	17	34	48	31
Accrington Stanley	38	11	8	19	45	59	30
Glossop	38	8	11	19	46	70	27
Formby	38	9	9	20	41	79	25
Netherfield	38	7	9	22	42	80	23
Lancaster City	38	8	5	25	46	90	21
Penrith	38	4	4	30	36	99	12

Formby and Prescot Cables both had 2 points deducted.

Division Two

Clitheroe	34	19	13	2	70	33	51
Irlam Town	34	21	9	4	60	24	51
Warrington Town	34	17	14	3	59	29	48
Ashton United	34	17	7	10	56	55	41
Droylsden	34	15	10	9	51	47	40
Wren Rovers	34	15	9	10	53	41	39
Great Harwood Town	34	17	4	13	49	44	38
Chadderton	34	13	9	12	47	46	35
Colne Dynamoes	34	9	14	11	45	40	32
Atherton Laburnum Rovers	34	13	6	15	42	43	32
Nantwich Town	34	13	5	16	50	47	31
Ford Motors	34	11	8	15	44	45	30
Skelmersdale United	34	11	8	15	39	56	30
Rossendale United	34	10	9	15	51	53	29
Salford	34	11	5	18	46	64	27
Darwen	34	7	6	21	32	62	20
Padiham	34	8	5	21	42	74	19
Ellesmere Port & Neston	34	5	7	22	34	67	15

Padiham and Ellesmere Port & Neston both had 2 points deducted.

Division Three

Kirkby Town	34	26	5	3	83	30	57
Colwyn Bay	34	22	10	2	75	32	54
Newton	34	16	10	8	56	33	42
Urmston Town	34	14	10	10	42	39	38
Blackpool Mechanics	34	15	7	12	61	48	37
Lytham	34	14	7	13	54	45	35
Atherton Collieries	34	13	8	13	44	44	34
Ashton Town	34	13	7	14	62	56	33
Oldham Dew	34	11	10	13	51	44	32
Bolton ST	34	12	8	14	55	73	32
Maghull	34	12	7	15	56	51	31
Cheadle Town	34	12	7	15	46	62	31
Bacup Borough	34	11	8	15	54	59	30
Ashton Athletic	34	12	6	16	45	61	30
Daisy Hill	34	10	9	15	51	61	27
Whitworth Valley	34	10	7	17	51	71	27
Nelson	34	9	4	21	43	80	22
Prestwich Heys	34	7	4	23	35	75	16

Daisy Hill and Prestwich Heys both had 2 points deducted.
Oldham Dew changed their name to Oldham Town.
Ashton Town and Urmston Town both left and joined the Manchester League Division One. Lytham also left and Huyton Town joined.

1985-86

Division One

Clitheroe	38	20	14	4	61	30	54
Congleton Town	38	22	10	6	51	29	54
Eastwood Hanley	38	22	9	7	68	45	53
Stalybridge Celtic	38	21	10	7	62	39	52
Fleetwood Town	38	21	10	7	70	34	50
Irlam Town	38	16	14	8	66	45	46
Leek Town	38	20	6	12	64	44	46
Curzon Ashton	38	18	9	11	52	50	45
Burscough	38	15	10	13	45	35	40
St. Helens Town	38	15	8	15	65	55	38
Accrington Stanley	38	13	11	14	62	60	37
Leyland Motors	38	13	8	17	62	67	34
Winsford United	38	14	6	18	55	68	34
Radcliffe Borough	38	12	9	17	48	49	33
Bootle	38	11	7	20	46	54	29
Penrith	38	9	8	21	46	63	26
Netherfield	38	8	10	20	38	76	26
Glossop	38	7	10	21	37	69	24
Prescot Cables	38	5	9	24	33	68	19
Formby	38	5	8	25	35	86	18

Fleetwood Town had 2 points deducted.

Division Two

Kirkby Town	34	24	7	3	85	30	55
Rossendale United	34	20	8	6	81	36	48
Wren Rovers	34	18	8	8	60	46	44
Warrington Town	34	17	9	8	62	48	43
Colwyn Bay	34	17	8	9	74	53	42
Chadderton	34	15	12	7	66	48	42
Colne Dynamoes	34	15	9	10	59	43	39
Great Harwood Town	34	13	10	11	38	45	36
Skelmersdale United	34	14	5	15	58	53	33
Droylsden	34	13	7	14	48	56	33
Atherton Laburnum Rovers	34	12	6	16	49	61	30
Lancaster City	34	10	9	15	57	66	29
Ellesmere Port & Neston	34	9	9	16	45	61	27
Ashton United	34	11	5	18	46	64	25
Darwen	34	8	8	18	48	57	24
Salford	34	9	4	21	38	72	22
Ford Motors	34	5	10	19	36	64	20
Nantwich Town	34	5	8	21	31	78	18

Ashton United had 2 points deducted.

Division Three

Blackpool Mechanics	28	22	2	4	77	33	44
Oldham Town	28	14	9	5	56	29	37
Maghull	28	15	6	7	62	36	36
Daisy Hill	28	13	7	8	62	45	33
Atherton Collieries	28	13	7	8	48	37	33
Bolton ST	28	12	7	9	42	34	29
Cheadle Town	28	9	10	9	42	26	28
Bacup Borough	28	10	8	10	36	40	28
Padiham	28	8	10	10	44	45	26
Prestwich Heys	28	10	6	12	53	66	26
Newton	28	7	10	11	43	48	24
Whitworth Valley	28	7	8	13	42	48	22
Huyton Town	28	7	7	14	41	71	21
Nelson	28	7	7	14	36	65	19
Ashton Athletic	28	1	6	21	24	85	8

Blackpool Mechanics, Bolton ST and Nelson all had 2 points deducted.
Ashton Athletic and Prestwich Heys both moved to the Manchester League Division One and Bolton ST and Huyton Town also left. Flixton and Ashton Town both joined from the Manchester League, Flixton from the Premier Division and Ashton Town from Division One.

1986-87

Division One

Stalybridge Celtic	38	25	8	5	74	39	58
Accrington Stanley	38	19	15	4	63	32	53
Clitheroe	38	20	12	6	76	47	52
Kirkby Town	38	22	4	12	71	48	48
Bootle	38	19	10	9	52	38	48
St. Helens Town	38	19	9	10	65	37	47
Winsford United	38	19	8	11	55	39	46
Fleetwood Town	38	16	13	9	61	49	45
Penrith	38	16	10	12	62	59	42
Rossendale United	38	14	11	13	66	59	39
Congleton Town	38	13	11	14	38	39	37
Burscough	38	11	11	16	58	54	33
Leyland Motors	38	13	7	18	52	56	33
Eastwood Hanley	38	10	11	17	40	50	31
Radcliffe Borough	38	11	8	19	46	57	30
Leek Town	38	9	12	17	42	55	30
Netherfield	38	12	5	21	45	73	29
Irlam Town	38	4	13	21	36	74	21
Curzon Ashton	38	4	12	22	35	78	20
Glossop	38	5	8	25	33	87	18

The 12 clubs in bold type above, plus Droylsden and Lancaster City from Division Two, left to become founder members of the Northern Premier League's new Division One.

Division Two

Droylsden	34	20	8	6	79	42	48
Warrington Town	34	16	13	5	48	34	45
Ashton United	34	19	6	9	73	45	44
Wren Rovers	34	18	8	8	65	39	44
Colwyn Bay	34	17	9	8	61	43	43
Darwen	34	15	8	11	45	47	38
Chadderton	34	14	9	11	52	47	37
Colne Dynamoes	34	14	8	12	57	44	36
Skelmersdale United	34	13	10	11	52	53	36
Ellesmere Port & Neston	34	15	5	14	68	54	35
Formby	34	13	7	14	54	55	33
Blackpool Mechanics	34	12	8	14	56	64	32
Lancaster City	34	12	7	15	55	53	31
Prescot Cables	34	12	6	16	46	48	28
Great Harwood Town	34	9	8	17	36	59	24
Oldham Town	34	7	9	18	38	57	23
Atherton Laburnum Rovers	34	8	5	21	32	61	21
Salford	34	1	8	25	17	89	10

Prescot Cables and Great Harwood Town both had 2 points deducted.
The 10 clubs in bold type above (not including Droylsden and Lancaster City) were promoted to Division One.

Division Three

Atherton Collieries	24	16	4	4	46	22	36
Flixton	24	15	5	4	58	29	35
Maghull	24	14	2	8	44	29	30
Nelson	24	12	6	6	37	29	30
Newton	24	11	5	8	42	36	27
Ford Motors	24	9	8	7	38	27	26
Bacup Borough	24	10	6	8	27	27	26
Cheadle Town	24	9	5	10	33	44	23
Daisy Hill	24	6	7	11	21	42	17
Padiham	24	4	8	12	35	39	16
Nantwich Town	24	5	6	13	26	42	16
Ashton Town	24	4	9	11	29	39	15
Whitworth Valley	24	3	5	16	17	48	11

Daisy Hill and Ashton Town both had 2 points deducted.
Division Three disbanded, its clubs all being promoted to Division Two along with newcomers Maine Road (from the Manchester League), Newcastle Town (from the Mid-Cheshire League) and Vauxhall GM (from the West Cheshire League).

1987-88

Division One

Colne Dynamoes	34	24	7	3	71	14	55
Rossendale United	34	24	7	3	68	23	55
Clitheroe	34	18	10	6	51	20	46
Colwyn Bay	34	20	7	7	60	42	45
St. Helens Town	34	18	6	10	61	36	42
Ellesmere Port & Neston	34	17	5	12	55	48	39
Darwen	34	14	10	10	55	45	38
Warrington Town	34	16	5	13	68	47	37
Kirkby Town	34	11	13	10	57	54	35
Burscough	34	14	7	13	45	51	35
Leyland Motors	34	10	11	13	53	53	31
Prescot Cables	34	10	11	13	34	45	29
Bootle	34	12	5	17	43	61	29
Formby	34	6	10	18	32	63	22
Salford	34	8	6	20	33	66	22
Skelmersdale United	34	4	11	19	34	64	19
Atherton Laburnum Rovers	34	4	7	23	31	78	15
Glossop	34	5	4	25	30	71	14

Colwyn Bay and Prescot Cables both had 2 points deducted.
Kirkby Town changed their name to Knowsley United.

Division Two

Ashton United	42	32	6	4	107	30	70
Flixton	42	27	10	5	94	38	64
Wren Rovers	42	26	9	7	92	51	61
Newcastle Town	42	26	7	9	81	39	59
Maine Road	42	23	4	15	74	48	50
Maghull	42	18	11	13	73	66	47
Vauxhall GM	42	15	16	11	58	50	46
Atherton Collieries	42	20	6	16	63	63	46
Whitworth Valley	42	15	12	15	50	60	42
Ashton Town	42	17	8	17	64	70	40
Oldham Town	42	13	11	18	44	51	37
Cheadle Town	42	13	11	18	47	62	35
Chadderton	42	13	9	20	55	71	35
Great Harwood Town	42	14	8	20	52	66	34
Blackpool Mechanics	42	12	10	20	57	77	34
Nelson	42	12	10	20	49	76	34
Ford Motors	42	12	9	21	59	70	33
Daisy Hill	42	12	8	22	55	66	32
Padiham	42	10	14	18	53	76	32
Newton	42	10	12	20	47	84	30
Nantwich Town	42	8	13	21	41	68	29
Bacup Borough	42	8	8	26	38	71	22

Ashton Town, Bacup Borough, Cheadle Town, Great Harwood Town, Newton and Padiham all had 2 points deducted.
Whitworth Valley moved to the Manchester League Division One, Ford Motors moved to the Liverpool County Combination and Nelson moved to the West Lancashire League Division Two.

1988-89

Division One

Rossendale United	34	24	8	2	84	27	56
Knowsley United	34	21	8	5	85	43	50
St. Helens Town	34	20	8	6	60	25	48
Colwyn Bay	34	19	9	6	77	45	47
Darwen	34	19	9	6	64	36	47
Warrington Town	34	16	10	8	47	37	42
Flixton	34	15	8	11	61	44	38
Leyland Motors	34	15	8	11	53	44	38
Bootle	34	14	4	16	49	54	32
Burscough	34	11	10	13	40	51	32
Ellesmere Port & Neston	34	9	12	13	36	42	30
Clitheroe	34	8	12	14	38	41	28
Skelmersdale United	34	8	9	17	39	68	25
Atherton Laburnum Rovers	34	9	6	19	47	74	24
Prescot Cables	34	7	9	18	36	60	23
Salford	34	7	8	19	33	70	22
Ashton United	34	7	6	21	37	72	18
Formby	34	3	4	27	24	77	10

Ashton United had 2 points deducted.
Ellesmere Port & Neston disbanded.

Division Two

Vauxhall GM	34	25	8	1	68	17	58
Maine Road	34	22	7	5	96	40	51
Chadderton	34	20	9	5	71	29	49
Wren Rovers	34	19	10	5	77	45	48
Nantwich Town	34	20	4	10	66	28	44
Newcastle Town	34	15	10	9	53	37	40
Great Harwood Town	34	16	6	12	52	40	38
Maghull	34	12	13	9	46	44	37
Bacup Borough	34	11	12	11	55	57	34
Daisy Hill	34	12	6	16	36	49	30
Atherton Collieries	34	9	11	14	52	58	29
Padiham	34	9	10	15	39	57	28
Glossop	34	10	7	17	42	60	27
Cheadle Town	34	10	7	17	46	67	27
Oldham Town	34	6	11	17	46	66	23
Blackpool Mechanics	34	9	5	20	46	72	23
Ashton Town	34	4	11	19	31	68	19
Newton	34	1	5	28	23	111	7

Daisy Hill changed their name to Westhoughton Town.

Three points were awarded for a win from the next season.

1989-90

Division One

Warrington Town	34	22	6	6	69	31	72
Knowsley United	34	21	6	7	68	45	69
Colwyn Bay	34	16	12	6	79	50	60
Vauxhall GM	34	16	9	9	50	42	57
Clitheroe	34	17	6	11	48	47	57
Darwen	34	15	9	10	40	34	54
Nantwich Town	34	13	5	16	50	52	44
St. Helens Town	34	10	13	11	50	48	43
Ashton United	34	11	10	13	39	45	43
Prescot Cables	34	10	11	13	49	54	41
Bootle	34	11	8	15	44	58	41
Flixton	34	11	7	16	37	47	40
Leyland Motors	34	10	7	17	55	64	37
Atherton Laburnum Rovers	34	8	13	13	43	58	37
Skelmersdale United	34	8	11	15	48	59	35
Salford	34	8	11	15	31	47	35
Burscough	34	8	12	14	38	41	33
Chadderton	34	7	12	15	39	55	33

Burscough had 3 points deducted.
Penrith and Eastwood Hanley joined after relegation from the Northern Premier League. Prescot Cables changed their name to Prescot, Leyland Motors changed their name to Leyland DAF-SGL and Salford changed their name to Salford City.

Division Two

Maine Road	30	22	4	4	84	35	70
Bacup Borough	30	21	5	4	76	30	68
Blackpool Mechanics	30	17	6	7	59	30	57
Wren Rovers	30	16	7	7	72	38	55
Great Harwood Town	30	16	6	8	52	29	54
Cheadle Town	30	13	8	9	54	45	47
Maghull	30	13	6	11	40	43	45
Atherton Collieries	30	12	7	11	34	38	43
Oldham Town	30	11	5	14	47	51	38
Ashton Town	30	9	7	14	42	57	34
Padiham	30	9	6	15	44	53	33
Formby	30	7	7	16	33	57	28
Newcastle Town	30	8	4	18	38	65	28
Glossop	30	8	3	19	34	58	27
Westhoughton Town	30	8	3	19	36	62	27
Newton	30	5	6	19	29	83	21

Wren Rovers changed their name to Blackpool Rovers.
Bradford Park Avenue joined from the Central Midlands League, Bamber Bridge joined from the Preston & District League, Castleton Gabriels joined from the Manchester League and Kidsgrove Athletic joined from the Mid-Cheshire League. Padiham moved to the West Lancashire League and Newton moved to the West Cheshire League.

1990-91

Division One

Knowsley United	36	25	8	3	95	37	83
Colwyn Bay	36	22	10	4	85	32	76
Ashton United	36	20	7	9	00	45	67
Eastwood Hanley	36	16	12	8	42	29	60
Vauxhall GM	36	15	10	11	42	36	55
Prescot	36	13	12	11	57	55	51
Flixton	36	14	7	15	48	72	49
St. Helens Town	36	13	9	14	52	47	48
Maine Road	36	13	9	14	58	61	48
Skelmersdale United	36	12	11	13	56	49	47
Nantwich Town	36	13	8	15	43	56	47
Leyland DAF-SGL	36	12	10	14	51	53	46
Bootle	36	10	9	17	55	64	39
Bacup Borough	36	9	12	15	38	47	39
Clitheroe	36	10	8	18	50	63	38
Darwen	36	9	11	16	44	62	38
Penrith	36	10	8	18	41	65	38
Atherton Laburnum Rovers	36	9	11	16	42	68	38
Salford City	36	6	10	20	30	68	28

Leyland DAF-SGL left.

Division Two

Great Harwood Town	34	27	5	2	81	22	86
Blackpool Rovers	34	25	4	5	84	33	78
Bradford Park Avenue	34	20	9	5	72	41	69
Bamber Bridge	34	20	6	8	78	46	66
Blackpool Mechanics	34	18	7	9	51	30	61
Newcastle Town	34	16	12	6	48	30	60
Cheadle Town	34	17	3	14	55	54	54
Glossop	34	12	10	12	47	42	46
Burscough	34	12	8	14	39	51	44
Westhoughton Town	34	11	10	13	50	64	43
Castleton Gabriels	34	11	9	14	42	47	42
Chadderton	34	10	6	18	51	61	36
Maghull	34	9	8	17	37	54	35
Kidsgrove Athletic	34	7	10	17	37	65	31
Ashton Town	34	9	2	23	43	86	29
Oldham Town	34	8	4	22	35	66	27
Formby	34	5	9	20	46	63	24
Atherton Collieries	34	6	4	24	37	78	22

Blackpool Rovers and Oldham Town both had 1 point deducted.
Squires Gate and Holker Old Boys both joined from the West Lancashire League.

1991-92

Division One

Ashton United	34	24	5	5	61	31	77
Great Harwood Town	34	22	8	4	68	38	74
Eastwood Hanley	34	18	9	7	54	35	63
Blackpool Rovers	34	16	7	11	73	57	55
Prescot	34	15	6	13	48	43	51
Penrith	34	15	5	14	57	58	50
Skelmersdale United	34	11	11	12	48	52	44
Flixton	34	11	9	14	46	50	42
Clitheroe	34	11	9	14	44	55	42
Darwen	34	10	11	13	56	55	41
Atherton Laburnum Rovers	34	11	8	15	38	45	41
Nantwich Town	34	11	10	13	44	49	40
Vauxhall GM	34	10	10	14	42	51	40
Bacup Borough	34	9	11	14	41	45	38
St. Helens Town	34	9	9	16	49	55	36
Maine Road	34	9	9	16	40	60	36
Bradford Park Avenue	34	10	5	19	57	68	35
Bootle	34	9	8	17	41	61	35
					907	*908*	

Nantwich Town had 3 points deducted.
Vauxhall GM moved to the West Cheshire League.

Division Two

Bamber Bridge	34	25	3	6	97	39	78
Newcastle Town	34	23	6	5	69	26	75
Blackpool Mechanics	34	20	9	5	75	34	69
Burscough	34	19	7	8	82	46	64
Formby	34	17	5	12	49	39	56
Glossop	34	15	9	10	61	44	54
Salford City	34	14	9	11	57	41	51
Castleton Gabriels	34	14	9	11	54	43	51
Cheadle Town	34	15	6	13	53	50	51
Kidsgrove Athletic	34	14	7	13	44	45	49
Chadderton	34	14	6	14	50	48	48
Oldham Town	34	11	8	15	49	62	41
Atherton Collieries	34	12	4	18	51	64	40
Squires Gate	34	11	5	18	45	60	38
Holker Old Boys	34	10	6	18	37	53	36
Maghull	34	7	2	25	38	90	23
Ashton Town	34	4	7	23	47	101	19
Westhoughton Town	34	5	4	25	33	106	19

Glossop changed their name to Glossop North End. Stantondale joined from the Liverpool County Combination, North Trafford joined from the Mid-Cheshire League, Burnley Bank Hall and Nelson both joined from the West Lancashire League, K Chell joined from the West Midland Regional League, Irlam Town joined from the Northern Premier League and Ellesmere Port Town joined as a new club.

1992-93

Division One

Atherton Laburnum Rovers	42	33	7	2	75	25	106
Bamber Bridge	42	24	11	7	81	37	83
Chadderton	42	24	11	7	99	64	83
Prescot	42	20	12	10	68	44	72
Newcastle Town	42	20	8	14	70	57	68
Bradford Park Avenue	42	19	8	15	54	43	65
Clitheroe	42	17	8	17	61	40	59
St. Helens Town	42	16	11	15	79	62	59
Salford City	42	15	13	14	58	61	58
Burscough	42	16	10	16	58	68	58
Flixton	42	14	15	13	50	42	57
Blackpool Rovers	42	16	9	17	66	64	57
Nantwich Town	42	14	15	13	60	60	57
Penrith	42	15	11	16	62	67	56
Bacup Borough	42	14	13	15	66	59	55
Glossop North End	42	16	9	17	70	67	54
Darwen	42	14	10	18	54	61	52
Eastwood Hanley	42	14	10	18	45	57	52
Maine Road	42	12	9	21	55	63	45
Kidsgrove Athletic	42	9	8	25	53	94	35
Skelmersdale United	42	7	10	25	45	84	31
Blackpool Mechanics	42	2	4	36	27	137	10

Glossop North End had 3 points deducted.
Rossendale United joined after relegation from the Northern Premier League.

Division Two

Maghull	34	21	9	4	77	26	72
Bootle	34	20	8	6	89	49	68
Oldham Town	34	20	6	8	79	47	66
Ellesmere Port Town	34	16	9	9	65	46	57
Stantondale	34	16	9	9	59	49	57
Castleton Gabriels	34	15	10	9	61	48	55
North Trafford	34	14	9	11	67	63	51
Formby	34	14	9	11	49	49	51
Atherton Collieries	34	14	7	13	63	67	49
Burnley Bank Hall	34	14	4	16	87	77	46
Westhoughton Town	34	14	3	17	65	75	42
Cheadle Town	34	12	7	15	44	48	40
Squires Gate	34	11	5	18	56	73	38
K Chell	34	10	8	16	52	72	38
Holker Old Boys	34	8	13	13	57	60	37
Ashton Town	34	8	8	18	51	74	32
Nelson	34	7	7	20	47	82	28
Irlam Town	34	4	5	25	47	110	17

Cheadle Town and Westhoughton Town both had 3 points deducted.
Burnley Bank Hall left and Haslingden joined from the West Lancashire League.

1993-94

Division One

Atherton Laburnum Rovers	42	25	13	4	83	34	88
Rossendale United	42	25	9	8	76	46	84
Burscough	42	22	13	7	107	50	79
Nantwich Town	42	22	11	9	80	54	77
Eastwood Hanley	42	22	11	9	75	52	77
Bootle	42	21	10	11	77	61	73
Penrith	42	20	11	11	62	44	71
Blackpool Rovers	42	19	10	13	64	57	67
Clitheroe	42	19	9	14	75	58	66
Kidsgrove Athletic	42	16	10	16	70	61	58
St. Helens Town	42	14	13	15	60	55	55
Prescot	42	14	13	15	46	47	55
Maine Road	42	14	13	15	58	64	55
Newcastle Town	42	14	10	18	66	67	52
Bradford Park Avenue	42	12	12	18	54	79	48
Darwen	42	12	8	22	38	61	44
Glossop North End	42	12	8	22	58	86	44
Salford City	42	11	10	21	50	67	43
Chadderton	42	10	8	24	49	85	38
Bacup Borough	42	9	9	24	57	85	36
Skelmersdale United	42	8	8	26	55	92	32
Flixton	42	9	5	28	35	90	32

Division Two

Haslingden	34	26	5	3	117	39	83
North Trafford	34	24	2	8	95	36	74
Holker Old Boys	34	23	3	8	75	40	72
Stantondale	34	20	8	6	88	45	68
Castleton Gabriels	34	19	6	9	55	46	63
Nelson	34	16	8	10	75	52	56
Atherton Collieries	34	15	9	10	58	40	54
Maghull	34	15	8	11	70	46	53
Ellesmere Port Town	34	14	8	12	62	63	50
Formby	34	12	11	11	59	50	47
Oldham Town	34	13	6	15	61	68	45
Cheadle Town	34	11	9	14	69	62	42
Blackpool Mechanics	34	10	5	19	50	69	35
Westhoughton Town	34	9	3	22	53	100	30
Ashton Town	34	7	8	19	42	91	29
Irlam Town	34	8	4	22	41	73	28
K Chell	34	4	6	24	35	97	18
Squires Gate	34	1	9	24	20	108	12

North Trafford changed their name to Trafford and Westhoughton Town changed their name to Daisy Hill. Ellesmere Port Town and K Chell both disbanded.
Tetley Walker joined from the Warrington & District League.

1994-95

Division One

Bradford Park Avenue	42	30	4	8	96	43	94
Clitheroe	42	27	9	6	104	49	90
St. Helens Town	42	27	8	7	86	42	89
Trafford	42	27	5	10	98	50	86
Newcastle Town	42	24	7	11	75	57	79
Glossop North End	42	23	8	11	88	59	77
Blackpool Rovers	42	22	7	13	81	64	73
Burscough	42	19	15	8	102	65	72
Prescot	42	16	8	18	47	47	56
Penrith	42	16	7	19	72	72	55
Chadderton	42	15	7	20	56	70	52
Maine Road	42	14	9	19	68	81	51
Eastwood Hanley	42	14	8	20	75	81	50
Holker Old Boys	42	13	11	18	63	72	50
Kidsgrove Athletic	42	14	8	20	66	78	50
Nantwich Town	42	14	7	21	85	83	49
Darwen	42	14	5	23	65	82	47
Rossendale United	42	12	11	19	60	82	47
Bootle	42	11	10	21	46	68	43
Skelmersdale United	42	10	7	25	67	118	37
Salford City	42	9	9	24	45	85	36
Bacup Borough	42	3	6	33	35	132	15

Mossley joined after relegation from the Northern Premier League.

Division Two

Flixton	30	21	6	3	98	32	69
Oldham Town	30	20	6	4	83	34	66
Tetley Walker	30	18	5	7	75	46	59
Atherton Collieries	30	18	4	8	67	41	58
Stantondale	30	18	3	9	58	43	57
Nelson	30	13	8	9	64	44	47
Haslingden	30	14	4	12	76	64	46
Blackpool Mechanics	30	12	8	10	72	57	44
Maghull	30	11	8	11	58	46	41
Formby	30	11	6	13	57	53	39
Cheadle Town	30	10	7	13	48	52	37
Castleton Gabriels	30	9	9	12	56	75	36
Daisy Hill	30	6	8	16	53	73	26
Ashton Town	30	6	2	22	39	92	20
Irlam Town	30	5	3	22	30	98	18
Squires Gate	30	2	5	23	30	114	11

Irlam Town left. Middlewich Athletic (ex-Mid-Cheshire League), Vauxhall GM (ex-West Cheshire League) and Ramsbottom United (ex- Manchester League) all joined.

1995-96

Division One

Flixton	42	28	8	6	85	30	92
Newcastle Town	42	26	7	9	88	42	85
Trafford	42	26	5	11	89	45	83
Mossley	42	24	8	10	87	59	80
Burscough	42	23	8	11	77	40	77
Bootle	42	23	5	14	74	55	74
Clitheroe	42	20	12	10	63	44	72
St. Helens Town	42	19	13	10	71	53	70
Nantwich Town	42	20	7	15	64	59	67
Prescot	42	17	11	14	70	66	62
Holker Old Boys	42	19	4	19	77	72	61
Glossop North End	42	15	15	12	55	48	60
Kidsgrove Athletic	42	15	9	18	61	64	54
Eastwood Hanley	42	12	15	15	60	57	51
Maine Road	42	12	14	16	60	71	50
Chadderton	42	14	8	20	52	69	50
Blackpool Rovers	42	11	9	22	49	74	42
Penrith	42	9	12	21	57	69	39
Darwen	42	9	10	23	57	77	37
Salford City	42	10	5	27	49	93	35
Rossendale United	42	6	10	26	32	114	28
Skelmersdale United	42	5	3	34	45	121	18

Prescot changed their name to Prescot Cables.

Division Two

Vauxhall GM	34	28	4	2	112	25	88
Atherton Collieries	34	25	5	4	90	44	80
Tetley Walker	34	22	7	5	76	35	73
Castleton Gabriels	34	19	5	10	77	52	62
Nelson	34	17	9	8	78	55	60
Cheadle Town	34	17	5	12	67	49	56
Haslingden	34	15	9	10	69	45	54
Maghull	34	16	3	15	55	42	51
Oldham Town	34	14	8	12	75	74	50
Middlewich Athletic	34	12	7	15	45	74	43
Daisy Hill	34	12	4	18	46	66	40
Ramsbottom United	34	11	6	17	60	65	39
Formby	34	10	7	17	59	76	37
Stantondale	34	11	4	19	47	75	37
Blackpool Mechanics	34	8	8	18	56	74	32
Ashton Town	34	8	3	23	53	102	27
Squires Gate	34	5	7	22	37	82	22
Bacup Borough	34	4	3	27	35	102	15

Garswood United joined from the Mid-Cheshire League, Leek County School Old Boys joined from the Midland League and Colne joined as a new club.

1996-97

Division One

Trafford	42	29	7	6	99	38	94
Newcastle Town	42	27	7	8	71	31	88
Clitheroe	42	23	14	5	75	36	83
Penrith	42	23	10	9	75	49	79
Burscough	42	22	9	11	68	48	75
Eastwood Hanley	42	20	10	12	64	51	70
Mossley	42	20	8	14	79	58	68
Blackpool Rovers	42	17	16	9	70	47	67
Prescot Cables	42	17	11	14	68	60	62
Vauxhall GM	42	14	15	13	70	69	57
Nantwich Town	42	14	11	17	74	74	53
Bootle	42	15	8	19	62	73	53
Glossop North End	42	14	11	17	56	67	53
St. Helens Town	42	14	6	22	65	79	48
Atherton Collieries	42	12	9	21	63	85	45
Kidsgrove Athletic	42	10	14	18	53	73	44
Rossendale United	42	11	9	22	51	76	42
Chadderton	42	10	11	21	49	80	41
Holker Old Boys	42	10	9	23	60	80	39
Maine Road	42	9	11	22	49	85	38
Darwen	42	9	10	23	49	82	37
Salford City	42	8	12	22	53	82	36

Penrith moved to the Northern League and Eastwood Hanley disbanded. Atherton Laburnum Rovers and Warrington Town joined after relegation from the Northern Premier League.

Division Two

Ramsbottom United	38	27	6	5	100	34	87
Haslingden	38	27	6	5	90	32	87
Garswood United	38	26	5	7	90	38	83
Tetley Walker	38	24	5	9	105	58	77
Castleton Gabriels	38	22	8	8	78	39	74
Leek County School Old Boys	38	22	7	9	67	49	73
Formby	38	21	6	11	86	57	69
Maghull	38	17	7	14	52	50	58
Cheadle Town	38	15	8	15	59	63	53
Skelmersdale United	38	14	10	14	72	66	52
Nelson	38	14	10	14	64	72	52
Stantondale	38	11	12	15	59	69	45
Middlewich Athletic	38	13	6	19	54	65	45
Squires Gate	38	12	4	22	44	79	40
Daisy Hill	38	10	5	23	47	76	35
Bacup Borough	38	9	6	23	48	83	33
Ashton Town	38	6	14	18	53	77	32
Blackpool Mechanics	38	7	5	26	48	88	26
Oldham Town	38	6	7	25	48	113	25
Colne	38	6	5	27	35	91	23

Woodley Sports joined from the Manchester League and Fleetwood Freeport joined as a new club.

1997-98

Division One

Kidsgrove Athletic	42	32	3	7	127	50	99
Burscough	42	29	7	6	101	30	94
Newcastle Town	42	23	16	3	82	32	85
Vauxhall GM	42	24	9	9	91	52	81
St. Helens Town	42	22	12	8	91	59	78
Clitheroe	42	21	10	11	72	51	73
Prescot Cables	42	19	11	12	72	57	68
Glossop North End	42	19	7	16	78	69	64
Mossley	42	16	14	12	67	52	62
Nantwich Town	42	17	6	19	71	79	57
Maine Road	42	15	10	17	56	70	55
Chadderton	42	15	8	19	63	59	53
Rossendale United	42	15	6	21	61	80	51
Blackpool Rovers	42	13	9	20	68	84	48
Atherton Laburnum Rovers	42	12	11	19	54	73	47
Haslingden	42	12	10	20	68	95	46
Ramsbottom United	42	12	9	21	58	85	45
Salford City	42	13	4	25	64	92	43
Warrington Town	42	10	10	22	56	72	40
Holker Old Boys	42	7	12	23	46	96	33
Darwen	42	6	13	23	42	93	31
Atherton Collieries	42	7	9	26	42	100	30

Workington joined after relegation from the Northern Premier League. Blackpool Rovers and Haslingden left.

Division Two

Oldham Town	40	27	8	5	118	49	89
Skelmersdale United	40	26	7	7	111	50	85
Leek County School Old Boys	40	26	7	7	76	38	85
Cheadle Town	40	24	9	7	108	58	81
Woodley Sports	40	22	7	11	118	56	73
Formby	40	22	7	11	90	63	73
Bootle	40	19	15	6	82	60	72
Garswood United	40	19	10	11	98	62	67
Tetley Walker	40	19	9	12	98	62	66
Castleton Gabriels	40	18	7	15	86	59	61
Maghull	40	16	10	14	67	62	58
Fleetwood Freeport	40	15	11	14	73	55	56
Nelson	40	17	5	18	69	76	56
Bacup Borough	40	13	8	19	58	83	47
Squires Gate	40	11	9	20	72	88	42
Daisy Hill	40	11	9	20	60	86	42
Middlewich Athletic	40	11	8	21	48	90	41
Colne	40	8	7	25	48	91	31
Ashton Town	40	6	6	28	73	137	24
Stantondale	40	4	4	32	50	146	16
Blackpool Mechanics	40	2	5	33	33	165	11

Middlewich Athletic reformed as Middlewich Town and moved to the Mid-Cheshire League, Garswood United moved to the Mid-Cheshire League and Stantondale also left. Abbey Hey joined from the Manchester League and Curzon Ashton joined from the Northern Counties (East) League.

1998-99

Division One

Workington	40	27	9	4	86	28	90
Mossley	40	27	7	6	91	38	88
Vauxhall GM	40	26	7	7	92	40	85
Newcastle Town	40	25	9	6	86	33	84
Kidsgrove Athletic	40	24	7	9	90	47	79
Prescot Cables	40	21	9	10	78	44	72
Skelmersdale United	40	21	8	11	82	48	71
St. Helens Town	40	22	5	13	77	58	71
Leek County School Old Boys	40	14	11	15	52	58	53
Salford City	40	15	7	18	63	73	52
Ramsbottom United	40	14	8	18	54	64	50
Clitheroe	40	14	6	20	68	58	48
Maine Road	40	14	6	20	50	71	48
Rossendale United	40	14	5	21	59	81	47
Nantwich Town	40	12	6	22	54	68	42
Glossop North End	40	12	6	22	53	81	42
Cheadle Town	40	12	6	22	56	97	42
Atherton Laburnum Rovers	40	10	9	21	45	73	39
Atherton Collieries	40	9	7	24	50	88	34
Bootle	40	9	7	24	41	84	34
Holker Old Boys	40	4	3	33	21	116	15

Vauxhall GM changed their name to Vauxhall Motors
Great Harwood Town joined after relegation from the Northern Premier League.

Division Two

Fleetwood Freeport	36	21	8	7	102	34	71
Abbey Hey	36	20	6	10	70	35	66
Squires Gate	36	17	14	5	53	31	65
Warrington Town	36	18	9	9	82	46	63
Woodley Sports	36	17	10	9	60	38	61
Castleton Gabriels	36	17	10	9	71	56	61
Formby	36	17	7	12	81	59	58
Darwen	36	13	12	11	64	53	51
Chadderton	36	11	17	8	42	38	50
Tetley Walker	36	14	8	14	62	64	50
Bacup Borough	36	11	14	11	47	61	47
Daisy Hill	36	12	9	15	51	63	45
Nelson	36	11	11	14	51	49	44
Curzon Ashton	36	12	7	17	56	58	43
Maghull	36	11	10	15	50	70	43
Colne	36	11	7	18	53	70	40
Ashton Town	36	11	6	19	35	59	39
Oldham Town	36	5	7	24	35	99	22
Blackpool Mechanics	36	4	6	26	40	122	18

Maghull moved to the West Cheshire League and Alsager joined from the Midland League.

1999-2000

Division One

Vauxhall Motors	42	29	7	6	101	32	94
Newcastle Town	42	26	7	9	82	35	85
Ramsbottom United	42	23	10	9	87	53	79
Mossley	42	23	10	9	80	50	79
Rossendale United	42	23	9	10	77	46	78
Skelmersdale United	42	22	9	11	91	53	75
Fleetwood Freeport	42	21	10	11	75	45	73
Prescot Cables	42	21	10	11	83	55	73
St. Helens Town	42	20	13	9	81	59	73
Clitheroe	42	21	7	14	75	49	70
Salford City	42	17	7	18	70	69	58
Atherton Collieries	42	16	6	20	58	68	54
Kidsgrove Athletic	42	14	9	19	47	66	51
Abbey Hey	42	14	8	20	50	75	50
Nantwich Town	42	13	9	20	60	73	48
Great Harwood Town	42	12	9	21	55	81	45
Glossop North End	42	10	11	21	52	73	41
Cheadle Town	42	8	13	21	49	85	37
Maine Road	42	9	10	23	59	100	37
Leek County School Old Boys	42	8	10	24	49	101	34
Bootle	42	6	8	28	29	90	26
Atherton Laburnum Rovers	42	4	12	26	51	103	24

Flixton joined after relegation from the Northern Premier League.

Division Two

Woodley Sports	34	24	6	4	85	29	78
Curzon Ashton	34	24	6	4	78	26	78
Nelson	34	21	8	5	77	31	71
Darwen	34	20	6	8	69	35	66
Bacup Borough	34	15	11	8	68	42	56
Squires Gate	34	16	7	11	70	49	55
Tetley Walker	34	16	4	14	56	70	52
Castleton Gabriels	34	15	6	13	67	67	51
Warrington Town	34	14	8	12	66	44	50
Chadderton	34	12	12	10	52	57	48
Formby	34	12	8	14	52	68	44
Alsager	34	11	8	15	48	64	41
Colne	34	12	2	20	44	70	38
Holker Old Boys	34	8	11	15	59	73	35
Blackpool Mechanics	34	9	6	19	49	74	33
Daisy Hill	34	7	5	22	41	75	26
Oldham Town	34	4	6	24	43	86	18
Ashton Town	34	5	2	27	30	94	17

Padiham joined from the West Lancashire League.
Stone Dominoes joined from the Midland League.

2000-01

Division One

Rossendale United	42	29	5	8	114	44	92
Clitheroe	42	27	8	7	105	47	89
Ramsbottom United	42	28	4	10	85	44	88
St. Helens Town	42	26	9	7	98	40	87
Fleetwood Freeport	42	26	4	12	90	50	82
Kidsgrove Athletic	42	24	10	8	81	46	82
Salford City	42	23	10	9	87	41	79
Prescot Cables	42	24	5	13	94	54	77
Newcastle Town	42	20	7	15	69	45	67
Mossley	42	19	7	16	73	56	64
Curzon Ashton	42	18	9	15	67	66	63
Skelmersdale United	42	17	8	17	69	69	59
Woodley Sports	42	16	9	17	69	69	57
Abbey Hey	42	15	6	21	76	92	51
Maine Road	42	15	3	24	75	102	48
Nantwich Town	42	10	9	23	46	79	39
Atherton Collieries	42	11	6	25	43	88	39
Glossop North End	42	9	4	29	41	111	31
Great Harwood Town	42	7	9	26	44	93	30
Flixton	42	5	13	24	47	100	28
Leek County School Old Boys	42	5	12	25	39	89	27
Cheadle Town	42	5	9	28	42	129	24

Congleton Town and Winsford United joined after relegation from the Northern Premier League.

Division Two

Warrington Town	38	24	7	7	90	31	79
Tetley Walker	38	24	5	9	83	41	77
Atherton Laburnum Rovers	38	24	3	11	88	50	75
Nelson	38	21	11	6	89	44	74
Squires Gate	38	21	7	10	75	47	70
Blackpool Mechanics	38	21	6	11	85	47	69
Alsager	38	19	8	11	48	42	65
Padiham	38	20	4	14	83	71	64
Daisy Hill	38	18	6	14	78	80	60
Chadderton	38	17	7	14	68	58	58
Darwen	38	16	7	15	72	66	55
Formby	38	15	8	15	65	56	53
Stone Dominoes	38	15	6	17	62	63	51
Bacup Borough	38	13	9	16	59	60	48
Holker Old Boys	38	14	5	19	67	79	47
Bootle	38	11	8	19	70	76	41
Castleton Gabriels	38	10	7	21	52	90	37
Ashton Town	38	8	3	27	46	98	27
Colne	38	4	4	30	37	107	16
Oldham Town	38	3	3	32	38	149	12

Alsager changed their name to Alsager Town and Tetley Walker left. Stand Athletic joined from the Manchester League and Norton United joined from the Midland League.

2001-02

Division One

Kidsgrove Athletic	44	31	9	4	125	47	102
Prescot Cables	44	29	10	5	110	42	97
Salford City	44	29	10	5	91	40	97
St. Helens Town	44	28	6	10	101	44	90
Newcastle Town	44	22	11	11	97	66	77
Clitheroe	44	22	10	12	73	53	76
Winsford United	44	19	12	13	72	71	69
Mossley	44	18	14	12	82	63	68
Skelmersdale United	44	19	5	20	87	89	62
Woodley Sports	44	16	12	16	58	65	60
Warrington Town	44	16	11	17	78	72	59
Ramsbottom United	44	15	10	19	75	73	55
Curzon Ashton	44	16	7	21	74	72	55
Fleetwood Freeport	44	13	13	18	70	86	52
Nantwich Town	44	12	15	17	63	90	51
Congleton Town	44	13	11	20	71	79	50
Atherton Collieries	44	13	8	23	66	91	47
Abbey Hey	44	12	11	21	62	101	47
Glossop North End	44	13	7	24	78	105	46
Atherton Laburnum Rovers	44	11	11	22	62	88	44
Flixton	44	11	9	24	61	112	42
Maine Road	44	8	7	29	68	115	31
Great Harwood Town	44	5	11	28	39	99	26

Fleetwood Freeport changed their name to Fleetwood Town.

Division Two

Stand Athletic	40	30	5	5	110	47	95
Alsager Town	40	24	9	7	77	31	81
Squires Gate	40	24	9	7	103	60	81
Stone Dominoes	40	25	3	12	71	40	78
Formby	40	21	14	5	76	39	77
Bootle	40	19	7	14	82	64	64
Norton United	40	19	7	14	56	51	64
Blackpool Mechanics	40	18	9	13	69	48	63
Nelson	40	18	9	13	73	63	63
Leek County School Old Boys	40	17	8	15	62	65	59
Darwen	40	15	10	15	77	73	55
Bacup Borough	40	13	13	14	52	66	52
Padiham	40	14	8	18	69	66	50
Colne	40	14	8	18	61	72	50
Chadderton	40	15	5	20	65	81	50
Ashton Town	40	13	6	21	65	85	45
Cheadle Town	40	10	8	22	66	85	38
Castleton Gabriels	40	10	3	27	61	95	33
Holker Old Boys	40	7	9	24	43	79	30
Daisy Hill	40	8	4	28	49	114	28
Oldham Town	40	7	4	29	50	113	25

Bootle and Formby both moved to the Liverpool County Combination.

2002-03

Division One

Prescot Cables	42	30	6	6	110	38	96
Clitheroe	42	28	8	6	97	38	92
Mossley	42	27	7	8	100	41	88
Newcastle Town	42	23	12	7	83	52	81
Skelmersdale United	42	22	8	12	91	51	74
Nantwich Town	42	19	11	12	90	74	68
St. Helens Town	42	17	14	11	77	60	65
Congleton Town	42	19	8	15	72	62	65
Salford City	42	17	12	13	84	63	63
Fleetwood Town	42	17	9	16	73	70	60
Alsager Town	42	15	11	16	61	67	56
Squires Gate	42	13	12	17	58	71	51
Abbey Hey	42	12	13	17	56	73	49
Atherton Laburnum Rovers	42	11	12	19	65	86	45
Ramsbottom United	42	11	11	20	73	83	44
Warrington Town	42	11	11	20	48	66	44
Woodley Sports	42	11	9	22	62	85	42
Curzon Ashton	42	11	9	22	60	87	42
Atherton Collieries	42	11	7	24	52	85	40
Glossop North End	42	10	9	23	55	104	39
Flixton	42	10	8	24	44	112	38
Winsford United	42	10	7	25	48	91	37

Trafford joined after relegation from the Northern Premier League.

Division Two

Bacup Borough	34	25	2	7	91	32	77
Stone Dominoes	34	24	3	7	94	34	75
Maine Road	34	23	2	9	74	55	71
Padiham	34	20	5	9	69	42	65
Holker Old Boys	34	18	7	9	65	42	61
Great Harwood Town	34	15	7	12	64	61	52
Nelson	34	13	12	9	50	40	51
Darwen	34	14	7	13	59	64	49
Norton United	34	14	6	14	50	52	48
Colne	34	14	5	15	65	53	47
Ashton Town	34	12	9	13	49	53	45
Castleton Gabriels	34	10	8	16	43	60	38
Cheadle Town	34	10	8	16	39	56	38
Blackpool Mechanics	34	9	10	15	39	52	37
Leek County School Old Boys	34	8	9	17	46	57	33
Daisy Hill	34	7	5	22	42	93	26
Oldham Town	34	4	12	18	40	86	24
Chadderton	34	5	5	24	33	80	20

Stand Athletic resigned in mid-season and their record was deleted when it was: 12 5 4 3 24 17 9

Formby joined from the Liverpool County Combination and Eccleshall joined from the Midland League.

2003-04

Division One

Clitheroe	42	29	5	8	88	55	92
Mossley	42	28	8	6	109	54	89
Fleetwood Town	42	26	8	8	84	51	86
Woodley Sports	42	26	5	11	99	56	83
Warrington Town	42	20	10	12	72	59	70
Newcastle Town	42	21	6	15	94	67	69
Curzon Ashton	42	19	10	13	84	79	64
Skelmersdale United	42	19	6	17	79	64	63
Alsager Town	42	16	15	11	54	47	63
Stone Dominoes	42	18	8	16	57	60	62
Congleton Town	42	15	16	11	62	50	61
Atherton Laburnum Rovers	42	17	7	18	77	76	58
Nantwich Town	42	15	11	16	73	66	53
Bacup Borough	42	15	8	19	68	72	53
Salford City	42	14	11	17	62	66	53
Trafford	42	14	8	20	72	91	50
Ramsbottom United	42	12	12	18	71	92	48
Glossop North End	42	9	9	24	51	95	36
St. Helens Town	42	10	6	26	51	81	33
Squires Gate	42	7	12	23	52	83	33
Abbey Hey	42	7	8	27	46	90	29
Atherton Collieries	42	6	9	27	48	99	23

Mossley, Curzon Ashton, Nantwich Town, St. Helens Town all had 3 points deducted. Atherton Collieries had 4 points deducted.

Division Two

Colne	38	26	6	6	102	41	84
Maine Road	38	23	5	10	99	58	74
Formby	38	21	9	8	86	48	72
Great Harwood Town	38	15	14	9	68	44	59
Flixton	38	16	11	11	76	60	59
Darwen	38	17	11	10	81	67	59
Ashton Town	38	16	11	11	66	60	59
Winsford United	38	15	11	12	66	62	56
Holker Old Boys	38	15	8	15	82	76	53
Nelson	38	14	11	13	55	64	53
Leek County School Old Boys	38	14	8	16	72	63	50
Padiham	38	14	8	16	63	80	50
Oldham Town	38	13	9	16	69	74	48
Blackpool Mechanics	38	13	7	18	45	59	46
Norton United	38	11	12	15	66	72	45
Cheadle Town	38	12	9	17	55	69	45
Eccleshall	38	10	14	14	56	65	44
Chadderton	38	7	11	20	42	63	32
Daisy Hill	38	7	10	21	33	82	31
Castleton Gabriels	38	6	5	27	53	128	23

Darwen had 3 points deducted.
Cammell Laird joined from the West Cheshire League, Silsden joined from the West Riding County Amateur League and New Mills joined from the Manchester League.

2004-05

Division One

Fleetwood Town	42	31	6	5	107	42	99
Newcastle Town	42	28	8	6	94	51	92
St. Helens Town	42	21	13	8	75	48	76
Curzon Ashton	42	23	7	12	66	45	76
Ramsbottom United	42	22	9	11	70	47	75
Skelmersdale United	42	21	11	10	94	57	74
Alsager Town	42	19	11	12	65	47	68
Maine Road	42	20	7	15	76	69	67
Bacup Borough	42	19	8	15	52	47	65
Colne	42	18	10	14	75	61	64
Stone Dominoes	42	17	12	13	73	64	63
Trafford	42	16	8	18	69	59	56
Glossop North End	42	15	10	17	79	75	55
Abbey Hey	42	16	6	20	51	69	54
Atherton Laburnum Rovers	42	14	6	22	64	82	48
Nantwich Town	42	12	8	22	71	91	44
Squires Gate	42	12	8	22	38	64	44
Salford City	42	11	9	22	68	90	42
Congleton Town	42	9	7	26	54	88	34
Formby	42	8	8	26	47	99	32
Atherton Collieries	42	8	7	27	57	102	31
Great Harwood Town	42	8	9	25	48	96	29

Great Harwood Town had 4 points deducted.

Division Two

Cammell Laird	36	27	6	3	142	34	87
Silsden	36	25	5	6	93	42	77
Winsford United	36	23	7	6	72	28	76
Padiham	36	21	7	8	84	56	70
Norton United	36	17	12	7	63	40	60
Nelson	36	16	11	9	75	52	59
Ashton Town	36	13	8	15	61	62	47
Daisy Hill	36	12	10	14	61	68	46
New Mills	36	13	6	17	51	74	45
Blackpool Mechanics	36	12	9	15	49	67	42
Eccleshall	36	11	8	17	47	58	41
Cheadle Town	36	11	7	18	47	80	40
Oldham Town	36	10	12	14	54	56	39
Leek County School Old Boys	36	9	10	17	59	68	37
Holker Old Boys	36	10	7	19	65	81	37
Darwen	36	13	5	18	39	56	35
Chadderton	36	7	7	22	40	94	28
Flixton	36	14	6	16	72	79	27
Castleton Gabriels	36	4	5	27	32	111	17

Silsden, Norton United, Blackpool Mechanics and Oldham Town all had 3 points deducted.
Darwen had 9 points deducted. Flixton had 21 points deducted.
FC United of Manchester joined as a new club.

2005-06

Division One

Cammell Laird	42	35	3	4	126	36	102
Skelmersdale United	42	28	7	7	119	48	91
Alsager Town	42	27	7	8	87	43	88
Nantwich Town	42	26	6	10	91	37	84
Salford City	42	23	10	9	79	46	79
Newcastle Town	42	21	9	12	97	52	72
Curzon Ashton	42	20	8	14	72	66	68
St. Helens Town	42	20	7	15	70	68	67
Colne	42	22	3	17	84	70	63
Maine Road	42	17	10	15	65	56	61
Abbey Hey	42	14	12	16	61	70	54
Congleton Town	42	15	8	19	50	63	53
Squires Gate	42	12	15	15	43	62	51
Silsden	42	16	8	18	76	75	50
Trafford	42	13	13	16	71	56	49
Glossop North End	42	12	11	19	62	78	47
Bacup Borough	42	13	8	21	44	62	47
Ramsbottom United	42	9	18	15	45	60	45
Atherton Collieries	42	7	9	26	43	93	30
Atherton Laburnum Rovers	42	7	8	27	40	115	29
Stone Dominoes	42	5	5	32	39	146	20
Formby	42	4	7	31	43	105	19

Trafford had 3 points deducted.
Cammell Laird, Colne and Silsden each had 6 points deducted.

Division Two

FC United of Manchester	36	27	6	3	111	35	87
Flixton	36	24	7	5	93	37	79
Nelson	36	23	5	8	82	53	74
Winsford United	36	19	8	9	65	41	65
Padiham	36	19	5	12	76	52	62
Great Harwood Town	36	18	8	10	51	33	62
Ashton Town	36	17	7	12	59	57	58
Norton United	36	13	12	11	45	47	51
Blackpool Mechanics	36	13	10	13	48	51	49
Oldham Town	36	14	6	16	46	49	48
Eccleshall	36	13	7	16	50	64	46
New Mills	36	13	7	16	46	62	46
Chadderton	36	13	8	15	51	62	44
Cheadle Town	36	14	6	16	55	53	42
Holker Old Boys	36	11	8	17	58	74	41
Darwen	36	11	2	23	47	61	35
Leek County School Old Boys	36	7	7	22	51	82	28
Daisy Hill	36	7	6	23	38	75	27
Castleton Gabriels	36	2	3	31	38	122	1

Chadderton had 3 points deducted. Cheadle Town had 6 points deducted. Castleton Gabriels had 8 points deducted.
Great Harwood Town disbanded. Bootle joined from the Liverpool County Combination, Ashton Athletic joined from the Manchester League and Runcorn Linnets joined as a new club.

2006-07

Division One

FC United of Manchester	42	36	4	2	157	36	112
Curzon Ashton	42	31	6	5	116	38	99
Nantwich Town	42	29	8	5	108	41	95
Salford City	42	26	9	7	103	55	87
Trafford	42	24	11	7	94	46	83
Maine Road	42	22	7	13	79	58	73
Atherton Collieries	42	19	13	10	72	55	70
Ramsbottom United	42	19	7	16	78	63	64
Glossop North End	42	19	6	17	71	71	63
Congleton Town	42	18	8	16	75	62	62
Colne	42	16	13	13	75	70	61
Newcastle Town	42	16	10	16	70	63	58
Flixton	42	15	11	16	72	67	56
Silsden	42	16	6	20	66	79	54
Bacup Borough	42	11	13	18	50	65	46
Atherton Laburnum Rovers	42	11	9	22	65	106	42
Abbey Hey	42	10	10	22	44	83	40
Squires Gate	42	10	8	24	56	97	38
St. Helens Town	42	10	6	26	47	92	36
Nelson	42	7	6	29	41	113	27
Formby	42	6	4	32	43	111	22
Stone Dominoes	42	2	3	37	36	147	9

Division Two

Winsford United	34	23	7	4	82	35	76
Runcorn Linnets	34	24	4	6	77	35	76
Padiham	34	21	6	7	75	39	69
New Mills	34	21	6	7	74	42	69
Chadderton	34	18	7	9	59	35	61
Oldham Town	34	17	5	12	69	54	56
Darwen	34	14	10	10	56	45	52
Ashton Town	34	15	7	12	55	56	52
Leek County School Old Boys	34	14	8	12	51	52	50
Bootle	34	14	8	12	63	48	46
Eccleshall	34	12	6	16	45	46	42
Cheadle Town	34	9	8	17	41	60	35
Blackpool Mechanics	34	10	6	18	39	48	30
Holker Old Boys	34	6	11	17	47	81	29
Daisy Hill	34	7	8	19	38	78	29
Ashton Athletic	34	6	10	18	38	62	28
Norton United	34	6	7	21	37	73	25
Castleton Gabriels	34	5	4	25	38	95	19

Bootle had 4 points deducted.
Blackpool Mechanics had 6 points deducted.
Kirkham & Wesham joined from the West Lancashire League.

2007-08

Division One

Trafford	38	30	5	3	102	35	95
Salford City	38	26	6	6	75	35	84
Newcastle Town	38	24	7	7	95	45	79
Maine Road	38	20	8	10	75	45	68
Colne	38	19	11	8	69	45	68
Squires Gate	38	19	9	10	52	43	66
Glossop North End	38	20	5	13	72	46	65
Flixton	38	17	7	14	65	65	58
Congleton Town	38	17	6	15	73	60	57
Winsford United	38	16	8	14	60	47	56
Silsden	38	15	10	13	65	57	55
Runcorn Linnets	38	14	6	18	53	64	48
Formby	38	14	3	21	52	60	42
St. Helens Town	38	11	8	19	64	93	41
Atherton Collieries	38	10	10	18	44	67	40
Ramsbottom United	38	9	10	19	41	59	37
Abbey Hey	38	6	9	23	45	106	27
Bacup Borough	38	5	11	22	35	69	26
Atherton Laburnum Rovers	38	5	9	24	38	86	24
Nelson	38	5	8	25	42	90	23

Formby had 3 points deducted.

Division Two

New Mills	34	28	3	3	107	23	87
Kirkham & Wesham	34	24	5	5	88	31	77
Ashton Athletic	34	20	7	7	68	35	67
Oldham Town	34	19	7	8	79	44	64
Chadderton	34	19	4	11	55	52	61
Bootle	34	18	6	10	86	53	60
Leek County School Old Boys	34	16	7	11	57	51	55
Norton United	34	13	11	10	47	52	50
Blackpool Mechanics	34	11	12	11	47	45	45
Stone Dominoes	34	12	8	14	60	59	44
Darwen	34	13	5	16	55	65	44
Padiham	34	11	8	15	50	48	41
Ashton Town	34	12	4	18	53	80	40
Cheadle Town	34	10	6	18	44	80	33
Eccleshall	34	8	6	20	41	69	30
Holker Old Boys	34	8	2	24	41	82	26
Castleton Gabriels	34	6	6	22	46	97	24
Daisy Hill	34	2	5	27	28	86	11

THE MANCHESTER LEAGUE

Background and Summary

The Manchester League was formed in 1890 but in its first few years, it received little attention from the local press. League tables were rarely printed and those that were often contained errors.

Considerable research has been done to try and find tables for every year but until extra sources are found, it will not be possible to complete this. After the turn of the century though, the league's catchment area extended and amongst the clubs who played their first XI's in the competition were Oldham Athletic, Rochdale, Macclesfield, Northwich Victoria, Altrincham and Witton Albion. It was then much more widely reported, up to its closure in 1912.

Many of the published tables contained errors. Additional research has succeeded in correcting many of these, those figures that still do not balance are shown in italics below the relevant column.

1890-91

St. Bride's	17	13	2	2	57	15	28
Whalley Range	16	10	3	3	54	23	23
Lancashire College	15	10	2	3	41	23	22
Stretford	15	10	1	4	51	27	21
Tonge	17	9	3	5	46	23	21
St. Mark's	17	7	3	7	48	58	17
Press	16	7	0	9	32	36	12
Dalton	15	5	1	9	30	45	11
Stockport	16	2	0	14	16	38	4
West End	15	1	1	13	12	50	3
	159	*74*	*16*	*69*	*387*	*338*	*162*

Press had 2 points deducted for fielding an ineligible player.
Remaining games are thought not to have been played.

1891-93

No record has been found of the league operating in 1891-92 or 1892-93 and when it was reinstated in 1893-94, it was referred to as the 'new Manchester League'. The only one of the 1890-91 clubs to enter the league in 1893-94 were Stretford.

1893-94

Stretford	20	15	3	2	75	22	33
Talbot	20	14	4	2	70	23	32
Hulme	20	11	3	6	50	36	25
Rusholme	20	9	6	5	45	28	24
Harpurhey	20	10	0	10	50	40	20
Beswick & Old Trafford	20	6	7	7	25	27	19
Fallowfield	20	7	4	9	42	47	18
Didsbury	20	6	3	11	31	69	15
Manchester St. Mary's	20	6	2	12	28	52	14
Burnage	20	5	3	12	42	56	13
Broadheath	20	2	3	15	17	75	7

Beswick disbanded at the end of October when their playing record stood as follows: 5 0 0 5 8 31 0

Old Trafford replaced them. Beswick Rovers also withdrew and their record was deleted. Burnage left and Higher Crumpsall, Manchester Amateurs, Molyneux (Longsight) and Moss Side joined.

1894-95

Talbot	26	19	2	5	105	41	40
Stretford	26	16	6	4	62	27	38
Higher Crumpsall	26	17	3	6	84	42	37
Molyneux (Longsight)	26	15	5	6	76	42	35
Hulme	26	15	3	8	62	30	33
Manchester St. Mary's	26	12	4	10	58	54	28
Fallowfield	26	12	3	11	68	43	27
Rusholme	26	9	7	10	66	52	25
Broadheath	26	9	4	13	35	64	22
Moss Side	26	9	3	14	50	70	21
Harpurhey	26	7	6	13	48	50	20
Didsbury	26	9	1	16	38	75	19
Manchester Amateurs	26	7	1	18	24	101	15
Old Trafford	26	1	2	23	16	102	4
					792	*793*	

Didsbury, Higher Crumpsall, Manchester Amateurs and Old Trafford all left. Ladybarn Lads Club, Levenshulme, Lymm and Reddish joined.

1895-96

Talbot	24	18	1	5	72	28	37
Fallowfield	24	17	2	5	74	27	36
Reddish	21	13	3	5	57	41	29
Stretford	24	13	1	10	65	39	27
Levenshulme	23	11	4	8	56	43	26
Rusholme	22	12	1	9	51	47	25
Harpurhey	21	10	3	8	66	49	23
Broadheath	21	9	1	11	46	59	19
Molyneux (Longsight)	18	8	3	7	34	48	19
Hulme	23	5	3	15	43	71	13
Lymm	23	4	5	14	29	74	13
Manchester St. Mary's	22	5	2	15	24	58	12
Moss Side	22	3	3	16	29	63	9
					646	*647*	

Ladybarn Lads Club withdrew and their record was deleted. Molyneux (Longsight) also withdrew but their record remained. Remaining games may not have been played. Harpurhey left but Tonge joined from the Lancashire Alliance and Higher Crumpsall and Longsight also joined.

1896-97

Tonge were champions but no tables have been found for this season. 33 results have been discovered and the part table compiled from these is below, shown in estimated finishing order:

Tonge (Champions)	3	3	0	0	13	2	6
Levenshulme	4	4	0	0	17	2	8
Broadheath	10	7	2	1	30	17	16
Rusholme & New Mills	3	1	2	0	4	2	4
Lymm	12	5	2	5	27	25	12
Talbot	6	2	2	2	12	13	6
Fallowfield	3	1	1	1	10	11	3
Hulme	4	2	0	2	8	9	4
Longsight	3	1	0	2	2	8	2
Manchester St. Mary's	4	0	2	2	5	9	2
Stretford	7	1	1	5	12	21	3
Reddish	2	0	0	2	2	5	0
Moss Side	2	0	0	2	2	11	0
Higher Crumpsall	3	0	0	3	1	10	0

Rusholme withdrew on 23rd March 1897 and their fixtures were taken over by New Mills. Longsight and Manchester St. Mary's left and Eccles and Prestwich joined.

1897-98

Tonge were champions but no tables have been found for this season. 44 results have been discovered and the part table compiled from these is below, shown in estimated finishing order:

Tonge (Champions)	6	5	0	1	27	7	10
Prestwich	7	5	1	1	17	11	11
Lymm	13	8	1	4	31	19	17
Reddish	5	3	0	2	6	7	6
Moss Side	7	4	0	3	18	13	8
Stretford	9	5	0	4	22	20	10
Broadheath	10	5	1	4	22	22	11
Higher Crumpsall	2	1	0	1	2	2	2
Levenshulme	3	1	1	1	4	8	3
Fallowfield	8	3	0	5	17	17	6
Hulme	3	1	0	2	2	7	2
Talbot	5	1	0	4	6	9	2
Eccles	5	0	0	5	3	16	0
New Mills	5	0	0	5	1	20	0

Eccles, Higher Crumpsall, Hulme, Levenshulme, New Mills and Reddish left. Marple, Newton Heath Athletic, Seedley, South-West Manchester and Urmston joined.

1898-99

The published final table gave only games played and points won as shown below:

	Played	Points
Newton Heath Athletic	22	37
Tonge	22	34
Broadheath	22	31
Lymm	22	26
Talbot	22	25
South-West Manchester	22	22
Prestwich	22	22
Seedley	22	19
Stretford	22	18
Fallowfield	22	13
Urmston	22	9
Moss Side	22	9
	264	*265*

Marple are thought to have had their record deleted after not completing their fixtures.

The latest published detail table found, dated 28th April 1899, was as shown below:

Newton Heath Athletic	20	17	2	1	56	11	36
Tonge	19	13	3	3	61	33	29
Broadheath	19	12	3	4	50	20	27
Lymm	18	12	3	3	53	27	27
Talbot	19	9	4	6	40	26	22
Prestwich	21	8	4	9	47	46	20
South-West Manchester	20	6	6	8	25	35	18
Stretford	19	6	4	9	49	55	16
Seedley	18	6	1	11	38	57	13
Fallowfield	19	6	1	12	23	46	13
Urmston	19	3	5	11	28	47	11
Moss Side	20	4	2	14	22	56	10
Marple	15	1	2	12	19	52	4

Fallowfield and Seedley left. Buxton joined from The Combination and Oughtrington Park, Sale Holmfield and St. Mary's Park (Walkden) also joined.

1899-1900

Tonge	26	23	2	1	110	16	48
Newton Heath Athletic	26	20	3	3	112	32	43
Broadheath	26	19	1	6	54	30	39
Buxton	24	12	7	5	58	51	31
Talbot	26	10	7	9	50	46	27
Lymm	26	9	7	10	54	61	25
South-West Manchester	26	10	5	11	40	57	25
Sale Holmfield	25	11	2	12	46	50	24
Stretford	26	7	7	12	41	51	21
Urmston	26	6	7	13	25	50	19
Prestwich	26	7	2	17	32	49	16
Oughtrington Park	25	6	4	15	30	57	16
Moss Side	26	6	4	16	32	62	16
St. Mary's Park (Walkden)	26	3	4	19	21	83	10
					705	*695*	

Two games were not played.
Moss Side, South-West Manchester, St. Mary's Park (Walkden) and Urmston left.
Northwich Victoria joined from the Cheshire League, Macclesfield joined from the North Staffordshire League, Oldham Athletic joined from the Manchester Alliance, Middleton joined from the Lancashire League and Hyde joined from the Stockport & District League.

1900-01

Tonge	28	23	2	3	94	32	48
Northwich Victoria	28	20	4	4	75	36	44
Newton Heath Athletic	28	19	2	7	78	35	40
Sale Holmfield	28	15	5	8	66	41	35
Hyde	27	14	5	8	79	41	33
Broadheath	27	13	4	10	75	59	30
Talbot	28	12	6	10	48	44	30
Buxton	28	12	4	12	54	46	28
Macclesfield	28	10	3	15	60	75	23
Oughtrington Park	28	8	6	14	46	64	22
Oldham Athletic	28	9	4	15	40	68	22
Lymm	28	7	4	15	42	64	20
Stretford	28	7	6	15	36	66	20
Middleton	28	8	5	15	47	66	19
Prestwich	28	1	1	26	18	128	3
	418	*178*	*61*	*177*	*858*	*865*	*417*

Middleton had 2 points deducted for a breach of the rules.
Stretford moved to the Manchester Federation and Oughtrington Park and Prestwich also left. Berry's Association joined from the Lancashire Combination and Failsworth and Heywood also joined.

1901-02

Hyde	26	17	6	3	74	27	40
Newton Heath Athletic	26	17	6	3	76	26	40
Northwich Victoria	26	16	2	8	61	53	34
Sale Holmfield	26	13	7	6	61	37	33
Tonge	26	13	4	9	79	47	30
Oldham Athletic	26	13	4	9	59	46	30
Berry's Association	26	12	4	10	55	52	28
Failsworth	26	10	4	12	64	54	24
Talbot	26	11	2	13	47	50	24
Heywood	26	8	4	14	59	66	20
Buxton	26	7	6	13	43	70	20
Broadheath	26	6	6	14	40	72	18
Macclesfield	26	8	1	17	44	68	17
Lymm	26	2	2	22	24	118	6

Hyde beat Newton Heath Athletic in a Championship play-off.
Middleton resigned during the season and their record was deleted.
Heywood moved to the Lancashire Combination and Lymm moved to the Manchester Federation. Levenshulme joined from the Manchester Federation, Denton joined from the North Cheshire League and Hooley Hill joined from the North Cheshire League.

1902-03

Northwich Victoria	26	20	4	2	60	22	44
Failsworth	26	16	3	7	87	42	35
Newton Heath Athletic	25	16	3	6	71	36	35
Oldham Athletic	26	15	4	7	57	31	34
Berry's Association	26	14	3	9	68	41	31
Hyde	26	14	1	11	70	47	29
Buxton	26	12	2	12	47	53	26
Sale Holmfield	26	9	6	11	46	63	24
Broadheath	26	9	5	12	43	55	23
Denton	24	8	4	12	41	53	20
Macclesfield	26	8	3	15	36	63	19
Tonge	26	6	7	13	25	68	19
Hooley Hill	25	5	2	18	40	62	12
Talbot	25	3	4	18	19	68	10
	359	*155*	*51*	*153*	*710*	*704*	*361*

Levenshulme disbanded on 4th February 1903 and their record was deleted.
Broadheath changed their name to Altrincham. Talbot moved to the Manchester Federation. Stretford joined from the Manchester Federation and Glossop United and Hollinwood also joined.

1903-04

Berry's Association	28	19	2	7	91	42	40
Northwich Victoria	28	17	4	7	69	40	38
Oldham Athletic	28	15	7	6	71	40	37
Sale Holmfield	28	15	3	10	75	50	33
Denton	28	13	7	8	72	47	33
Newton Heath Athletic	28	14	4	10	65	50	32
Failsworth	28	13	5	10	75	50	31
Tonge	28	15	1	12	57	54	31
Hyde	28	12	4	12	73	55	28
Altrincham	28	12	4	12	56	55	28
Macclesfield	28	9	8	11	49	57	26
Glossop United	28	9	3	16	40	74	21
Hooley Hill	28	8	4	16	52	72	20
Buxton	28	7	1	20	45	71	15
Stretford	28	4	1	23	21	135	9
	420	*182*	*58*	*180*	*911*	*892*	*422*

Hollinwood withdrew and their record was deleted.
Oldham Athletic moved to the Lancashire Combination.
Witton Albion joined from The Combination and Oughtrington Park also joined.

1904-05

Altrincham	30	18	8	4	66	43	44
Buxton	30	16	6	8	63	40	38
Denton	30	16	5	9	83	49	37
Sale Holmfield	30	14	9	7	66	39	37
Tonge	30	11	14	5	60	33	36
Failsworth	30	14	8	8	63	41	36
Northwich Victoria	30	13	10	7	47	43	36
Berry's Association	30	13	6	11	61	55	32
Witton Albion	30	9	12	9	44	41	30
Macclesfield	30	7	11	12	48	55	25
Hyde	30	9	7	14	40	53	25
Hooley Hill	30	9	6	15	47	53	24
Newton Heath Athletic	30	8	6	16	53	72	22
Stretford	30	8	5	17	54	78	21
Glossop United & Heywood United	30	6	7	17	45	91	19
Oughtrington Park	30	8	2	20	47	101	18

Heywood United took over Glossop United's fixtures in mid-season.
Failsworth moved to the Lancashire Combination and Oughtrington Park also left. Pendlebury joined from the Manchester Federation and Salford United joined as a new club.

1905-06

Denton	30	22	1	7	88	38	45
Sale Holmfield	30	15	10	5	53	30	40
Altrincham	30	16	5	9	81	51	37
Northwich Victoria	30	17	3	10	67	58	37
Tonge	30	15	5	10	67	57	35
Macclesfield	30	15	4	11	58	58	34
Heywood United	30	14	5	11	62	58	33
Pendlebury	30	10	10	10	74	53	30
Witton Albion	30	10	8	12	47	45	28
Berry's Association	30	10	6	14	53	71	26
Buxton	30	9	7	14	36	46	25
Hyde	30	10	4	16	48	81	24
Hooley Hill	30	9	4	17	57	65	22
Salford United	30	10	2	18	54	74	22
Newton Heath Athletic	30	9	4	17	45	73	22
Stretford	30	7	6	17	45	77	20

Hyde moved to the Lancashire Combination and Chadderton joined.

1906-07

Altrincham	28	18	7	3	70	30	43
Macclesfield	28	19	4	5	75	39	42
Witton Albion	28	18	5	5	49	30	41
Sale Holmfield	28	13	8	7	53	38	34
Salford United	28	10	10	8	61	39	30
Northwich Victoria	28	12	6	10	59	51	30
Tonge	28	12	6	10	51	45	30
Denton	28	12	5	11	52	44	29
Pendlebury	28	10	9	9	57	51	29
Stretford	28	11	4	13	39	55	26
Berry's Association	28	7	7	14	40	66	21
Heywood United	28	8	4	16	54	63	20
Buxton	28	7	5	16	39	57	19
Hooley Hill	28	4	7	17	35	68	15
Newton Heath Athletic	28	3	5	20	32	90	11

Chadderton resigned during the season and their record was deleted. Heywood United and Pendlebury both moved to the Lancashire Combination. Rochdale joined as a new club and Eccles Borough and Ramsbottom also joined.

1907-08

Denton	30	21	5	4	108	48	47
Northwich Victoria	30	15	10	5	75	53	40
Eccles Borough	30	16	7	7	59	44	39
Macclesfield	30	16	5	9	63	39	37
Tonge	30	14	8	8	67	46	36
Altrincham	30	13	6	11	63	53	32
Witton Albion	30	12	8	10	52	54	32
Sale Holmfield	30	14	3	13	70	53	31
Ramsbottom	30	10	8	12	61	68	28
Rochdale	30	10	8	12	49	63	28
Buxton	30	10	7	13	35	52	27
Hooley Hill	30	8	9	13	56	59	25
Salford United	30	9	5	16	49	68	23
Berry's Association	30	9	5	16	46	66	23
Stretford	30	5	10	15	43	75	20
Newton Heath Athletic	30	3	6	21	33	88	12

Eccles Borough and Rochdale both moved to the Lancashire Combination and Stretford also left. Tyldesley Albion joined from the Lancashire Alliance and Hazel Grove and New Mills also joined.

1908-09

Macclesfield	30	18	6	6	78	43	42
Northwich Victoria	30	17	4	9	73	51	38
Altrincham	30	16	4	10	82	56	36
Tonge	30	16	3	11	54	45	35
New Mills	30	13	8	9	73	45	34
Hazel Grove	30	13	8	9	62	47	34
Sale Holmfield	29	15	3	11	65	56	33
Salford United	30	14	5	11	61	55	33
Witton Albion	30	13	5	12	67	59	31
Tyldesley Albion	30	12	6	12	74	67	30
Denton	30	11	7	12	70	67	29
Ramsbottom	30	12	5	13	61	81	29
Hooley Hill	30	11	6	13	57	54	28
Berry's Association	29	10	5	14	52	53	25
Buxton	30	7	4	19	38	74	18
Newton Heath Athletic	30	0	3	27	34	148	3

Hurst and Rusholme joined.

1909-10

Salford United	34	20	6	8	79	44	46
Hurst	34	19	8	7	70	41	46
Altrincham	34	20	5	9	82	41	45
Macclesfield	34	18	6	10	86	45	42
Tonge	34	20	2	12	66	41	42
Denton	34	18	6	10	75	60	42
Northwich Victoria	34	18	4	12	81	65	40
Tyldesley Albion	34	15	8	11	65	50	38
Witton Albion	34	15	6	13	74	71	36
Buxton	34	15	5	14	60	51	35
Hooley Hill	34	11	13	10	67	62	35
Berry's Association	34	14	5	15	58	67	33
Hazel Grove	34	11	9	14	58	69	31
New Mills	34	10	9	15	53	66	29
Ramsbottom	34	12	5	17	66	86	29
Rusholme	34	8	3	23	49	91	19
Sale Holmfield	34	4	6	24	28	93	14
Newton Heath Athletic	34	3	4	27	31	105	10

Salford United beat Hurst in a Championship Play-Off.

Denton left to continue in the Lancashire Combination, where they had taken over Pendlebury's fixtures during the 1909-10 season. Newton Heath Athletic moved to the Manchester Federation and Ramsbottom and Sale Holmfield also left. Crewe Alexandra Reserves and Nantwich both joined from The Combination.

1910-11

Macclesfield	30	20	8	2	61	30	48
Altrincham	30	19	4	7	81	38	42
Crewe Alexandra Reserves	30	17	8	5	74	36	42
Northwich Victoria	30	16	5	9	75	41	37
Tyldesley Albion	30	15	5	10	62	55	35
Hurst	30	14	4	12	69	66	32
Hazel Grove	30	11	10	9	47	52	32
Buxton	30	13	5	12	57	56	31
Witton Albion	30	11	7	12	68	64	29
Berry's Association	30	11	6	13	62	72	28
Rusholme	30	11	4	15	67	76	26
Hooley Hill	30	7	11	12	41	56	25
Nantwich	30	8	6	16	60	83	22
New Mills	30	6	6	18	49	71	18
Salford United	30	7	3	20	43	85	17
Tonge	30	5	6	19	42	76	16
					958	*957*	

Altrincham and Tyldesley Albion moved to the Lancashire Combination and Berry's Association, New Mills, Salford United, Tonge and Rushholme also left.

Chester Reserves joined from The Combination and Eccles Borough Reserves, Rochdale Reserves and Stalybridge Celtic Reserves joined.

1911-12

Hurst	24	18	4	2	82	30	40
Northwich Victoria	24	14	5	5	51	32	33
Witton Albion	24	13	5	6	58	32	31
Macclesfield	24	12	5	7	51	34	29
Eccles Borough Reserves	24	11	3	10	48	39	25
Stalybridge Celtic Reserves	24	10	3	11	55	53	23
Chester Reserves	24	10	3	11	40	50	23
Nantwich	23	11	1	11	40	45	23
Crewe Alexandra Reserves	23	10	1	12	39	47	21
Hooley Hill	24	7	3	14	46	65	17
Rochdale Reserves	24	6	4	14	45	70	16
Buxton	22	5	4	13	30	66	14
Hazel Grove	24	5	3	16	48	70	13

Two games were not played.

The Manchester League closed in 1912. Hurst, Macclesfield, Nantwich, Northwich Victoria, Rochdale Reserves, Stalybridge Celtic Reserves and Witton Albion all joined the Lancashire Combination and Crewe Alexandra Reserves joined the North Staffordshire League.

The Manchester League was reformed in 1920 but with a much lower level membership.

THE NORFOLK & SUFFOLK LEAGUE

FORMATION

Unusually, the initiative for the Norfolk & Suffolk League came not from a group of clubs, but from an individual, Mr. J. Sterry, a prominent Lowestoft fish merchant who wished to make a gesture to commemorate his 50 years in the business. Early in April 1897, Mr. Sterry donated a 50 guinea (£52.50) cup to be competed for annually on a league basis between 8 leading clubs in the counties of Norfolk & Suffolk – Kings Lynn, Norwich C.E.Y.M.S., North Walsham Athletic, Yarmouth Fearnoughts, Ipswich Town, Beccles Caxton, Lowestoft Town and Kirkley. The Norfolk & Suffolk League disappeared in 1964 when it merged with the East Anglian League to form the Anglian Combination but even today, the Sterry Cup is awarded annually to the Combination champions.

Only six of Mr. Sterry's eight intended members took part in the league's first season. Ipswich Town declined the invitation to compete as they considered league football to be incompatible with the true amateur spirit with which they played the game, although they did join the league two years later. North Walsham Athletic were also absent but in their case it was more than 20 years before their name appeared in the league. The name of Yarmouth Fearnoughts never actually appeared in the league either as the club merged that summer with Yarmouth Royal Artillery and so instead entered the league as a brand new club called Great Yarmouth Town. Four years later, another club had their first taste of league football in the Norfolk & Suffolk League when the newly-formed Norwich City became members.

Three of the league's founder members, Beccles Caxton, Kirkley and Lowestoft Town had already played league football in Division One of the North Suffolk League, in which they also continued but for Kings Lynn and Norwich C.E.Y.M.S., the Norfolk & Suffolk League was their first league competition.

Many of the published tables contained errors, some of which have been corrected. Those which remain are shown in italics below the relevant columns.

1897-98

Lowestoft Town	10	4	5	1	17	11	13
Kings Lynn	10	4	4	2	16	12	12
Beccles Caxton	10	6	0	4	17	16	12
Great Yarmouth Town	10	4	2	4	15	18	10
Kirkley	10	3	2	5	19	13	8
Norwich C.E.Y.M.S.	10	2	1	7	13	26	5
					97	*96*	

1898-99

Lowestoft Town	10	7	1	2	21	9	15
Kirkley	10	5	2	3	15	9	12
Great Yarmouth Town	10	4	4	2	17	12	12
Kings Lynn	10	4	2	4	12	10	10
Norwich C.E.Y.M.S.	10	4	1	5	18	17	9
Beccles Caxton	10	0	2	8	3	28	2
					86	*85*	

Bury St. Edmunds joined from the West Suffolk League and Ipswich Town joined, not having previously played in a league.

1899-1900

Norwich C.E.Y.M.S.	14	10	3	1	34	14	23
Kings Lynn	14	10	2	2	44	10	22
Lowestoft Town	13	7	0	6	28	19	16
Ipswich Town	14	5	4	5	22	21	14
Great Yarmouth Town	14	6	2	6	24	27	14
Kirkley	14	5	2	7	17	23	12
Bury St. Edmunds	13	4	1	8	11	27	9
Beccles Caxton	14	1	0	13	11	50	2

Lowestoft Town vs Bury St. Edmunds was abandoned after 10 minutes. Bury were unable to raise a team to replay the game and the points were therefore awarded to Lowestoft.

1900-01

Lowestoft Town	14	10	4	0	35	6	24
Kings Lynn	14	10	3	1	51	10	23
Norwich C.E.Y.M.S.	14	8	4	2	51	16	20
Great Yarmouth Town	14	6	2	6	43	21	14
Ipswich Town	14	6	1	7	32	26	13
Kirkley	14	5	3	6	20	32	13
Bury St. Edmunds	14	1	1	12	7	77	3
Beccles Caxton	14	0	2	12	9	60	2

1901-02

Lowestoft Town	12	9	1	2	38	15	19
Norwich C.E.Y.M.S.	12	8	1	3	37	16	17
Ipswich Town	12	7	1	4	30	25	15
Kirkley	12	5	1	6	21	19	11
Kings Lynn	12	4	1	7	15	30	9
Great Yarmouth Town	12	3	2	7	14	23	8
Beccles Caxton	12	2	1	9	10	37	5

Bury St. Edmunds withdrew and their record was deleted. Their record at the time of withdrawal was: 5 0 0 5 4 38 0

A newly formed club called Norwich City joined.

1902-03

Lowestoft Town	14	11	1	2	54	15	23
Ipswich Town	14	8	1	5	34	24	17
Norwich City	14	8	0	6	34	33	16
Norwich C.E.Y.M.S.	14	7	2	5	28	28	16
Great Yarmouth Town	14	7	1	6	25	21	15
Kings Lynn	14	5	3	6	36	36	13
Kirkley	14	4	3	7	18	18	11
Beccles Caxton	14	0	1	13	11	65	1

Beccles Caxton left but continued in the North Suffolk League.

Cromer joined.

1903-04

Lowestoft Town	14	9	3	2	34	18	21
Kirkley	14	7	2	5	33	18	16
Norwich City	14	5	5	4	32	20	15
Kings Lynn	14	6	3	5	26	27	15
Norwich C.E.Y.M.S.	14	5	2	7	23	28	12
Ipswich Town	14	4	3	7	28	37	11
Cromer	14	5	1	8	19	41	11
Great Yarmouth Town	14	4	3	7	17	23	11

Beccles Caxton rejoined while continuing in the North Suffolk League.

1904-05

Norwich City	16	10	4	2	33	16	24
Lowestoft Town	16	9	2	5	34	26	20
Norwich C.E.Y.M.S.	16	9	1	6	37	23	19
Great Yarmouth Town	16	8	3	5	29	25	19
Ipswich Town	16	9	0	7	32	21	18
Kings Lynn	16	7	3	6	41	31	17
Kirkley	16	5	1	10	21	40	11
Cromer	16	3	2	11	21	39	8
Beccles Caxton	16	4	0	12	17	44	8

During the season, Norwich City were found by the F.A. to be a professional club and at the end of the season they moved to the Southern League, placing their reserves in the Norfolk & Suffolk League.

1905-06

Kings Lynn	14	9	4	1	75	14	22
Norwich C.E.Y.M.S.	14	10	1	3	43	20	21
Cromer	14	7	1	6	35	24	15
Great Yarmouth Town	14	6	3	5	32	35	15
Ipswich Town	14	5	3	6	27	27	13
Lowestoft Town	14	5	2	7	19	44	12
Kirkley	14	3	4	7	22	44	10
Beccles Caxton	14	1	2	11	21	66	4

Norwich City Reserves withdrew after playing 6 games as the league could not agree to the number of professionals that Norwich wished to include in their games.

1906-07

Norwich C.E.Y.M.S.	14	10	3	1	31	13	23
Cromer	14	8	2	4	35	22	18
Great Yarmouth Town	14	6	5	3	32	24	17
Kings Lynn	14	7	2	5	38	16	16
Ipswich Town	14	6	3	5	30	25	15
Lowestoft Town	14	4	2	8	19	42	10
Kirkley	14	2	5	7	19	31	9
Beccles Caxton	14	1	2	11	19	50	4

Ipswich Town left and joined the Southern Amateur League and Carrow Works joined.

1907-08

Kings Lynn	13	9	2	2	44	12	20
Carrow Works	14	7	4	3	25	13	18
Cromer	14	9	0	5	28	24	18
Kirkley	14	5	3	6	27	29	13
Norwich C.E.Y.M.S.	14	6	1	7	24	26	13
Great Yarmouth Town	14	6	0	8	33	32	12
Lowestoft Town	13	5	2	6	17	29	12
Beccles Caxton	14	1	2	11	20	48	4
					218	*213*	

Kings Lynn versus Lowestoft was not played.
Gorleston joined from the Yarmouth & District League.

1908-09

Cromer	16	11	3	2	42	21	25
Kings Lynn	16	11	3	2	50	26	25
Gorleston	16	11	2	3	48	22	24
Kirkley	16	7	2	7	31	32	16
Norwich C.E.Y.M.S.	16	6	3	7	20	31	15
Great Yarmouth Town	16	5	2	9	39	38	12
Carrow Works	16	4	3	9	15	29	11
Lowestoft Town	16	5	1	10	20	40	11
Beccles Caxton	16	2	1	13	17	53	5
					282	*292*	

1909-10

Kings Lynn	16	12	2	2	61	21	26
Norwich C.E.Y.M.S.	16	10	3	3	37	17	23
Cromer	16	9	3	4	38	20	21
Great Yarmouth Town	16	8	4	4	37	27	20
Lowestoft Town	16	7	4	5	30	26	18
Kirkley	16	5	5	6	34	37	15
Carrow Works	16	5	0	11	20	33	10
Gorleston	16	1	4	11	18	36	6
Beccles Caxton	16	2	1	13	13	71	5

16th Lancers (based at the Britannia Barracks in Norwich) joined.

1910-11

Norwich C.E.Y.M.S.	18	14	3	1	62	11	31
Cromer	18	13	1	4	64	26	27
Kings Lynn	18	12	3	3	56	32	27
16th Lancers	18	10	2	6	46	21	22
Great Yarmouth Town	17	7	3	7	34	37	17
Carrow Works	17	6	3	8	32	39	15
Kirkley	18	7	1	10	23	39	15
Lowestoft Town	18	3	5	10	23	52	11
Gorleston	18	3	4	11	32	48	10
Beccles Caxton	18	1	1	16	12	79	3

Carrow Works versus Yarmouth was not played.

1911-12

16th Lancers	18	14	3	1	70	16	31
Kings Lynn	18	14	2	2	48	16	30
Cromer	18	11	0	7	55	26	22
Great Yarmouth Town	18	10	2	6	44	43	22
Norwich C.E.Y.M.S.	18	9	2	7	42	25	20
Kirkley	18	7	2	9	22	32	16
Lowestoft Town	18	5	4	9	25	41	14
Carrow Works	18	5	1	12	24	30	11
Gorleston	18	2	5	11	15	26	9
Beccles Caxton	18	2	1	15	12	83	5
					357	*338*	

16th Lancers left.

1912-13

Kings Lynn	14	11	1	2	62	14	23
Cromer	14	9	3	2	52	19	21
Carrow Works	14	9	1	4	41	18	19
Gorleston	14	7	4	3	35	23	18
Norwich C.E.Y.M.S.	14	4	6	4	23	21	14
Kirkley	14	2	3	9	9	47	7
Lowestoft Town	14	2	1	11	16	64	5
Beccles Caxton	14	1	3	10	10	42	5

Great Yarmouth Town actually topped the table at the end of the season with the following record: 16 13 0 3 66 18 26
However it was found that a regular member of their side was a player called Von Malakowski whose home was in Drayton near Norwich, whereas league rules stated that players had to "live" within five miles of the club they played for. Yarmouth argued that the player worked and had lodgings in Yarmouth and so "lived" in the town but this was not accepted. Von Malakowski's parents were German and at a time when there was lots of anti-German feeling, his case would have found few sympathisers. Yarmouth were therefore stripped of the title, their record expunged and the final table recalculated, leaving Kings Lynn as champions, as shown above.
Norwich St. James joined from the Norwich & District League and Mortons Athletic and 12th Lancers (based at the Britannia Barracks in Norwich) also joined.

1913-14

Great Yarmouth Town	20	18	1	1	79	15	37
Norwich C.E.Y.M.S.	20	15	0	5	48	27	30
Cromer	18	14	1	3	59	23	29
Kings Lynn	20	11	2	7	40	40	24
Gorleston	20	8	2	10	59	45	18
Mortons Athletic	20	8	2	10	27	27	18
Norwich St. James	20	9	0	11	42	46	18
Carrow Works	20	7	2	11	41	52	16
Lowestoft Town	20	6	2	12	30	50	14
Kirkley	18	3	2	13	13	50	8
Beccles Caxton	20	1	2	17	11	74	4

12th Lancers withdrew in December when they were posted abroad.
The two games between Kirkley and Cromer were not played following a dispute between the two clubs about gate receipts for their F.A. Cup game at Cromer on 11th October.
Kirkley disbanded at the end of the season when their ground was required for building land.

1914-19

Despite the outbreak of war in August 1914, the league did start the 1914-15 season. However the competition was abandoned in early October and did not restart until the 1919-20 season.
When the league restarted after the war, Kirkley were defunct, Carrow Works joined the Norwich & District League instead and Norwich St. James and Beccles Caxton also did not rejoin. There were three new members: Beccles Town, Norwich City Reserves (from the East Anglian League) and Norwich Federation.

1919-20

Norwich City Reserves	18	15	3	0	51	14	31
Kings Lynn	18	10	2	6	35	20	22
Great Yarmouth Town	18	9	4	5	32	21	22
Gorleston	18	9	3	6	34	24	21
Cromer	18	8	3	7	38	24	19
Beccles Town	18	6	6	6	24	34	16
Lowestoft Town	18	5	5	8	27	34	15
Norwich C.E.Y.M.S.	18	4	6	8	17	29	14
Mortons Athletic	18	5	4	9	21	36	14
Norwich Federation	18	0	2	16	13	49	2
					292	*285*	

Norwich City Reserves and Beccles Town each had 2 points deducted for fielding ineligible players.
Norwich City Reserves moved to the Southern League – English Section. Bury United joined from the Ipswich & District League, Carrow Works joined from the Norwich & District League and Thetford Recreation and North Walsham Athletic also joined.

1920-21

Gorleston	24	17	4	3	67	24	38
Mortons Athletic	24	11	9	4	49	22	31
Kings Lynn	24	13	4	7	62	33	30
Cromer	24	12	4	8	60	46	28
Great Yarmouth Town	24	11	6	7	41	38	28
Lowestoft Town	24	11	5	8	51	38	27
Bury United	24	11	4	9	53	38	26
Carrow Works	24	8	5	11	33	41	21
Norwich C.E.Y.M.S.	24	7	6	11	50	40	20
Norwich Federation	24	7	5	12	38	79	19
Thetford Recreation	24	6	6	12	35	59	18
North Walsham Athletic	24	5	6	13	32	78	16
Beccles Town	24	4	2	18	33	70	10
					604	*606*	

Norwich Federation left. Leiston Works Athletic joined from the Ipswich & District League and Sheringham also joined.

1921-22

Kings Lynn	26	16	9	1	72	18	41
Gorleston	26	19	1	6	80	26	39
Norwich C.E.Y.M.S.	26	15	6	5	51	31	36
Lowestoft Town	26	14	5	7	76	33	33
Mortons Athletic	26	14	5	7	44	37	33
Cromer	26	13	5	8	64	38	31
Great Yarmouth Town	26	11	8	7	42	31	30
Beccles Town	26	10	3	13	31	41	23
Leiston Works Athletic	26	9	4	13	47	63	22
Carrow Works	26	8	5	13	38	54	21
Sheringham	26	7	4	15	36	55	18
Bury United	26	4	7	15	38	76	15
Thetford Recreation	26	5	5	16	19	47	15
North Walsham Athletic	26	3	1	22	12	98	7
					650	*648*	

1922-23

Kings Lynn	26	21	2	3	102	26	44
Gorleston	26	20	3	3	84	34	43
Cromer	26	19	2	5	81	36	40
Lowestoft Town	26	16	3	7	65	41	35
Great Yarmouth Town	26	12	3	11	58	61	27
Sheringham	26	10	6	10	43	37	26
Bury United	26	11	2	13	40	52	24
Norwich C.E.Y.M.S.	26	9	5	12	36	50	23
Beccles Town	26	9	3	14	36	51	21
Mortons Athletic	26	8	3	15	37	48	19
Carrow Works	26	7	4	15	40	65	18
Leiston Works Athletic	26	6	3	17	31	69	15
North Walsham Athletic	26	6	3	17	40	88	15
Thetford Recreation	26	5	4	17	20	55	14

Bury United changed name to Bury Town. North Walsham Athletic left and joined the Norwich & District League and City Wanderers joined.

1923-24

Kings Lynn	26	19	3	4	93	30	41
Gorleston	26	17	5	4	88	37	39
Cromer	26	15	6	5	70	35	36
City Wanderers	26	16	3	7	69	41	35
Great Yarmouth Town	26	15	4	7	70	39	34
Lowestoft Town	26	14	2	10	59	42	30
Bury Town	26	10	5	11	49	51	25
Sheringham	26	10	4	12	47	62	24
Norwich C.E.Y.M.S.	26	8	5	13	37	52	21
Carrow Works	26	9	3	14	30	55	21
Beccles Town	26	8	2	16	41	85	18
Thetford Recreation	26	6	6	14	25	57	18
Leiston Works Athletic	26	6	3	17	35	68	15
Mortons Athletic	26	3	1	22	27	86	7

Mortons Athletic left and Kirkley joined from the East Anglian League – Division Two.

1924-25

Kings Lynn	26	23	2	1	108	21	48
Lowestoft Town	26	17	4	5	90	33	38
Carrow Works	26	17	3	6	65	40	37
Gorleston	26	16	3	7	75	51	35
Great Yarmouth Town	26	14	5	7	78	46	33
Cromer	26	13	5	8	61	42	31
City Wanderers	26	12	6	8	61	66	30
Kirkley	26	10	3	13	40	47	23
Bury Town	26	10	3	13	37	50	23
Norwich C.E.Y.M.S.	26	8	4	14	46	58	20
Leiston Works Athletic	26	7	5	14	49	68	19
Beccles Town	26	6	2	18	36	73	14
Sheringham	26	3	3	20	25	74	9
Thetford Recreation	26	1	2	23	15	91	4
					786	*760*	

1925-26

Gorleston	26	22	3	1	128	41	47
Lowestoft Town	26	20	3	3	82	31	43
Kings Lynn	26	14	4	8	72	46	32
Great Yarmouth Town	26	15	1	10	85	62	31
Carrow Works	26	13	4	9	55	45	30
Norwich C.E.Y.M.S.	26	12	3	11	55	72	27
Cromer	26	11	2	13	55	62	24
Thetford Recreation	26	9	4	13	58	78	22
City Wanderers	26	9	3	14	47	58	21
Kirkley	26	9	2	15	59	76	20
Beccles Town	26	8	2	16	58	70	18
Bury Town	26	8	2	16	52	80	18
Leiston Works Athletic	26	7	2	17	50	97	16
Sheringham	26	7	1	18	45	99	15
					901	*917*	

Thetford Recreation changed name to Thetford Town.
Leiston Works Athletic left and joined the Ipswich & District League.

1926-27

Great Yarmouth Town	24	17	6	1	78	30	40
Lowestoft Town	24	18	3	3	94	29	39
Gorleston	24	18	2	4	82	48	38
Kings Lynn	24	14	3	7	81	38	31
Norwich C.E.Y.M.S.	24	9	6	9	75	58	24
Cromer	24	9	6	9	62	72	24
Thetford Town	24	9	5	10	49	52	23
Sheringham	24	7	7	10	56	54	21
City Wanderers	24	7	4	13	45	64	18
Bury Town	24	6	3	15	40	74	15
Kirkley	24	5	5	14	46	89	15
Carrow Works	24	6	2	16	39	74	14
Beccles Town	24	4	2	18	40	108	10
					787	*790*	

City Wanderers left.

1927-28

Great Yarmouth Town	22	20	0	2	85	29	40
Gorleston	22	15	2	5	82	27	32
Kings Lynn	22	13	1	8	72	47	27
Lowestoft Town	22	11	3	8	66	36	25
Norwich C.E.Y.M.S.	22	9	5	8	58	52	23
Kirkley	22	11	1	10	52	52	23
Carrow Works	22	8	5	9	47	50	21
Sheringham	22	9	3	10	47	67	21
Cromer	22	8	2	12	53	57	18
Thetford Town	22	6	5	11	33	61	17
Bury Town	22	4	4	14	39	64	12
Beccles Town	22	2	1	19	22	112	5
					656	*654*	

Norwich Y.M.C.A. joined from the Norwich & District League.

1928-29

Lowestoft Town	24	16	6	2	95	30	38
Gorleston	24	18	2	4	82	33	38
Great Yarmouth Town	24	15	7	2	65	28	37
Cromer	24	16	2	6	78	55	34
Norwich Y.M.C.A.	24	12	6	6	78	49	30
Kings Lynn	24	12	2	10	61	67	26
Sheringham	24	10	3	11	61	51	23
Thetford Town	24	11	1	12	51	55	23
Kirkley	24	7	4	13	57	66	18
Carrow Works	24	6	4	14	34	59	16
Norwich C.E.Y.M.S.	24	5	5	14	40	58	15
Bury Town	24	4	4	16	45	91	12
Beccles Town	24	1	0	23	12	112	2
					759	*754*	

Kirkley merged with Waveney Athletic and changed their name to Kirkley & Waveney.
Bury Town left and joined the Essex & Suffolk Border League.

1929-30

Gorleston	22	18	2	2	89	33	38
Great Yarmouth Town	22	16	2	4	66	20	34
Kings Lynn	22	15	2	5	78	25	32
Kirkley & Waveney	22	15	1	6	67	31	31
Lowestoft Town	22	13	2	7	54	29	28
Norwich Y.M.C.A.	22	11	4	7	61	53	26
Cromer	22	8	6	8	53	53	22
Norwich C.E.Y.M.S.	22	8	3	11	62	56	19
Sheringham	22	7	2	13	44	73	16
Thetford Town	22	3	6	13	37	70	12
Carrow Works	22	1	1	20	16	74	3
Beccles Town	22	1	1	20	23	133	3

Carrow Works left and Boulton & Paul joined from the Norwich & District League.

1930-31

Lowestoft Town	22	18	2	2	66	20	38
Gorleston	22	14	0	8	83	39	28
Kings Lynn	22	12	4	6	60	36	28
Norwich C.E.Y.M.S.	22	13	1	8	70	50	27
Boulton & Paul	22	11	4	7	64	48	26
Kirkley & Waveney	22	11	3	8	68	40	25
Cromer	22	11	3	8	52	54	25
Great Yarmouth Town	22	10	3	9	61	50	23
Norwich Y.M.C.A.	22	8	2	12	59	71	18
Thetford Town	22	5	2	15	46	78	12
Sheringham	22	5	2	15	43	84	12
Beccles Town	22	1	0	21	21	123	2

1931-32

Gorleston	22	17	1	4	85	31	35
Lowestoft Town	22	14	2	6	52	33	30
Kings Lynn	22	13	3	6	57	26	29
Norwich C.E.Y.M.S.	22	13	3	6	87	59	29
Sheringham	22	11	3	8	55	52	25
Boulton & Paul	22	12	1	9	56	54	25
Great Yarmouth Town	22	11	2	9	54	50	24
Cromer	22	7	5	10	59	72	19
Norwich Y.M.C.A.	22	7	5	10	40	55	19
Kirkley & Waveney	22	6	3	13	53	67	15
Thetford Town	22	4	3	15	35	71	11
Beccles Town	22	1	1	20	16	88	3
					649	*658*	

Kirkley & Waveney changed their name to Kirkley. Beccles Town left and Bury Town joined from the Essex & Suffolk Border League.

1932-33

Gorleston	22	17	3	2	75	26	37
Lowestoft Town	22	15	2	5	62	35	32
Norwich C.E.Y.M.S.	22	14	3	5	68	41	31
Kings Lynn	22	12	3	7	58	36	27
Great Yarmouth Town	22	10	2	10	45	37	22
Cromer	22	8	5	9	49	59	20
Bury Town	22	9	2	11	51	76	20
Sheringham	22	5	8	9	46	59	18
Boulton & Paul	22	6	5	11	39	46	17
Norwich Y.M.C.A.	22	5	6	11	39	49	16
Kirkley	22	6	4	12	36	57	16
Thetford Town	22	2	3	17	18	65	7

Cromer had 1 point deducted for a breach of the league rules.

1933-34

Gorleston	22	17	4	1	74	22	38
Great Yarmouth Town	22	16	4	2	69	19	36
Kirkley	22	12	4	6	63	47	28
Kings Lynn	22	8	8	6	55	42	24
Thetford Town	22	10	4	8	49	52	24
Norwich Y.M.C.A.	22	8	4	10	35	41	20
Lowestoft Town	22	7	6	9	37	45	20
Sheringham	22	6	6	10	49	48	18
Norwich C.E.Y.M.S.	22	8	2	12	40	54	18
Bury Town	22	7	1	14	43	66	15
Cromer	22	6	2	14	49	79	14
Boulton & Paul	22	2	5	15	27	75	9

Frosts Athletic joined from the Norwich & District League and Norwich City "A" also joined.

1934-35

Gorleston	26	19	4	3	82	21	42
Lowestoft Town	26	17	5	4	75	36	39
Norwich City "A"	26	17	4	5	53	25	38
Great Yarmouth Town	26	14	4	8	76	39	32
Norwich C.E.Y.M.S.	26	14	2	10	67	53	30
Frosts Athletic	26	11	6	9	48	39	28
Kirkley	26	12	4	10	53	49	28
Kings Lynn	26	13	1	12	70	58	27
Thetford Town	26	10	5	11	41	51	25
Bury Town	26	7	7	12	65	100	21
Sheringham	26	6	5	15	41	61	17
Norwich Y.M.C.A.	26	6	4	16	34	69	16
Boulton & Paul	26	4	4	18	32	91	12
Cromer	26	3	3	20	43	88	9

Bury Town, Gorleston, Great Yarmouth Town, Kings Lynn, Lowestoft Town and Thetford Town all left to become founder members of the Eastern Counties League.
Bungay Town, Dereham Town, Diss Town, Fakenham Town, Holt United, Norwich St. Barnabas and Swaffham Town all joined from the Norwich & District League and Eastern Counties United and Norwich Electricity also joined.
Kirkley were absorbed by Lowestoft Town.

1935-36

Norwich C.E.Y.M.S.	30	24	3	3	86	24	51
Norwich City "A"	30	20	6	4	109	27	46
Frosts Athletic	30	18	6	6	74	36	42
Eastern Counties United	30	17	4	9	98	70	38
Sheringham	30	16	5	9	65	48	37
Norwich St. Barnabas	30	13	6	11	71	65	32
Holt United	30	15	1	14	71	69	31
Cromer	30	13	4	13	58	77	30
Norwich Y.M.C.A.	30	10	9	11	59	51	29
Fakenham Town	30	12	3	15	50	65	27
Diss Town	30	8	8	14	34	55	24
Boulton & Paul	30	8	7	15	47	55	23
Norwich Electricity	30	10	3	17	53	93	23
Dereham Town	30	5	8	17	51	74	18
Bungay Town	30	6	5	19	47	92	17
Swaffham Town	30	5	2	23	50	120	12
					1023	*1021*	

Swaffham Town left.

1936-37

Norwich City "A"	28	19	5	4	86	41	43
Cromer	28	18	2	8	78	44	38
Eastern Counties United	28	15	7	6	85	56	37
Frosts Athletic	28	15	6	7	72	59	36
Norwich Y.M.C.A.	28	15	4	9	62	50	34
Holt United	28	13	5	10	69	51	31
Bungay Town	28	14	3	11	68	63	31
Sheringham	28	14	2	12	64	52	30
Norwich Electricity	28	12	5	11	68	64	29
Norwich C.E.Y.M.S.	28	12	4	12	74	55	28
Norwich St. Barnabas	28	10	7	11	56	55	27
Dereham Town	28	10	3	15	47	73	23
Fakenham Town	28	6	4	18	63	93	16
Diss Town	28	4	1	23	26	97	9
Boulton & Paul	28	3	2	23	28	93	8

Cromer and Norwich C.E.Y.M.S. moved to the Eastern Counties League and Norwich City "A" also left. Thetford Town joined from the Eastern Counties League and R.A.F. Bircham Newton and R.A.F. Feltwell also joined. Eastern Counties United became Eastern Coachworks and Norwich Electricity became Electricity Works.

1937-38

Eastern Coachworks	28	21	3	4	76	27	45
Holt United	28	19	5	4	70	23	43
Frosts Athletic	28	16	7	5	79	29	39
Sheringham	28	17	4	7	73	46	38
Norwich Y.M.C.A.	28	11	7	10	58	57	29
Diss Town	28	11	6	11	53	48	28
Bungay Town	28	13	2	13	53	50	28
Thetford Town	28	12	4	12	54	64	28
Electricity Works	28	10	7	11	55	56	27
Fakenham Town	28	11	4	13	69	74	26
Boulton & Paul	28	10	6	12	43	54	26
Dereham Town	28	10	5	13	52	67	25
R.A.F. Bircham Newton	28	5	4	19	45	84	14
Norwich St. Barnabas	28	3	6	19	43	85	12
R.A.F. Feltwell	28	3	6	19	30	85	12
					853	*849*	

R.A.F. Marham joined.

1938-39

Holt United	30	26	1	3	118	38	53
Bungay Town	30	19	5	6	77	44	43
Fakenham Town	30	18	6	6	104	56	42
Eastern Coachworks	30	15	7	8	82	50	37
Frosts Athletic	30	16	4	10	100	47	36
Electricity Works	30	16	2	12	69	56	34
Norwich Y.M.C.A.	30	12	6	12	48	60	30
Norwich St. Barnabas	30	12	6	12	69	94	30
Thetford Town	30	10	7	13	69	64	27
R.A.F. Marham	30	11	5	14	73	76	27
Boulton & Paul	30	9	7	14	59	69	25
Sheringham	30	9	7	14	52	80	25
Dereham Town	30	8	5	17	50	90	21
R.A.F. Feltwell	30	8	4	18	65	91	20
Diss Town	30	9	2	19	39	80	20
R.A.F. Bircham Newton	30	4	2	24	48	127	10

1939-46

The league did not operate. When it restarted after the war, Frosts Athletic, Norwich St. Barnabas, Norwich Y.M.C.A., R.A.F. Bircham Newton, R.A.F. Feltwell and R.A.F. Marham did not rejoin. Norwich C.E.Y.M.S. and Cromer joined from the Eastern Counties League, Gothic joined from the East Anglian League and C.N.S.O.B.U. and Wymondham Town also joined.

1946-47

Bungay Town	28	24	4	0	128	32	52
Norwich C.E.Y.M.S.	28	23	2	3	107	38	48
Gothic	28	22	2	4	113	34	46
C.N.S.O.B.U.	28	16	1	11	113	73	33
Cromer	28	14	5	9	102	74	33
Holt United	28	12	6	10	80	67	30
Wymondham Town	28	12	5	11	83	74	29
Eastern Coachworks	28	13	1	14	81	78	27
Diss Town	28	12	3	13	79	77	27
Dereham Town	28	11	4	13	80	76	26
Thetford Town	28	11	4	13	68	95	26
Sheringham	28	9	5	14	58	87	23
Fakenham Town	28	4	3	21	53	133	11
Boulton & Paul	28	2	3	23	33	113	7
Electricity Works	28	1	0	27	22	143	2
					1200	*1194*	

1947-48

Bungay Town	28	23	2	3	111	23	48
Norwich C.E.Y.M.S.	28	22	2	4	93	37	46
Eastern Coachworks	28	14	9	5	77	40	37
Gothic	28	16	5	7	70	47	37
Holt United	28	15	3	10	63	47	33
C.N.S.O.B.U.	28	13	6	9	68	51	32
Cromer	28	12	5	11	84	72	29
Thetford Town	28	11	4	13	69	69	26
Diss Town	28	11	4	13	58	69	26
Fakenham Town	28	8	9	11	69	82	25
Dereham Town	28	10	4	14	58	63	24
Sheringham	28	8	4	16	50	73	20
Wymondham Town	28	5	5	18	49	80	15
Electricity Works	28	5	3	20	34	114	13
Boulton & Paul	28	4	1	23	30	121	9
					983	*988*	

Leiston joined from the Ipswich & District League.

1948-49

Bungay Town	30	25	1	4	116	32	51
Cromer	30	24	2	4	103	42	50
Eastern Coachworks	30	19	3	8	97	50	41
Gothic	30	18	5	7	89	51	41
Thetford Town	30	17	5	8	76	52	39
Holt United	30	13	4	13	80	70	30
Leiston	30	13	4	13	78	85	30
Norwich C.E.Y.M.S.	30	13	3	14	72	70	29
Fakenham Town	30	12	5	13	75	79	29
Boulton & Paul	30	11	5	14	52	69	27
C.N.S.O.B.U.	30	10	3	17	63	70	23
Sheringham	30	8	7	15	49	61	23
Wymondham Town	30	10	2	18	61	107	22
Dereham Town	30	8	4	18	58	84	20
Diss Town	30	7	3	20	63	108	17
Electricity Works	30	1	6	23	27	135	8
					1159	*1165*	

Electricity Works left and Beccles Town joined.

1949-50

Gothic	30	22	3	5	95	37	47
Bungay Town	30	18	6	6	92	41	42
Leiston	30	20	0	10	90	59	40
Cromer	30	17	3	10	66	47	37
Diss Town	30	16	3	11	89	57	35
Beccles Town	30	14	3	13	65	55	31
Eastern Coachworks	30	13	5	12	53	61	31
Norwich C.E.Y.M.S.	30	12	6	12	68	67	30
C.N.S.O.B.U.	30	12	5	13	65	65	29
Thetford Town	30	12	5	13	59	66	29
Fakenham Town	30	10	8	12	56	82	28
Holt United	30	9	8	13	64	78	26
Boulton & Paul	30	5	11	14	49	69	21
Dereham Town	30	5	10	15	51	80	20
Wymondham Town	30	5	7	18	45	92	17
Sheringham	30	5	7	18	41	92	17

1950-51

Gothic	30	25	3	2	109	32	53
Boulton & Paul	30	19	5	6	65	33	43
Beccles Town	30	19	1	10	110	66	39
Dereham Town	30	17	5	8	77	47	39
Cromer	30	16	6	8	72	57	38
Bungay Town	30	15	5	10	76	56	35
Diss Town	30	12	7	11	69	73	31
Eastern Coachworks	30	11	6	13	52	76	28
C.N.S.O.B.U.	30	12	2	16	74	78	26
Norwich C.E.Y.M.S.	30	12	1	17	58	72	25
Fakenham Town	30	9	5	16	57	81	23
Wymondham Town	30	8	6	16	72	87	22
Sheringham	30	8	5	17	46	61	21
Leiston	30	8	5	17	66	107	21
Thetford Town	30	7	6	17	47	80	20
Holt United	30	4	8	18	51	95	16

1951-52

Bungay Town	30	23	3	4	98	34	49
Thetford Town	30	20	2	8	82	31	42
Beccles Town	30	19	3	8	89	48	41
Gothic	30	17	3	10	79	58	37
C.N.S.O.B.U.	30	16	2	12	79	68	34
Fakenham Town	30	13	6	11	61	58	32
Cromer	30	12	7	11	42	61	31
Boulton & Paul	30	13	4	13	48	44	30
Holt United	30	12	4	14	67	70	28
Wymondham Town	30	12	3	15	59	79	27
Eastern Coachworks	30	10	6	14	51	61	26
Sheringham	30	11	3	16	42	64	25
Leiston	30	10	3	17	64	84	23
Dereham Town	30	8	5	17	40	66	21
Diss Town	30	5	8	17	43	82	18
Norwich C.E.Y.M.S.	30	7	2	21	41	75	16
					985	*983*	

North Walsham Athletic joined from the East Anglian League.

1952-53

Beccles Town	32	26	3	3	120	44	55
Thetford Town	32	24	3	5	104	40	51
Bungay Town	32	19	8	5	90	40	46
North Walsham Athletic	32	19	8	5	104	64	46
C.N.S.O.B.U.	32	18	3	11	86	64	39
Sheringham	32	13	7	12	63	64	33
Norwich C.E.Y.M.S.	32	12	8	12	63	63	32
Cromer	32	11	7	14	70	82	29
Gothic	32	11	6	15	78	76	28
Holt United	32	10	6	16	65	89	26
Boulton & Paul	32	11	4	17	45	80	26
Dereham Town	32	9	7	16	51	73	25
Fakenham Town	32	11	2	19	65	88	24
Wymondham Town	32	10	3	19	69	90	23
Diss Town	32	9	5	18	69	98	23
Eastern Coachworks	32	8	5	19	55	90	21
Leiston	32	6	5	21	48	100	17

Leiston moved to the Ipswich & District League. Thorpe Village joined from the East Anglian League and Norwich Electricity also joined. North Walsham Athletic changed their name to North Walsham Town.

1953-54

North Walsham Town	34	23	7	4	112	47	53
Thetford Town	34	23	6	5	132	70	52
Sheringham	34	23	4	7	97	54	50
Gothic	34	19	7	8	104	68	45
Bungay Town	34	18	6	10	95	65	42
Thorpe Village	34	18	6	10	108	79	42
Beccles Town	34	17	6	11	90	68	40
Wymondham Town	34	17	4	13	80	88	38
C.N.S.O.B.U.	34	15	4	15	75	82	34
Eastern Coachworks	34	13	6	15	64	71	32
Holt United	34	12	4	18	73	102	28
Fakenham Town	34	11	5	18	74	101	27
Dereham Town	34	10	5	19	54	84	25
Diss Town	34	10	4	20	60	85	24
Norwich C.E.Y.M.S.	34	10	2	22	56	92	22
Cromer	34	8	6	20	66	110	22
Norwich Electricity	34	7	6	21	67	88	20
Boulton & Paul	34	6	4	24	52	105	16

1954-55

Thetford Town	34	27	4	3	163	43	58
Thorpe Village	34	22	5	7	106	63	49
Beccles Town	34	22	2	10	102	68	46
Gothic	34	17	8	9	96	58	42
Bungay Town	34	17	7	10	98	69	41
North Walsham Town	34	19	2	13	111	95	40
Diss Town	34	16	6	12	113	87	38
Wymondham Town	34	16	5	13	96	99	37
Sheringham	34	12	11	11	84	76	35
C.N.S.O.B.U.	34	14	4	16	83	87	32
Norwich C.E.Y.M.S.	34	11	7	16	66	104	29
Boulton & Paul	34	11	5	18	81	107	27
Norwich Electricity	34	9	9	16	81	110	27
Holt United	34	11	3	20	75	100	25
Fakenham Town	34	10	5	19	79	107	25
Dereham Town	34	9	3	22	60	116	21
Cromer	34	8	4	22	59	115	20
Eastern Coachworks	34	7	6	21	47	97	20
					1600	*1601*	

1955-56

Gothic	34	27	3	4	100	51	57
Diss Town	34	22	4	8	101	50	48
Thetford Town	34	22	4	8	128	77	48
Bungay Town	34	22	2	10	108	78	46
C.N.S.O.B.U.	34	20	3	11	112	67	43
Sheringham	34	18	6	10	99	62	42
North Walsham Town	34	18	6	10	97	80	42
Thorpe Village	34	17	4	13	93	87	38
Beccles Town	34	14	6	14	90	84	34
Fakenham Town	34	15	3	16	75	73	33
Holt United	34	11	5	18	94	101	27
Wymondham Town	34	12	3	19	84	99	27
Boulton & Paul	34	8	7	19	61	93	23
Eastern Coachworks	34	8	7	19	48	86	23
Norwich C.E.Y.M.S.	34	11	1	22	61	110	23
Dereham Town	34	9	4	21	51	78	22
Cromer	34	8	4	22	52	103	20
Norwich Electricity	34	5	6	23	53	123	16
					1507	*1502*	

1956-57

Gothic	34	28	3	3	121	48	59
North Walsham Town	34	22	5	7	101	66	49
Sheringham	34	21	6	7	123	51	48
C.N.S.O.B.U.	34	20	6	8	122	78	46
Wymondham Town	34	20	4	10	127	80	44
Diss Town	34	16	9	9	111	61	41
Thetford Town	34	16	6	12	105	76	38
Cromer	34	14	7	13	78	83	35
Bungay Town	34	14	2	18	90	88	30
Beccles Town	34	12	6	16	72	98	30
Norwich C.E.Y.M.S.	34	11	7	16	58	89	29
Fakenham Town	34	12	4	18	71	88	28
Holt United	34	11	4	19	69	88	26
Norwich Electricity	34	10	6	18	65	94	26
Boulton & Paul	34	9	6	19	70	92	24
Dereham Town	34	9	4	21	73	128	22
Thorpe Village	34	8	3	23	63	123	19
Eastern Coachworks	34	8	2	24	48	129	18
					1567	*1560*	

1957-58

Sheringham	34	24	7	3	105	36	55
Thetford Town	34	25	3	6	118	54	53
C.N.S.O.B.U.	34	22	5	7	99	54	49
Gothic	34	22	3	9	106	59	47
North Walsham Town	34	21	4	9	102	65	46
Bungay Town	34	20	2	12	83	60	42
Fakenham Town	34	16	6	12	91	65	38
Wymondham Town	34	16	6	12	76	88	38
Boulton & Paul	34	16	4	14	102	85	36
Diss Town	34	14	6	14	95	69	34
Thorpe Village	34	11	5	18	66	94	27
Dereham Town	34	11	4	19	78	104	26
Norwich C.E.Y.M.S.	34	10	5	19	59	90	25
Beccles Town	34	11	1	22	51	115	23
Cromer	34	8	5	21	61	101	21
Holt United	34	8	4	22	67	102	20
Eastern Coachworks	34	8	2	24	52	125	18
Norwich Electricity	34	5	4	25	43	110	14
					1454	*1476*	

1958-59

Gothic	34	29	4	1	125	41	62
C.N.S.O.B.U.	34	23	4	7	113	40	50
Diss Town	34	23	4	7	136	71	50
Bungay Town	34	20	5	9	104	69	45
Beccles Town	34	19	4	11	88	68	42
Boulton & Paul	34	17	5	12	91	76	39
Eastern Coachworks	34	15	8	11	69	76	38
Sheringham	34	17	3	14	91	68	37
Fakenham Town	34	15	7	12	93	82	37
Norwich C.E.Y.M.S.	34	11	9	14	66	71	31
Dereham Town	34	15	1	18	83	104	31
North Walsham Town	34	12	4	18	80	98	28
Wymondham Town	34	10	8	16	69	94	28
Thetford Town	34	11	4	19	59	78	26
Thorpe Village	34	9	6	19	73	109	24
Cromer	34	8	5	21	58	97	21
Norwich Electricity	34	7	2	25	54	116	16
Holt United	34	1	5	28	50	144	7

1959-60

C.N.S.O.B.U.	34	23	5	6	113	42	51
Bungay Town	34	25	1	8	97	44	51
Gothic	34	23	3	8	129	50	49
Dereham Town	34	21	4	9	97	74	46
Diss Town	34	20	4	10	118	85	44
Thetford Town	34	17	7	10	111	75	41
North Walsham Town	34	18	3	13	107	93	39
Boulton & Paul	34	15	8	11	99	79	38
Cromer	34	15	6	13	70	67	36
Fakenham Town	34	15	4	15	76	80	34
Norwich C.E.Y.M.S.	34	15	4	15	69	70	34
Beccles Town	34	11	6	17	95	106	28
Thorpe Village	34	10	5	19	72	82	25
Wymondham Town	34	10	5	19	70	89	25
Sheringham	34	8	7	19	75	100	23
Norwich Electricity	34	5	8	21	59	138	18
Holt United	34	5	7	22	51	113	17
Eastern Coachworks	34	3	5	26	40	161	11
	612	*259*	*92*	*261*			*610*

Holt United left and Gorleston joined from the Eastern Counties League.

1960-61

Gothic	34	31	3	0	132	40	65
Bungay Town	34	25	4	5	127	54	54
Thetford Town	34	24	1	9	103	52	49
Gorleston	34	20	7	7	77	50	47
Diss Town	34	19	7	8	131	69	45
Sheringham	34	17	10	7	93	63	44
Dereham Town	34	19	3	12	105	86	41
C.N.S.O.B.U.	34	14	11	9	96	66	39
Fakenham Town	34	15	5	14	91	84	35
Norwich C.E.Y.M.S.	34	13	7	14	61	58	33
Cromer	34	11	8	15	70	105	30
Boulton & Paul	34	12	4	18	87	82	28
North Walsham Town	34	8	5	21	48	83	21
Eastern Coachworks	34	6	9	19	56	102	21
Wymondham Town	34	9	3	22	55	102	21
Beccles Town	34	7	5	22	71	137	19
Thorpe Village	34	6	4	24	56	116	16
Norwich Electricity	34	1	2	31	44	154	4

Beccles Town and Eastern Coachworks left.

1961-62

Gothic	30	22	4	4	98	29	48
C.N.S.O.B.U.	30	18	9	3	103	52	45
Bungay Town	30	18	4	8	78	58	40
Dereham Town	30	18	4	8	85	67	40
Gorleston	30	13	7	10	75	58	33
Diss Town	30	15	2	13	95	57	32
Boulton & Paul	30	13	6	11	85	83	32
North Walsham Town	30	13	5	12	80	70	31
Norwich C.E.Y.M.S.	30	12	7	11	69	58	31
Fakenham Town	30	13	4	13	72	82	30
Thetford Town	30	12	5	13	74	83	29
Sheringham	30	8	9	13	72	71	25
Norwich Electricity	30	10	1	19	95	113	21
Thorpe Village	30	8	3	19	53	108	19
Cromer	30	6	4	20	43	87	16
Wymondham Town	30	3	2	25	37	138	8

1962-63

C.N.S.O.B.U.	24	17	4	3	78	33	38
Gothic	24	14	5	5	61	40	33
Bungay Town	24	14	4	6	70	46	32
Gorleston	24	13	6	5	38	30	32
Diss Town	24	14	2	8	71	51	30
Thetford Town	24	13	2	9	70	65	28
Dereham Town	24	12	3	9	54	55	27
Norwich Electricity	24	12	2	10	70	72	26
Norwich C.E.Y.M.S.	24	8	6	10	45	48	22
Cromer	24	8	6	10	59	74	22
Sheringham	24	9	3	12	58	87	21
Fakenham Town	24	8	2	14	64	88	18
Thorpe Village	24	6	5	13	34	61	17
North Walsham Town	24	6	4	14	35	69	16
Boulton & Paul	24	4	5	15	50	86	13
Wymondham Town	24	3	3	18	34	76	9
					891	*981*	

The season was reduced to 24 games due to the severe winter weather. Bungay Town, Gothic and Thetford Town moved to the Eastern Counties League. Reepham Town and Sprowston Athletic joined.

1963-64

C.N.S.O.B.U.	28	22	4	2	138	43	48
Norwich Electricity	28	20	2	6	85	38	42
Sheringham	28	20	2	6	93	63	42
Diss Town	28	15	5	8	91	60	35
Cromer	28	13	8	7	72	60	34
Norwich C.E.Y.M.S.	28	13	5	10	60	50	31
Reepham Town	28	13	4	11	71	90	30
Boulton & Paul	28	11	6	11	53	66	28
Gorleston	28	12	3	13	71	55	27
Dereham Town	28	8	8	12	77	75	24
Thorpe Village	28	7	4	17	52	82	18
Sprowston Athletic	28	6	6	16	53	94	18
North Walsham Town	28	6	5	17	59	90	17
Wymondham Town	28	5	5	18	46	93	15
Fakenham Town	28	5	1	22	49	110	11
					1070	*1069*	

At the end of the season, the Norfolk & Suffolk League merged with the East Anglian League to form the Anglian Combination. C.N.S.O.B.U., Cromer Town, Fakenham Town, Gorleston, North Walsham Town, Reepham Town, Sheringham and Thorpe Village were placed in Senior Section "A" while Boulton & Paul, Dereham Town, Diss Town, Norwich C.E.Y.M.S., Norwich Electricity, Sprowston Athletic and Wymondham Town were placed in Senior Section "B" of the new competition.

WARWICKSHIRE COMBINATION

Background and Summary

The massive influence of the city of Birmingham and its leagues meant that for many years Warwickshire had no county league of its own. Just after the war, there was a Warwickshire and West Midland Alliance but the very name gives away the fact that most of its members were based in the Birmingham conurbation and this league did not always keep the Warwickshire part of its title. In the 1952-53 season it had a 15 club Southern Section but more than half of that section's members were based in Birmingham or even to the north of the city and some of the remainder wanted a more local fixture list. As a result, the South Warwickshire League came into being in 1953. In its first season it had only nine members and so the fixture list was supplemented by a cup competition in which the clubs played each other again in a league format. However the popularity of the new league allowed it to expand its membership to 19 clubs in 1954-55, when it adopted the name "Warwickshire Combination".

The nine founder members of the South Warwickshire League were Cubbington Albion, Flavels, Saltisford Rovers, Warwick Town, Warwickshire Constabulary and the reserve sides of Banbury Spencer, Bedworth Town, Cheltenham Town and Lockheed (Leamington). Of these Lockheed Reserves, Saltisford Rovers and Warwick Town had played in the Warwickshire and West Midland Alliance in 1952-53.

The league contained several junior clubs, some of whom - Evesham United, Cinderford Town, Coventry Amateurs (later Coventry Sporting) and Saltisford Rovers (as R.C. Warwick) - later grew and joined the Southern League. Other members included the third or fourth sides of Football League clubs and some reserve sides of Southern and Birmingham League clubs. This last category expanded in 1960 when the Birmingham League adopted a policy of including first teams only and so the Warwickshire Combination expanded to two regional divisions. However after a few years, the reserve sides formed their own league while the neighbouring Worcestershire Combination continued to expand. Squeezed by these two factors, the Warwickshire Combination closed in 1967.

Several of the published tables contained errors. Additional research has succeeded in correcting some of these. Those totals that still do not balance are shown below the relevant columns in italics.

1953-54

South Warwickshire League

League championship

Cheltenham Town Reserves	16	11	3	2	61	21	25
Cubbington Albion	16	11	1	4	45	33	23
Lockheed (Leamington) Reserves	16	9	3	4	51	25	21
Saltisford Rovers	16	6	4	6	39	40	16
Bedworth Town Reserves	16	7	0	9	40	54	14
Banbury Spencer Reserves	16	6	1	9	42	49	13
Warwick Town	16	5	2	9	44	58	12
Flavels	16	3	4	9	36	51	10
Warwickshire Constabulary	16	4	2	10	33	55	10
					391	*386*	

Cup competition

Cheltenham Town Reserves	16	13	1	2	56	18	27
Lockheed (Leamington) Reserves	16	8	2	6	37	23	18
Saltisford Rovers	16	7	4	5	45	28	18
Cubbington Albion	16	5	8	3	32	23	18
Flavels	16	8	1	7	30	31	17
Warwick Town	16	6	3	7	35	44	15
Banbury Spencer Reserves	16	4	5	7	29	51	13
Warwickshire Constabulary	16	3	4	9	29	45	10
Bedworth Town Reserves	16	3	2	11	20	49	8
					313	*312*	

Cheltenham Town Reserves left. West Bromwich Albion "A" joined from the Birmingham Combination, Nuneaton Borough Reserves joined from the Staffordshire County League (South), Stratford Town Reserves joined from the Warwickshire & West Midlands Alliance, Birch Coppice Colliery Reserves joined from the Tamworth & Trent Valley League and Ansley Hall Colliery, Aston Villa "B", Birmingham City "A", Coventry City "A", Rootes Athletic, Rugby Town Reserves and Worcester City "A" also joined.

After abortive discussions concerning a merger with the Birmingham Combination, the league changed its name to Warwickshire Combination during the 1954-55 season.

1954-55

Warwickshire Combination

West Bromwich Albion "A"	36	30	2	4	166	41	62
Birmingham City "A"	36	27	5	4	163	39	59
Warwick Town	36	21	7	8	114	73	49
Rugby Town Reserves	36	18	12	6	87	64	48
Worcester City "A"	36	19	6	11	88	67	44
Nuneaton Borough Reserves	36	17	9	10	78	69	43
Banbury Spencer Reserves	36	16	7	13	86	81	39
Aston Villa "B"	36	12	13	11	56	51	37
Coventry City "A"	36	15	6	15	74	79	36
Lockheed (Leamington) Reserves	36	15	6	15	101	72	34
Rootes Athletic	36	14	6	16	91	82	34
Bedworth Town Reserves	36	14	6	16	61	60	34
Cubbington Albion	36	12	7	17	59	96	31
Flavels	36	12	5	19	80	90	29
Stratford Town Reserves	36	9	6	21	46	74	24
Warwickshire Constabulary	36	10	3	23	79	119	23
Ansley Hall Colliery	36	8	5	23	40	77	21
Saltisford Rovers	36	7	5	24	57	131	19
Birch Coppice Colliery Reserves	36	6	6	24	40	136	18
	684	*282*	*122*	*280*	*1566*	*1501*	*684*

Lockheed (Leamington) Reserves had 2 points deducted for fielding an ineligible player.
West Bromwich Albion's "B" side joined the league instead of the "A" side who moved to the Birmingham League. Birch Coppice Colliery Reserves left and were replaced by their first team who moved from the Birmingham League. Coventry Amateurs joined from the Warwickshire & West Midlands Alliance.

1955-56

Lockheed (Leamington) Reserves	38	29	3	6	137	49	61
Birmingham City "A"	38	26	7	5	125	44	59
Banbury Spencer Reserves	38	27	2	9	140	57	56
Bedworth Town Reserves	38	25	4	9	116	39	54
Rugby Town Reserves	38	25	3	10	100	54	53
Aston Villa "B"	38	18	10	10	97	79	46
West Bromwich Albion "B"	38	17	7	14	85	65	41
Coventry City "A"	38	17	7	14	72	67	41
Saltisford Rovers	38	14	12	12	87	90	40
Rootes Athletic	38	14	11	13	74	76	39
Nuneaton Borough Reserves	38	16	4	18	64	80	36
Warwick Town	38	15	5	18	83	80	35
Flavels	38	15	5	18	66	75	35
Birch Coppice Colliery	38	13	8	17	80	100	34
Worcester City "A"	38	13	5	20	65	94	31
Cubbington Albion	38	10	8	20	62	90	28
Stratford Town Reserves	38	11	5	22	64	117	27
Coventry Amateurs	38	7	5	26	46	108	19
Ansley Hall Colliery	38	6	5	27	54	114	17
Warwickshire Constabulary	38	3	6	29	61	188	12
	760	*321*	*122*	*317*	*1678*	*1666*	*764*

Flavels moved to the Coventry Works League and Stratford Town Reserves also left, replacing their "A" team in the Warwickshire & West Midlands Alliance. Kenilworth Rangers joined from the Warwickshire and West Midlands Alliance.

1956-57

Birmingham City "A"	36	29	2	5	133	45	60
Kenilworth Rangers	36	28	3	5	134	34	59
Coventry City "A"	36	19	12	5	98	53	50
Lockheed (Leamington) Reserves	36	20	7	9	91	56	47
Rugby Town Reserves	36	20	6	10	115	69	46
Warwick Town	36	20	5	11	105	73	45
West Bromwich Albion "B"	36	19	3	14	89	65	41
Saltisford Rovers	36	16	8	12	110	98	40
Bedworth Town Reserves	36	15	8	13	81	72	38
Nuneaton Borough Reserves	36	16	6	14	92	65	38
Cubbington Albion	36	16	5	15	68	69	37
Aston Villa "B"	36	15	6	15	91	73	36
Rootes Athletic	36	12	10	14	89	74	34
Banbury Spencer Reserves	36	13	1	22	82	93	27
Coventry Amateurs	36	8	6	22	49	73	22
Ansley Hall Colliery	36	9	3	24	79	121	21
Birch Coppice Colliery	36	7	7	22	68	124	21
Worcester City "A"	36	6	3	27	71	178	15
Warwickshire Constabulary	36	3	1	32	51	221	7
					1696	*1656*	

Worcester City "A" moved to the Worcestershire Combination and Birch Coppice Colliery also left. Birmingham City and Coventry City placed their "B" sides in the league instead of their "A" sides, who moved to the Birmingham League. Smethwick Town joined from the Birmingham Youths and Old Boys League and Hinckley Athletic Reserves joined from the Leicestershire Senior League.

1957-58

Warwick Town	36	29	3	4	151	52	61
Banbury Spencer Reserves	36	22	7	7	105	52	51
Birmingham City "B"	36	21	9	6	99	53	51
Kenilworth Rangers	36	22	6	8	127	58	50
Lockheed (Leamington) Reserves	36	21	1	14	114	69	43
West Bromwich Albion "B"	36	17	9	10	98	73	43
Rugby Town Reserves	36	18	5	13	87	62	41
Smethwick Town	36	18	5	13	116	80	41
Hinckley Athletic Reserves	36	17	6	13	103	66	40
Cubbington Albion	36	15	6	15	84	98	36
Saltisford Rovers	36	14	7	15	85	96	35
Rootes Athletic	36	15	4	17	77	92	34
Nuneaton Borough Reserves	36	14	5	17	88	97	33
Bedworth Town Reserves	36	11	9	16	59	114	31
Aston Villa "B"	36	13	4	19	82	89	30
Coventry City "B"	36	10	4	22	71	113	24
Coventry Amateurs	36	9	5	22	63	88	23
Warwickshire Constabulary	36	3	3	30	54	184	9
Ansley Hall Colliery	36	3	2	31	42	177	8
					1705	*1713*	

Ansley Hall Colliery moved to the West Midland Alliance and Coventry City "B", Nuneaton Borough Reserves and Warwickshire Constabulary also left. Stratford Town Reserves joined from the Warwickshire and West Midlands Alliance and Sterling Metals also joined.

1958-59

Birmingham City "B"	32	22	4	6	122	55	48
Lockheed (Leamington) Reserves	32	23	1	8	109	48	47
Warwick Town	32	19	7	6	99	50	45
Aston Villa "B"	32	21	3	8	95	48	45
Banbury Spencer Reserves	32	19	7	6	81	56	45
Cubbington Albion	32	18	5	9	85	65	41
Smethwick Town	32	17	5	10	76	69	39
West Bromwich Albion "B"	32	18	2	12	91	50	38
Hinckley Athletic Reserves	32	17	4	11	85	62	38
Rugby Town Reserves	32	16	5	11	94	61	37
Kenilworth Rangers	32	14	3	15	78	87	31
Rootes Athletic	32	10	4	18	57	81	24
Coventry Amateurs	32	6	9	17	58	83	21
Saltisford Rovers	32	7	6	19	73	115	20
Bedworth Town Reserves	32	4	4	24	51	108	12
Stratford Town Reserves	32	4	1	27	47	111	9
Sterling Metals	32	0	4	28	23	166	4
					1324	*1315*	

Rugby Town Reserves left and Easington Sports joined.

1959-60

Aston Villa "B"	32	26	3	3	122	43	55
Lockheed (Leamington) Reserves	32	21	4	7	95	37	46
Banbury Spencer Reserves	32	20	5	7	85	51	45
Hinckley Athletic Reserves	32	21	2	9	92	45	44
Birmingham City "B"	32	17	7	8	92	53	41
Warwick Town	32	17	4	11	84	67	38
Rootes Athletic	32	15	5	12	64	56	35
Easington Sports	32	14	6	12	85	65	34
West Bromwich Albion "B"	32	14	2	16	68	61	30
Stratford Town Reserves	32	12	6	14	69	78	30
Cubbington Albion	32	12	5	15	91	89	29
Coventry Amateurs	32	14	1	17	54	66	29
Kenilworth Rangers	32	11	5	16	60	90	27
Saltisford Rovers	32	10	5	17	67	88	25
Smethwick Town	32	8	2	22	54	115	18
Bedworth Town Reserves	32	6	3	23	55	107	15
Sterling Metals	32	0	3	29	32	151	3
					1269	*1262*	

Smethwick Town moved to the West Midlands Alliance and Sterling Metals also left but nine new clubs joined increasing membership to 24. The league was split into two 12 club divisions, Eastern and Western, with Baddesley Liberals from the West Midlands Alliance and

West Bromwich Albion "C" joining the Eastern Division while Netherton Town from the West Midlands Alliance and the reserves of Cheltenham Town, Hereford United, Wellington Town and Worcester City moved to the Western Division from the Birmingham League. Gloucester City Reserves and Rugby Town Reserves also joined the Western Division.

1960-61

Eastern Division

Rootes Athletic	22	16	4	2	83	33	36
Banbury Spencer Reserves	22	14	2	6	48	29	30
Cubbington Albion	22	12	4	6	63	41	28
Coventry Amateurs	22	11	4	7	39	34	26
Stratford Town Reserves	22	8	7	7	50	52	23
West Bromwich Albion "C"	22	10	2	10	50	46	22
Baddesley Liberals	22	8	3	11	63	54	19
Saltisford Rovers	22	7	5	10	41	54	19
Warwick Town	22	7	5	10	31	57	19
Easington Sports	22	6	3	13	45	60	15
Bedworth Town Reserves	22	6	2	14	27	58	14
Kenilworth Rangers	22	5	3	14	34	56	13

Baddesley Liberals, Bedworth Town Reserves, Kenilworth Rangers and West Bromwich Albion "C" left. Lockheed (Leamington) Reserves transferred from the Western Division. Forest of Arden joined from the Leamington League.

Western Division

Wellington Town Reserves	22	14	3	5	55	26	31
Hereford United Reserves	22	13	4	5	65	37	30
Birmingham City "B"	22	13	3	6	71	40	29
Cheltenham Town Reserves	22	13	2	7	59	40	28
Worcester City Reserves	22	13	1	8	51	37	27
Rugby Town Reserves	22	10	5	7	62	39	25
Hinckley Athletic Reserves	22	9	4	9	34	40	22
West Bromwich Albion "B"	22	9	3	10	70	61	21
Netherton Town	22	7	6	9	31	46	20
Aston Villa "B"	22	7	3	12	31	40	17
Lockheed (Leamington) Reserves	22	4	2	16	25	49	10
Gloucester City Reserves	22	2	0	20	17	116	4

Birmingham City "B" and Gloucester City Reserves left. Kidderminster Harriers Reserves joined from the West Midlands Alliance and Nuneaton Borough Reserves and Sankeys (Wellington) Reserves also joined.

1961-62

Eastern Division

Rootes Athletic	18	13	3	2	54	25	29
Cubbington Albion	18	13	1	4	63	29	27
Coventry Amateurs	18	11	2	5	50	32	24
Stratford Town Reserves	18	9	3	6	45	42	21
Lockheed (Leamington) Reserves	18	9	1	8	38	32	19
Saltisford Rovers	18	7	4	7	42	44	18
Banbury Spencer Reserves	18	8	1	9	41	34	17
Easington Sports	18	4	3	11	30	52	11
Forest of Arden	18	2	5	11	33	60	9
Warwick Town	18	2	1	15	24	70	5

Forest of Arden moved to the Stratford League. Evesham United joined from the Birmingham League, Alcester Town joined from the Redditch League and Bedworth Town Reserves also joined.

Western Division

Worcester City Reserves	22	15	3	4	39	18	33
Hereford United Reserves	22	14	3	5	61	29	31
Nuneaton Borough Reserves	22	11	6	5	45	31	28
Sankeys (Wellington) Reserves	22	12	3	7	47	43	27
Wellington Town Reserves	22	12	1	9	46	30	25
Rugby Town Reserves	22	10	3	9	35	30	23
Cheltenham Town Reserves	22	11	0	11	60	53	22
Kidderminster Harriers Reserves	22	8	4	10	37	47	20
Aston Villa "B"	22	8	3	11	43	50	19
Hinckley Athletic Reserves	22	8	1	13	51	61	17
Netherton Town	22	3	5	14	22	50	11
West Bromwich Albion "B"	22	2	4	16	27	71	8

Stafford Rangers Reserves joined from the Staffordshire County League (South) and Lydbrook Athletic also joined.

1962-63

Eastern Division

Evesham United	22	19	3	0	111	24	41
Rootes Athletic	22	19	1	2	99	26	39
Lockheed (Leamington) Reserves	22	10	8	4	45	22	28
Cubbington Albion	22	12	2	8	55	47	26
Coventry Amateurs	22	10	2	10	47	49	22
Banbury Spencer Reserves	22	8	3	11	49	55	19
Alcester Town	22	8	3	11	48	73	19
Stratford Town Reserves	22	8	2	12	39	55	18
Bedworth Town Reserves	22	6	5	11	44	66	17
Warwick Town	22	7	1	14	33	71	15
Easington Sports	22	5	4	13	44	56	14
Saltisford Rovers	22	2	2	18	29	99	6

Western Division

Cheltenham Town Reserves	26	18	4	4	71	35	40
Worcester City Reserves	26	16	6	4	63	31	38
Wellington Town Reserves	26	15	2	9	61	41	32
Rugby Town Reserves	26	14	4	8	54	46	32
Nuneaton Borough Reserves	26	13	4	9	53	35	30
Lydbrook Athletic	26	13	4	9	54	45	30
Stafford Rangers Reserves	26	15	0	11	51	45	30
Hereford United Reserves	26	11	6	9	53	37	28
West Bromwich Albion "B"	26	11	2	13	42	54	24
Hinckley Athletic Reserves	26	9	6	11	31	50	24
Kidderminster Harriers Reserves	26	9	2	15	52	61	20
Sankeys (Wellington) Reserves	26	6	4	16	48	61	16
Aston Villa "B"	26	5	6	15	33	64	16
Netherton Town	26	1	2	23	21	82	4

Netherton Town left and Cinderford Town joined.

1963-64

Eastern Division

Evesham United	22	17	3	2	97	22	37
Lockheed (Leamington) Reserves	22	15	7	0	62	25	37
Banbury Spencer Reserves	22	14	3	5	65	30	31
Cubbington Albion	22	11	4	7	59	49	26
Coventry Amateurs	22	10	3	9	46	36	23
Warwick Town	22	10	3	9	37	62	23
Saltisford Rovers	22	10	2	10	48	45	22
Rootes Athletic	22	9	2	11	49	49	20
Stratford Town Reserves	22	7	4	11	59	67	18
Easington Sports	22	5	2	15	44	76	12
Alcester Town	22	4	2	16	29	72	10
Bedworth Town Reserves	22	1	3	18	21	83	5

Rootes Athletic moved to the Coventry Works League and Easington Sports also left. Castle Rovers joined from the Kings Norton League and Feckenham United joined from the Redditch League. Evesham United and Lockheed (Leamington) Reserves transferred to the Western Division.

Western Division

Worcester City Reserves	26	20	4	2	80	25	44
Hereford United Reserves	26	17	3	6	71	36	37
Nuneaton Borough Reserves	26	14	6	6	59	33	34
Cheltenham Town Reserves	26	16	2	8	52	36	34
Cinderford Town	26	14	5	7	88	44	33
Lydbrook Athletic	26	10	8	8	36	39	28
Wellington Town Reserves	26	12	3	11	51	52	27
Aston Villa "B"	26	12	3	11	49	53	27
Kidderminster Harriers Reserves	26	11	2	13	55	62	24
Stafford Rangers Reserves	26	9	4	13	48	61	22
West Bromwich Albion "B"	26	4	7	15	39	70	15
Sankeys (Wellington) Reserves	26	5	5	16	33	71	15
Rugby Town Reserves	26	4	5	17	29	57	13
Hinckley Athletic Reserves	26	4	3	19	37	88	11

Aston Villa "B", West Bromwich Albion "B" and the reserves of Kidderminster Harriers, Rugby Town, Sankeys (Wellington) and Stafford Rangers left.

1964-65

Eastern Division

Club	P	W	D	L	F	A	Pts
Castle Rovers	18	14	3	1	67	22	31
Saltisford Rovers	18	12	4	2	49	21	28
Banbury Spencer Reserves	18	10	4	4	59	28	24
Stratford Town Reserves	18	6	4	8	33	43	16
Coventry Amateurs	18	6	4	8	29	39	16
Feckenham United	18	7	1	10	40	48	15
Cubbington Albion	18	6	3	9	32	51	15
Alcester Town	18	6	2	10	44	47	14
Warwick Town	18	4	5	9	21	40	13
Bedworth Town Reserves	18	3	2	13	20	55	8

Western Division

Club	P	W	D	L	F	A	Pts
Cinderford Town	18	11	5	2	42	19	27
Worcester City Reserves	18	10	3	5	66	34	23
Evesham United	18	10	2	6	46	30	22
Wellington Town Reserves	18	9	1	8	55	45	19
Hereford United Reserves	18	9	1	8	48	46	19
Nuneaton Borough Reserves	18	7	4	7	34	38	18
Lockheed (Leamington) Reserves	18	6	4	8	27	33	16
Lydbrook Athletic	18	7	2	9	24	36	16
Hinckley Athletic Reserves	18	2	6	10	22	40	10
Cheltenham Town Reserves	18	4	2	12	34	77	10

Banbury Spencer changed their name to Banbury United. Cinderford Town moved to the West Midlands Regional League. Alcester Town, Castle Rovers and Evesham United moved to the Worcestershire Combination. Feckenham United and the Reserves of Cheltenham Town, Hinckley Athletic, Lockheed (Leamington), Nuneaton Borough and Wellington Town also left. Walsgrave Lodge and Warwickshire Constabulary joined. The League consolidated into a single 12 club division.

1965-66

Club	P	W	D	L	F	A	Pts
Saltisford Rovers	22	16	5	1	71	13	37
Banbury United Reserves	22	15	3	4	63	28	33
Lydbrook Athletic	22	15	3	4	49	27	33
Hereford United Reserves	22	13	6	3	54	25	32
Coventry Amateurs	22	10	5	7	45	29	25
Worcester City Reserves	22	10	3	9	71	42	23
Warwick Town	22	10	2	10	48	47	22
Walsgrave Lodge	22	8	3	11	42	54	19
Bedworth Town Reserves	22	3	6	13	24	54	12
Warwickshire Constabulary	22	5	2	15	28	86	12
Stratford Town Reserves	22	4	1	17	37	66	9
Cubbington Albion	22	3	1	18	27	88	7

Stratford Town Reserves moved to the Warwickshire and West Midlands Alliance, Banbury United Reserves moved to the Hellenic League and Worcester City Reserves also left. Fisher & Ludlow joined from the Birmingham Works League and Aston Villa "B" and Redditch B.A. also joined.

1966-67

Club	P	W	D	L	F	A	Pts
Hereford United Reserves	22	19	2	1	92	17	40
Saltisford Rovers	22	18	3	1	76	21	39
Warwickshire Constabulary	22	12	3	7	77	53	27
Walsgrave Lodge	22	12	2	8	62	43	26
Lydbrook Athletic	22	11	2	9	60	48	24
Aston Villa "B"	22	9	5	8	62	42	23
Fisher & Ludlow	22	10	3	9	43	41	23
Coventry Amateurs	22	8	4	10	43	50	20
Bedworth Town Reserves	22	7	5	10	37	52	19
Warwick Town	22	4	4	14	26	72	12
Redditch B.A.	22	3	0	19	30	82	6
Cubbington Albion	22	2	1	19	18	105	5

Saltisford Rovers and Warwick Town merged as Warwick Saltisford Rovers and resigned to join the West Midlands Regional League. Bedworth Town Reserves also resigned to join the West Midlands Regional League and Aston Villa "B", Cubbington Albion and Redditch B.A. also resigned leaving 6 existing members.

Applications were received from 5 new clubs – Redditch Transport, Ross All Whites, Rugby St. Johns, Saunders Hall and Warley Reserves who were a new club. However at the A.G.M. in June 1967 it was revealed that Fisher & Ludlow and Walsgrave Lodge had also resigned and that Redditch Transport had withdrawn their application, reducing membership for 1967-68 to 8 clubs. Several clubs were unhappy with this and Coventry Amateurs and Hereford United Reserves were successful with late applications to the West Midlands Regional League.

Of the remaining 6 clubs, only Saunders Hall and Warwickshire Constabulary remained committed to the Warwickshire Combination and so the league was officially wound up at a special meeting on Thursday 6th July, 1967.

THE WESSEX LEAGUE

FORMATION

The Wessex League was formed in 1986 to provide a platform for ambitious clubs from Hampshire and the surrounding area who might wish to progress to the Southern League. Its 17 founder members were:NAFC Totton, Brockenhurst, Eastleigh, Havant Town, Horndean, Lymington Town, Newport (I.O.W.), Portals Athletic, Portsmouth Royal Navy, Romsey Town and Sholing Sports, all from Division One of the Hampshire League, plus:

Bashley from Division Two of the Hampshire League; Bournemouth and Wellworthy Athletic from Division Three of the Hampshire League; Road Sea Southampton from the Southern League Premier Division; Steyning Town who were Sussex County League champions and Thatcham Town from the London-Spartan League.

Some published tables contained errors which have been corrected in the tables below.

1986-87

Bashley	32	24	3	5	71	30	75
Road Sea Southampton	32	22	7	3	70	26	73
AFC Totton	32	20	7	5	62	21	67
Newport (I.O.W.)	32	15	8	9	51	36	53
Havant Town	32	15	7	10	57	48	52
Thatcham Town	32	15	6	11	53	33	51
Wellworthy Athletic	32	14	6	12	48	50	48
Eastleigh	32	14	6	12	40	42	48
Sholing Sports	32	10	8	14	41	45	38
Lymington Town	32	10	8	14	31	37	38
Steyning Town	32	10	8	14	45	47	37
Portals Athletic	32	9	9	14	37	46	36
Portsmouth Royal Navy	32	11	2	19	43	58	35
Horndean	32	8	8	16	42	55	32
Bournemouth	32	7	9	16	33	59	28
Romsey Town	32	7	7	18	25	61	28
Brockenhurst	32	4	5	23	34	89	17

Steyning Town had 1 point deducted.
Road Sea Southampton disbanded and Portals Athletic left.
East Cowes Victoria Athletic, Folland Sports and Christchurch joined from the Hampshire League and Wimborne Town joined from the Western League.

1987-88

Bashley	36	26	6	4	91	26	84
Havant Town	36	24	8	4	91	31	80
Romsey Town	36	22	3	11	69	46	69
Newport (I.O.W.)	36	19	8	9	71	37	65
Christchurch	36	17	11	8	50	40	62
Wimborne Town	36	17	8	11	68	53	59
Sholing Sports	36	15	12	9	50	45	57
AFC Totton	36	16	8	12	52	37	56
East Cowes Victoria Athletic	36	15	10	11	49	32	55
Bournemouth	36	14	8	14	55	38	50
Thatcham Town	36	14	7	15	50	53	49
Eastleigh	36	13	8	15	36	39	47
Folland Sports	36	13	7	16	42	48	46
Horndean	36	12	9	15	52	58	45
Wellworthy Athletic	36	12	8	16	46	53	44
Portsmouth Royal Navy	36	11	4	21	39	72	37
Steyning Town	36	6	8	22	24	81	26
Brockenhurst	36	2	8	26	23	93	14
Lymington Town	36	0	7	29	27	103	7

Lymington Town and Wellworthy Athletic merged to form AFC Lymington.
Steyning Town moved to the Combined Counties League.

1988-89

Bashley	32	26	4	2	87	24	82
Havant Town	32	21	8	3	67	26	71
Newport (I.O.W.)	32	20	6	6	67	32	66
Thatcham Town	32	17	7	8	60	26	58
AFC Lymington	32	16	9	7	51	32	57
Wimborne Town	32	14	6	12	59	55	48
Romsey Town	32	9	16	7	47	39	43
East Cowes Victoria Athletic	32	11	8	13	44	48	41
Eastleigh	32	10	10	12	39	34	40
Folland Sports	32	10	10	12	46	42	40
Horndean	32	11	5	16	45	70	38
Bournemouth	32	10	6	16	49	64	36
Christchurch	32	9	7	16	40	71	34
AFC Totton	32	8	9	15	39	58	33
Sholing Sports	32	6	6	20	29	65	24
Brockenhurst	32	3	11	18	17	52	20
Portsmouth Royal Navy	32	5	4	23	25	73	19

Bashley moved to the Southern League.
B.A.T. Sports joined from the Hampshire League, Fleet Town joined from the Chiltonian League and Bemerton Heath Harlequins joined as a new club after a merger of three junior clubs: Bemerton Athletic, Moon F.C. and Bemerton Boys.

1989-90

Romsey Town	36	25	6	5	84	31	81
Newport (I.O.W.)	36	24	7	5	82	29	79
B.A.T. Sports	36	21	7	8	74	35	70
Wimborne Town	36	20	8	8	83	48	68
AFC Lymington	36	19	8	9	68	44	65
AFC Totton	36	17	8	11	58	45	59
Thatcham Town	36	15	12	9	56	45	57
Bemerton Heath Harlequins	36	16	8	12	61	47	56
Sholing Sports	36	16	8	12	57	51	56
Bournemouth	36	15	9	12	69	70	54
Havant Town	36	13	8	15	49	50	47
Folland Sports	36	13	6	17	42	47	45
East Cowes Victoria Athletic	36	11	10	15	47	54	43
Eastleigh	36	10	11	15	60	66	41
Christchurch	36	10	9	17	47	59	39
Horndean	36	10	6	20	56	75	36
Brockenhurst	36	5	8	23	35	98	23
Fleet Town	36	5	5	26	22	86	20
Portsmouth Royal Navy	36	4	2	30	38	108	14

Folland Sports changed their name to Aerostructures Sports & Social.
Newport (I.O.W.) moved to the Southern League. Swanage Town & Herston joined from the Western League and Ryde Sports joined from the Hampshire League.

1990-91

Havant Town	38	24	8	6	76	30	80
Swanage Town & Herston	38	24	6	8	88	41	78
Bournemouth	38	24	4	10	69	33	76
Romsey Town	38	20	11	7	59	35	71
Wimborne Town	38	22	4	12	80	45	70
Thatcham Town	38	19	11	8	68	32	68
Brockenhurst	38	17	8	13	56	51	59
B.A.T. Sports	38	16	10	12	54	48	58
AFC Lymington	38	16	9	13	60	50	57
Fleet Town	38	17	6	15	64	57	57
Ryde Sports	38	17	6	15	62	55	57
Eastleigh	38	13	8	17	40	62	47
East Cowes Victoria Athletic	38	12	10	16	45	52	46
AFC Totton	38	13	6	19	54	70	45
Christchurch	38	11	10	17	37	55	43
Aerostructures Sports & Social	38	11	6	21	32	62	39
Portsmouth Royal Navy	38	10	5	23	51	102	35
Bemerton Heath Harlequins	38	7	11	20	42	59	32
Sholing Sports	38	6	8	24	39	84	26
Horndean	38	5	5	28	39	92	20

Havant Town moved to the Southern League.

1991-92

Wimborne Town	36	25	5	6	82	37	80
AFC Lymington	36	23	5	8	73	39	74
Thatcham Town	36	22	4	10	85	45	70
Romsey Town	36	21	6	9	72	42	69
Swanage Town & Herston	36	20	7	9	78	38	67
Bournemouth	36	20	6	10	73	48	66
Ryde Sports	36	18	8	10	61	51	62
Bemerton Heath Harlequins	36	17	10	9	51	38	61
Aerostructures Sports & Social	36	18	5	13	59	40	59
Eastleigh	36	18	4	14	61	53	58
Fleet Town	36	13	10	13	59	55	49
Brockenhurst	36	12	9	15	47	52	45
Christchurch	36	9	11	16	39	54	38
East Cowes Victoria Athletic	36	9	9	18	36	72	36
Sholing Sports	36	9	7	20	43	81	34
B.A.T. Sports	36	9	4	23	41	57	31
AFC Totton	36	7	8	21	43	71	29
Horndean	36	5	3	28	33	109	18
Portsmouth Royal Navy	36	4	5	27	30	84	17

Gosport Borough joined from the Southern League and Whitchurch United joined from the Hampshire League.

1992-93

AFC Lymington	40	30	7	3	111	27	97
Wimborne Town	40	30	5	5	101	27	95
Bemerton Heath Harlequins	40	27	7	6	77	33	88
Thatcham Town	40	24	10	6	104	45	82
Gosport Borough	40	20	12	8	83	48	72
Ryde Sports	40	21	4	15	79	61	67
Bournemouth	40	18	11	11	83	58	65
Fleet Town	40	17	10	13	79	51	61
Eastleigh	40	17	9	14	68	54	60
Brockenhurst	40	17	7	16	60	56	58
Horndean	40	15	9	16	63	66	54
Aerostructures Sports & Social	40	13	14	13	55	57	53
Christchurch	40	14	7	19	60	73	49
Swanage Town & Herston	40	11	11	18	65	78	44
Whitchurch United	40	12	6	22	57	80	42
AFC Totton	40	12	6	22	56	82	42
Portsmouth Royal Navy	40	10	10	20	52	83	40
B.A.T. Sports	40	9	9	22	59	83	36
Sholing Sports	40	7	10	23	46	94	31
East Cowes Victoria Athletic	40	8	4	28	52	106	28
Romsey Town	40	3	2	35	20	168	11

Romsey Town moved to the Hampshire League. Andover joined from the Southern League, Downton joined from the Hampshire League and Petersfield Town joined as a new club after Petersfield United had disbanded and resigned from the Isthmian League.

1993-94

Wimborne Town	42	34	5	3	126	41	107
Andover	42	27	8	7	137	48	89
AFC Lymington	42	27	5	10	83	33	86
Thatcham Town	42	25	7	10	96	51	82
Gosport Borough	42	23	10	9	87	55	79
Fleet Town	42	21	9	12	82	48	72
Bemerton Heath Harlequins	42	19	11	12	72	56	68
Brockenhurst	42	17	12	13	70	64	63
B.A.T. Sports	42	17	10	15	66	66	61
Christchurch	42	15	13	14	55	58	58
Bournemouth	42	16	6	20	67	78	54
Ryde Sports	42	14	10	18	61	77	52
Portsmouth Royal Navy	42	13	10	19	59	78	49
East Cowes Victoria Athletic	42	14	7	21	78	114	49
Eastleigh	42	12	12	18	47	54	48
Downton	42	12	10	20	59	82	46
Horndean	42	13	6	23	56	95	45
Petersfield Town	42	11	7	24	64	96	40
Aerostructures Sports & Social	42	11	6	25	41	84	39
Swanage Town & Herston	42	10	7	25	53	89	37
AFC Totton	42	9	9	24	43	90	36
Whitchurch United	42	11	2	29	51	96	35

Sholing Sports resigned because of ground problems after playing just one game. Whitchurch United moved to the Hampshire League. Cowes Sports joined from the Hampshire League.

1994-95

Fleet Town	42	32	4	6	116	42	100
Bournemouth	42	31	5	6	109	33	98
Thatcham Town	42	29	9	4	105	44	96
Bemerton Heath Harlequins	42	24	8	10	75	48	80
Wimborne Town	42	21	15	6	100	53	78
Brockenhurst	42	24	4	14	87	59	76
Andover	42	23	5	14	122	69	74
AFC Lymington	42	17	10	15	85	67	61
AFC Totton	42	18	6	18	69	70	60
Gosport Borough	42	17	7	18	85	64	58
Portsmouth Royal Navy	42	16	8	18	65	66	56
Ryde Sports	42	16	6	20	81	88	54
B.A.T. Sports	42	15	8	19	62	82	53
Eastleigh	42	14	9	19	66	73	51
Cowes Sports	42	14	8	20	61	87	50
East Cowes Victoria Athletic	42	13	10	19	65	72	49
Aerostructures Sports & Social	42	12	10	20	62	79	46
Christchurch	42	12	8	22	58	95	44
Swanage Town & Herston	42	10	6	26	49	115	36
Downton	42	7	11	24	45	85	32
Petersfield Town	42	8	5	29	59	163	29
Horndean	42	6	4	32	49	121	22

Fleet Town moved to the Southern League and Horndean moved to the Hampshire League. Whitchurch United joined from the Hampshire League.

1995-96

Thatcham Town	40	28	8	4	73	27	92
AFC Lymington	40	28	7	5	100	31	91
Ryde Sports	40	25	8	7	92	41	83
Eastleigh	40	21	13	6	83	50	76
Christchurch	40	21	8	11	66	49	71
Wimborne Town	40	20	6	14	85	61	66
Bournemouth	40	17	13	10	85	40	64
Bemerton Heath Harlequins	40	18	8	14	67	63	62
Andover	40	18	7	15	101	70	61
East Cowes Victoria Athletic	40	17	8	15	60	60	59
Gosport Borough	40	16	9	15	59	58	57
Downton	40	16	6	18	65	73	54
Whitchurch United	40	12	13	15	66	76	49
AFC Totton	40	10	13	17	55	66	43
B.A.T. Sports	40	10	12	18	44	58	42
Cowes Sports	40	11	7	22	38	76	40
Portsmouth Royal Navy	40	10	8	22	52	84	38
Aerostructures Sports & Social	40	9	10	21	41	71	37
Brockenhurst	40	11	4	25	42	74	37
Petersfield Town	40	8	4	28	53	93	28
Swanage Town & Herston	40	6	4	30	32	138	22

Swanage Town & Herston moved to the Dorset Combination. Romsey Town joined from the Hampshire League.

1996-97

AFC Lymington	40	35	5	0	112	22	110
Wimborne Town	40	26	7	7	97	42	85
Thatcham Town	40	26	5	9	91	45	79
Ryde Sports	40	25	4	11	77	50	79
Bemerton Heath Harlequins	40	23	9	8	69	45	78
Andover	40	19	12	9	80	42	69
Eastleigh	40	19	8	13	71	56	65
Downton	40	18	7	15	72	70	61
Cowes Sports	40	15	14	11	65	55	59
Portsmouth Royal Navy	40	16	4	20	65	79	52
Gosport Borough	40	15	5	20	56	66	50
Aerostructures Sports & Social	40	13	9	18	45	66	48
Bournemouth	40	14	5	21	50	72	47
Brockenhurst	40	13	7	20	54	73	46
Whitchurch United	40	12	7	21	58	81	43
Christchurch	40	13	4	23	49	72	43
East Cowes Victoria Athletic	40	10	7	23	53	72	37
Romsey Town	40	10	7	23	52	94	37
B.A.T. Sports	40	8	9	23	43	74	33
AFC Totton	40	8	8	24	54	87	32
Petersfield Town	40	8	5	27	42	92	29

Thatcham Town had 4 points deducted.
Petersfield Town moved to the Hampshire League.
AFC Newbury joined from the Hampshire League.

1997-98

AFC Lymington	38	29	5	4	94	27	92
Andover	38	24	9	5	99	46	81
AFC Newbury	38	22	7	9	72	35	73
Eastleigh	38	20	11	7	74	31	71
Bemerton Heath Harlequins	38	19	11	8	69	38	68
Cowes Sports	38	20	6	12	67	51	66
Wimborne Town	38	18	9	11	89	63	63
AFC Totton	38	15	10	13	58	41	55
Bournemouth	38	16	7	15	64	68	55
Thatcham Town	38	16	6	16	64	54	54
Christchurch	38	15	6	17	55	69	51
East Cowes Victoria Athletic	38	13	11	14	46	42	50
Portsmouth Royal Navy	38	13	7	18	64	79	46
B.A.T. Sports	38	12	7	19	60	82	43
Gosport Borough	38	9	10	19	48	65	37
Aerostructures Sports & Social	38	9	10	19	50	77	37
Brockenhurst	38	9	9	20	43	83	36
Downton	38	7	10	21	36	66	31
Whitchurch United	38	7	8	23	37	78	29
Romsey Town	38	5	5	28	40	134	20

Ryde Sports resigned and their record at the time was deleted:

	17	0	2	15	16	69	2

AFC Lymington merged with New Milton Town of Division Two of the Hampshire League to form Lymington & New Milton. Aerostructures Sports & Social changed their name to Hamble Aerostructures Sports & Social Club. Andover moved to the Southern League and Romsey Town moved to the Hampshire League. Fareham Town joined from the Southern League and Moneyfields joined from the Hampshire League.

1998-99

Lymington & New Milton	38	27	6	5	92	31	87
Thatcham Town	38	23	9	6	92	46	78
AFC Newbury	38	22	11	5	81	39	77
Eastleigh	38	22	8	8	69	43	74
Christchurch	38	22	7	9	72	53	73
Wimborne Town	38	18	14	6	81	34	68
Cowes Sports	38	19	8	11	77	54	65
Moneyfields	38	17	8	13	69	62	59
AFC Totton	38	15	10	13	60	50	55
Bemerton Heath Harlequins	38	17	4	17	59	54	55
Brockenhurst	38	14	7	17	52	61	49
Bournemouth	38	12	10	16	46	63	46
Fareham Town	38	11	12	15	58	67	45
Gosport Borough	38	11	11	16	66	71	44
B.A.T. Sports	38	10	13	15	55	65	43
East Cowes Victoria Athletic	38	10	4	24	48	103	34
Hamble Aerostructures S.S.C.	38	6	9	23	37	68	27
Portsmouth Royal Navy	38	6	9	23	42	81	27
Whitchurch United	38	5	11	22	36	76	26
Downton	38	4	7	27	40	111	19

Andover joined from the Southern League.

1999-2000

Wimborne Town	40	32	4	4	126	33	100
Lymington & New Milton	40	31	7	2	115	27	100
Andover	40	25	7	8	147	60	82
AFC Totton	40	24	8	8	93	30	80
B.A.T. Sports	40	24	8	8	88	48	80
Moneyfields	40	22	9	9	76	64	75
Eastleigh	40	20	8	12	67	46	68
AFC Newbury	40	17	12	11	67	51	63
Cowes Sports	40	17	11	12	73	55	62
Bemerton Heath Harlequins	40	17	9	14	75	66	60
Fareham Town	40	14	14	12	72	71	56
Christchurch	40	16	7	17	68	67	55
Thatcham Town	40	15	7	18	62	69	52
Gosport Borough	40	8	12	20	40	70	36
Downton	40	10	6	24	74	113	36
Hamble Aerostructures S.S.C.	40	7	11	22	44	89	32
Whitchurch United	40	7	10	23	53	89	31
Brockenhurst	40	7	7	26	43	114	28
Bournemouth	40	7	8	25	54	110	27
Portsmouth Royal Navy	40	5	10	25	47	114	25
East Cowes Victoria Athletic	40	5	5	30	43	141	20

Bournemouth had 2 points deducted.
East Cowes Victoria Athletic moved to the Hampshire League.
Fleet Town joined from the Southern League, Swanage Town & Herston joined from the Dorset Combination and Blackfield & Langley joined from the Hampshire League.

2000-01

Andover	44	37	5	2	153	33	116
Lymington & New Milton	44	34	6	4	106	29	108
Wimborne Town	44	28	9	7	111	52	93
Fleet Town	44	29	3	12	91	56	90
AFC Totton	44	26	9	9	87	47	87
Thatcham Town	44	24	9	11	81	58	81
Eastleigh	44	23	10	11	87	48	79
Gosport Borough	44	23	8	13	74	44	77
Brockenhurst	44	23	7	14	93	72	76
Cowes Sports	44	22	4	18	80	70	70
Bemerton Heath Harlequins	44	15	9	20	63	70	54
AFC Newbury	44	15	8	21	71	78	53
B.A.T. Sports	44	14	10	20	52	75	52
Bournemouth	44	13	12	19	51	65	51
Fareham Town	44	12	10	22	48	74	46
Moneyfields	44	12	9	23	52	76	45
Christchurch	44	11	12	21	55	80	45
Hamble Aerostructures S.S.C.	44	10	14	20	39	70	44
Whitchurch United	44	8	13	23	37	72	37
Swanage Town & Herston	44	11	4	29	52	123	37
Blackfield & Langley	44	7	8	29	32	95	29
Downton	44	6	8	30	45	103	26
Portsmouth Royal Navy	44	4	11	29	37	107	23

Portsmouth Royal Navy moved to the Hampshire League.
Portland United joined from the Dorset Combination.

2001-02

Andover	44	30	6	8	138	53	96
Fleet Town	44	29	9	6	107	59	95
AFC Totton	44	29	7	8	104	50	94
Gosport Borough	44	26	11	7	101	41	89
Lymington & New Milton	44	26	6	12	94	47	84
Brockenhurst	44	27	2	15	99	57	83
AFC Newbury	44	22	12	10	87	51	78
Wimborne Town	44	21	14	9	82	53	77
Moneyfields	44	23	7	14	98	64	76
Fareham Town	44	21	13	10	72	54	76
Bemerton Heath Harlequins	44	18	11	15	103	84	65
Thatcham Town	44	19	8	17	94	77	65
Eastleigh	44	18	9	17	91	71	63
Portland United	44	17	8	19	81	66	59
Christchurch	44	16	7	21	61	80	55
Cowes Sports	44	15	9	20	66	73	54
Blackfield & Langley	44	16	5	23	82	121	53
Bournemouth	44	14	7	23	61	84	49
B.A.T. Sports	44	13	8	23	46	67	47
Whitchurch United	44	5	5	34	27	116	20
Downton	44	5	4	35	42	139	19
Hamble Aerostructures S.S.C.	44	4	4	36	33	119	16
Swanage Town & Herston	44	3	6	35	31	174	15

Fleet Town had 1 point deducted. Fleet Town moved to the Southern League and Swanage Town & Herston moved to the Dorset Combination. Alton Town joined from the Hampshire League.

2002-03

Eastleigh	42	32	7	3	115	32	103
Gosport Borough	42	27	7	8	94	43	88
AFC Totton	42	27	6	9	96	47	87
Wimborne Town	42	26	7	9	113	44	85
Fareham Town	42	22	10	10	78	47	76
Lymington & New Milton	42	22	8	12	89	56	74
Andover	42	22	7	13	95	63	73
Portland United	42	20	8	14	81	62	68
Thatcham Town	42	18	13	11	68	58	67
Moneyfields	42	18	6	18	73	68	60
B.A.T. Sports	42	18	6	18	57	65	60
AFC Newbury	42	17	6	19	77	72	57
Christchurch	42	15	10	17	58	68	55
Bournemouth	42	15	9	18	57	67	54
Cowes Sports	42	13	13	16	57	55	52
Hamble Aerostructures S.S.C.	42	13	12	17	58	60	51
Alton Town	42	14	9	19	71	80	51
Bemerton Heath Harlequins	42	13	5	24	59	83	44
Downton	42	10	7	25	41	105	37
Brockenhurst	42	7	5	30	50	118	26
Blackfield & Langley	42	4	6	32	37	134	18
Whitchurch United	42	4	3	35	27	124	15

Eastleigh moved to the Southern League and Winchester City joined from the Hampshire League.

2003-04

Winchester City	42	35	3	4	151	35	108
Wimborne Town	42	31	6	5	105	45	99
Gosport Borough	42	29	5	8	96	40	92
Lymington & New Milton	42	29	3	10	98	38	90
AFC Newbury	42	26	4	12	94	53	82
Andover	42	25	4	13	100	65	79
Fareham Town	42	24	6	12	71	38	78
AFC Totton	42	18	10	14	76	55	64
Brockenhurst	42	19	7	16	49	74	64
Thatcham Town	42	16	10	16	70	72	58
Christchurch	42	17	6	19	63	62	57
Bemerton Heath Harlequins	42	16	7	19	77	79	55
Hamble Aerostructures S.S.C.	42	16	7	19	51	76	55
Cowes Sports	42	15	8	19	51	59	53
B.A.T. Sports	42	13	7	22	57	68	46
Portland United	42	14	4	24	58	86	46
Moneyfields	42	11	8	23	51	83	41
Alton Town	42	12	2	28	55	110	38
Downton	42	8	7	27	43	106	31
Bournemouth	42	8	6	28	41	86	30
Blackfield & Langley	42	7	7	28	51	99	28
Whitchurch United	42	7	5	30	38	117	26

VTFC (ex-Hampshire League Premier Division) and Hamworthy United (ex-Dorset Premier League) joined.

The League added a third division by absorbing the Hampshire League. The existing clubs formed Division One except for Blackfield & Langley and Whitchurch United who went into the new Division Two which also included the other 17 clubs from the Hampshire League Premier Division:
AFC Aldermaston, Amesbury Town, Andover New Street, Bishops Waltham Town, Brading Town, East Cowes Victoria Athletic, Fawley, Horndean, Hythe & Dibden, Liss Athletic, Locks Heath, Lymington Town, Petersfield Town, Poole Town, Ringwood Town, Stockbridge and United Services Portsmouth (ex-Portsmouth Royal Navy); plus Alresford Town (Hampshire League Division One), Romsey Town (Hampshire League Division Two) and Shaftesbury (Dorset Premier League).
Division Three was formed by the other 13 members of the Hampshire League Division One and 9 from Division Two. From Division One: AFC Portchester, Clanfield, Colden Common, Farnborough North End, Fleet Spurs, Fleetlands, Hayling United, Laverstock & Ford, Micheldever, Overton United, Paulsgrove, Tadley Calleva and Verwood Town. From Division Two: Dave Coleman, Hamble Club, Ludgershall Sports, Netley Central Sports, Ordnance Survey, Otterbourne, QK Southampton, RS Basingstoke and Yateley Green. The remaining 5 clubs from the Hampshire League Division Two: Broughton, Durley, East Lodge, M & T Awbridge and Mottisfont, helped form a new Hampshire League for 2004-05.

2004-05

Division One

Lymington & New Milton	42	31	6	5	123	41	99
Winchester City	42	31	4	7	134	38	97
Thatcham Town	42	24	13	5	95	51	85
Gosport Borough	42	25	9	8	75	49	84
Andover	42	24	8	10	100	67	80
AFC Newbury	42	23	8	11	80	45	77
Wimborne Town	42	20	12	10	82	53	72
AFC Totton	42	19	10	13	69	59	67
B.A.T. Sports	42	17	12	13	63	60	63
Moneyfields	42	14	14	14	62	57	56
Bournemouth	42	16	8	18	54	65	56
VTFC	42	16	7	19	69	80	55
Cowes Sports	42	16	6	20	70	69	54
Bemerton Heath Harlequins	42	15	6	21	64	72	51
Hamworthy United	42	14	9	19	51	72	51
Fareham Town	42	13	9	20	50	63	46
Christchurch	42	12	8	22	64	80	44
Brockenhurst	42	12	5	25	52	79	41
Alton Town	42	9	10	23	50	90	37
Portland United	42	8	6	28	35	104	30
Hamble Aerostructures S.S.C.	42	6	7	29	36	121	25
Downton	42	7	3	32	50	113	24

Fareham Town had 2 points deducted.
Lymington & New Milton moved to the Isthmian League Division One.

Division Two

Lymington Town	42	35	3	4	121	28	108
Poole Town	42	33	4	5	123	29	103
Locks Heath	42	24	10	8	79	43	82
Romsey Town	42	23	8	11	84	55	77
Petersfield Town	42	21	10	11	77	49	73
Liss Athletic	42	21	8	13	106	77	71
Blackfield & Langley	42	20	9	13	89	61	69
Stockbridge	42	19	9	14	91	71	66
Horndean	42	18	12	12	85	76	66
Alresford Town	42	20	4	18	85	74	64
Ringwood Town	42	20	3	19	89	84	63
Whitchurch United	42	17	5	20	72	77	56
Shaftesbury	42	15	9	18	65	85	54
Hythe & Dibden	42	15	7	20	75	105	52
Amesbury Town	42	14	7	21	76	99	49
Brading Town	42	13	8	21	75	84	46
East Cowes Victoria Athletic	42	12	9	21	71	85	45
Andover New Street	42	12	6	24	45	100	42
United Services Portsmouth	42	9	6	27	58	103	33
Bishops Waltham Town	42	7	12	23	46	104	33
Fawley	42	9	4	29	54	111	31
AFC Aldermaston	42	7	3	32	50	116	24

Division Three

Colden Common	38	28	4	6	123	39	88
Hayling United	38	26	8	4	104	30	86
Farnborough North End	38	26	7	5	111	38	85
Fleetlands	38	23	6	9	115	42	75
Paulsgrove	38	22	7	9	93	46	73
Otterbourne	38	23	3	12	88	36	72
Overton United	38	22	6	10	88	52	72
Tadley Calleva	38	21	7	10	84	43	69
Micheldever	38	18	11	9	82	49	65
Clanfield	38	16	12	10	72	70	60
Laverstock & Ford	38	14	10	14	73	59	52
Netley Central Sports	38	13	7	18	71	66	46
Ordnance Survey	38	11	9	18	44	55	42
AFC Portchester	38	11	6	21	65	83	39
Hamble Club	38	9	11	18	51	86	38
Verwood Town	38	8	6	24	54	95	46
Fleet Spurs	38	6	11	21	59	98	29
Ludgershall Sports	38	7	3	28	48	118	24
QK Southampton	38	4	4	30	41	178	16
Yateley Green	38	2	2	34	30	213	8

Tadley Calleva had 1 point deducted.
Dave Coleman resigned and their record at the time was deleted:

7	3	0	4	12	24	9

RS Basingstoke resigned and their record at the time was deleted:

21	4	7	10	24	51	19

Ludgershall Sports moved to the Hampshire League and Yateley Green also left.

2005-06

Division One

Winchester City	42	34	5	3	112	31	107
Thatcham Town	42	29	7	6	92	37	94
Andover	42	27	5	10	120	64	86
AFC Totton	42	25	9	8	101	40	84
Gosport Borough	42	23	10	9	85	44	79
Hamworthy United	42	21	12	9	65	40	75
Bournemouth	42	21	10	11	72	45	73
Poole Town	42	21	8	13	79	60	71
Fareham Town	42	19	10	13	74	61	67
Christchurch	42	17	9	16	72	62	60
Moneyfields	42	14	16	12	48	49	58
Wimborne Town	42	15	10	17	60	61	55
VTFC	42	13	15	14	65	66	54
Bemerton Heath Harlequins	42	14	8	20	70	86	50
Hamble Aerostructures S.S.C.	42	14	7	21	50	56	49
Cowes Sports	42	12	10	20	48	67	46
Lymington Town	42	10	14	18	42	71	44
B.A.T. Sports	42	10	6	26	61	109	36
AFC Newbury	42	9	8	25	35	96	35
Alton Town	42	8	9	25	51	99	33
Brockenhurst	42	4	6	32	42	93	18
Portland United	42	2	6	34	32	139	12

B.A.T. Sports and AFC Newbury were relegated to Division Two (formerly Division Three).
Winchester City, Thatcham Town and Andover moved to the Southern League and Portland United moved to the Dorset Premier League.

Division Two

Locks Heath	42	31	5	6	96	28	98
Hayling United	42	27	8	7	99	39	89
Brading Town	42	27	7	8	96	50	88
Downton	42	27	6	9	108	64	87
Liss Athletic	42	26	5	11	99	57	83
Horndean	42	22	6	14	95	67	72
Fawley	42	20	9	13	76	53	69
Stockbridge	42	18	13	11	82	52	67
Ringwood Town	42	20	6	16	81	71	66
United Services Portsmouth	42	18	11	13	86	72	65
Farnborough North End	42	19	6	17	93	76	63
East Cowes Victoria Athletic	42	16	10	16	76	70	58
Romsey Town	42	15	11	16	59	61	56
Blackfield & Langley	42	14	13	15	81	69	55
Petersfield Town	42	12	8	22	58	91	44
Shaftesbury	42	10	10	22	53	96	46
Hythe & Dibden	42	11	7	24	50	98	40
Andover New Street	42	10	9	23	61	96	39
Amesbury Town	42	10	4	28	55	109	34
Alresford Town	42	8	9	25	49	86	33
Bishops Waltham Town	42	7	7	28	57	112	28
Whitchurch United	42	5	8	29	44	137	23

Warminster Town joined from the Wiltshire League.

Division Three

Paulsgrove	30	20	6	4	91	34	66
Laverstock & Ford	30	19	6	5	62	37	63
Verwood Town	30	19	3	8	73	42	60
Colden Common	30	17	5	8	86	45	56
Netley Central Sports	30	16	5	9	62	41	53
Fleetlands	30	15	7	8	59	36	52
Tadley Calleva	30	16	4	10	52	40	52
Otterbourne	30	14	6	10	56	45	48
AFC Aldermaston	30	12	5	13	64	68	41
Overton United	30	11	7	12	54	53	40
AFC Portchester	30	11	4	15	57	61	37
Ordnance Survey	30	10	6	14	69	68	36
Clanfield	30	11	3	16	56	62	36
Fleet Spurs	30	8	3	19	60	75	27
QK Southampton	30	2	3	25	24	123	9
Hamble Club	30	1	3	26	17	112	6

Micheldever resigned and their record at the time was deleted:

23	3	1	19	24	102	10

Ordnance Survey changed their name to Stoneham. Netley Central Sports left and joined the Hampshire League. Wellow joined from the Southampton League.

2006-07

Divisions were renamed to Premier, One and Two

Premier Division

Gosport Borough	38	27	8	3	87	27	89
AFC Totton	38	27	8	3	89	31	89
VTFC	38	24	8	6	76	44	80
Poole Town	38	23	4	11	88	41	73
Bournemouth	38	20	10	8	69	38	70
Wimborne Town	38	19	10	9	82	54	67
Moneyfields	38	21	3	14	69	46	66
Fareham Town	38	18	12	8	95	57	65
Cowes Sports	38	17	9	12	61	50	60
Brading Town	38	15	7	16	74	80	52
Bemerton Heath Harlequins	38	13	9	16	55	73	48
Lymington Town	38	13	8	17	49	48	47
Brockenhurst	38	10	11	17	52	66	41
Christchurch	38	9	10	19	47	63	37
Hamworthy United	38	9	10	19	49	70	37
Horndean	38	11	1	26	51	104	34
Alton Town	38	9	7	22	59	87	33
Downton	38	7	10	21	48	89	31
Ringwood Town	38	5	8	25	34	85	23
Hamble Aerostructures S.S.C.	38	5	3	30	24	105	18

Fareham Town and Alton Town each had 1 point deducted.
Gosport Borough were promoted to the Southern League from which Lymington & New Milton were relegated, changing their name to New Milton Town.

Division One

Hayling United	36	27	4	5	116	32	85
Alresford Town	36	23	8	5	53	28	77
Romsey Town	36	22	6	8	68	36	72
Locks Heath	36	21	7	8	78	40	70
Fawley	36	18	7	11	78	57	61
Verwood Town	36	17	9	10	73	46	60
Stockbridge	36	17	8	11	64	54	59
Warminster Town	36	16	9	11	63	48	57
Shaftesbury	36	15	9	12	58	47	54
United Services Portsmouth	36	12	10	14	76	68	46
Farnborough North End	36	11	13	12	40	56	46
Laverstock & Ford	36	12	9	15	55	65	45
Liss Athletic	36	11	10	15	59	73	42
Hythe & Dibden	36	9	9	18	54	81	36
East Cowes Victoria Athletic	36	10	6	20	49	101	36
Blackfield & Langley	36	9	5	22	66	104	32
Petersfield Town	36	7	6	23	50	98	27
Amesbury Town	36	5	10	21	57	78	25
Andover New Street	36	5	5	26	37	82	20

Liss Athletic had 1 point deducted.

Division Two

Fleetlands	30	25	2	3	101	18	77
Tadley Calleva	30	23	5	2	103	33	74
Wellow	30	19	6	5	77	36	63
AFC Portchester	30	16	4	10	68	45	52
B.A.T. Sports	30	15	6	9	61	49	51
Otterbourne	30	15	6	9	60	50	51
Overton United	30	14	6	10	66	55	48
Paulsgrove	30	14	3	13	69	63	45
Clanfield	30	10	7	13	60	59	37
Colden Common	30	11	3	16	66	76	36
Fleet Spurs	30	10	5	15	55	58	35
Whitchurch United	30	10	4	16	48	61	34
AFC Aldermaston	30	10	4	16	61	78	34
Stoneham	30	9	6	15	51	76	33
Hamble Club	30	1	4	25	29	130	7
QK Southampton	30	0	5	25	18	106	5

AFC Newbury resigned and their record at the time was deleted:

7	2	1	4	7	23	7

Bishops Waltham Town resigned and their record was deleted:

7	1	0	6	4	28	3

BAT Sports changed their name to Totton & Eling, Stoneham changed their name to AFC Stoneham and Wellow left. Division Two was reformed as the Hampshire Premier League for 2007-08. As well as the 9 remaining clubs and Bishops Waltham Town who rejoined, there were 7 new members: Headley United (ex-Aldershot & District League), Ludwig Leisure (Basingstoke), Lyndhurst STJS, Sporting BTC and Winchester Castle, (all ex-Hampshire League), Team Solent (ex-Southampton League) and relegated Locks Heath.

2007-08

Premier Division

Club	P	W	D	L	F	A	Pts
AFC Totton	44	33	7	4	120	39	106
VTFC	44	32	6	6	106	35	102
Wimborne Town	44	30	6	8	125	33	96
Poole Town	44	29	9	6	120	35	96
Bournemouth	44	27	12	5	92	40	93
Brockenhurst	44	23	11	10	87	55	80
Moneyfields	44	24	7	13	82	45	79
Fareham Town	44	22	9	13	87	65	75
Cowes Sports	44	20	13	11	91	59	73
Hamworthy United	44	19	8	17	55	54	65
Horndean	44	15	13	16	76	73	58
Hayling United	44	15	9	20	66	101	54
Bemerton Heath Harlequins	44	15	8	21	74	101	53
Alton Town	44	15	7	22	66	89	52
Brading Town	44	13	12	19	67	85	51
Christchurch	44	15	5	24	67	80	50
Hamble Aerostructures S.S.C.	44	11	14	19	47	72	47
Romsey Town	44	12	7	25	68	98	43
New Milton Town	44	11	8	25	58	88	41
Lymington Town	44	11	7	26	63	103	39
Alresford Town	44	9	8	27	48	88	35
Ringwood Town	44	5	9	30	45	124	24
Downton	44	1	3	40	29	177	6

Lymington Town had 1 point deducted.

Division One

Club	P	W	D	L	F	A	Pts
Tadley Calleva	40	33	3	4	134	45	102
Laverstock & Ford	40	29	3	8	124	59	90
Farnborough North End	40	26	9	5	101	30	87
Verwood Town	40	23	6	11	94	63	75
Totton & Eling	40	22	8	10	80	50	74
Fawley	40	22	5	13	94	44	71
Warminster Town	40	20	11	9	89	48	71
Petersfield Town	40	21	7	12	90	53	70
United Services Portsmouth	40	21	6	13	98	65	69
Blackfield & Langley	40	18	10	12	70	57	64
Amesbury Town	40	16	5	19	100	86	53
Shaftesbury	40	14	9	17	73	63	51
Stockbridge	40	11	12	17	47	61	45
Fleet Spurs	40	12	6	22	64	95	42
AFC Portchester	40	11	9	20	59	86	42
Liss Athletic	40	8	10	22	58	95	34
Whitchurch United	40	8	10	22	51	97	34
East Cowes Victoria Athletic	40	8	10	22	50	103	34
Andover New Street	40	9	5	26	54	117	32
Hythe & Dibden	40	6	9	25	42	125	27
AFC Aldermaston	40	4	3	33	31	161	15

Hampshire Premier League

Club	P	W	D	L	F	A	Pts
AFC Stoneham	32	25	3	4	102	42	78
Otterbourne	32	24	5	3	87	28	77
Clanfield	32	22	2	8	93	43	68
Paulsgrove	32	19	5	8	93	43	62
Locks Heath	32	17	6	9	73	45	57
Fleetlands	32	15	8	9	65	47	53
Team Solent	32	16	2	14	52	57	50
Headley United	32	14	6	12	67	79	48
Sporting BTC	32	11	6	15	39	50	39
QK Southampton	32	11	6	15	40	64	39
Colden Common	32	10	5	17	56	80	35
Lyndhurst STJS	32	10	4	18	46	64	34
Winchester Castle	32	9	4	19	58	81	31
Hamble Club	32	8	7	17	38	74	31
Overton United	32	7	5	20	46	78	26
Bishops Waltham Town	32	8	2	22	33	65	26
Ludwig Leisure (Basingstoke)	32	6	4	22	38	86	22

Fleetlands did not play 3 games so the results were decided by the management committee as follows:
Bishops Waltham Town (H) – Win for Fleetlands
Team Solent (A) – Win for Team Solent
Overton United (A) – Draw.
These results were included in the final table as above but no adjustment was made to the clubs' For and Against goals records.

THE CORINTHIAN LEAGUE

FORMATION

During the Second World War, a number of clubs in the South-East found themselves playing unfamiliar opponents. Some clubs from such competitions as the London League and Spartan League mixed in with more senior clubs from the Isthmian and Athenian Leagues and this experience meant that when normal football resumed in 1945, they wished to play in a higher standard league than previously. The Isthmian and Athenian Leagues still had their full quota of members and so nine of those ambitious clubs – Epsom Town, Erith & Belvedere, Grays Athletic, London Fire Forces, Maidenhead United, Slough United, Twickenham, Walton & Hersham and Windsor & Eton – formed an entirely new competition, the Corinthian League.

In the last pre-war season: Epsom Town and Grays Athletic had been members of the London League, Maidenhead United and Windsor & Eton had been members of the Spartan League and Erith & Belvedere had played in the Kent League.

Walton & Hersham was a new club formed by the 1945 amalgamation of pre-war clubs Hersham, who lost their ground during the war, and Walton-on-Thames. Both of these two clubs had been members of the London League for the cancelled 1939-40 season.

Slough United had been formed in 1943 by the amalgamation of Slough F.C., who were pre-war members of the Spartan League and Slough Centre who had been pre-war members of the Windsor, Slough & District Junior League.

Twickenham had been formed in 1943 and played in the Middlesex Senior League from 1943-45. The final founder member was London Fire Forces who had no regular ground of their own and played all Corinthian League games away.

Some of the published tables contained errors but additional research has succeeded in correcting these.

1945-46

Grays Athletic	16	14	2	0	59	14	30
Slough United	16	13	1	2	54	24	27
Erith & Belvedere	16	9	2	5	50	28	20
Windsor & Eton	16	8	1	7	56	49	17
Maidenhead United	16	7	0	9	43	44	14
Epsom Town	16	6	1	9	28	37	13
Walton & Hersham	16	5	2	9	31	53	12
Twickenham	16	4	1	11	31	67	9
London Fire Forces	16	1	0	15	16	52	2

Epsom Town left after Epsom F.C. (who re-formed in 1945), reclaimed their ground which they had leased to Epsom Town while they were inactive. As they had nowhere to play, Epsom Town disbanded while Epsom F.C. continued in the London League.
Twickenham left after their hopes of ground-sharing at Brentford came to nothing and so they dropped back to the Middlesex Senior League.
London Fire Forces were also asked to resign as they had no ground.
Carshalton Athletic, Edgware Town and Uxbridge joined from the London League, Hounslow Town joined from the Spartan League, Bedford Avenue joined from the United Counties League, Hastings & St. Leonard's and Eastbourne joined from the Southern Amateur League.

1946-47

Walton & Hersham	24	19	2	3	88	35	40
Slough United	24	15	4	5	92	49	34
Windsor & Eton	24	14	4	6	83	49	32
Uxbridge	24	13	4	7	92	53	30
Grays Athletic	24	12	5	7	70	59	29
Erith & Belvedere	24	12	2	10	68	51	26
Hounslow Town	24	9	4	11	57	55	22
Maidenhead United	24	8	5	11	50	67	21
Hastings & St. Leonard's	24	6	7	11	42	68	19
Eastbourne	24	8	2	14	57	80	18
Carshalton Athletic	24	6	6	12	59	91	18
Edgware Town	24	6	2	16	40	76	14
Bedford Avenue	24	4	1	19	51	116	9

Slough United demerged, Slough Town continuing in Slough United's place in the Corinthian League while Slough Centre joined the Spartan League. Chesham United joined from the Spartan League.

1947-48

Walton & Hersham	26	17	4	5	82	40	38
Hounslow Town	26	16	2	8	68	46	34
Erith & Belvedere	26	15	3	8	67	38	33
Carshalton Athletic	26	15	2	9	70	53	32
Grays Athletic	26	13	5	8	68	56	31
Edgware Town	26	12	5	9	55	46	29
Hastings & St. Leonard's	26	12	3	11	72	57	27
Maidenhead United	26	10	5	11	45	52	25
Eastbourne	26	10	4	12	55	68	24
Uxbridge	26	10	3	13	53	62	23
Chesham United	26	6	9	11	48	60	21
Windsor & Eton	26	9	3	14	42	75	21
Slough Town	26	7	4	15	50	51	18
Bedford Avenue	26	4	0	22	35	106	8

Bedford Avenue moved to the Central Amateur League and Worthing joined from the Sussex County League.

1948-49

Walton & Hersham	24	19	1	4	82	32	39
Uxbridge	24	14	5	5	52	36	33
Hounslow Town	24	13	6	5	67	45	32
Erith & Belvedere	24	13	5	6	54	39	31
Grays Athletic	24	12	4	8	73	58	28
Slough Town	24	10	6	8	55	38	26
Worthing	24	7	7	10	49	60	21
Chesham United	24	8	5	11	42	75	21
Maidenhead United	24	8	4	12	34	48	20
Carshalton Athletic	24	7	3	14	48	59	17
Edgware Town	24	4	8	12	35	43	16
Eastbourne	24	6	4	14	49	68	16
Windsor & Eton	24	6	0	18	35	74	12

Hastings & St. Leonard's withdrew after playing one game because of ground difficulties following the formation of the new professional club, Hastings United. Their single game, a 6-0 defeat away to Hounslow Town, was deleted from the table.
Epsom joined from the London League.

1949-50

Hounslow Town	26	19	3	4	86	37	41
Walton & Hersham	26	18	4	4	69	31	40
Erith & Belvedere	26	14	6	6	59	30	34
Uxbridge	26	15	3	8	65	47	33
Worthing	26	12	4	10	57	50	28
Grays Athletic	26	10	8	8	63	62	28
Eastbourne	26	10	7	9	52	46	27
Slough Town	26	10	7	9	46	51	27
Edgware Town	26	10	5	11	50	53	25
Maidenhead United	26	7	8	11	43	46	22
Chesham United	26	7	8	11	53	59	22
Carshalton Athletic	26	8	4	14	56	75	20
Epsom	26	2	5	19	38	95	9
Windsor & Eton	26	3	2	21	34	89	8

Walton & Hersham moved to the Athenian League and Windsor & Eton moved to the Metropolitan League. Tilbury joined from the London League and Maidstone United joined from the Kent League.

1950-51

Slough Town	26	17	4	5	65	33	38
Hounslow Town	26	17	3	6	80	41	37
Erith & Belvedere	26	13	5	8	59	43	31
Edgware Town	26	14	2	10	65	52	30
Maidenhead United	26	13	3	10	57	49	29
Grays Athletic	26	11	5	10	68	54	27
Chesham United	26	11	4	11	69	61	26
Tilbury	26	11	4	11	42	44	26
Uxbridge	26	10	4	12	64	62	24
Worthing	26	11	2	13	52	75	24
Carshalton Athletic	26	8	4	14	65	75	20
Eastbourne	26	8	3	15	47	65	19
Epsom	26	8	2	16	61	94	18
Maidstone United	26	6	3	17	58	104	15

1951-52

Hounslow Town	26	21	1	4	84	28	43
Grays Athletic	26	19	5	2	77	35	43
Slough Town	26	19	3	4	85	37	41
Erith & Belvedere	26	14	1	11	56	50	29
Carshalton Athletic	26	10	7	9	67	59	27
Chesham United	26	12	2	12	64	62	26
Tilbury	26	11	4	11	46	58	26
Eastbourne	26	9	7	10	53	53	25
Epsom	26	9	4	13	45	65	22
Worthing	26	8	6	12	44	68	22
Uxbridge	26	8	5	13	59	58	21
Edgware Town	26	5	5	16	37	60	15
Maidstone United	26	3	7	16	40	80	13
Maidenhead United	26	5	1	20	28	72	11

1952-53

Carshalton Athletic	26	19	1	6	70	44	39
Hounslow Town	26	16	4	6	84	46	36
Epsom	26	16	2	8	72	39	34
Maidstone United	26	14	4	8	58	53	32
Uxbridge	26	12	5	9	40	41	29
Grays Athletic	26	11	6	9	58	47	28
Edgware Town	26	11	6	9	65	54	28
Tilbury	26	10	5	11	46	42	25
Maidenhead United	26	9	5	12	44	50	23
Slough Town	26	7	7	12	39	53	21
Eastbourne	26	7	7	12	40	58	21
Erith & Belvedere	26	8	4	14	43	50	20
Chesham United	26	5	4	17	33	64	14
Worthing	26	6	2	18	29	80	14

1953-54

Carshalton Athletic	26	17	5	4	75	41	39
Edgware Town	26	17	4	5	75	41	38
Hounslow Town	26	13	8	5	75	45	34
Maidstone United	26	13	7	6	60	43	33
Eastbourne	26	11	5	10	47	45	27
Grays Athletic	26	12	2	12	62	50	26
Tilbury	26	10	6	10	60	56	26
Erith & Belvedere	26	10	6	10	45	55	26
Uxbridge	26	11	3	12	45	56	25
Epsom	26	11	1	14	54	64	23
Worthing	26	7	6	13	52	66	20
Maidenhead United	26	7	4	15	46	71	18
Slough Town	26	5	7	14	49	60	17
Chesham United	26	4	4	18	38	90	12

Yiewsley joined from the Delphian League.

1954-55

Hounslow Town	28	22	3	3	80	37	47
Grays Athletic	28	18	3	7	74	41	39
Carshalton Athletic	28	17	4	7	65	38	38
Slough Town	28	12	10	6	58	49	34
Uxbridge	28	11	8	9	62	46	30
Maidenhead United	28	11	6	11	50	63	28
Yiewsley	28	12	3	13	49	46	27
Edgware Town	28	10	7	11	58	60	27
Chesham United	28	12	3	13	56	73	27
Erith & Belvedere	28	10	8	10	57	56	26
Worthing	28	10	4	14	54	62	24
Maidstone United	28	9	5	14	48	50	23
Tilbury	28	9	5	14	47	56	23
Eastbourne	28	3	7	18	24	63	13
Epsom	28	3	6	19	41	83	12

Erith & Belvedere had 2 points deducted.
Hounslow Town moved to the Athenian League.

1955-56

Maidstone United	26	19	3	4	74	37	41
Yiewsley	26	15	5	6	62	31	35
Uxbridge	26	14	5	7	56	34	33
Slough Town	26	14	5	7	59	38	33
Epsom	26	14	3	9	58	42	31
Grays Athletic	26	13	3	10	48	48	29
Maidenhead United	26	12	4	10	56	47	28
Carshalton Athletic	26	12	3	11	50	41	27
Tilbury	26	9	6	11	43	55	24
Edgware Town	26	7	7	12	30	49	21
Worthing	26	7	5	14	57	71	19
Eastbourne	26	6	4	16	29	54	16
Erith & Belvedere	26	6	2	18	32	69	14
Chesham United	26	6	1	19	36	74	13

Carshalton Athletic moved to the Athenian League. Wembley joined from the Delphian League and Dorking joined from the Surrey Senior League.

1956-57

Yiewsley	28	18	6	4	73	35	42
Grays Athletic	28	16	8	4	81	43	40
Maidenhead United	28	17	5	6	88	50	39
Epsom	28	18	2	8	76	37	38
Maidstone United	28	15	6	7	80	40	36
Slough Town	28	12	9	7	63	42	33
Eastbourne	28	12	6	10	67	56	30
Uxbridge	28	12	6	10	54	52	30
Wembley	28	9	8	11	53	55	26
Erith & Belvedere	28	11	3	14	51	66	25
Edgware Town	28	8	5	15	48	72	21
Dorking	28	7	5	16	51	80	19
Tilbury	28	8	3	17	31	78	19
Chesham United	28	4	5	19	38	83	13
Worthing	28	2	5	21	34	99	9

Maidstone United moved to the Athenian League and Tilbury moved to the London League. Dagenham joined from the Delphian League and Horsham joined from the Metropolitan League.

1957-58

Maidenhead United	28	20	3	5	65	39	43
Slough Town	28	18	6	4	72	41	42
Grays Athletic	28	17	6	5	82	28	40
Yiewsley	28	13	8	7	56	36	34
Edgware Town	28	13	5	10	59	54	31
Uxbridge	28	12	7	9	57	53	31
Dagenham	28	11	8	9	38	40	30
Epsom	28	12	5	11	64	60	29
Erith & Belvedere	28	11	2	15	44	57	24
Eastbourne	28	7	9	12	40	50	23
Wembley	28	9	4	15	48	54	22
Chesham United	28	9	4	15	40	50	22
Horsham	28	6	5	17	50	77	17
Dorking	28	4	9	15	37	63	17
Worthing	28	6	3	19	48	98	15

Grays Athletic moved to the Athenian League and Yiewsley moved to the Southern League. Leatherhead joined from the Delphian League.

1958-59

Dagenham	26	19	2	5	70	36	40
Maidenhead United	26	14	7	5	63	38	35
Slough Town	26	14	5	7	75	41	33
Wembley	26	13	4	9	61	44	30
Leatherhead	26	13	4	9	58	54	30
Dorking	26	9	8	9	45	40	26
Uxbridge	26	11	3	12	58	63	25
Edgware Town	26	11	3	12	49	67	25
Horsham	26	9	5	12	66	68	23
Erith & Belvedere	26	8	7	11	43	53	23
Chesham United	26	8	6	12	45	57	22
Epsom	26	8	6	12	44	57	22
Eastbourne	26	5	7	14	28	50	17
Worthing	26	5	3	18	45	82	13

Letchworth Town and Wokingham Town both joined from the Delphian League.

1959-60

Uxbridge	30	20	4	6	72	40	44
Maidenhead United	30	16	6	8	70	40	38
Dorking	30	17	3	10	69	47	37
Epsom	30	17	2	11	70	55	36
Letchworth Town	30	14	6	10	68	62	34
Dagenham	30	13	7	10	50	40	33
Slough Town	30	14	4	12	54	53	32
Horsham	30	13	5	12	68	64	31
Wokingham Town	30	11	7	12	62	51	29
Worthing	30	11	7	12	70	74	29
Erith & Belvedere	30	10	9	11	62	66	29
Leatherhead	30	12	3	15	56	63	27
Chesham United	30	11	4	15	45	60	26
Wembley	30	11	3	16	56	77	25
Eastbourne	30	8	4	18	41	67	20
Edgware Town	30	4	2	24	37	91	10

Epsom merged with Ewell & Stoneleigh F.C. and changed their name to Epsom & Ewell.

1960-61

Maidenhead United	30	19	5	6	65	39	43
Chesham United	30	19	2	9	73	38	40
Edgware Town	30	17	6	7	70	40	40
Dagenham	30	18	3	9	82	55	39
Horsham	30	17	3	10	85	77	37
Uxbridge	30	15	5	10	50	40	35
Worthing	30	14	5	11	85	67	33
Letchworth Town	30	15	3	12	64	66	33
Dorking	30	12	6	12	64	61	30
Erith & Belvedere	30	10	7	13	59	57	27
Eastbourne	30	10	6	14	50	59	26
Epsom & Ewell	30	11	3	16	46	77	25
Leatherhead	30	9	4	17	68	93	22
Wokingham Town	30	8	5	17	44	60	21
Wembley	30	6	6	18	51	80	18
Slough Town	30	4	3	23	48	95	11

1961-62

Maidenhead United	30	23	3	4	77	31	49
Chesham United	30	19	4	7	64	34	42
Horsham	30	18	3	9	88	57	39
Edqware Town	30	15	7	8	47	40	37
Dagenham	30	16	3	11	65	49	35
Uxbridge	30	14	5	11	47	41	33
Erith & Belvedere	30	14	5	11	56	57	33
Slough Town	30	12	5	13	47	49	29
Wokingham Town	30	11	6	13	50	49	28
Leatherhead	30	10	7	13	63	52	27
Letchworth Town	30	8	9	13	55	65	25
Worthing	30	10	5	15	52	67	25
Eastbourne	30	8	6	16	39	57	22
Dorking	30	8	6	16	55	90	22
Epsom & Ewell	30	8	2	20	47	81	18
Wembley	30	7	2	21	40	73	16

1962-63

Leatherhead	30	22	5	3	88	36	49
Erith & Belvedere	30	18	6	6	61	32	42
Wokingham Town	30	18	5	7	53	41	41
Dagenham	30	15	8	7	64	47	38
Uxbridge	30	15	7	8	73	51	37
Letchworth Town	30	16	3	11	75	50	35
Maidenhead United	30	12	9	9	61	46	33
Slough Town	30	12	9	9	62	54	33
Chesham United	30	11	6	13	66	59	28
Worthing	30	12	4	14	63	78	28
Dorking	30	9	6	15	56	70	24
Horsham	30	10	3	17	50	74	23
Edgware Town	30	9	5	16	43	66	23
Eastbourne	30	7	5	18	43	76	19
Epsom & Ewell	30	5	5	20	31	82	15
Wembley	30	4	4	22	46	73	12

The Corinthian League closed as a separate competition in 1963, being absorbed into the Athenian League as its new First Division (second tier). 14 of the Corinthian League's 16 clubs made up the new division, the exceptions being Dagenham and Maidenhead United who moved up to the Athenian League's newly named Premier Division.

THE DELPHIAN LEAGUE

The Delphian League was formed in 1951 on the initiative of Dagenham and of Woodford Town and was aimed at clubs who wanted to play at a higher level than the Spartan League but had been unable to gain entry into the Corinthian League.

The 14 founder members were Aylesbury United, Berkhamsted Town, Bishops Stortford, Brentwood & Warley, Slough Centre, Stevenage Town, Wembley, Willesden and Yiewsley, all of whom joined from the Spartan League; Cheshunt, Rainham Town and Woodford Town, all of whom joined from the London League and Dagenham and Leatherhead, both of whom joined from the Metropolitan League. Some of the published tables contained errors but additional research has succeeded in correcting these.

1951-52

Brentwood & Warley	26	16	4	6	65	37	36
Dagenham	26	16	3	7	68	35	35
Yiewsley	26	14	5	7	70	48	33
Leatherhead	26	14	4	8	51	43	32
Woodford Town	26	12	7	7	59	44	31
Aylesbury United	26	12	6	8	67	40	30
Rainham Town	26	13	3	10	41	43	29
Slough Centre	26	10	6	10	58	61	26
Willesden	26	10	3	13	48	50	23
Bishops Stortford	26	10	3	13	55	80	23
Berkhamsted Town	26	9	3	14	47	58	21
Stevenage Town	26	6	7	13	50	75	19
Cheshunt	26	5	6	15	46	69	16
Wembley	26	2	6	18	30	72	10

Hemel Hempstead and Upminster both joined from the Spartan League, Upminster changing name to Hornchurch & Upminster.

1952-53

Dagenham	30	22	3	5	78	34	47
Aylesbury United	30	18	3	9	70	43	39
Yiewsley	30	14	11	5	62	48	39
Slough Centre	30	16	4	10	60	35	36
Stevenage Town	30	17	2	11	63	51	36
Brentwood & Warley	30	15	5	10	60	50	35
Woodford Town	30	14	6	10	66	52	34
Rainham Town	30	14	3	13	47	41	31
Leatherhead	30	12	7	11	53	59	31
Hornchurch & Upminster	30	12	5	13	48	48	29
Berkhamsted Town	30	11	6	13	57	71	28
Wembley	30	8	7	15	52	58	23
Cheshunt	30	9	4	17	48	66	22
Hemel Hempstead	30	7	3	20	46	77	17
Bishops Stortford	30	6	5	19	47	94	17
Willesden	30	4	8	18	29	59	16

Willesden moved to the Parthenon League.

1953-54

Aylesbury United	28	18	5	5	97	45	41
Dagenham	28	18	4	6	64	35	40
Rainham Town	28	17	6	5	64	40	40
Wembley	28	14	4	10	52	49	32
Slough Centre	28	13	5	10	58	52	31
Bishops Stortford	28	12	4	12	64	56	28
Stevenage Town	28	12	4	12	65	61	28
Woodford Town	28	11	5	12	41	59	27
Yiewsley	28	11	4	13	51	45	26
Brentwood & Warley	28	8	9	11	55	62	25
Berkhamsted Town	28	9	7	12	54	61	25
Cheshunt	28	10	5	13	50	59	25
Hemel Hempstead	28	9	5	14	48	66	23
Hornchurch & Upminster	28	6	6	16	46	72	18
Leatherhead	28	4	3	21	45	92	11

Yiewsley moved to the Corinthian League and Tufnell Park Edmonton joined from the Spartan League.

1954-55

Bishops Stortford	28	22	3	3	98	39	47
Dagenham	28	19	3	6	82	29	41
Aylesbury United	28	18	1	9	77	43	37
Rainham Town	28	16	4	8	66	47	36
Slough Centre	28	15	5	8	62	46	35
Hemel Hempstead	28	14	1	13	56	53	29
Woodford Town	28	11	6	11	55	58	28
Wembley	28	11	4	13	48	40	26
Stevenage Town	28	10	6	12	53	72	26
Tufnell Park Edmonton	28	9	6	13	41	61	24
Leatherhead	28	8	5	15	48	65	21
Hornchurch & Upminster	28	9	3	16	49	68	21
Berkhamsted Town	28	9	3	16	42	70	21
Cheshunt	28	6	3	19	37	76	13
Brentwood & Warley	28	4	5	19	36	83	13

Cheshunt had 2 points deducted for fielding an ineligible player.
Hemel Hempstead changed their name to Hemel Hempstead Town.
Cheshunt moved to the London League and Ware joined from the Spartan League.

1955-56

Team	P	W	D	L	F	A	Pts
Dagenham	28	20	3	5	83	28	43
Wembley	28	18	6	4	72	32	42
Rainham Town	28	18	3	7	71	45	39
Bishops Stortford	28	16	5	7	84	43	37
Aylesbury United	28	14	4	10	57	63	32
Hornchurch & Upminster	28	13	5	10	60	59	31
Hemel Hempstead Town	28	11	8	9	61	56	30
Leatherhead	28	11	5	12	53	63	27
Tufnell Park Edmonton	28	9	7	12	51	59	25
Ware	28	8	9	11	63	73	25
Berkhamsted Town	28	10	3	15	53	72	23
Woodford Town	28	8	7	13	52	74	23
Slough Centre	28	6	6	16	50	68	18
Brentwood & Warley	28	5	3	20	42	80	13
Stevenage Town	28	2	8	18	35	72	12

Stevenage Town merged with Stevenage Rangers to form Stevenage FC. Slough Centre disbanded and Wembley moved to the Corinthian League. Letchworth Town joined from the Spartan League.

1956-57

Team	P	W	D	L	F	A	Pts
Dagenham	26	18	5	3	66	29	41
Rainham Town	26	15	4	7	68	45	34
Brentwood & Warley	26	14	6	6	68	46	34
Aylesbury United	26	11	7	8	55	41	29
Bishops Stortford	26	13	3	10	70	56	29
Ware	26	13	2	11	78	65	28
Letchworth Town	26	12	3	11	57	47	27
Hornchurch & Upminster	26	12	3	11	47	44	27
Leatherhead	26	11	4	11	57	67	26
Hemel Hempstead Town	26	8	6	12	50	56	22
Stevenage	26	6	7	13	39	70	19
Tufnell Park Edmonton	26	5	8	13	40	59	18
Berkhamsted Town	26	6	5	15	35	64	17
Woodford Town	26	5	3	18	43	84	13

Dagenham moved to the Corinthian League. Aveley joined from the London League and Wokingham Town joined from the Metropolitan League.

1957-58

Team	P	W	D	L	F	A	Pts
Letchworth Town	28	22	4	2	96	27	48
Aveley	28	18	4	6	77	46	40
Rainham Town	28	17	5	6	67	45	39
Brentwood & Warley	28	15	5	8	78	47	35
Aylesbury United	28	14	6	8	69	49	34
Leatherhead	28	14	4	10	77	56	32
Hornchurch & Upminster	28	13	5	10	50	38	31
Bishops Stortford	28	12	6	10	62	54	30
Tufnell Park Edmonton	28	11	6	11	44	53	28
Woodford Town	28	8	6	14	44	66	22
Ware	28	8	5	15	41	60	21
Wokingham Town	28	8	5	15	44	69	21
Hemel Hempstead Town	28	6	5	17	30	72	17
Stevenage	28	5	3	20	40	79	13
Berkhamsted Town	28	4	1	23	24	82	9

Leatherhead moved to the Corinthian League and Harrow Town joined from the Spartan League.

1958-59

Team	P	W	D	L	F	A	Pts
Brentwood & Warley	28	21	1	6	74	39	43
Hornchurch & Upminster	28	19	2	7	73	41	40
Woodford Town	28	15	6	7	60	39	36
Harrow Town	28	14	7	7	70	40	35
Bishops Stortford	28	15	5	8	64	50	35
Rainham Town	28	14	5	9	64	41	33
Aylesbury United	28	16	1	11	57	48	33
Aveley	28	13	5	10	58	52	31
Ware	28	10	7	11	52	49	27
Wokingham Town	28	11	2	15	63	54	24
Tufnell Park Edmonton	28	9	5	14	55	50	23
Letchworth Town	28	7	8	13	52	70	22
Hemel Hempstead Town	28	6	5	17	44	77	17
Stevenage	28	5	4	19	39	94	14
Berkhamsted Town	28	3	1	24	30	111	7

Letchworth Town and Wokingham Town both moved to the Corinthian League and Hornchurch & Upminster moved to the Athenian League. Hertford Town joined from the Spartan League.

1959-60

Team	P	W	D	L	F	A	Pts
Brentwood & Warley	24	17	3	4	56	23	37
Hertford Town	24	17	1	6	55	22	35
Harrow Town	24	13	7	4	52	32	33
Bishops Stortford	24	14	3	7	52	35	31
Aylesbury United	24	13	4	7	50	37	30
Woodford Town	24	12	3	9	39	29	27
Rainham Town	24	10	7	7	45	35	27
Aveley	24	8	7	9	41	42	23
Ware	24	8	4	12	38	54	20
Stevenage	24	6	5	13	34	50	17
Tufnell Park Edmonton	24	6	4	14	36	53	16
Hemel Hempstead Town	24	3	3	18	23	63	9
Berkhamsted Town	24	2	3	19	22	68	7

Tufnell Park Edmonton changed name to Edmonton and Stevenage changed name to Stevenage. Windsor & Eton joined from the Metropolitan League and Histon joined from the Spartan League.

1960-61

Team	P	W	D	L	F	A	Pts
Hertford Town	28	20	5	3	65	27	45
Brentwood & Warley	28	21	1	6	86	32	43
Windsor & Eton	28	17	4	7	64	43	38
Hemel Hempstead Town	28	14	5	9	59	44	33
Bishops Stortford	28	14	2	12	67	63	30
Harrow Town	28	12	6	10	65	63	30
Aveley	28	13	3	12	69	55	29
Rainham Town	28	11	4	13	53	46	26
Aylesbury United	28	10	4	14	57	64	24
Histon	28	10	4	14	58	71	24
Ware	28	8	6	14	55	74	22
Edmonton	28	8	5	15	47	64	21
Stevenage Town	28	7	7	14	44	61	21
Woodford Town	28	8	5	15	38	68	21
Berkhamsted Town	28	3	7	18	35	87	13

Woodford Town and Rainham Town both moved to the Metropolitan League. Harlow Town joined from the London League.

1961-62

Team	P	W	D	L	F	A	Pts
Hertford Town	26	18	5	3	84	32	41
Hemel Hempstead Town	26	14	9	3	64	29	37
Bishops Stortford	26	14	6	6	62	36	34
Brentwood & Warley	26	12	8	6	63	55	32
Aylesbury United	26	11	8	7	46	40	30
Windsor & Eton	26	10	7	9	66	53	27
Aveley	26	9	8	9	50	43	26
Edmonton	26	8	9	9	45	43	25
Stevenage Town	26	9	7	10	53	65	25
Berkhamsted Town	26	9	4	13	34	58	22
Ware	26	7	7	12	36	58	21
Harlow Town	26	5	8	13	28	39	18
Harrow Town	26	3	7	16	33	62	13
Histon	26	5	3	18	39	90	13

Tilbury and Wingate both joined from the London League.

1962-63

Table as at 8th March 1963 when the competition was abandoned because the severe winter had caused so many postponements there was no realistic possibility of the league programme being completed.

Team	P	W	D	L	F	A	Pts
Hertford Town	17	13	3	1	61	19	29
Bishops Stortford	17	9	5	3	38	29	23
Aveley	17	8	5	4	34	29	21
Stevenage Town	15	7	4	4	21	24	18
Tilbury	16	6	5	5	32	29	17
Windsor & Eton	17	6	5	6	37	35	17
Edmonton	14	7	2	5	40	20	16
Harlow Town	11	7	1	3	25	7	15
Aylesbury United	14	5	5	4	32	29	15
Hemel Hempstead Town	12	5	3	4	31	18	13
Berkhamsted Town	16	6	1	9	27	25	13
Ware	15	5	2	8	28	33	12
Brentwood & Warley	17	5	1	11	27	49	11
Harrow Town	12	3	3	6	23	32	9
Histon	18	4	1	13	21	67	9
Wingate	16	1	4	11	21	53	6

An Emergency Competition was then organised to decide the league title:

Western Section

Edmonton	7	5	1	1	25	6	11
Windsor & Eton	7	4	2	1	14	10	10
Berkhamsted Town	7	3	3	1	16	12	9
Hemel Hempstead Town	7	3	2	2	13	9	8
Harrow Town	7	4	0	3	11	10	8
Aylesbury United	7	2	0	5	12	21	4
Wingate	7	2	0	5	9	17	4
Stevenage Town	7	0	2	5	8	23	2

Eastern Section

Hertford Town	7	5	1	1	15	4	11
Bishops Stortford	7	5	1	1	13	8	11
Harlow Town	7	4	1	2	14	10	9
Aveley	7	4	0	3	11	11	8
Tilbury	7	2	2	3	13	13	6
Ware	7	1	3	3	13	17	5
Histon	7	1	2	4	7	14	4
Brentwood & Warley	7	0	2	5	7	16	2

Championship Play-Off – First Leg

Hertford Town 1, Edmonton 1

Championship Play-Off – Second Leg

Edmonton 4, Hertford Town 1 (after extra time).

Edmonton won 5-2 on aggregate and were declared champions.

The Delphian League closed as a separate competition in 1963, being absorbed into the Athenian League as its new Second Division (third tier). 15 of the Delphian League's 16 clubs made up the new division, the exception being Stevenage Town who turned professional and joined the Southern League.

EARLY LEAGUES IN THE EAST MIDLANDS

The East Midlands embraced league football very early. In 1888, Derby County and Notts County were founders of the Football League while Long Eaton Rangers, Derby Junction, Derby Midland and Notts Rangers, along with such clubs as Grimsby Town, Small Heath (later Birmingham City) and Newton Heath (later Manchester United) were founders of the Football Combination. This league though failed to complete the season and was replaced in 1889-90 by the Football Alliance (see page 4 of this book).

However, the Alliance began operations with only 12 members, whereas the Combination had tried to accommodate 20. Those clubs excluded from the Alliance were already committed to professionalism and so had to find new leagues to play in to ensure sufficient attractive revenue-earning games. Long Eaton Rangers were amongst the 12 admitted to the Alliance but the other three East Midland clubs were not and for the 1889-90 season, they were amongst the founder members of the Midland League. The Midland League, like the Football League and Football Alliance, was an immediate success and so in 1890, further new competitions were formed in the area. (The tables of the Midland League are included in the 2002 edition of Non-League Tables, a few copies of which remain on sale from Soccer Books Limited).

The most important of the new leagues was the Midland Alliance which was in effect a Second Division of the Midland League. Its more successful clubs moved up to the Midland League and included Doncaster Rovers and Loughborough, both of whom later played in the Football League. The consistent loss of its better clubs though weakened the Midland Alliance and it closed in 1893.

The Notts & District League had started in 1889 and ran until 1908, when it was succeeded by the Notts & Derbyshire League. The Derbyshire Senior League started in 1890 and lasted until 1898 and there were also other generally, lower level leagues: the Derbyshire Alliance (from 1891), Notts Alliance (from 1894), Mid-Derbyshire League (from c. 1898) and Derby & District League.

In 1911, the Central Alliance was formed, principally by clubs from the Notts & Derbyshire League, but embracing a wider geographical area. Meanwhile, the Derbyshire Senior League reformed in 1911, thus contributing to the closure of the Notts & Derbyshire League in 1912. The Central Alliance, like its predecessor the Midland Alliance, often lost its best clubs to the Midland League, and the formation in 1924 of yet another new league - the Midland Combination, which catered principally for Football League Reserve sides - hastened its demise. It closed in 1925.

Below are the tables of the most important of those early leagues – the Midland Alliance (1890-1893), the Derbyshire Senior League (1890-1898), the Notts & District League (1889-1908), the Notts & Derbyshire League (1908-1912) and the Central Alliance (1911-1925).

Many of the published tables contained errors, some of which have been corrected. Those which remain are shown in italics below the relevant columns.

THE MIDLAND ALLIANCE

Of the 10 founder members, Sheffield had played in the Midland League in 1889-90 but for the other 9 founders, this was their first taste of league football. Notts County Rovers were Notts County's reserve team.

1890-91

Notts County Rovers	14	9	4	1	33	17	22
Doncaster Rovers	14	9	1	4	43	19	17
Loughborough	14	7	2	5	35	25	16
Grantham Rovers	14	5	4	5	33	30	14
Heanor Town	14	5	2	7	32	41	12
Newark	14	4	4	6	26	37	12
Notts Olympic	14	3	3	8	20	39	9
Sheffield	14	3	2	9	23	37	8

Doncaster Rovers had 2 points deducted for fielding an ineligible player.

Notts Jardines were suspended by the F.A. and their record at the time was deleted: 9 1 2 6 13 28 4

Rotherham Swifts withdrew and their record at the time was deleted: 6 1 0 5 8 22 2

Doncaster Rovers, Loughborough and Grantham Rovers all moved to the Midland League. Mansfield Town (not the present club) joined from the Notts League and Derby County Wanderers (Derby County's Reserves), Lincoln City Swifts (Lincoln City's Reserves), Long Eaton Athletic and Grantham Town also joined.

1891-92

Derby County Wanderers	18	15	1	2	88	19	31
Mansfield Town	18	13	2	3	43	19	28
Notts County Rovers	18	11	2	5	49	34	24
Newark	18	10	2	6	55	42	22
Heanor Town	18	8	2	8	46	37	18
Lincoln City Swifts	18	6	3	9	26	43	15
Long Eaton Athletic	18	4	4	10	37	38	12
Grantham Town	18	3	5	10	29	51	11
Sheffield	18	4	3	11	25	64	11
Notts Olympic	18	2	4	12	19	64	8
					417	*411*	

Derby County's reserve side changed their name from Derby County Wanderers to Derby Town. Mansfield Town and Newark both moved to the Midland League.

Matlock joined from the Derbyshire Senior League, Sheffield United Strollers (Sheffield United's reserve side) joined from the Hallamshire League and Nottingham Forest Swifts (Nottingham Forest's reserve side) and Mansfield Greenhalgh's also joined.

1892-93

Derby Town	20	16	2	2	69	15	34
Sheffield United Strollers	20	12	3	5	66	26	27
Mansfield Greenhalgh's	20	11	4	5	46	32	26
Nottingham Forest Swifts	20	11	4	5	36	33	26
Heanor Town	20	11	3	6	41	18	25
Notts County Rovers	20	9	2	9	41	43	20
Matlock	20	9	1	10	41	46	19
Lincoln City Swifts	20	8	3	9	34	43	16
Notts Olympic	20	6	2	12	34	73	14
Sheffield	20	1	3	16	18	67	5
Long Eaton Athletic	20	1	3	16	14	52	5
					440	*448*	

Lincoln City Swifts had 3 points deducted for misconduct.

Grantham Town withdrew after one game (where they lost 16-0 to Notts County Rovers) and their record was deleted.

Derby Town, Heanor Town and Matlock moved to the Derbyshire Senior League, Sheffield and Sheffield United Strollers moved to the Sheffield & Hallamshire Cup (played on a league basis), Mansfield Greenhalgh's moved to the Midland League and Notts Olympic moved to the Notts & District League. Lincoln City Swifts, Long Eaton Athletic, Nottingham Forest Swifts and Notts County Rovers also left and the Midland Alliance closed.

THE DERBYSHIRE SENIOR LEAGUE

Formed in 1890 with 8 founder members, none of whom had previously played in a league. Missing games are believed not to have been played.

1890-91

Matlock	13	11	1	1	42	17	23
Clay Cross Town	14	9	0	5	43	20	18
Belper Town	14	8	1	5	36	25	17
Tibshelf Colliery	13	6	2	5	36	28	14
Riddings St. James	14	6	1	7	29	35	13
Ilkeston Town	14	5	0	9	34	49	10
Ripley Town	13	5	0	8	27	40	10
Wirksworth Town	13	1	1	11	19	50	3
					266	*264*	

Blackwell Colliery, Codnor Park and Langley Mill Rangers joined.

1891-92

Matlock	20	15	3	2	68	33	33
Belper Town	20	14	0	6	97	46	28
Blackwell Colliery	20	12	2	6	75	42	26
Clay Cross Town	18	12	1	5	57	34	25
Tibshelf Colliery	20	8	4	8	75	75	18
Riddings St. James	20	7	4	9	49	51	18
Langley Mill Rangers	20	8	1	11	52	56	17
Wirksworth Town	20	6	3	11	40	47	15
Ripley Town	20	7	1	12	38	61	13
Ilkeston Town	18	6	1	11	25	60	9
Codnor Park	20	2	2	16	35	67	6
					611	*572*	

Tibshelf Colliery and Ripley Town both had 2 points deducted.

Ilkeston Town had 4 points deducted.

Matlock left and joined the Midland Alliance. Alfreton Town joined from the Derbyshire Alliance and South Normanton Colliery also joined.

1892-93

Blackwell Colliery	21	18	1	2	112	30	37
Langley Mill Rangers	21	16	1	4	107	32	33
Ilkeston Town	21	14	2	5	94	36	30
Clay Cross Town	22	13	2	7	73	29	28
Codnor Park	22	7	8	7	54	48	22
Belper Town	19	9	2	8	70	52	20
Riddings St. James	22	8	4	10	41	57	20
Wirksworth Town	21	6	3	12	36	95	15
South Normanton Colliery	22	6	2	14	59	71	14
Ripley Town	22	6	2	14	31	101	14
Tibshelf Colliery	19	4	2	13	41	78	10
Alfreton Town	20	4	1	15	25	107	9
					743	*736*	

Alfreton Town moved to the Derbyshire Alliance and Ripley Town, South Normanton Colliery and Tibshelf Colliery also left. Derby Junction joined from the Midland League, Derby Town (Derby County Reserves), Heanor Town and Matlock all joined from the Midland Alliance and North Wingfield and Staveley Wanderers also joined.

1893-94

Heanor Town	26	22	1	3	143	27	45
Derby Town	26	17	5	4	69	33	39
Ilkeston Town	26	16	6	4	111	44	38
Langley Mill Rangers	26	14	4	8	89	61	32
Blackwell Colliery	26	13	5	8	73	42	31
Matlock	26	13	5	8	60	50	31
Riddings St. James	26	10	7	9	73	53	27
Clay Cross Town	26	13	0	13	75	77	26
Staveley Wanderers	26	11	2	13	66	75	24
Derby Junction	26	9	6	11	50	67	24
North Wingfield	26	7	4	15	42	68	18
Codnor Park	26	5	2	19	43	90	12
Belper Town	26	4	4	18	41	101	12
Wirksworth Town	26	2	1	23	18	165	5

Ilkeston Town and Heanor Town both moved to the Midland League, and were replaced by their reserve teams, Derby Town moved to the Midland League, changing their name to Derby County Reserves and Matlock also moved to the Midland League. Langley Mill Rangers, Staveley Wanderers and Wirksworth Town also left. Derby St. Andrews, Ripley Town and Swadlincote joined.

1894-95

Swadlincote	21	18	2	1	91	20	38
Blackwell Colliery	22	16	2	4	100	42	34
Riddings St. James	22	11	5	6	45	39	27
Belper Town	21	9	5	7	41	29	23
Clay Cross Town	21	10	2	9	52	64	22
Heanor Town Reserves	21	9	3	9	48	51	21
Derby Junction	21	9	2	10	51	57	20
North Wingfield	22	9	2	11	48	62	20
Derby St. Andrews	21	5	6	10	42	46	16
Ilkeston Town Reserves	21	7	0	14	44	53	14
Ripley Town	22	6	2	14	36	80	14
Codnor Park	21	3	1	17	30	86	7
					628	*629*	

Clay Cross Town, Derby Junction, Derby St. Andrews and North Wingfield left.
Derby County Reserves joined from the Midland League and Gresley Rovers also joined.

1895-96

Swadlincote	18	14	2	2	59	18	30
Belper Town	18	12	4	2	56	17	28
Gresley Rovers	18	11	1	6	53	22	23
Derby County Reserves	18	10	3	5	45	27	23
Blackwell Colliery	18	8	2	8	32	30	18
Ripley Town	18	6	5	7	34	46	17
Heanor Town Reserves	18	4	4	10	19	39	12
Ilkeston Town Reserves	18	5	1	12	31	50	11
Riddings St. James	18	4	3	11	26	55	11
Codnor Park	18	2	3	13	9	60	7

Blackwell Colliery, Codnor Park and Heanor Town Reserves left. Matlock joined from the Midland League and Langley Mill Pottery and Long Eaton Rangers Reserves also joined.

1896-97

Derby County Reserves	17	14	2	1	84	11	30
Swadlincote	17	11	3	3	45	21	25
Riddings St. James	16	10	3	3	20	15	23
Gresley Rovers	15	8	0	7	45	20	16
Belper Town	16	7	2	7	24	28	16
Matlock	15	7	1	7	35	40	15
Ripley Town	16	6	2	8	24	37	14
Long Eaton Rangers Reserves.	16	3	5	8	15	34	11
Ilkeston Town Reserves	17	5	0	12	30	52	10
Langley Mill Pottery	17	0	2	15	10	72	2
					332	*330*	

Gresley Rovers, Langley Mill Pottery, Ripley Town and Swadlincote left. Chesterfield Reserves and Sheepbridge Works joined.

1897-98

Chesterfield Reserves	12	10	0	2	42	14	20
Ilkeston Town Reserves	12	9	1	2	32	11	19
Derby County Reserves	12	7	0	5	30	14	14
Long Eaton Rangers Reserves	12	6	1	5	26	23	13
Belper Town	12	3	2	7	18	19	8
Riddings St. James	12	2	2	8	9	39	6
Matlock	12	2	0	10	15	52	4

Sheepbridge Works withdrew and their record was deleted.
The Derbyshire Senior League closed in 1898 with Derby County Reserves moving to the Midland League.

THE NOTTS & DISTRICT LEAGUE

Formed in 1889 but final tables have proved elusive in its early years and so in those cases, the latest tables found are shown. Missing games may not have been played.

1889-90

No table found.

1890-91 (Goals record not given)

Mansfield Town	17	13	4	0	x	x	30
Kimberley	18	10	5	3	x	x	25
Nottingham Forest Reserves	18	11	3	4	x	x	25
Ruddington	18	8	3	7	x	x	19
Sneinton Wanderers	18	6	6	6	x	x	18
Bulwell United	18	5	7	6	x	x	17
Radcliffe-on-Trent	17	6	3	8	x	x	15
Sutton Zingari	18	5	4	9	x	x	14
St. Andrews Institute	18	4	5	9	x	x	13

This Mansfield Town is not the present club.
Notts Wanderers were expelled but results against them were allowed to stand. Their recordat the time was Played 16, Lost16, No points.

1891-92

No table found.

1892-93

Hucknall St. Johns	16	11	2	3	50	25	23
Newstead Byron	15	9	3	3	38	16	21
Ruddington	16	8	1	7	32	25	17
Kimberley	16	7	3	6	31	25	17
Sutton Town	16	7	3	6	27	22	17
Bulwell United	15	6	4	5	27	24	16
Newark Swifts	14	5	1	8	28	41	11
Stapleford	16	3	3	10	22	30	9
Radcliffe-on-Trent	16	3	1	12	18	53	7
		59	*21*	*60*	*273*	*261*	

Hucknall St. Johns had 1 point deducted.
Newark Swifts left and Hucknall Portland, Notts Olympic, Bestwood Institute and Gedling Grove joined.

1893-94

Newstead Byron	22	18	2	2	79	21	38
Hucknall Portland	22	16	3	3	67	26	35
Hucknall St. Johns	22	12	6	4	69	27	30
Stapleford	22	10	7	5	44	29	27
Sutton Town	20	12	2	6	63	36	26
Kimberley	22	10	4	8	50	43	24
Bulwell United	21	10	1	10	57	36	21
Ruddington	22	8	4	10	41	49	20
Radcliffe-on-Trent	21	5	2	14	28	80	12
Notts Olympic	21	4	2	15	26	66	10
Bestwood Institute	19	2	4	13	28	53	8
Gedling Grove	22	1	3	18	22	108	5

Gedling Grove and Radcliffe-on-Trent left. Beeston St. Johns, Langley Mill Rangers, Nottingham Forest Reserves and Notts County Reserves joined.

1894-95

Bulwell United	23	16	4	3	62	32	36
Hucknall St. Johns	24	15	4	5	70	31	34
Hucknall Portland	23	14	4	5	64	34	32
Nottingham Forest Reserves	23	13	3	7	59	34	29
Langley Mill Rangers	22	11	4	7	49	36	26
Kimberley	20	10	3	7	59	35	23
Newstead Byron	21	10	3	8	37	33	23
Notts County Reserves	21	9	4	8	56	33	22
Sutton Town	24	9	4	11	51	59	22
Ruddington	22	5	2	15	31	72	12
Stapleford	22	3	5	14	24	46	11
Notts Olympic	20	2	2	16	20	76	6
	265	*117*	*42*	*106*	*582*	*521*	*276*

Bestwood Institute were suspended but results against them were allowed to stand, hence the imbalance in the column totals above.
Beeston St. Johns withdrew and their record was deleted. Eastwood Town and Mansfield Reserves joined.

1895-96

Hucknall St. Johns	24	17	4	3	69	19	38
Nottingham Forest Reserves	24	16	5	3	55	16	37
Sutton Town	24	13	5	6	57	35	31
Hucknall Portland	24	14	0	10	48	39	28
Newstead Byron	22	10	6	6	59	34	26
Bulwell United	24	12	2	10	52	38	26
Stapleford	22	12	1	9	51	37	25
Langley Mill Rangers	23	7	5	11	38	46	19
Eastwood Town	24	8	3	13	46	52	19
Kimberley	23	6	5	12	38	47	17
Mansfield Reserves	24	7	3	14	32	64	17
Notts County Reserves	24	6	4	14	37	61	16
Notts Olympic	22	2	1	19	22	117	3
					604	*605*	

Notts Olympic had 2 points deducted.
Ruddington withdrew during the season and their record was deleted.
Notts Olympic left. Beeston Humber and Red Hill United joined and Mansfield joined from the Midland League, replacing their Reserves.

1896-97

Hucknall St. Johns	26	19	4	3	72	19	42
Nottingham Forest Reserves	26	18	5	3	74	28	41
Mansfield	26	14	6	6	52	27	34
Bulwell United	26	13	6	7	71	52	32
Eastwood Town	25	13	3	9	59	47	29
Notts County Reserves	26	13	3	10	48	42	29
Newstead Byron	24	12	2	10	53	53	26
Sutton Town	25	8	8	9	35	44	24
Langley Mill Rangers	25	8	3	14	50	63	19
Red Hill United	26	7	5	14	43	65	19
Beeston Humber	25	5	6	14	33	53	16
Stapleford	26	6	4	16	36	64	16
Kimberley	26	5	6	15	32	62	16
Hucknall Portland	26	6	3	17	37	79	15
					695	*698*	

Sutton Town left and Newark joined.

1897-98

Hucknall St. Johns	26	20	1	5	64	29	41
Nottingham Forest Reserves	26	15	8	3	60	30	38
Newark	26	17	2	7	65	33	36
Eastwood Town	26	15	4	7	60	41	34
Notts County Reserves	26	15	3	8	66	37	33
Bulwell United	26	12	7	7	64	49	31
Langley Mill Rangers	26	9	7	10	46	50	25
Red Hill United	26	9	6	11	49	60	24
Mansfield	26	6	10	10	32	42	22
Hucknall Portland	26	7	4	15	44	72	18
Stapleford	26	6	4	16	37	68	16
Beeston Humber	26	5	6	15	32	68	16
Newstead Byron	24	5	5	14	30	49	15
Kimberley	24	4	3	17	33	50	11
					682	*678*	

Beeston Humber and Eastwood Town left.
Kirkby Town, Stanton Hill Victoria and Sutton Town joined.

1898-99

Nottingham Forest Reserves	23	21	1	1	90	16	43
Newark	24	14	4	6	68	36	32
Mansfield	23	14	3	6	43	18	31
Notts County Reserves	24	14	3	7	56	37	31
Sutton Town	24	12	2	10	45	26	26
Stapleford	22	10	4	8	41	34	24
Bulwell United	24	11	0	13	44	54	22
Newstead Byron	24	10	1	13	45	62	21
Hucknall Portland	24	10	1	13	39	56	21
Langley Mill Rangers	24	9	2	13	44	59	20
Red Hill United	24	8	3	13	42	58	19
Stanton Hill Victoria	24	5	3	16	31	67	13
Kirkby Town	24	2	1	21	28	101	5
					616	*624*	

Hucknall St. Johns resigned and their record was deleted.
Kimberley resigned and their record atthe time was also deleted:

18	2	4	12	30	55	8

Newark moved to the Midland League and Langley Mill Rangers and Mansfield also left. Arnold, Grantham Avenue, Mansfield Foresters and Old Brinsley Priory joined.

1899-1900

Bulwell United	23	17	4	2	70	31	38
Stanton Hill Victoria	26	16	4	6	63	44	36
Red Hill United	24	14	3	7	44	38	31
Nottingham Forest Reserves	24	12	6	6	46	24	30
Grantham Avenue	25	13	4	8	78	49	30
Newstead Byron	23	11	5	7	48	37	27
Sutton Town	24	10	7	7	43	36	27
Notts County Reserves	22	11	1	10	46	39	23
Arnold	25	9	4	12	42	43	22
Mansfield Foresters	22	6	4	12	40	44	16
Stapleford	23	4	4	15	34	56	12
Hucknall Portland	24	4	1	19	27	80	9
Kirkby Town	15	3	1	11	21	50	7
Old Brinsley Priory	14	2	2	10	19	43	6
					621	*614*	

Kirkby Town and Old Brinsley Priory both withdrew during the season but their records were allowed to stand. Hucknall Portland changed their name to Hucknall.
Mansfield Foresters left and Kimberley and Mansfield joined.

1900-01

Newstead Byron	21	14	3	4	62	27	31
Sutton Town	22	12	6	4	50	28	30
Notts County Reserves	20	13	3	4	45	17	29
Hucknall	20	12	4	4	60	23	28
Grantham Avenue	21	11	2	8	57	37	24
Arnold	20	7	6	7	37	24	20
Mansfield	21	8	4	9	38	44	20
Nottingham Forest Reserves	19	9	0	10	42	35	18
Bulwell United	17	6	2	9	32	41	14
Stapleford	21	5	4	12	26	43	14
Red Hill United	19	1	5	13	18	78	7
Kimberley	21	2	3	16	15	82	7
					482	*479*	

Stanton Hill Victoria withdrew and their record was deleted. Hucknall changed their name to Hucknall Town, Mansfield and Red Hill United left and Gresley Rovers joined.

1901-02

Nottingham Forest Reserves	18	14	3	1	66	18	31
Notts County Reserves	18	11	4	3	45	21	26
Arnold	18	7	6	5	32	26	20
Gresley Rovers	17	8	2	7	57	26	18
Sutton Town	18	8	2	8	43	42	18
Hucknall Town	18	6	4	8	27	44	16
Grantham Avenue	17	7	1	9	33	40	15
Stapleford	18	5	4	9	27	43	14
Kimberley	16	4	4	8	21	38	12
Bulwell United	18	2	2	14	18	68	6
					369	*366*	

Newstead Byron withdrew and their record was deleted. Gresley Rovers moved to the Derby & District League and Hucknall Town and Kimberley also left.

1902-03

First Series

Notts County Reserves	12	8	1	3	35	16	17
Sutton Town	12	7	1	4	31	17	15
Nottingham Forest Reserves	12	6	3	3	25	15	15
Grantham Avenue	12	7	1	4	21	25	15
Arnold	12	3	6	3	17	17	12
Stapleford	12	2	1	9	16	34	5
Bulwell United	12	2	1	9	14	35	5

Second Series

Nottingham Forest Reserves	12	11	0	1	34	6	22
Notts County Reserves	12	8	1	3	26	11	17
Arnold	11	7	1	3	18	13	15
Sutton Town	12	4	2	6	29	24	10
Grantham Avenue	11	3	2	6	19	27	8
Stapleford	11	2	2	7	11	27	6
Bulwell United	9	0	0	9	6	35	0

Championship Play-Off

Nottingham Forest Reserves 3 Notts County Reserves 0

Nottingham Forest Reserves moved to the Midland League and Bulwell United also left. Kimberley St. Johns, Lawrence's Athletic, Linby, Mansfield Mechanics, Mansfield Woodhouse, Newark Reserves and Southwell joined.

1903-04

Notts County Reserves	21	16	2	3	62	19	34
Arnold	22	15	1	6	41	19	31
Sutton Town	21	12	3	6	53	30	27
Mansfield Woodhouse	22	11	3	8	51	36	25
Linby	21	11	3	7	31	27	25
Grantham Avenue	22	9	5	8	41	30	23
Mansfield Mechanics	22	8	5	9	36	37	21
Newark Reserves	22	9	3	10	27	28	21
Kimberley St. Johns	20	8	1	11	23	44	17
Lawrence's Athletic	21	6	3	12	34	50	15
Southwell	22	4	3	15	22	53	11
Stapleford	21	4	1	16	16	57	9
	257	*113*	*33*	*111*	*437*	*430*	*259*

Notts County Reserves moved to the Midland League and Lawrence's Athletic also left. Hucknall Constitutional and Notts Jardines joined.

1904-05

Arnold	22	14	4	4	70	29	32
Sutton Town	22	13	6	3	54	23	32
Notts Jardines	22	13	4	5	65	29	30
Linby	22	12	4	6	51	32	28
Hucknall Constitutional	22	10	7	5	44	34	27
Mansfield Woodhouse	22	8	9	5	34	29	25
Stapleford	22	10	5	7	49	49	25
Mansfield Mechanics	22	7	6	9	36	43	20
Grantham Avenue	22	6	7	9	37	34	19
Kimberley St. Johns	22	5	1	16	25	58	11
Newark Reserves	22	3	4	15	29	69	10
Southwell	22	3	0	19	18	82	6
		104	*57*	*103*	*512*	*511*	*265*

Championship Play-off

Arnold 1 Sutton Town 0 (played at Mansfield)

Grantham Avenue moved to the Midland League and Linby, Southwell and Stapleford also left. Southwell St. Mary's and Stanton Hill Victoria joined.

1905-06

Sutton Town	18	14	1	3	53	12	29
Hucknall Constitutional	18	11	4	3	32	15	26
Kimberley St. Johns	18	8	4	6	30	29	20
Mansfield Mechanics	18	9	1	8	38	26	19
Arnold	18	7	4	7	31	26	18
Newark Reserves	18	9	4	5	32	27	18
Notts Jardines	18	7	3	8	36	38	17
Mansfield Woodhouse	17	7	2	8	30	36	16
Stanton Hill Victoria	18	3	2	13	29	43	8
Southwell St. Mary's	17	1	1	15	13	72	3

Newark Reserves had 4 points deducted.

Championship Match:

Sutton Town 2 Rest of the League 1

Hucknall Constitutional, Newark Reserves and Southwell St. Mary's left. Eastwood Rangers, Langley Mill, Mansfield Wesley, Notts Olympic, Notts Rangers, Southwell and Sutton Junction joined.

1906-07

Sutton Town	26	22	3	1	76	28	47
Mansfield Mechanics	26	20	3	3	78	20	43
Langley Mill	26	17	2	7	54	34	36
Mansfield Woodhouse	26	13	2	11	53	42	28
Notts Olympic	26	9	8	9	41	38	26
Mansfield Wesley	26	10	5	11	55	57	25
Kimberley St. Johns	25	8	8	9	33	34	24
Sutton Junction	26	9	5	12	39	38	23
Stanton Hill Victoria	26	9	5	12	41	46	23
Eastwood Rangers	26	9	3	14	51	52	21
Arnold	25	7	5	13	58	55	19
Notts Jardines	26	7	5	14	39	61	19
Southwell	26	6	7	13	35	77	19
Notts Rangers	26	2	5	19	25	75	9
					678	*657*	

Arnold versus Kimberley St. Johns was not played due to Arnold ground suspension. Mansfield Woodhouse, Notts Jardines and Notts Rangers left. Notts County Reserves joined from the Midland League and Mansfield Woodhouse Rangers also joined.

1907-08

Notts County Reserves	24	21	0	3	107	20	42
Mansfield Mechanics	24	18	2	4	77	27	38
Sutton Town	24	17	2	5	62	26	36
Sutton Junction	24	13	2	9	49	46	28
Mansfield Wesley	24	12	3	9	67	56	27
Eastwood Rangers	24	12	3	9	46	39	27
Stanton Hill Victoria	24	12	2	10	45	35	26
Notts Olympic	24	8	6	10	43	54	22
Mansfield Woodhouse Rangers	20	9	2	9	31	39	20
Kimberley St. Johns	24	6	2	16	33	68	14
Langley Mill	21	4	1	16	24	69	9
Arnold	20	3	2	15	17	58	6
Southwell	23	1	1	21	17	81	3

Arnold had 2 points deducted.

Notts County Reserves moved to the Midland League and Mansfield Mechanics, Sutton Town, Sutton Junction, Mansfield Wesley, Eastwood Rangers and Stanton Hill Victoria all moved to the Notts & Derbyshire League. The league then closed down.

THE NOTTS & DERBYSHIRE LEAGUE

Formed in 1908, this league was effectively a merger of the Notts & District and Mid-Derbyshire Leagues. Of its 20 founder members, 7 came from the Notts & District League – Sutton Town, Mansfield Mechanics, Mansfield Wesley, Eastwood Rangers, Stanton Hill Victoria, Sutton Junction and Mansfield Woodhouse Rangers.
Another 10 came from the Mid-Derbyshire League – Ilkeston United, Blackwell Colliery, Derby County Reserves, Alfreton Town, Belper Town, Pinxton Colliery, Ripley Athletic, Heanor United, South Normanton Colliery and Ripley Town. The other 3 founders were Long Eaton St. Helen's, Tibshelf Colliery and Clay Cross Works.

1908-09

Ilkeston United	36	25	5	6	101	35	55
Sutton Town	36	21	12	3	94	46	54
Mansfield Mechanics	36	22	8	6	83	40	52
Mansfield Wesley	36	19	6	11	95	73	44
Blackwell Colliery	36	18	6	12	84	60	42
Derby County Reserves	36	18	4	14	67	48	40
Alfreton Town	36	17	6	13	96	84	40
Eastwood Rangers	36	16	6	14	77	61	38
Stanton Hill Victoria	36	13	10	13	56	64	36
Belper Town	36	13	6	17	64	65	32
Pinxton Colliery	36	12	8	16	57	80	32
Ripley Athletic	36	11	9	16	53	72	31
Long Eaton St. Helen's	36	12	6	18	68	73	30
Heanor United	36	11	7	18	67	92	29
Sutton Junction	36	12	5	19	59	86	29
South Normanton Colliery	36	10	8	18	53	75	28
Tibshelf Colliery	36	10	5	21	56	99	25
Ripley Town	36	9	6	21	40	80	24
Clay Cross Works	36	8	7	21	41	78	23

Mansfield Woodhouse Rangers were suspended and then disbanded.
Their record was deleted: 27 2 4 21 30 112 8
Ripley Town and Ripley Athletic merged to form Ripley Town & Athletic.

1909-10

Mansfield Mechanics	34	21	8	5	72	35	48
Eastwood Rangers	34	19	9	6	76	50	47
Ilkeston United	34	18	8	8	81	34	44
Ripley Town & Athletic	34	18	7	9	61	38	43
Alfreton Town	34	19	5	10	83	55	43
Sutton Town	34	18	6	10	89	46	42
Sutton Junction	34	14	8	12	63	50	36
Blackwell Colliery	34	15	4	15	63	72	34
Long Eaton St. Helen's	34	13	7	14	70	65	33
Heanor United	34	13	6	15	75	72	32
Derby County Reserves	34	13	7	14	76	78	31
South Normanton Colliery	34	11	8	15	59	77	30
Belper Town	34	11	9	14	63	62	29
Pinxton Colliery	34	11	8	15	46	65	28
Clay Cross Works	34	9	10	15	47	74	26
Stanton Hill Victoria	34	9	5	20	47	87	23
Mansfield Wesley	34	6	7	21	35	81	17
Tibshelf Colliery	34	5	4	25	40	105	12

Mansfield Mechanics, Derby County Reserves, Belper Town, Pinxton Colliery, Clay Cross Works, Mansfield Wesley and Tibshelf Colliery all had 2 points deducted. Mansfield Wesley changed their name to Mansfield Town (the present club).

1910-11

Mansfield Mechanics	34	24	6	4	79	42	54
Ilkeston United	34	21	6	7	84	37	48
Sutton Junction	34	21	3	10	81	43	45
Alfreton Town	34	18	7	9	88	48	43
Derby County Reserves	34	18	6	10	87	45	40
Heanor United	34	16	7	11	68	60	39
Eastwood Rangers	34	15	8	11	76	64	38
Pinxton Colliery	34	15	7	12	60	62	37
Mansfield Town	34	15	6	13	66	58	36
Stanton Hill Victoria	34	13	8	13	44	46	34
Sutton Town	34	12	9	13	61	59	33
Long Eaton St. Helen's	34	11	6	17	60	74	28
Tibshelf Colliery	34	9	9	16	63	66	27
Blackwell Colliery	34	9	7	18	66	89	25
Ripley Town & Athletic	34	11	2	21	48	75	24
Belper Town	34	8	6	20	47	84	22
South Normanton Colliery	34	8	6	20	43	91	20
Clay Cross Works	34	6	3	25	32	101	15
					1153	*1144*	

Derby County Reserves and South Normanton Colliery both had 2 points deducted.
Mansfield Mechanics, Ilkeston United, Sutton Junction, Derby County Reserves, Mansfield Town, Sutton Town and Long Eaton St. Helen's left to become founder members of the Central Alliance. Alfreton Town, Belper Town, Clay Cross Worksand Heanor United also left. Shirebrook, Hardwick Colliery, Chesterfield Reserves and Birchwood Colliery joined.

1911-12

Ripley Town & Athletic	20	14	3	3	46	25	31
Pinxton Colliery	20	11	6	3	48	25	28
Shirebrook	20	9	6	5	42	33	24
Hardwick Colliery	20	9	4	7	36	32	22
Tibshelf Colliery	20	8	6	6	42	32	20
Stanton Hill Victoria	20	6	7	7	35	27	19
Blackwell Colliery	20	8	3	9	39	34	19
Eastwood Rangers	20	7	4	9	35	39	18
South Normanton Colliery	20	7	2	11	31	48	16
Chesterfield Reserves	20	4	4	12	28	47	12
Birchwood Colliery	20	4	1	15	26	66	9

Tibshelf Colliery had 2 points deducted.

A subsidiary competition was organised but Chesterfield Reserves did not take part:

Subsidiary Competition – North

Shirebrook	10	8	1	1	24	5	17
Hardwick Colliery	10	5	1	4	18	15	11
Stanton Hill Victoria	10	3	4	3	14	10	10
Blackwell Colliery	10	4	2	4	15	16	10
Tibshelf Colliery	10	3	3	4	11	19	9
South Normanton Colliery	10	1	1	8	11	28	3

Subsidiary Competition – South

Eastwood Rangers	6	5	0	1	23	4	10
Ripley Town & Athletic	6	4	0	2	15	8	8
Pinxton Colliery	6	2	0	4	7	17	4
Birchwood Colliery	6	1	0	5	6	22	2

Championship Play-off

Shirebrook 2 Eastwood Rangers 1

Eastwood Rangers, Ripley Town & Athletic, Shirebrook and Stanton Hill Victoria moved to the Central Alliance and Blackwell Colliery, Chesterfield Reserves, Hardwick Colliery, South Normanton Colliery and Tibshelf Colliery moved to the Derbyshire Senior League. The league then closed down.

THE CENTRAL ALLIANCE

Formed in 1911 with 12 founder members, 7 of which came from the Notts & Derbyshire League – Derby County Reserves, Ilkeston United, Long Eaton St. Helen's, Mansfield Mechanics, Mansfield Town, Sutton Junction and Sutton Town. The other founders were Nottingham Forest Reserves from the Midland League, Grantham from the Midland Amateur League, Peterborough G.N. Loco from the Northamptonshire League, Walsall Reserves from the Southern League Division Two and Grantham Avenue. In the 1911-12 season, Walsall continued as members of the Southern League - Division Two but arranged their fixtures on different dates to their Birmingham League games and so were able to use their first team to fulfil both sets of fixtures.

1911-12

Derby County Reserves	22	17	5	0	67	17	39
Sutton Town	22	14	4	4	56	30	32
Sutton Junction	22	14	2	6	69	39	30
Mansfield Mechanics	22	9	8	5	41	28	26
Walsall Reserves	22	9	7	6	36	36	25
Nottingham Forest Reserves	22	9	6	7	46	36	24
Ilkeston United	22	7	7	8	51	29	21
Grantham Avenue	22	6	6	10	30	48	18
Grantham	22	7	2	13	32	67	16
Long Eaton St. Helens	22	2	9	11	28	45	13
Mansfield Town	22	6	0	16	35	62	12
Peterborough G.N. Loco	22	2	4	16	36	90	8

Nottingham Forest Reserves left.
Eastwood Rangers, Ripley Town & Athletic, Shirebrook and Stanton Hill Victoria all joined from the Notts & Derbyshire League, Leicester Fosse Reserves joined from the Midland League, Kettering joined from the Southern League - Division Two and Gresley Rovers joined from the Leicestershire Senior League.

1912-13

Long Eaton St. Helens	32	23	4	5	72	36	50
Sutton Junction	32	20	7	5	84	44	47
Sutton Town	32	18	9	5	68	43	45
Leicester Fosse Reserves	32	19	5	8	76	38	43
Mansfield Mechanics	32	17	7	8	65	40	41
Ilkeston United	32	16	6	10	64	43	38
Derby County Reserves	32	15	7	10	60	42	37
Shirebrook	32	14	4	14	54	66	32
Grantham	32	11	6	15	61	60	28
Mansfield Town	32	13	2	17	50	54	28
Kettering	32	11	4	17	66	77	26
Gresley Rovers	32	11	6	15	48	52	22
Peterborough G.N. Loco	32	7	7	18	49	74	21
Ripley Town & Athletic	32	8	5	19	37	63	21
Grantham Avenue	32	8	5	19	40	73	21
Eastwood Rangers	32	7	4	21	51	84	18
Walsall Reserves	32	6	8	18	40	86	18
					985	*975*	

Walsall Reserves had 2 points deducted for fielding an ineligible player.
Gresley Rovers had 6 points deducted for fielding ineligible players.

Stanton Hill Victoria withdrew on 12th April 1913 and their record at the time was deleted: 20 4 1 15 25 64 7
2 points having been deducted for fielding an ineligible player.
Peterborough G.N. Loco moved to the Peterborough & District League, Ripley Town & Athletic moved to the Derbyshire Senior League and Walsall Reserves and Eastwood Rangers also left. Notts County Reserves joined from the Midland League and Holwell Works and Leicester Imperial joined from the Leicestershire Senior League.

1913-14

Shirebrook	30	22	5	3	76	33	49
Grantham Avenue	30	17	6	7	52	34	40
Sutton Town	30	18	2	10	66	40	38
Ilkeston United	30	15	7	8	64	41	37
Leicester Fosse Reserves	30	17	4	9	74	43	36
Long Eaton St. Helens	30	14	6	10	49	45	34
Sutton Junction	30	14	2	14	56	65	30
Grantham	30	12	5	13	51	61	29
Notts County Reserves	30	12	3	15	51	54	27
Gresley Rovers	30	10	6	14	46	53	26
Derby County Reserves	30	11	3	16	49	48	25
Kettering	30	10	5	15	35	62	25
Mansfield Mechanics	30	8	8	14	47	52	22
Leicester Imperial	30	7	6	17	38	61	20
Mansfield Town	30	6	7	17	38	62	19
Holwell Works	30	8	3	19	36	70	19
					828	*824*	

Leicester Fosse Reserves and Mansfield Mechanics both had 2 points deducted.
Long Eaton St. Helens changed their name to Long Eaton Town.
Mansfield Town were not re-elected as they had not brought their ground up to standard and they joined the reformed Notts & Derbyshire League for 1914-15. Holwell Works also left.
Loughborough Corinthians joined from the Leicestershire Senior League and Peterborough City also joined.

1914-15

Notts County Reserves	30	21	4	5	75	32	46
Shirebrook	30	17	8	5	51	23	42
Derby County Reserves	30	18	3	9	82	55	39
Gresley Rovers	30	14	8	8	59	35	36
Ilkeston United	30	14	8	8	55	38	36
Loughborough Corinthians	30	14	4	12	53	52	32
Sutton Junction	30	13	4	13	62	53	30
Mansfield Mechanics	30	13	4	13	63	55	30
Long Eaton Town	30	11	7	12	42	49	29
Kettering	30	11	3	16	55	59	25
Grantham Town	30	9	6	15	41	58	24
Leicester Imperial	30	7	10	13	25	60	24
Sutton Town	30	7	8	15	46	54	22
Grantham Avenue	30	9	4	17	47	89	22
Leicester Fosse Reserves	30	8	7	15	46	45	21
Peterborough City	30	6	8	16	33	74	18
					835	*831*	

Leicester Fosse Reserves and Peterborough City both had 2 points deducted.
Derby County Reserves, Gresley Rovers, Kettering and Grantham left but rejoined the league in 1919. Leicester Fosse Reserves also left and rejoined in 1919 having changed their name to Leicester City Reserves.
Notts County Reserves left and joined the Midland League in 1919.
Grantham Avenue left and did not reform after the war and Leicester Imperial and Peterborough City also left. Mansfield Town and New Hucknall Colliery both joined from the Notts & Derbyshire League.

1915-16

First Series

Ilkeston United	16	11	2	3	55	26	24
New Hucknall Colliery	16	9	3	4	36	20	21
Loughborough Corinthians	16	9	1	6	38	28	19
Shirebrook	16	7	3	6	18	27	17
Sutton Town	16	7	2	7	28	26	16
Mansfield Town	16	7	0	9	33	33	14
Mansfield Mechanics	16	5	2	9	35	35	12
Long Eaton Town	16	5	1	10	28	43	11
Sutton Junction	16	5	0	11	27	60	10

Ilkeston United did not play in the Second Series and they joined the Derbyshire Senior League in 1919. Loughborough Corinthians and Long Eaton Town also did not take part in the Second Series.

Second Series

Mansfield Town	10	10	0	0	42	7	20
Shirebrook	9	6	0	3	20	14	12
New Hucknall Colliery	9	5	1	3	42	10	11
Sutton Town	10	4	1	5	35	20	9
Sutton Junction	9	1	0	8	10	56	2
Mansfield Mechanics	9	1	0	8	6	48	2

Two games were not played.

The league then closed down until 1919.

1919-20

When the league reformed after the war, Mansfield Mechanics did not rejoin but all of the other 1915-16 members did. They were joined by Derby County Reserves, Gresley Rovers, Kettering, Grantham and Leicester City Reserves, all of whom had been members in 1914-15. There were also three new members, Hucknall Byron and Wellbeck Colliery and also Chesterfield Reserves, who had been members of the Derbyshire Senior League in 1914-15 and joined after adding Municipal to their name.

Mansfield Town	30	19	3	8	81	41	41
Ilkeston United	30	16	8	6	51	36	40
Kettering	30	16	6	8	52	43	38
Leicester City Reserves	30	13	11	6	64	46	37
Derby County Reserves	30	14	7	9	73	57	35
Gresley Rovers	30	15	4	11	62	48	34
Sutton Town	30	14	5	11	78	67	33
Wellbeck Colliery	30	12	7	11	45	41	31
Loughborough Corinthians	30	13	4	13	62	53	28
New Hucknall Colliery	30	11	5	14	57	54	27
Hucknall Byron	30	9	7	14	47	61	25
Shirebrook	30	9	8	13	46	54	24
Grantham	30	10	4	16	53	65	24
Sutton Junction	30	10	4	16	47	83	24
Long Eaton Town	30	5	12	13	37	52	22
Chesterfield Municipal Reserves	30	3	7	20	37	91	13

Loughborough Corinthians and Shirebrook each had two points deducted.
Chesterfield Municipal changed their name to Chesterfield.
R.A.F. Cranwell and Retford Town joined.

1920-21

Leicester City Reserves	34	28	1	5	132	29	57
Shirebrook	34	23	3	8	76	46	49
Gresley Rovers	34	18	7	9	69	46	43
Ilkeston United	34	17	8	9	73	39	42
Mansfield Town	34	18	6	10	75	56	42
Derby County Reserves	34	15	9	10	64	54	39
Sutton Town	34	15	8	11	82	61	38
Chesterfield Reserves	34	16	6	12	59	55	38
Wellbeck Colliery	34	12	8	14	71	76	32
Grantham	34	13	6	15	70	88	32
Kettering	34	12	7	15	70	62	31
Retford Town	34	12	6	16	55	70	30
Loughborough Corinthians	34	12	4	18	60	71	28
Hucknall Byron	34	10	7	17	37	59	27
Long Eaton Town	34	9	9	16	50	76	27
Sutton Junction	34	9	3	22	56	95	21
New Hucknall Colliery	34	5	10	19	41	80	20
R.A.F. Cranwell	34	6	4	24	45	122	16

Mansfield Town moved to the Midland League, Derby County Reserves moved to the Central League and R.A.F. Cranwell also left. Heanor Town joined from the Derbyshire Senior League, Coalville Swifts joined from the Leicestershire Senior League and Alfreton Town joined, having only just reformed after the war.

1921-22

Leicester City Reserves	34	27	4	3	132	19	58
Ilkeston United	34	21	7	6	89	44	49
Heanor Town	34	22	3	9	70	38	47
Kettering	34	21	3	10	86	58	45
Chesterfield Reserves	34	17	6	11	83	53	40
Gresley Rovers	34	18	3	13	68	49	39
Wellbeck Colliery	34	15	7	12	77	62	37
Grantham	34	14	9	11	49	46	37
Sutton Town	34	14	2	18	63	72	30
Loughborough Corinthians	34	13	4	17	48	63	30
Long Eaton Town	34	12	6	16	39	65	30
Coalville Swifts	34	11	7	16	51	72	29
Alfreton Town	34	13	2	19	68	78	28
Retford Town	34	10	7	17	53	77	27
New Hucknall Colliery	34	10	6	18	56	94	26
Shirebrook	34	7	10	17	37	66	24
Sutton Junction	34	6	6	22	35	92	18
Hucknall Byron	34	7	4	23	28	84	18

Chesterfield Reserves moved to the Midland League and Newark Town joined.

1922-23

Leicester City Reserves	32	24	4	4	107	34	52
Alfreton Town	32	21	4	7	96	40	46
Kettering	32	18	3	11	80	51	39
Ilkeston United	32	15	7	10	59	45	37
Loughborough Corinthians	32	16	5	11	70	56	37
Retford Town	32	14	8	10	67	55	36
Shirebrook	32	11	12	9	59	46	34
Long Eaton Town	32	13	6	13	61	74	32
Sutton Town	32	13	4	15	49	55	30
Gresley Rovers	32	12	5	15	61	54	29
Heanor Town	32	9	11	12	54	63	29
Grantham	32	10	9	13	36	48	29
Newark Town	32	10	9	13	38	57	29
Coalville Swifts	32	10	7	15	50	61	27
New Hucknall Colliery	32	10	6	16	51	81	26
Hucknall Byron	32	6	5	21	32	103	17
Sutton Junction	32	4	7	21	33	80	15

Wellbeck Colliery resigned during April and their record at the time was deleted: 26 10 2 14 36 54 22

Kettering and Leicester City Reserves moved to the Southern League, Sutton Town moved to the Midland League and New Hucknall Colliery also left. R.A.F. Cranwell joined.

1923-24

Alfreton Town	26	18	5	3	95	31	41
Newark Town	26	16	5	5	63	39	37
Grantham	26	12	7	7	48	37	31
Shirebrook	26	13	4	9	61	37	30
Retford Town	26	11	6	9	53	48	28
Gresley Rovers	26	10	7	9	55	45	27
Coalville Swifts	26	12	3	11	54	48	27
Ilkeston United	26	9	7	10	33	37	25
Heanor Town	26	9	5	12	42	37	23
Long Eaton Town	26	8	7	11	46	57	23
Hucknall Byron	26	8	7	11	35	57	23
Loughborough Corinthians	26	8	5	13	45	59	21
Sutton Junction	26	8	3	15	33	65	19
R.A.F. Cranwell	26	3	3	20	35	102	9
					698	*699*	

Coalville Swifts, Ilkeston United, Retford Town and Shirebrook left. Matlock Town joined from the Derbyshire Senior League.

1924-25

Grantham	20	12	6	2	39	20	30
Loughborough Corinthians	20	13	2	5	65	33	28
Newark Town	20	13	2	5	40	31	28
Alfreton Town	20	11	4	5	53	26	26
Gresley Rovers	20	11	1	8	45	33	23
Heanor Town	20	10	3	7	39	35	23
Matlock Town	20	7	1	12	42	42	15
Long Eaton Town	20	5	5	10	27	37	15
Hucknall Byron	20	4	4	12	26	47	12
R.A.F. Cranwell	20	4	4	12	27	61	12
Sutton Junction	20	2	4	14	22	60	8

A subsidiary competition was organised but Long Eaton Town and Sutton Junction did not take part:

Subsidiary Competition – Division A

Loughborough Corinthians	8	6	1	1	24	14	13
Gresley Rovers	8	5	2	1	21	15	12
Heanor Town	8	1	3	4	15	18	5
Alfreton Town	8	1	3	4	12	19	5
Matlock Town	8	1	3	4	15	21	5

Subsidiary Competition – Division B

Grantham	6	4	0	2	16	6	8
Newark Town	6	3	2	1	12	4	8
Hucknall Byron	6	2	1	3	9	20	5
R.A.F. Cranwell	6	1	1	4	7	14	3

Alfreton Town, Grantham, Long Eaton Town, Loughborough Corinthians and Newark Town all moved to the Midland League. Heanor Town, Matlock Town and Sutton Junction all moved to the Derbyshire Senior League and Gresley Rovers moved to the Leicestershire Senior League.

The Central Alliance then closed and was not revived until 1948.